Praise for *Global Environmental Constitutionalism in the Anthropocene*

'The first comprehensive treatise of the burgeoning literature on global environmental constitutionalism, this book is incredibly well researched, insightful and inspirational. A landmark publication for years to come.'
Professor Klaus Bosselmann, University of Auckland, New Zealand

'With humanity poised on the precipice of an environmental abyss, we need intellectual visionaries to design and build the bridge to a sustainable future. With *Global Environmental Constitutionalism in the Anthropocene*, Professor Louis Kotzé demonstrates that he not only possesses such vision, but can articulate it in a clear, concise, and compelling fashion. While Kotzé acknowledges the formidable magnitude of the challenges we face, his book identifies prospective solutions and thus offers a much-needed beacon of hope.'
Professor David Boyd, Simon Fraser University, Canada

'Professor Kotzé's *Global Environmental Constitutionalism in the Anthropocene* serves as a tempered *tour de force* for using constitutionalism to re-imagine how global juridical and governance structures can be deployed in new ways to save the planet. Kotzé makes the strong case that global environmental constitutionalism already provides means for transformative environmental progress, that is, if we are up to the task. The book is an essential addition to the growing dialogic canon of environmental constitutionalism. It proposes new cognates and constructs in the global conversation about how constitutionalism in general and environmental constitutionalism in particular can serve as a necessary if not sufficient mechanism for advancing sustainability, improving environmental outcomes, and respecting human dignity. Perhaps most importantly, Kotzé fashions a compelling and convincing rebuttal to the Anthropocene itself, reinforcing the notion that we are the change we seek.'
Professor James May and Professor Erin Daly, Widener University, Delaware Law School, United States

'This book is a brilliant exposition of the intersection between two emerging yet crucial concepts in global environmental thought. It is a groundbreaking contribution to the fields of international law, constitutional law and environmental law. Kotzé sheds new light on the most important challenges of our time, and the most promising pathways for meeting them.'
Professor Lynda Collins, Centre for Environmental Law and Global Sustainability, University of Ottawa, Canada

'The realisation that humans have become an Earth-shaping force of geological proportions is only now permeating the social sciences. The often conservative legal disciplines are among the most obstinate, yet important, areas of knowledge where this re-conceptualisation is needed. The penetrating and insightful study of Professor Kotzé is therefore of great importance in that it focuses on a critical legal discipline, constitutional law, and succeeds in fleshing out the implications and potential of environmental constitutionalism from a global governance perspective.'
Professor Jorge E Viñuales, Harold Samuel Chair of Law and Environmental Policy, University of Cambridge, United Kingdom

'Louis Kotzé's book is a ground breaking, timely and imaginative interrogation of two increasingly influential framings of the current global ecological situation. Bringing

together the 'Anthropocene' and 'global environmental constitutionalism', Kotzé confronts the juridical implications of the Anthropocene imaginary by providing the first systematic treatment of the concepts of environmental constitutionalism and global environmental constitutionalism and by charting a new constitutionalized framework for human ecological responsibility. This thought-provoking text is highly recommended reading.
Professor Anna Grear, Professor of Law and Legal Theory, Cardiff University, United Kingdom

'This is a book about responsibility in the age of the Anthropocene. It identifies the core issues of the current socio-ecological crisis, points out priorities, and proposes interventions. Kotzé delivers a compelling argument that humanity finds itself in a rare global constitutional moment that requires us to reimagine the law at a planetary scale and to create, enact, and advance global environmental constitutionalism.'
Professor Maria Ivanova, University of Massachusetts, United States

'Professor Kotze eloquently and persuasively contends that in order to respond to the challenges of the new era of the Anthropocene, it is necessary to construct a new legal framework, which unites environmental and constitutional principles at a global level. Comprehensive, engaging, and ambitious, this book will be a seminal work in this field for years to come.'
Professor John H Knox, United Nations Special Rapporteur on Human Rights and the Environment; Henry C Lauerman Professor of International Law, Wake Forest University, United States

GLOBAL ENVIRONMENTAL CONSTITUTIONALISM IN THE ANTHROPOCENE

There is persuasive evidence suggesting we are on the brink of human-induced ecological disaster that could change life on Earth as we know it. There is also a general consensus among scientists about the pace and extent of global ecological decay, including a realisation that humans are central to causing the global socio-ecological crisis. This new epoch has been called the Anthropocene. Considering the many benefits that constitutional environmental protection holds out in domestic legal orders, it is likely that a constitutionalised form of global environmental law and governance would be better able to counter the myriad exigencies of the Anthropocene. This book seeks to answer this central question: from the perspective of the Anthropocene, what is environmental constitutionalism and how could it be extrapolated to formulate a global framework? In answering this question, this book offers the first systematic conceptual framework for global environmental constitutionalism in the epoch of the Anthropocene.

Global Environmental Constitutionalism in the Anthropocene

Louis J Kotzé

HART PUBLISHING

OXFORD AND PORTLAND, OREGON

2016

Hart Publishing
An imprint of Bloomsbury Publishing Plc

Hart Publishing Ltd	Bloomsbury Publishing Plc
Kemp House	50 Bedford Square
Chawley Park	London
Cumnor Hill	WC1B 3DP
Oxford OX2 9PH	UK
UK	

www.hartpub.co.uk
www.bloomsbury.com

Published in North America (US and Canada) by
Hart Publishing
c/o International Specialized Book Services
920 NE 58th Avenue, Suite 300
Portland, OR 97213-3786
USA

www.isbs.com

HART PUBLISHING, the Hart/Stag logo, BLOOMSBURY and the
Diana logo are trademarks of Bloomsbury Publishing Plc

First published 2016

© Louis J Kotzé

Louis J Kotzé has asserted his right under the Copyright, Designs and Patents Act 1988 to be identified as
Author of this work.

All rights reserved. No part of this publication may be reproduced or transmitted in any form or by any means,
electronic or mechanical, including photocopying, recording, or any information storage or retrieval system,
without prior permission in writing from the publishers.

While every care has been taken to ensure the accuracy of this work, no responsibility for loss or damage occasioned
to any person acting or refraining from action as a result of any statement in it can be accepted by the authors,
editors or publishers.

All UK Government legislation and other public sector information used in the work is Crown Copyright ©.
All House of Lords and House of Commons information used in the work is Parliamentary Copyright ©. This
information is reused under the terms of the Open Government Licence v3.0 (http://www.nationalarchives.gov.uk/
doc/open-government-licence/version/3) excepted where otherwise stated.

All Eur-lex materials used in the work is © European Union,
http://eur-lex.europa.eu/, 1998–2015.

British Library Cataloguing-in-Publication Data
A catalogue record for this book is available from the British Library.

ISBN: HB: 978-1-50990-758-8
       ePDF: 978-1-50990-761-8
       ePub: 978-1-50990-759-5

Library of Congress Cataloging-in-Publication Data

Names: Kotzé, Louis J., author.
Title: Global environmental constitutionalism in the anthropocene / Louis J Kotzé.
Description: Portland, Oregon : Hart Publishing, 2016. | Includes bibliographical
references and index.
Identifiers: LCCN 2016019863 (print) | LCCN 2016020004 (ebook) | ISBN 9781509907588
(hardback : alk. paper) | ISBN 9781509907595 (Epub)
Subjects: LCSH: Environmental law, International. | Climatic changes—Effect of human beings
on. | Climatic changes—Law and legislation. | Constitutional law.
Classification: LCC K3585.5 .K68 2016 (print) | LCC K3585.5 (ebook) | DDC 344.04/6—dc23
LC record available at https://lccn.loc.gov/2016019863

Typeset by Compuscript Ltd, Shannon
Printed and bound in Great Britain by
TJ International Ltd, Padstow

For Francois Venter:
A Dean, a scholar and a constitutionalist.

PREFACE

It is not a matter of mere coincidence that this book, which focuses on constitutionalism, was written by a South African. I was just entering university in the 1990s when Nelson Mandela was set free and the country was standing at the edge of a ravine into which it could either fall or build a bridge to cross. We chose to build a bridge. What followed was a new dawn in South Africa's deeply troubled history that saw sweeping political transformations that engulfed the country and sought to change it to its core. This post-apartheid transformation was principally driven by a constitutional revolution. Constitutionalism created the juridical, political and social foundations and mechanisms to commence dismantling the remnants of colonialism, deeply embedded structures of white apartheid privilege, naked racism and unspeakable injustices perpetrated against a majority of the country's population for far too long. It was constitutionalism that created hope, provided opportunities for reconciliation and the possibility to start again. While South Africa's constitutional revolution is not yet complete, the power of constitutionalism became clear to us all.

Today, humanity is confronted by events that, according to various scientific accounts, are set to affect the continuation of life on Earth. The climate is changing, biodiversity is being lost at alarming rates, inter- and intra-species injustices are intensifying and a host of ecological cycles are being flung in such disarray that the possibility for recovery seems remote. Similar events of ecological upheaval have occurred during earlier stages in Earth's geological history, with one significant difference: the current socio-ecological crisis is not being caused by volcanoes or meteors, but by humans. It is in this context that scientists have recently suggested the Earth system might have entered a new geological epoch called the Anthropocene. In the Anthropocene humanity takes centre stage as a geological agent for the first time, elevated to such a position by anthropogenic impacts on the Earth system since at least the European Industrial revolution; and reflecting underlying structures of privilege placing particular human interests above any meaningful concern for the preservation of the interdependent community of life. Similar to South Africa's constitutional moment, humanity now stands at the edge of what could possibly be the most decisive point in human-Earth history: we can make a conscious and deliberate effort to address the Anthropocene's socio-ecological crises, or we can remain on the same path that led us to the gaping ravine we are now facing.

In this book I employ the increasingly popular framework of the Anthropocene to make out a case in support of using constitutionalism as a means to re-imagine and to reform those global juridical and governance structures that, by design and purpose, have been complicit in the genesis of the Anthropocene's socio-ecological crisis. Importantly, it will be these very same law and governance structures that will form part of future regulatory responses to Anthropocene exigencies. The value of domestic constitutional environmental protection (or environmental constitutionalism), and its potential to ensure better socio-ecological care, is by now undisputed. But environmental constitutionalism has not yet been translated in any meaningful way to the global environmental law and governance domain. Departing from the familiar domestic constitutionalism narrative, this book attempts to think about environmental constitutionalism in global terms by opening up hitherto closed epistemic spaces that shut out the possibility of more radical constitutional transformations of the global environmental law and governance order. In so doing, I hope to show that these global constitutional transformations are both possible and capable of contributing by reforming the laws and governance institutions that could help humanity build a bridge to cross the Anthropocene's ravine.

Many of the ideas that found their way into this book have been discussed with numerous colleagues and friends around the world who are too many to list here. I am grateful for their continuous support and for the growing interest that is shown in our collective and gradually maturing environmental constitutionalism project. I wish to thank in particular the following people for their special contributions: Jonathan Verschuuren and Francois Venter for their extensive critical comments on each chapter; James May, Erin Daly and David Boyd for their inspiration and for sharing their extensive knowledge on environmental constitutionalism; Anna Grear for her vision and unparallelled ability to force critical thought; Duncan French for opening up the complex world of international environmental law; Erika de Wet for sharing her knowledge on global constitutionalism; and my dean, Nicola Smit for giving me the freedom to do what I love. On a personal level my sincere thanks goes to Anél du Plessis, Gerhard van Huyssteen, Klaus Zweckberger and my parents Mart and Flip Kotzé, for their support and encouragement.

Most of this book was written during several research visits to the Max Planck Institute for Comparative Public Law and International Law, Heidelberg, Germany. I am grateful to the Institute and to its world-class library staff for accommodating me. Hart Publishing has been truly exceptional. Thank you to Sinead Moloney, Emily Braggins and their extraordinarily supportive and professional publishing team. Finally, the book would not have been possible without the generous financial assistance provided by the following institutions: the South African National Research Foundation as part of a Competitive Funding for Rated Researchers Project entitled *Environmental Constitutionalism*; the North-West University's Vice-rector for Research, Strategic Research Development Grant; and the Alexander von Humboldt Foundation. All views and errors are my own.

Louis J Kotzé
Potchefstroom, February 2016

TABLE OF CONTENTS

Preface vii

1. Introduction 1
    I. Human Domination 1
    II. The Anthropocene's Global Socio-Ecological Crisis 4
    III. The Anthropocene's Global Socio-Ecological
         Crisis and the Law 6
    IV. Constitutionalism and the Anthropocene 7
    V. Environmental Constitutionalism 11
    VI. Global Aspects of Environmental Constitutionalism 14
    VII. Global Environmental Constitutionalism Through
         the Lens of the Anthropocene 16
    VIII. About this Book 17
    IX. Original Contribution 20

2. Law and the Anthropocene's Global
   Socio-Ecological Crisis 21
    I. Introduction 21
    II. About this Chapter 23
    III. The Anthropocene and the History of Earth 24
    IV. Turning Rock into Air: A Brief History
         of the Anthropocene 26
    V. The Anthropocene: What Lies Behind a Word? 32
    VI. The Anthropocene and Regulatory Institutions 38
    VII. Conclusion 41

3. Constitutionalism 43
    I. Introduction 43
    II. About this Chapter 44
    III. Constitutional Concepts 47
        A. Constitution 48
        B. Constitutionalism 50
        C. Constitutionalisation 52
        D. The Constitutional State 54
    IV. The Turn Towards Constitutionalism
         and Counter-constitutionalism Considerations 57

V. General Elements of the Contemporary Constitutional State 61
   A. A Constitution 62
   B. The Rule of Law 65
   C. Separation of Powers 71
   D. Judicial Independence and Powers of Review 74
   E. Constitutional Supremacy 77
   F. Democracy 79
   G. Rights 82
VI. Conclusion 87

4. Global Aspects of Constitutionalism 89
   I. Introduction 89
   II. About this Chapter 90
   III. From the Local to the Global 91
       A. The Inappropriateness of Domestic Constitutionalism for the Global Sphere 91
       B. The Appropriateness of Domestic Constitutionalism for the Global Sphere 93
   IV. Why (Not) Constitutionalise the Global Order? 96
       A. Globalisation 96
       B. Fragmentation 98
       C. Enhanced Regulation for Global Problems 99
       D. Critiquing Global Constitutionalism 100
   V. Approaches to and Meaning of Global Constitutionalism: A Devil with Many Faces 102
       A. The Internationalist Approach 103
       B. The Regionalist Approach 104
       C. The International Regulatory Regime Approach 106
       D. Global Civil Society Constitutionalism 107
       E. Transnational Comparative Constitutionalism 109
       F. Towards a Singular Vision? 110
   VI. In Search of Constitutionalism's Features in the Global Sphere 111
       A. A Global Constitution 112
       B. Global Rule of Law 114
       C. Global Separation of Powers 116
       D. The Global Judiciary 118
       E. Global Constitutional Supremacy 121
       F. Global Democracy 125
       G. Global Rights 128
   VII. Conclusion 131

5. The Fundamentals of Environmental Constitutionalism............................133
   I. Introduction...133
   II. About this Chapter..134
   III. A Historical-conceptual Account of the Convergence
        Between Environmentalism and Constitutionalism 136
        A. Should Trees have Standing? 137
        B. Jonas and the Imperative of Responsibility..........................138
        C. Kloepfer's Environmental State..138
        D. Bosselmann's Ecological *Rechtsstaat*..................................140
        E. Verschuuren's Environmental
           Constitutional Democracy...142
        F. Steinberg and the Ecological Constitutional State...............143
        G. Green Constitutionalism..144
        H. Boyd's Environmental Rights Revolution............................145
        I. 'Thin' and 'Thick' Environmental
           Constitutionalism..146
        J. Environmental Constitutionalism as a
           Discursive-contemplative Framework..................................147
        K. Global Comparative Environmental
           Constitutionalism..148
        L. Structural and Fundamental Environmental
           Constitutionalism..150
   IV. A Contemporary Description of Environmental
       Constitutionalism 151
   V. Environmental Constitutionalism
      in Domestic Constitutional Orders...153
        A. Formal and Substantive Environmental
           Constitutions...154
        B. Environmental Rule of Law..159
        C. Separation of Environmental Governance Powers 162
        D. Judicial Independence and Powers of Review.....................165
        E. Constitutional Supremacy..168
        F. Democracy 169
        G. Environmental Rights...172
   VI. Conclusion...175

6. The Prospects of Environmental Constitutionalism
   in the Anthropocene...176
   I. Introduction...176
   II. About this Chapter..177
   III. Revisiting Law in the Anthropocene: The Urgency
        of Constitutional Transformations 178
        A. Law and Order: The Anthropocene's
           Constitutional Moment..178

		B.	The 'Global' Regulatory Space of the Anthropocene 184
		C.	Ethics, Vulnerability and Responsibility of Care 188
	IV.	The Prospects of Environmental Constitutionalism in the Anthropocene 192	
		A.	Higher-order Juridical Guarantees and Care 192
		B.	A Foundational Determinant of Secondary Regimes 193
		C.	Benchmarking Environmental Protection Through Transnationalism 194
		D.	Regulatory Longevity 195
		E.	Environmental Awareness and Societal Involvement 196
		F.	Inter-generational Reach 196
		G.	Legitimisation of Environmental Law and Governance 197
		H.	Levelling the Sustainable Development Playing Field 198
	V.	Conclusion 199	
7.	A Vision of Global Environmental Constitutionalism in the Anthropocene 201		
	I.	Introduction 201	
	II.	About this Chapter 202	
	III.	From Domestic to Global Environmental Constitutionalism 203	
	IV.	Global Environmental Constitutionalism's Five Approaches 206	
		A.	The Internationalist Approach 206
		B.	The Regionalist Approach 210
		C.	The International Environmental Regulatory Regime Approach 214
		D.	Global Civil Society Environmental Constitutionalism 217
		E.	Transnational Comparative Environmental Constitutionalism 221
	V.	The Elements of Global Environmental Constitutionalism 224	
		A.	A Global Environmental Constitution 224
		B.	Global Environmental Rule of Law 227
		C.	Separation of Global Environmental Governance Powers 229
		D.	The Global Environmental Judiciary 230

		E.	Global Environmental Democracy..237
		F.	Global Environmental Constitutional Supremacy..239
		G.	Global Environmental Rights 242
	VI.	Conclusion...245
8.	Conclusion 246

Bibliography..248
Index 271

1

Introduction

I. Human Domination

There is persuasive evidence suggesting we are on the brink of human-induced ecological disaster that could change life on Earth as we know it. The United Nations Environment Programme, in its authoritative *Global Environmental Outlook 5*, confirms that anthropogenic drivers of environmental change are 'growing, evolving and combining at such an accelerating pace, at such a large scale and with such widespread reach that they are exerting unprecedented pressure on the environment'.[1] While there is always the threat of single or multiple-event natural disasters occurring (such as volcanic eruptions, massive earthquakes or a meteor impact), the eventuality of human-induced ecological disasters is not a distant possibility; it is increasingly considered imminent.[2] Human-induced ecological disasters, such as climate change, refer to the collection of human impacts as well as to the cumulative totality and effects of these impacts on the Earth and its systems.[3] These disasters are not only 'environmental', but also reach into various other spheres of human experience as a result of threat multipliers that have cascading effects,[4] as climate change with its ability to ignite and aggravate social, economic and political dilemmas vividly illustrates.[5]

In the wake of dire warnings such as those from UNEP, there is an increasing realisation that we are living in a period in Earth's geological history that signifies human domination of the Earth and its complex systems.[6] The extent and effects of this human domination and environmental imprint is astounding and it is caused by 'global-scale forcing mechanisms' that might lead to state shifts in,

---

[1] United Nations Environment Programme (UNEP), 'Global Environment Outlook: Environment for the Future We Want' (*GEO 5*, 2012) www.unep.org/geo/geo5.asp 23.
[2] AD Barnosky et al, 'Approaching a State Shift in Earth's Biosphere' (2012) 486 *Nature* 52.
[3] J Zalasiewicz et al, 'Are we Now Living in the Anthropocene?' (2008) 18(2) *Geological Society of America Today* 4.
[4] T Ng, 'Safeguarding Peace and Security in our Warming World: A Role for the Security Council' (2010) 15 *Journal of Conflict and Security Law* 275, 283.
[5] See, among the many publications in this respect, J Verschuuren (ed), *Research Handbook on Climate Change Adaptation Law* (Cheltenham, Edward Elgar, 2013).
[6] PJ Crutzen and EF Stoermer, 'The "Anthropocene"' (2000) 41 *IGBP Global Change Newsletter* 17.

or critical transitions of, the Earth's biosphere.[7] These human forcing mechanisms are broadly divided into human population growth and resource consumption (the two main drivers underlying all other drivers); habitat transformation and fragmentation; energy production and consumption; and climate change.[8] Statistics suggest the following with respect to these forcing mechanisms:

Population growth: While the Earth's natural resources have not increased, the world population has grown from 2.5 billion in 1950 to 7 billion people today;[9] a number that is predicted to increase to 9.5 billion in 2050, and which will compound human demands exceeding the carrying capacity and critical thresholds of Earth systems.[10]

Consumption: During the twentieth century, global economic output grew more than 20-fold, while materials extraction expanded to approximately 60 billion tonnes per year, with global gross domestic product (GDP) increasing by a factor of 24.[11] These indicators of consumption have been showing no signs of abating into the twenty-first century.

Habitat transformation and fragmentation: Vast areas of the Earth's surface are being converted from natural forests to agricultural areas with 37.4 per cent of the planet's land surface being used for agricultural production and urban areas, while 50 per cent of wetlands have been lost as a result.[12]

Energy production and consumption: Humans are drastically modifying the way energy flows through the global ecosystem.[13] From 1992 to 2008, per-person energy consumption increased globally at a rate of 5 per cent annually, leading to significant spikes in greenhouse gas (GHG) emissions (ranging from 310 parts per million in 1950 to 391 parts per million in 2011, with half the total rise in atmospheric CO^2 since the pre-industrial era having occurred in the last 30 years).[14] The global carbon sink in the biosphere has also increased from approximately 2 billion tonnes of carbon per year in the 1960s to approximately 4 billion tonnes in 2005.[15]

---

[7] Barnosky et al suggest while planetary scale critical transitions have occurred previously in the biosphere, 'humans are now forcing another such transition, with the potential to transform Earth rapidly and irreversibly into a state unknown in human experience': Barnosky et al, 'Approaching a State Shift' (n 2) 52.

[8] ibid 53. Others use a broader range of human development indicators. eg Steffen et al show a significant spike in the post-Second World War period with respect to: population, total real gross domestic product, foreign direct investment, damming of rivers, water use, fertiliser consumption, urban population, paper consumption, number of McDonald's restaurants, number of motor vehicles, number of telephones and international travel: W Steffen et al, 'The Anthropocene: Conceptual and Historical Perspectives' (2011) 369 *Philosophical Transactions of the Royal Society* 842, 851.

[9] United Nations Department of Economic and Social Affairs Population Division, 'Population Estimates and Projections Section' (2015) esa.un.org/unpd/wpp/Excel-Data/population.htm.

[10] Geohive, 'Global Population Statistics' (2016) www.geohive.com/.

[11] UNEP, 'Global Environment Outlook' (n 1) 10–11.

[12] ibid 8, 139.

[13] Barnosky et al (n 2) 54.

[14] UNEP (n 1) 14.

[15] ibid 196, 197.

Climate change: Most recently in its Fifth Assessment Report, the Intergovernmental Panel on Climate Change (IPCC) determined with greater certainty than ever before that '[h]uman interference with the climate system is occurring' and that climate change is observably affecting various socio-ecological systems with possible disastrous consequences.[16] This prediction was subsequently corroborated by the World Meteorological Organization (WMO), which showed that in 2013, concentration of CO^2 in the atmosphere was 142 per cent of the pre-industrial era (1750), and of methane and nitrous oxide, 253 per cent and 121 per cent respectively.[17] The cumulative result is an unprecedented spike in the rate of ocean acidification, which could severely inhibit the ocean's functions as the primary driver of the planet's climate and attenuator of climate change.[18] With an expected 4°C warming, climate change is projected to become the dominant driver of impacts on ecosystems, superseding other drivers such as land-use change.[19]

Despite deliberate resistance from the neo-liberal growth-without-limits agenda,[20] there seems to be general consensus among scientists about the pace and extent of global socio-ecological decay, including a realisation that humans are central to causing this crisis. Representing a collective estimation that is based on the joint research of four major global research programmes,[21] the Amsterdam Declaration on Global Change of 2001, confirmed that the Earth system has moved well outside its range of natural variability exhibited over the last half million years.[22] Clearly, the human impact on the Earth system cannot today only be characterised simply as the degree in change compared to the pre-Industrial Revolution period, but increasingly also as a difference in the kind of changes that humans affect;[23] changes that might very well mark a distinct new geological period in the Earth's history. These changes physically manifest in and are exemplified by, among others, the damning of rivers and building of sluices; alteration

---

[16] Intergovernmental Panel on Climate Change (IPCC), '5th Assessment Report—Climate Change 2014: Impacts, Adaptation and Vulnerability (Technical Summary)' (2014) ipcc-wg2.gov/AR5/images/uploads/WGIIAR5-TS_FGDall.pdf 17.

[17] World Meteorological Organization, 'The State of Greenhouse Gasses in the Atmosphere Based on Global Observations through 2013' (2014) 10 *WMO Greenhouse Gas Bulletin* 1.

[18] World Meteorological Organization, 'Press Release Number 1002: Record Greenhouse Gas Levels Impact Atmosphere and Oceans' (9 September 2014) www.wmo.int/pages/mediacentre/press_releases/pr_1002_en.html.

[19] IPCC, '5th Assessment Report' (n 16) 18.

[20] See, for a particularly critical account, A Grear, *Redirecting Human Rights: Facing the Challenge of Corporate Legal Humanity* (New York, Palgrave Macmillan, 2010).

[21] These programmes include: the International Geosphere-Biosphere Programme (IGBP), the International Human Dimensions Programme on Global Environmental Change (IHDP), the World Climate Research Programme (WCRP) and the international biodiversity programme, DIVERSITAS. See International Geosphere-Biosphere Programme (IGBP) et al, 'The Amsterdam Declaration on Global Change' (2001) www.colorado.edu/AmStudies/lewis/ecology/gaiadeclar.pdf; and for a useful retrospective analysis, A Ignaciuk et al, 'Responding to Complex Societal Challenges: A Decade of Earth System Science Partnership (ESSP) Interdisciplinary Research' (2012) 4 *Current Opinion in Environmental Sustainability* 147.

[22] IGBP et al, 'Amsterdam Declaration' (n 21).

[23] K Scott, 'International Law in the Anthropocene: Responding to the Geoengineering Challenge' (2013) 34 *Michigan Journal of International Law* 309, 310, 315.

of the Earth's atmosphere as a result of GHG emissions which have reached their highest levels in 400,000 years; interference with natural oceanic cycles; and alteration of the Earth's surface through mining and other forms of land use such as urban sprawl.[24]

II. The Anthropocene's Global Socio-Ecological Crisis

This vaguely apocalyptic narrative underlies scientists' recent suggestion that we have probably entered a human-dominated geological epoch called the Anthropocene. The Anthropocene was first introduced in a 2000 publication by Eugene F Stoermer and Paul J Crutzen as a term of art expressing the geological significance of anthropogenic change.[25] Emphasising the central role of mankind as a major driving force in modifying the biosphere, the term Anthropocene suggests that the Earth is rapidly moving into a critically unstable state, with Earth systems gradually becoming less predictable, non-stationary and less harmonious as a result of the global human imprint on the biosphere.[26] In the Anthropocene, humanity has become a geological agent in much the same way as a volcano or meteor—able to change the Earth and its systems, and possibly even to cause a mass extinction.[27] The existence of a boundary that separates the current harmonious Holocene epoch (still formally viewed as being 'current')[28] from the human-dominated and unstable Anthropocene, has not been officially defined though.[29] A proposal to formalise the Anthropocene as an epoch of the geological timescale is being prepared by the Anthropocene Working Group for consideration by the International Commission on Stratigraphy.[30]

With its formal acceptance pending, the Anthropocene has meanwhile managed to grab the attention of a growing trans-disciplinary cohort of scholars and it

---

[24] See, generally, M Whitehead, *Environmental Transformations: A Geography of the Anthropocene* (New York, Routledge, 2014).
[25] Crutzen and Stoermer, 'The "Anthropocene"' (n 6) 17.
[26] LJ Kotzé, 'Rethinking Global Environmental Law and Governance in the Anthropocene' (2014) 32 *Journal of Energy and Natural Resources Law* 121.
[27] M Hodson and S Marvin, 'Urbanism in the Anthropocene: Ecological Urbanism or Premium Ecological Enclaves?' (2010) 14 *City* 299.
[28] It is argued that:

> Earth has endured changes sufficient to leave a global stratigraphic signature distinct from that of the Holocene or of previous Pleistocene interglacial phases, encompassing novel biotic, sedimentary, and geochemical change. These changes, although likely only in their initial phases, are sufficiently distinct and robustly established for suggestions of a Holocene-Anthropocene boundary in the recent historical past to be geologically reasonable.

Zalasiewicz et al, 'Are we Now Living in the Anthropocene?' (n 3) 4.

[29] AD Barnosky et al, 'Introducing the Scientific Consensus on Maintaining Humanity's Life Support Systems in the 21st Century: Information for Policy Makers' (2014) 1 *The Anthropocene Review* 78, 78.
[30] See Subcommission on Quaternary Stratigraphy, 'Working Group on the "Anthropocene"' (2015) quaternary.stratigraphy.org/workinggroups/anthropocene/.

has become a major academic enterprise, even recently culminating in the launch of two dedicated scientific journals.[31] The burgeoning trans-disciplinary and global interest that the Anthropocene is attracting suggests that it is becoming a popular lens through which to consider the pure scientific, and increasingly the social aspects of past, present and future global environmental change.[32] To date, much of the work on the Anthropocene remains in the sphere of the natural sciences, although Anthropocene debates are now increasingly penetrating the social sciences realm.[33] As Robinson puts it: determining the existence of the Anthropocene 'is a scientific one, not a socio-economic or cultural determination, yet its greatest implications may lie in the realm of the social sciences'.[34] In Baskin's view, this is so because 'the term [Anthropocene] needs to make sense to, and be embraced by, social scientists, with their typically messy, contested and historically contingent ways of understanding the workings of human societies'.[35] The body of work that is being done around the Anthropocene suggests that we are seeing the steady emergence of a trans-disciplinary platform upon which to bridge the prevailing divide between the social world of philosophy, anthropology, sociology, politics, law and economics on the one hand, and the material world of engineering and natural science on the other;[36] aptly reflecting, perhaps, the collapse of old epistemological distinctions in the face of the new, sobering reality of the Anthropocene.

In tandem with its instigating this trans-disciplinary scientific confluence, the Anthropocene is rapidly transcending its initial use as a 'mere rhetorical device',[37] permitting deeper epistemological and ontological enquiries into our regulatory interventions that seek to mediate the human-environment interface.[38] In doing so, the Anthropocene fulfils a useful function to the extent that it could assist the broader scientific community solidifying the idea of humanity as an Earth system driver; aiding understanding of anthropogenic Earth system processes;[39] and fostering deeper political, social and cultural awareness of human-induced

---

[31] These are *Anthropocene* and *The Anthropocene Review* available at www.journals.elsevier.com/anthropocene/ and anr.sagepub.com/ respectively.

[32] The Anthropocene 'is not just a new way to look at the past; it [also] strongly affects the future': L Robin and W Steffen, 'History for the Anthropocene' (2007) 5 *History Compass* 1694, 1699.

[33] Malm and Hornborg, eg, 'find it deeply paradoxical and disturbing that the growing acknowledgement of the impact of societal forces on the biosphere should be couched in terms of a narrative so completely dominated by natural science': A Malm and A Hornborg, 'The Geology of Mankind: A Critique of the Anthropocene Narrative' (2014) 1 *The Anthropocene Review* 62, 63.

[34] N Robinson, 'Fundamental Principles of Law for the Anthropocene?' (2014) 44 *Environmental Policy and Law* 13, 13.

[35] J Baskin, 'Paradigm Dressed as Epoch: The Ideology of the Anthropocene' (2015) 24 *Environmental Values* 9, 23.

[36] O Uhrqvist and E Lövbrand, 'Seeing and Knowing the Earth as a System: Tracing the History of the Earth System Science Partnership' (*Earth System Governance*, 3 December 2009) www.earthsystemgovernance.org/ac2009/papers/AC2009-0107.pdf.

[37] Scott, 'International Law in the Anthropocene' (n 23) 312.

[38] Kotzé, 'Rethinking Global Environmental Law' (n 26) 121.

[39] W Autin and J Holbrook, 'Is the Anthropocene an Issue of Stratigraphy or Pop Culture?' (2012) July *GSA Today* 60, 61.

environmental changes.[40] Realising within this context that '[n]avigating the anthropocene [sic] has … become a key challenge for policy-makers at all levels of decision-making … to prepare—politically, legally, socially and economically—for the adaptation to those global environmental changes that can no longer be avoided';[41] provides a central impetus and motivation to also commence with a wholesale re-evaluation of the socio-political, legal and broader regulatory interventions that humans use to mediate our relations with one another and with other non-human Earth system entities.

III. The Anthropocene's Global Socio-Ecological Crisis and the Law

To this end, the Anthropocene mindset is notably beginning to infiltrate the legal, and more specifically the environmental law discourse, providing a new perspective for (environmental) lawyers to consider the role of law in mediating the human-environment interface during a period of a global socio-ecological crisis. Realising that law 'is deeply implicated in the systems that have caused the end to the Holocene, and at once is central also to the reforms needed to cope with the emerging Anthropocene',[42] allows an opening up, as it were, of hitherto prohibitive closures in the law, of the legal discourse more generally and of the world order that the law seeks to maintain, to other understandings of global environmental change (such as the Anthropocene) and ways to mediate this change. These closures are countering the new type of thinking that is both required and at once instigated by the Anthropocene mindset because, as Grear understands it, the closures concern a world order that is hegemonic through which it produces limits and a stifling sense of monolithic ideology that closes down the space for other modes of being and thinking by resisting such interventions or engagements with its dominant structures and modes of operation.[43]

Increasingly (albeit hesitantly), from international environmental and human rights law to nature conservation and sustainable development law, the Anthropocene is pushing against these closures and finding a place in juridical

---

[40] ibid 60.

[41] F Biermann et al, 'Navigating the Anthropocene: The Earth System Governance Project Strategy Paper' (2010) 2 *Current Opinion in Environmental Sustainability* 202, 202.

[42] Robinson, 'Fundamental Principles' (n 34) 13. Looking at law through the lens of the Anthropocene could expose the historic and continuing contribution of law to enabling a multitude of Anthropocene causes and realities, including, among others: the enclosure of the commons; the dispossession of indigenous peoples under colonialism; the continuing corporate neo-colonialism and resulting ecological ravaging; and asymmetrically distributed patterns of advantage and disadvantage that prevail in society. See further, A Grear, 'Deconstructing Anthropos: A Critical Legal Reflection on "Anthropocentric" Law and Anthropocene "Humanity"' (2015) *Law and Critique* 1.

[43] A Grear, 'Human Bodies in Material Space: Lived Realities, Eco-crisis and the Search for Transformation' (2013) 4 *Journal of Human Rights and the Environment* 111.

discursive spaces that have historically been reserved for fragmented, issue-specific, and narrow legal enquiries that accommodate less alarmist expressions of urgency and that have tolerated weak commitments to ethical responsibility towards the environment.[44] This is occurring as a result of scholars gradually commencing re-imaginations, in the light of the Anthropocene, of the role of environmental law and of its components (such as human rights) and its aspects (such as state sovereignty and biodiversity); the role of ethics (such as the tenuous relationship between ecocentrism and anthropocentrism); and long-held doctrinal palliatives (such as sustainable development), that have traditionally formed the backbone of environmental law.[45] Throughout these re-imaginations, there is a steady realisation that our legal systems cannot continue to 'rely on the assumption, never questioned due to our experience so far, that the stable conditions of the Holocene will last forever'.[46] Law cannot continue to comfortably rest on foundations that evolved under the harmonious Holocene, because under the type of biospheric conditions in the Anthropocene, 'Holocene law' will arguably be unable to establish and maintain the type of societal ordering it typically would have sought to achieve under 'normal' Holocene conditions. The Anthropocene is therefore not only a possible new geological epoch; for law and environmental law scholars specifically, the Anthropocene, acting as a current cognitive framework, is providing a unique opportunity to question and to re-imagine the juristic interventions that must ultimately be better able to respond to the current global socio-ecological crisis.[47]

IV. Constitutionalism and the Anthropocene

One aspect of the law where the Anthropocene has not found any explicit expression is that of constitutionalism. This is surprising, considering that constitutionalism is a foundational, if not *the* foundational aspect of law and of legal and

---

[44] Some recent publications include: R Kim and K Bosselmann, 'International Environmental Law in the Anthropocene: Towards a Purposive System of Multilateral Environmental Agreements' (2013) 2 *Transnational Environmental Law* 285; N Robinson, 'Beyond Sustainability: Environmental Management for the Anthropocene Epoch' (2012) 12 *Journal of Public Affairs* 181; LJ Kotzé, 'Human Rights and the Environment in the Anthropocene' (2014) 1 *The Anthropocene Review* 1; LJ Kotzé, 'Transboundary Environmental Governance of Biodiversity in the Anthropocene' in LJ Kotzé and T Marauhn (eds), *Transboundary Governance of Biodiversity* (Boston, Brill, 2014); D Vidas et al, 'International Law for the Anthropocene: Shifting Perspectives in Regulation of the Oceans, Environment and Genetic Resources' (2015) 9 *Anthropocene* 1; LJ Kotzé, 'Constitutional Conversations in the Anthropocene: In Search of Environmental Jus Cogens Norms' (2016) *Netherlands Yearbook of International Law* (forthcoming); LJ Kotzé, 'The Anthropocene's Global Environmental Constitutional Moment' (2015) 24 *Yearbook of International Environmental Law*.
[45] ibid.
[46] R Showstack, 'Scientists Debate Whether the Anthropocene Should be a New Geological Epoch' (2013) 94(4) *Eos* 41, quoting a speech by Davor Vidas, on 'The Anthropocene—and International Law of the Holocene', at Fall Meeting of the American Geophysical Union, San Francisco, 6 Dec 2012.
[47] Kotzé (n 26) 121.

political systems globally, of nation states, and in the private sphere. In most basic terms, constitutionalism 'is a way to think about (or conceive of) basic rules of the political game',[48] in which law plays a critical role. In the words of Albert:

> Constitutionalism is ubiquitous. It informs how states behave in the international order, how governments treat their constituents, how communities order themselves, how groups relate to individuals, and how citizens interact with each other. Constitutionalism compels and constrains all dimensions of our everyday lives in ways large and small that we often do not fully appreciate, perhaps because constitutions take many forms that we do not generally associate with constitutionalism. Yet whether in the arts, sports, trade, entertainment, politics, or war, constitutionalism is both the point of departure and the port of call.[49]

Just as the contemporary evidence concerning the emergence of the Anthropocene serves as a reminder that humans live in uncertain times of ecological upheaval, history has shown that regulators and legislators, in uncertain times such as the present, seem to seek refuge in the familiar, the constant and the trusted. Constitutions have been an influential component of political history and the world order for centuries,[50] providing a familiar language of good rule and order by acting as a logical 'go to' solution to attempt wholesale reforms in the aftermath of wars, or in the political transitions of countries from offending pariah states to global participative democracies. The creation of the United Nations and its Constitution, the Charter of the United Nations 1945; the equally important Universal Declaration of Human Rights 1948;[51] as well as many domestic constitutions such as the Constitution of the Republic of South Africa 1996;[52] are examples of constitution-type innovations that resulted from 'constitutional moments' that sought to counter injustice, oppression, political mayhem and societal instability.[53]

---

[48] M Saward, 'Constituting Sustainability' (2008) 17(2) *The Good Society* 12, 14.
[49] R Albert, 'The Cult of Constitutionalism' (2012) 39 *Florida State University Law Review* 373, 374.
[50] F Venter, 'Die Staat, Staatsreg en Globalisering' (2008) 3 *Tydskrif vir die Suid-Afrikaanse Reg* 412, 416–20.
[51] As a response and counter measure to the atrocities and human rights abuses of the Second World War, the Universal Declaration of Human Rights 1948, recognises in its Preamble that 'disregard and contempt for human rights have resulted in barbarous acts which have outraged the conscience of mankind'.
[52] As is the case with the Charter of the United Nations and the Universal Declaration of Human Rights, post-apartheid South Africa makes clear its intentions to break from its past and to embark on a new future through its constitution:

> We ... adopt this Constitution as the supreme law of the Republic so as to [h]eal the divisions of the past and establish a society based on democratic values, social justice and fundamental human rights; [l]ay the foundations for a democratic and open society in which government is based on the will of the people and every citizen is equally protected by law; [i]mprove the quality of life of all citizens and free the potential of each person; and [b]uild a united and democratic South Africa able to take its rightful place as a sovereign state in the family of nations.

Preamble of the Constitution of the Republic of South Africa 1996.

[53] Kotzé, 'Anthropocene's Global Environmental Constitutional Moment' (n 44).

While the political and socio-legal transitions evinced by these examples have all been attained through written constitutions in a remarkably quick way, it is also possible for these transitions to come about over a longer period of time through unwritten constitutions or constitutional processes such as in the United Kingdom.[54]

Whether written or unwritten, abrupt or prolonged, from a regulatory perspective, the general trend to revert to constitutionalism as a means to creating order and instigating socio-political and legal reforms is unsurprising: constitutions remain the highest expression of legal ideals in any legal order, providing the clearest manifestation and evidence of a social order's values and guiding principles.[55] Constitutionalism is also a 'good word' that has 'favorable emotive properties',[56] thus reflecting on constitutionalism's 'majestic possibilities for fulfilling the maxim that humanity can sometimes achieve unimaginable triumphs unbefitting the sum of its parts'.[57] Or as Peters describes it, the term constitution 'has a positive appeal which is owed to the positive connotations of a legitimate constitution as a good order'[58] (although she recognises that illegitimate constitutions may also exist). Mindful of the risk of overstatement, as the foundation of polities, constitutionalism is probably peerless when it is invoked to achieve regulatory transitions, to provide for ordered co-existence, and to entrench the values and ideals of a society at the highest possible juridical level.

But constitutionalism is not without its critics. Constitutions and constitutionalism more broadly have been criticised for being too Western-oriented; for being too dependent on the contested notion of democracy; for the disproportional power that is afforded to courts to strengthen judicial review functions

---

[54] The United Kingdom is the famous example of a constitutional democracy without a written constitution. It has a difficult and *sui generis* constitution 'deriving from a tortuous sedimentation of common law, acts and conventional usage, partly legal and partly extra-legal': G Sartori, 'Constitutionalism: A Preliminary Discussion' (1962) 56 *American Political Science Review* 853, 853. McHarg refers to the United Kingdom approach as 'political constitutionalism' as opposed to the more traditional notion of liberal Western constitutionalism. Through the United Kingdom's political constitutionalism: 'Fundamental values are expressed and protected through institutional design and practices and the attitudes of constitutional actors. On this version of constitutionalism, ordinary statutes can gain constitutional status, and therefore a measure of political entrenchment, if they are regarded by relevant actors as being intended to effect a fundamental change in, or to protect some fundamental feature of, the governing system': A McHarg, 'Climate Change Constitutionalism? Lessons from the United Kingdom' (2011) 2 *Climate Law* 469, 475.

[55] Bosselmann believes that the constitutional level unquestionably is the highest juridical expression of values and guiding principles in a society: 'Unbestritten ist die Verfassungsebene das zentrale Feld der Auseinandersetzung um gesellschaftliche Wertorientierungen. Nirgendwo sonst bietet sich eine vergleichbare Ebene, auf dersich Werte und Leitprinzipien einer Gesellschaftsordung so deutlich zeigen wie auf der Ebeneder Verfassung': K Bosselmann, *Im Namen der Natur: Der Weg zum ökologischen Rechtsstaat* (Bern, Scherz, 1992) 190.

[56] Sartori, 'Constitutionalism' (n 54) 855.

[57] Albert, 'Cult of Constitutionalism' (n 49) 382.

[58] A Peters, 'Compensatory Constitutionalism: The Function and Potential of Fundamental International Norms and Structures' (2006) 19 *Leiden Journal of International Law* 579, 581.

(otherwise referred to as the countermajoritarian dilemma);[59] for its reluctance to acknowledge the role of non-state actors as important contributors to work towards a common (constitutional) governance goal; for being disingenuous by attempting to window dress without achieving any tangible results where it really matters;[60] and for being such an endless process that 'it becomes unreachable ... leading one to condone the reality [of the situation it seeks to ameliorate]'.[61]

Nevertheless, given the premium that is placed on constitutions the world over, and the many positive advances that have been made in terms of creating constitutional democracies with all that goes with that impulse, it would appear on balance as if constitutionalism has been and continues to be a generally positive aspect of law and governance. Because of the promise of 'goodness' it seems to hold, its legitimising effect and its guardian functions, the allure of constitutionalism seems to be gripping various areas of law and socio-legal-political projects. For example, the gradual movement towards constitutionalism is evident in the regional and public international law domain, where the constitutionalisation of international law and regional law (notably in the European Union)[62] has become a flourishing normative and analytical enterprise.[63] The movement that seeks to clothe global trade law and the World Trade Organization in constitutional terms is an example of an instance where a specific legal discipline (trade law) is increasingly a focus area of the global constitutionalism project.[64] More generally, the argument that there is a gradual (but incomplete) shift in the focus of the world order from state sovereignty towards a value-driven and individualistic approach, further emphasises that there is an increasing turn towards the promise of constitutionalism, also at the global level.[65] Therefore, while the worth of constitutionalism or a constitutionalised legal order should not be overstressed by suggesting that it is a magic cure for all ills of law and governance generally, the argument that

---

[59] Ekeli explains the 'unavoidable quantum of rule-making' underlying the countermajoritarian dilemma as follows: '[S]ome degree of law-making and policy-making discretion and power is inherent in judicial enforcement (i.e., interpretation and application) of laws. This means that if the people and their elected representatives employ judges to enforce laws, some power to govern will be transferred to the judges': KS Ekeli, 'Green Constitutionalism: The Constitutional Protection of Future Generations' (2007) 20 *Ratio Juris* 378, 383. For a more forceful and critical account, see M Mandel, 'A Brief History of the New Constitutionalism, or "How we Changed Everything so that Everything Would Remain the Same"' (1998) 32 *Israel Law Review* 250.

[60] DR Boyd, *The Environmental Rights Revolution: A Global Study of Constitutions, Human Rights, and the Environment* (Vancouver, UBC Press, 2012) 5.

[61] G Galindo, 'Constitutionalism Forever' (2010) 21 *Finnish Yearbook of International Law* 137, 155.

[62] See, eg, J Habermas, 'The Crisis of the European Union in the Light of a Constitutionalization of International Law' (2012) 23 *European Journal of International Law* 335.

[63] See among the many publications, R Macdonald and D Johnston (eds), *Towards World Constitutionalism: Issues in the Legal Ordering of the World Community* (Leiden, Martinus Nijhoff, 2005); and Ch 4 of this book.

[64] See, among the many publications in this respect, A Stone Sweet, 'Constitutionalism, Legal Pluralism and International Regimes' (2009) 16 *Indiana Journal of Global Legal Studies* 621; G De Búrca and J Scott (eds), *The EU and the WTO: Legal and Constitutional Issues* (Oxford, Hart Publishing, 2001); and Ch 4 of this book.

[65] Venter, 'Die Staat, Staatsreg en Globalisering' (n 50) 412.

a constitutionalised legal order is preferable, better, or more acceptable than one that is not constitutionalised, carries with it considerable weight.

As the central hypothesis of this book, considering its profound influence in shaping histories and futures, and mindful of its central role as an aspect of law and governance to create some kind of good regulatory order, it stands to reason that constitutionalism should also be a vital component of the global regulatory arsenal that is currently being shaped as a social-institutional[66] response to the Anthropocene's socio-ecological crisis. To put it differently, while the absence of constitutionalism does not necessary mean the absence of environmental protection,[67] a constitutionalised global environmental law and governance order would arguably be better able to respond to the Anthropocene's unprecedented exigencies than a non-constitutionalised one. This is premised on the belief that a constitutional approach to environmental protection, of which there are ample domestic examples, has improved a number of domestic environmental governance regimes and has made a positive contribution to both the quality of environmental law and governance on the one hand, and to the results that environmental law and governance seek to achieve on the other: '[w]hile no nation has yet achieved the holy grail of ecological sustainability ... evidence ... indicates that constitutional protection of the environment can be a powerful and potentially transformative step toward that elusive goal'.[68]

V. Environmental Constitutionalism

Is there a discernable trend towards the constitutionalisation of environmental protection in legal regimes that would enable one to identify the emergence of a specialised focused form of constitutionalism that is exclusively concerned with environmental matters? Since the Stockholm Conference in 1972,[69] many states have adopted environmental protection provisions in their domestic constitutions and today three-quarters of the world's constitutions contain references to environmental rights.[70] In addition to rights (since a constitutional approach to environmental protection casts a net reaching far wider than rights-based

---

[66] Law as an institution is broadly understood in terms of Young's description of institutions as part of 'sets of rules of the game or codes of conduct that serve to define social practices, assign roles to the participants in these practices, and guide the interactions among occupants of these roles ...': O Young, *International Governance: Protecting the Environment in a Stateless Society* (Ithaca, Cornell University Press, 1994) 3; and Ch 6 of this book.

[67] JR May and E Daly, *Global Environmental Constitutionalism*, Kindle edn (New York, Cambridge University Press, 2015) 862/11268.

[68] Boyd, *Environmental Rights Revolution* (n 60) 3.

[69] See, generally, E Daly, 'Constitutional Protection for Environmental Rights: The Benefits of Environmental Process' (2012) 17(2) *International Journal of Peace Studies* 71.

[70] Boyd (n 60) 47.

environmental protection and obligations as we shall see),[71] environmental awareness and broader environmental protection responsibilities are increasingly being articulated through constitutions and elevated to a higher juridical level through constitutions. Calling the world's governments to action, the World Conservation Strategy recognised as far back as 1980 that '[i]deally, a commitment to conserve … living resources should be incorporated in the constitution' that should entrench 'the obligation of the state to conserve living resources and the systems of which they are part, the rights of citizens to a stable and diversified environment, and the corresponding obligations of citizens to such an environment'.[72]

Constitutions are also creating institutions and alternative mechanisms to ensure greater environmental care. For example, in a pioneering attempt to constitutionalise climate change protection, the recent Tunisian Constitution[73] recognises 'the necessity of contributing to a secure climate and the protection of the environment to ensure the sustainability of … natural resources and the sustainability of a safe life for coming generations'.[74] For this purpose, it established the Sustainable Development and Rights of Future Generations Commission; a constitutional body that advises on social, economic, environmental and development planning.[75] Other popular non-rights based means by which to constitutionalise environmental protection include providing for and safeguarding sustainable development and its associated principles in a constitution as guiding principles, peremptory obligations or ideals; and by delineating specific state and non-state functions and duties with respect to environmental protection through directive principles or principles of state policy that work to galvanise, or to compel, legislative and executive activities to protect the environment.[76]

In sum, there is little disagreement today:

> about the importance of making some form of provision for environmental protection at the constitutional level, even if in the form of a state duty or objective rather than necessarily as a fundamental individual right. This is now indeed widely recognized. Globally, more than a hundred countries have constitutional environmental provisions of some kind; no recently promulgated constitution omits these, and many older constitutions are being amended to include them.[77]

---

[71] To be sure, '[s]pecific textual reference in the Constitution to an environmental right is not a prerequisite to the bestowal of constitutional protection': JYP Jnr, 'Toward a Constitutionally Protected Environment' (1970) 56 *Virginia Law Review* 458, 459.

[72] International Union for Conservation of Nature and Natural Resources (IUCN), 'World Conservation Strategy' (1980) portals.iucn.org/library/efiles/documents/WCS-004.pdf s 11.

[73] Constitution of the Tunisian Republic, 2014 (adopted on 24 January 2014). See for an unofficial English translation, The Jasmine Foundation, 'Constitution of the Tunisian Republic' (2014) www.jasmine-foundation.org/doc/unofficial_english_translation_of_tunisian_constitution_final_ed.pdf.

[74] See the Preamble and arts 12, 13, 44 and 45.

[75] Art 129.

[76] See also Daly, 'Constitutional Protection for Environmental Rights' (n 69) 71.

[77] T Hayward, *Constitutional Environmental Rights*, e-book (Oxford, Oxford University Press, 2005) ch 1, 3/15.

The deliberate reorientation of environmental protection towards and through constitutionalism that the foregoing evinces, suggests that a form of 'specialised constitutionalism'[78] exists which focuses specifically on the human-environment interface and which constitutes a particularly focused and specialised sub-division of the broader constitutionalism paradigm. To this end, 'environmental constitutionalism' has recently emerged as a new scholarly term of art, encapsulating in broad terms a constitutional approach to environmental protection.

Despite its emergence, as far as I have been able to establish from a survey of English, Afrikaans, German and Dutch texts, there exists neither a universally endorsed definition, nor a cogent theoretical or normative treatment of environmental constitutionalism (sometimes also termed 'green constitutionalism' although this term is not widely used).[79] Approaching this specialised form of constitutionalism from various angles (regulatory, comparative, empirically-evaluative and theoretical) some authors, however, have paid cursory attention to the issue.[80] Kysar generally describes environmental constitutionalism as the 'constitutionalization of environmental protection', and elsewhere as 'the constitutionalization of environmental law', which, he argues, remains largely a symbolic exercise in the regulatory scheme of things because constitutional provisions are sometimes weakly enforced and vaguely specified.[81] May and Daly take a global comparative approach and explain that:

> Environmental constitutionalism is a relatively recent phenomenon at the confluence of constitutional law, international law, human rights, and environmental law. It embodies the recognition that the environment is a proper subject for protection in constitutional texts and for vindication by constitutional courts worldwide.[82]

The authors admit that while it is difficult to determine exactly the conceptual and theoretical content, as well as the many different forms and components, of environmental constitutionalism, 'the constant is that environmental constitutionalism exists in just about every nook and cranny on the globe, with growing significance'.[83] Taking a theoretical view in an earlier work, I have suggested that where environmental care is couched in constitutionalist language, it is termed environmental constitutionalism, and is important and necessary for environmental protection because it provides the broader means to defend environment-related

---

[78] C Schwöbel, 'Situating the Debate on Global Constitutionalism' (2010) 8 *International Journal of Constitutional Law* 611, 632.

[79] Ekeli, 'Green Constitutionalism' (n 59) 378; and Ch 5 of this book.

[80] Commentators seem to accept the inevitable need for environmental constitutionalism, but stop short of delving deeper into the theory of this concept. eg while Gareau highlights the need of a global environmental constitutionalist order, he does not detail the meaning of environmental constitutionalism in the global context: BJ Gareau, 'Global Environmental Constitutionalism' (2013) 40 *Boston College Environmental Affairs Law Review* 403.

[81] DA Kysar, *Regulating from Nowhere: Environmental Law and the Search for Objectivity* (New Haven, Yale University Press, 2010) 229, 231.

[82] May and Daly, *Global Environmental Constitutionalism* (n 67) 178/11268.

[83] ibid 218/11268.

rights and interests, to restrict authority and private encroachment on these rights and interests, and to compel the state and even non-state actors to act affirmatively (collectively referred to as the duties to respect, protect and to fulfil constitutional obligations).[84]

Yet, these fragmentary accounts suggest that while domestic constitutional environmental protection has become a central part of most domestic legal regimes in the world, the discourse has not kept up with concomitantly developing a suitably systemised and unified notional framework within which to situate, explore and understand constitutional environmental protection. The evident reticence to critically engage with the concept of environmental constitutionalism and to provide any comprehensive and structured account thereof, creates various knowledge gaps in relation to, among others: a comprehensive notional understanding of environmental constitutionalism; the historical development trajectory and origin, motivation and rationale behind environmental constitutionalism; the scope and objectives of environmental constitutionalism as a strategy for better environmental protection and its various manifestations (for example, as a comparative research agenda, as an analytical perspective or as a normative programme); the distinct aspects of environmental constitutionalism; where environmental constitutionalism fits into, and what its relationship is with the broader constitutionalism paradigm; and the benefits and shortcomings of environmental constitutionalism, especially as a normative programme.

VI. Global Aspects of Environmental Constitutionalism

More importantly for present purposes, it remains unclear if and to what extent environmental constitutionalism could reach beyond the parochial state-bound understanding of constitutionalism, with a view to informing or even reforming a global environmental law and governance regime that should be better able to respond to the Anthropocene's global socio-ecological crisis. In other words, from a global constitutionalist perspective, it is unclear if there are elements of environmental constitutionalism present in the global environmental regulatory sphere; if they are, how they manifest; if they are absent whether and how they could come about; and how they should ideally be constructed to respond fully to the Anthropocene's global socio-ecological crisis.

In the current globalised age, '[g]lobal constitutionalism is the international legal term *du jour*',[85] and it is has become well-trodden scholarly ground.[86] Key

---

[84] LJ Kotzé, 'Arguing Global Environmental Constitutionalism' (2012) 1 *Transnational Environmental Law* 199, 208.

[85] C Schwöbel, *Global Constitutionalism in International Legal Perspective* (Leiden, Martinus Nijhoff, 2011) 1.

[86] See, among others, J Klabbers, A Peters and G Ulfstein (eds), *The Constitutionalization of International Law* (Oxford, Oxford University Press, 2009); and Ch 4 of this book.

themes that typically permeate the global constitutionalism debate include, among others: global constitutionalism acting as a limitation on a single locus of global power; increased participation and greater representation in global governance through a global constitutional approach; the creation of (a) global constitution(s) and corresponding institutions of global governance; legitimisation of global governance through a global constitutional approach; ensuring more effective global governance through the global institutionalisation of power and the regulation of that power; the development of (a) higher law(s) or constitutional norm(s) which place restrictions on states and non-state parties and which create accountability; the existence of a common universal value system based on fundamental rights; and the pursuit of the common interests of an internationally community.[87]

Apart from cursory attempts,[88] the global constitutionalism narrative has not meaningfully merged with the environmental constitutionalism narrative in any comprehensively structured way. As well, environmental protection has not yet found any meaningful place in the global constitutionalism domain and its discourse. The result is that the conceptual meaning, content, scope, manifestations and implications of global environmental constitutionalism remain at best at the periphery of the global constitutionalism debate and at worst, undetermined. It is unclear, for example: to what extent the domestic environmental constitutionalism and the global constitutionalism spaces are compatible and which elements of domestic environmental constitutionalism (such as the rule of law, rights and judicial review) could be replicated in the global sphere; what different scientific manifestations global environmental constitutionalism could take (for example, as a comparative research agenda, as an analytical perspective or as a normative programme); and the purpose of global environmental constitutionalism (for example, acting as a means of constituting and organising global environmental authority, and/or as a means of providing higher-order protective guarantees by fostering greater legitimacy in law and political orders and calling for certain forms of checks and balances). It is also unclear whether a global environmental constitution exists; if it does not, whether there is sufficient justification for its creation; and if there is, what specific form such a global environmental constitution should take.[89] The foregoing issues collectively express the analytical *problematique* as well as the focus of this book, which seeks to approach global environmental constitutionalism conceptually and to offer a systematic analysis of how environmental constitutionalism manifests globally and could eventually emerge in the light of the Anthropocene mindset.

---

[87] Schwöbel, *Global Constitutionalism* (n 85) 49.
[88] Kotzé, 'Arguing Global Environmental Constitutionalism' (n 84) 199.
[89] D Bodansky, 'Is There an International Environmental Constitution?' (2009) 16 *Indiana Journal of Global Legal Studies* 565.

VII. Global Environmental Constitutionalism Through the Lens of the Anthropocene

As far as the enquiry's analytical focus is concerned, approaching this *problematique* will require focusing on the normativity of global environmental constitutionalism. Global environmental constitutionalism normativity could mean many different things. In this book a normative approach is taken to mean an account of what global environmental constitutionalism is and what it should or could be like conceptually when viewed through the lens of the Anthropocene. Wiener et al state that a normative approach to global constitutionalism entails: 'a legal or moral conceptual framework that guides the interpretation, progressive development or political reform of legal and political practices beyond the state to reflect a commitment to constitutional standards'.[90] In terms of this approach, a normative conceptual approach to global environmental constitutionalism is an enquiry that seeks to determine the broader global constitutional framework that guides the interpretation, progressive development and/or political reform of legal and political process that relate to the environment, with a view to better reflecting a commitment to higher-order constitutional standards where existing regulatory regimes are non-existent or deficient to adequately institutionalise and fulfil environmental normative commitments and the ethical obligations of a society towards environmental protection.

Considering its paradigm-shifting potential, developing a normative conceptual framework for global environmental constitutionalism should occur within the analytical context of the Anthropocene and its imagery of a global socio-ecological crisis. Although the Anthropocene cannot lay any normative claims in the same way that law generally and constitutionalism specifically are able to, this book uses the Anthropocene as a system of thought that expresses a deep ethical need and justification for more thoroughgoing global constitutional interventions to enhance environmental protection as opposed to through 'mere' non-constitutional legal approaches to environmental protection, and/or to constitutional interventions that only occur domestically. To this end, the Anthropocene provides a useful analytical perspective from which to critically interrogate the conceptual normativity of global environmental constitutionalism and to understand and describe what global environmental constitutionalism is, what it should be, what it aims to do and how it could form part of the global regulatory agenda that must facilitate urgent intervention in the human-environment interface in the Anthropocene. This book therefore uses the Anthropocene to frame a notion of responsibility, at once acting as a context for the rise of global environmental constitutionalism; as a legitimisation for a global constitutional approach to environmental care; and as

---

[90] A Wiener et al, 'Global Constitutionalism: Human Rights, Democracy and the Rule of Law' (2012) 1 *Global Constitutionalism* 1, 7.

a means of emphasising the urgency of drastic global constitutional interventions that must address the Anthropocene's socio-ecological crisis.

In doing so this book likens the Anthropocene to an analytical lens through which we may view and understand the magnitude of the global impact of anthropogenic impacts on the Earth and its systems and the potential of constitutional interventions to mediate these impacts and their effects. The simile which likens the Anthropocene to a lens is reminiscent of Pease's like simile, in which she sees political theory frameworks as 'a pair of glasses whose different lenses allow us to view the distinct political, economic, and social characteristics and processes that shape world politics'.[91] She explains that:

> These lenses act as filters, directing attention toward (and away from) certain kinds of actors and focusing discussion on certain kinds of questions. Through these theoretical lenses, we see different reflections, different explanations regarding which actors—states, individuals, class, gender—should figure most prominently in our understanding of international relations.[92]

The Anthropocene could arguably fulfil a similar analytical function. It has the potential to raise new questions, and to identify new issues, emerging priorities, new relationships and, more importantly, new interventionist regulatory strategies that are couched in global environmental constitutionalism terms.

VIII. About this Book

In light of the foregoing, the present enquiry seeks to answer the following central question: considered through the powerful analytical framework of the Anthropocene, what is environmental constitutionalism and how could it be extrapolated to and understood in global terms? In seeking to answer this question, the book attempts to develop a systemised conceptual framework for global environmental constitutionalism that could provide structural guidance for future (empirical) analyses into the different components and manifestations of, and approaches to, global environmental constitutionalism alongside the Anthropocene's framework. The enquiry approaches the research question along the following argumentative lines and structure.

Accepting that the Anthropocene could probably be formally declared a new geological epoch in the near future, (and even if it were not, it will likely remain an influential aspect of the scientific discourse by continuing to act as an analytical framework), the discussion commences in Chapter 2 with an analysis of the Anthropocene and the implications of this proposed geological epoch for

---

[91] KS Pease, *International Organizations: Perspectives on Governance in the Twenty-First Century*, 3rd edn (Upper Saddle River, Pearson Prentice Hall, 2008) 1–2.
[92] ibid.

our regulatory, and more specifically, legal interventions that mediate the human-environment interface. The discussion will show that the idea of the Anthropocene is set to place unprecedented strain on perceptions of our legal institutions and that it creates a new position of responsibility for humans who are ironically uniquely situated to design normative frameworks that could respond to change the lethal behaviours that make us paradoxically so powerful and so vulnerable in relation to the biosphere. Highlighting the need for an apex judicial intervention through constitutionalism that is both unprecedented in its depth and global in its reach, this chapter will illustrate the extent to which the Anthropocene mindset will require of us to rethink our juridical regulatory interventions in global constitutional terms.

Considering the centrality of constitutionalism as a foundation of law and the idea that constitutionalism is a potent juridical construction through which humans could express their responsibility to the biosphere as ecological and as moral agents, Chapter 3 argues that constitutionalism should form the basis of a legal approach that aims to mediate the human-environment interface in the Anthropocene. In doing so, the discussion traces the profound influence that constitutionalism has had on societies over many decades. With a focus on the rationale, objectives, meaning, features or elements, and possible advantages and disadvantages that constitutionalism generally holds out as a normative regulatory intervention, the discussion aims to show that, as an apex form of law embedded in domestic legal frameworks, constitutionalism could exert the type of far-reaching and paradigm-changing regulatory influences on law, society and politics that would be necessary to help counter the Anthropocene's socio-ecological crisis. In doing so, while accepting that constitutionalism is not a panacea for all regulatory ills and certainly not for all Anthropocene exigencies in their entirety, and accepting that non-constitutional law will and must continue to form a fundamental component of the broader global environmental governance paradigm, this chapter will start building a case for the global constitutionalisation of environmental care in the Anthropocene.

Chapter 4 takes the generic and domestically-situated constitutionalism debate developed in Chapter 3 to the global level by critically analysing global constitutionalism; its meaning; its different manifestations and elements; its parallels with domestic constitutionalism; and its relevance for global environmental law and governance. The intention with this part is to sketch the global contours of constitutionalism that will be used to frame global environmental constitutionalism in Chapter 7.

Chapter 5 focuses on environmental constitutionalism as a concept and its manifestations in domestic jurisdictions. It describes the conceptual parameters of this emerging specialised form of constitutionalism with its tailor-made environmental focus on the environment, including a description of its historical conceptual development, current manifestations and descriptions of these manifestations and their elements. The central aim of this chapter is to present a cogent conceptual description of environmental constitutionalism, thus adding to existing analyses that, to date, have focused on the specific elements of domestic environmental constitutionalism from a predominantly comparative and rights-based point of view.[93]

Chapter 6 ties the ideas of the Anthropocene and constitutionalism by critically appraising the prospects of environmental constitutionalism as an apex juridical approach to mediate the human-environment interface in the Anthropocene. In doing so, it first offers a discussion of some of the implications of viewing law through the Anthropocene lens. Through this discussion it will be illustrated that the expectations of law, when it is situated in the Anthropocene's cognitive framework, are arguably so far-reaching that some form of constitutional law and constitutional transformation would be inevitable as part of the global juridical response to Anthropocene exigencies. Building on the previous chapter's findings, Chapter 6 also weighs the perceived advantages of environmental constitutionalism against its perceived disadvantages with a view to critically appraising the potential of a constitutional approach to environmental protection in the Anthropocene.

As an amalgamation of the different thoughts and findings that have been offered in all previous chapters, Chapter 7 endeavours to translate environmental constitutionalism to the global regulatory domain and to propose a more systematic and comprehensive understanding of global environmental constitutionalism, its possible manifestations, its components and approaches thereto. This chapter first constructs a motivation in support of opening closed epistemic spaces in the global constitutionalism and environmental discourses that could be more receptive to 'radical' ideas such as global constitutionalism and the Anthropocene. Taking a *lex lata* and *lex ferenda* stance, it then investigates the environmental aspects of the different approaches to global constitutionalism elaborated in Chapter 4 including: the internationalist approach, the regionalist approach, the international regulatory regime approach, the global civil society constitutionalism approach, and finally, the transnational comparative constitutionalism approach. With reference to the general features of the constitutional state, the chapter then discusses in detail how these features currently do, and ideally should, manifest in the global environmental constitutionalism paradigm. In doing so, a framework is constructed for envisioning global environmental constitutionalism in terms of its component parts, ie a global environmental constitution, global environmental rule of law, separation of global environmental powers, the global environmental judiciary, global environmental democracy, global environmental constitutional supremacy, and finally, global environmental rights.

---

[93] The two major works in this respect are, May and Daly (n 67) and Boyd (n 60).

Chapter 8 concludes the book and offers suggestions for a future research agenda.

IX. Original Contribution

This book's original contribution lies at three levels. First, it aims to provide a discursive space for the increasingly critical overlap between law and Anthropocene discussions by opening up the closures of law generally, and constitutionalism specifically, to the more radical imagery of the Anthropocene. Conversely, it aims to introduce constitutional thinking to the 'material' and natural science dominated world of the Anthropocene, with a view to creating a trans-disciplinary space where Anthropocene and legal debates are more comfortably aligned.

Second, to date, there is no systemised theoretical treatment of the concepts environmental constitutionalism and global environmental constitutionalism. Environmental constitutionalism and its related tracks are just starting to emerge in the environmental law literature; a deliberate emergence, but one that is not mature yet, at least not from a conceptual point of view. This paucity justifies a deeper and more comprehensive conceptual treatment of environmental constitutionalism and its global manifestations. The present enquiry is the first comprehensive and systematised contribution in this respect.

A third and related contribution lies in the book providing common ground for constitutional law and environmental law discourse to bridge the hitherto separated discursive tracks that these two legal disciplines have followed. The limited number of environmental law publications on global environmental constitutionalism has thus far not explored in any comprehensively systematised way the conceptual contours of global environmental constitutionalism. Discussions about the environment are also noticeably absent from the global constitutionalism domain. The majority of commentators in this area are international lawyers, political scientists and/or constitutional law scholars.[94] To date, the voice of environmental lawyers has been noticeably absent in the corridors of global constitutionalism. This book is a first attempt to link global constitutional and environmental law discourses more systematically and comprehensively.

---

[94] See the discussion in Ch 4.

2

Law and the Anthropocene's Global Socio-Ecological Crisis

I. Introduction

The world is in the midst of a global socio-ecological crisis. This much is evident from global state of the environment statistics that are well known and that have been equally well documented. Some prominent analyses include: UNEP's *Global Environmental Outlook 5*;[1] UNEP's *Vital Water Graphics: An Overview of the State of the World's Fresh and Marine Waters*;[2] the Food and Agricultural Organization's (FAO) *State of the World's Land and Water Resources for Food and Agriculture: Managing Systems at Risk*;[3] the Secretariat of the Convention on Biodiversity's *Global Biodiversity Outlook 3*;[4] the International Programme on the State of the Ocean' s (IPSO) *State of the Ocean Report, 2013*;[5] the European Environment Agency's (EEA) *The European Environment: State and Outlook 2010*;[6] the Assessment Reports produced by the Intergovernmental Panel on Climate Change (IPCC);[7] and the many in-country state of the environment reports.[8]

---

[1] United Nations Environment Programme (UNEP), 'Global Environment Outlook: Environment for the Future We Want' (*GEO 5*, 2012) www.unep.org/geo/geo5.asp 23.
[2] United Nations Environment Programme (UNEP), *Vital Water Graphics: An Overview of the State of the World's Fresh and Marine Waters*, 2nd edn (Nairobi, UNEP, 2008).
[3] Food and Agricultural Organization (FAO), *The State of the World's Land and Water Resources for Food and Agriculture: Managing Systems at Risk* (Abingdon, Earthscan, 2011).
[4] Secretariat of the Convention on Biodiversity, *Global Biodiversity Outlook 3* (Montreal, Secretariat of the Convention on Biodiversity, 2010).
[5] AD Rogers (ed), 'The Global State of the Ocean; Interactions between Stresses, Impacts and Some Potential Solutions. Synthesis Papers from the International Programme on the State of the Ocean 2011 and 2012 Workshops' (2013) 74 *Marine Pollution Bulletin* 491.
[6] European Environment Agency (EEA), *The European Environment: State and Outlook—Synthesis* (Luxembourg, Office for Official Publication of the European Union, 2010).
[7] See Intergovernmental Panel on Climate Change (IPCC), 'Assessment Reports' (2015) www.ipcc.ch/publications_and_data/publications_and_data_reports.shtml#1.
[8] See, eg, Australia's at Australian Government, Department of the Environment, 'State of the Environment (SoE) Reporting' (2011) www.environment.gov.au/topics/science-and-research/state-environment-reporting; and South Africa's at Republic of South Africa, Department of Environmental Affairs, 'State of the Environment' (2014) soer.deat.gov.za/State_of_the_Environment.html.

These reports collectively suggest that humans are significantly altering biogeochemical, or element cycles, such as nitrogen, phosphorus and sulphur that are fundamental to life on Earth; as well as causing unprecedented modifications of the water, energy and biological cycles.[9] Virtually all global environmental indicators have been rising exponentially, showing that 'the Earth system has clearly moved outside the envelope of Holocene variability'.[10] These indicators suggest major deterioration in all respects, including: an increase in greenhouse gas (CO^2, N^2O and CH^4) concentrations; rising ozone depletion; rising Northern hemisphere average surface temperature; an increase in the frequency of great floods; depletion of ocean ecosystems including fisheries; a rise in annual shrimp production as a proxy for coastal zone alteration; a rise in nitrogen with respect to coastal zone biogeochemistry; sustained loss of tropical rain forest and woodland; a rise in the amount of domesticated land; increased global biodiversity loss measured as the rate of species extinction; and expanding inter- and intra-species hierarchies and accompanying injustices.[11]

The extent of anthropogenic encroachments on the biosphere, as evinced by these indicators, is further exemplified in the broad terms of planetary boundaries that determine the self-regulating capacity of the Earth system (otherwise understood as biophysical thresholds). Developed by Rockström and his colleagues,[12] the boundary theory seeks to refocus our attention on the non-negotiable planetary preconditions that humanity needs to respect in order to avoid the risk of calamitous global environmental change. As a global environmental change threshold reference framework, planetary boundaries is signalling the fact that humanity is venturing into unchartered territory as far as the Earth system is concerned;[13] or an 'unsafe operating space' for humans in the Earth system.[14] A 'safe space' on the other hand is a value judgement based on how societies deal with risk and uncertainty and it expresses the current 'space' we live in that has more or less safely enveloped humanity for centuries. In terms of the boundary theory, when a boundary or biophysical threshold is crossed, humanity is entering an unsafe operating space,[15] which implies a risk of damaging or catastrophic loss of existing ecosystem functions or services across the biosphere.[16] As we are approaching and/or crossing these boundaries, we are simultaneously instigating a state shift in the Earth's biosphere that could cause critical planetary scale transitions as a

---

[9] W Steffen et al, 'The Anthropocene: Conceptual and Historical Perspectives' (2011) 369 *Philosophical Transactions of the Royal Society* 842, 843.
[10] ibid 850–51.
[11] ibid 852–53.
[12] J Rockström et al, 'Planetary Boundaries: Exploring the Safe Operating Space for Humanity' (2009) 14(2) *Ecology and Society* 1.
[13] PJ Crutzen and EF Stoermer, 'The "Anthropocene"' (2000) 41 *IGBP Global Change Newsletter* 17.
[14] Rockström et al, 'Planetary Boundaries' (n 12) 1.
[15] Steffen et al, 'The Anthropocene' (n 9) 860.
[16] B Brook et al, 'Does the Terrestrial Biosphere have Planetary Tipping Points?' (2013) 28(7) *Trends in Ecology and Evolution* 1, 1.

result of threshold effects that could change life on Earth as we know it.[17] Of the nine planetary boundaries,[18] it is estimated that three have already been crossed, ie climate change, rate of biodiversity loss and the nitrogen cycle.[19]

While the Earth and its systems have been impacted and altered before, this is the first time in Earth's history that humans are considered to act as geological agents capable of changing Earth and its natural systems in the same way that a meteorite, for example, is. We have the potential 'to transform Earth rapidly and irreversibly into a state unknown in human experience'.[20] As a cognitive response to this realisation of a human-induced global socio-ecological crisis, it has recently been informally suggested that we have left the Holocene and entered a new geological epoch called the Anthropocene; or the epoch of humankind. Preparatory work is currently underway to propose the formal acceptance of the Anthropocene to the International Commission on Stratigraphy as a new epoch.[21]

II. About this Chapter

This chapter will argue that the Anthropocene, whether it is formally established or not, is a powerful framework that allows us to re-interrogate our regulatory institutions, including juridical institutions, with a view to devising a different approach to mediating the human-environment interface. Consequent upon the Anthropocene's imagery of a global socio-ecological crisis, we would need an apex juridical normative regulatory approach (among other interventions) with elevated authority that is global in its reach and at once more deliberately geared towards instilling the degree of environmental care and moral responsibility that would be necessary to continue life on Earth. Subsequent chapters will argue that such an approach at the global level must, as a minimum, be anchored in constitutionalism.

In order to illustrate the influence that the Anthropocene likely will exert on how we view our regulatory institutions and to understand the responsibility framework it creates as an impetus for constructing more far-reaching juridical interventions that are cast in global constitutional terms, the discussion commences with a brief contextual background that situates the Anthropocene debate in the

---

[17] AD Barnosky et al, 'Approaching a State Shift in Earth's Biosphere' (2012) 486 *Nature* 52.
[18] Climate change; rate of biodiversity loss (terrestrial and marine); interference with the nitrogen and phosphorus cycles; stratospheric ozone depletion; ocean acidification; global freshwater use; change in land use; chemical pollution; and atmospheric aerosol loading.
[19] J Rockström et al, 'A Safe Operating Space for Humanity' (2009) 461 *Nature* 472.
[20] Barnosky et al, 'Approaching a State Shift' (n 17) 52. Some, however, question the theory of critical tipping points and state shifts. See, eg, Brook et al, 'Does the Terrestrial Biosphere have Planetary Tipping Points?' (n 16) 396–401.
[21] See Subcommission on Quaternary Stratigraphy, 'Working Group on the "Anthropocene"' (2015) quaternary.stratigraphy.org/workinggroups/anthropocene/, and Ch 1 of this book.

context of the Earth's geological history. The next part reflects on the controversial historical point of origin of the Anthropocene. The discussion will illustrate that pinpointing a specific Anthropocene onset date is merely auxiliary to the more important realisation that an historical account of the Anthropocene as a cognitive framework seeks to convey: the extent of biospheric human domination, the resulting global socio-ecological crisis, and the need for urgent regulatory intervention.

The next part delves deeper into the etymology of the Anthropocene, with a view to emphasising human responsibility for creating the conditions that have led to the Anthropocene's socio-ecological crisis and that give rise to human responsibility to address this crisis. The chapter concludes in the final part by interrogating the significance and consequences of the Anthropocene, as a framework, for our socio-political and legal institutions with a view to framing a justificatory basis for a more intrusive, far-reaching and deliberate global constitutional approach to environmental law and governance in later chapters.

III. The Anthropocene and the History of Earth

Considering that the Earth is approximately an unfathomable 5 billion years old, scientists usefully divide this vast expanse of geological time into geochronological units of descending order of length termed eons,[22] eras,[23] periods[24] and epochs.[25] The division's chronological function seeks to present Earth's history 'as an ordered sequence of events, each placed in its correct relative position and allocated its proper time span',[26] thus providing a framework for deciphering the history of the Earth.[27] As far as the current formally recorded division is concerned, we live in the Phanerozoic Eon, the Cenozoic Era, the Quaternary Period and the Holocene Epoch. The Holocene Epoch or 'Recent Whole' is the latest of Quaternary interglacial phases and it denotes the relatively stable period of the past 10,000–12,000 years that has been characterised by extraordinarily good living conditions that enabled the development of modern societies in a world of

---

[22] Including Pre-Cambrian and Phanerozoic eons.

[23] Including the Protozoic, Archaean, Paleozoic, Mesozoic and Cenozoic eras.

[24] Including the Cambrian, Ordovician, Silurian, Devonian, Carboniferous: Mississippian, Carboniferous: Pennsylvanian, Permian, Triassic, Jurassic, Cretaceous, Tertiary and Quaternary periods.

[25] Including the Age of Invertebrates, the Age of Fishes, the Age of Amphibians, the Age of Reptiles, the Paleocene, the Eocene, the Oligocene, the Miocene, the Pliocene, the Pleistocene and the Holocene. See, for a useful tabular summary, HyperPhysics, 'Geological Time Scale' (*Department of Physics and Astronomy, Georgia State University*, date unknown) hyperphysics.phy-astr.gsu.edu/hbase/geophys/geotime.html; and for a discussion F Fitch, S Forster and J Miller, 'Geological Time Scale' (1974) 37 *Reports on Progress in Physics* 1433.

[26] Fitch, Forster and Miller, 'Geological Time Scale' (n 25) 1436.

[27] F Gradstein and J Ogg, 'Geological Time Scale 2004—Why, How and Where Next!' (2004) 37 *Lethaia* 175, 175.

7 billion people.[28] To date, it is the only interglacial unit to have been officially accorded the status of an epoch.[29]

To formally establish the Anthropocene as the new geological epoch will require of scientists to find evidence of human-induced Earth system changes in the fossil record, such as evidence of cities and diversion of waterways, or a warming climate and radioactive traces of nuclear activities.[30] If accepted, the proposal will have the effect of amending formal time stratigraphic nomenclature which, from a geographic and stratigraphic point of view, will be significant considering that the keystone rationale of the Anthropocene is that humanity's (and not a volcano's or meteorite's) stratigraphic imprint would be discernible to future geologists.[31]

In this sense, the Anthropocene is different from any other period in geological history, since its geological agents are humans and not a 'natural' phenomenon. As well, its justification does not rest on the issue of exact equivalence to past epochs in a formal sense, but on physical and biological human-induced changes that could alter the Earth's geology.[32] Essentially then, a central issue surrounding the Anthropocene revolves around efforts to successfully unite human history with Earth's history: '[I]n the Anthropocene era, "men" make more than history, they make *geological* history'.[33]

A further novelty of its possible formal acceptance is that, instead of following the usual retrospective approach, it would be the first geochronical unit to have been proactively designated before it has ended; a consideration which is eliciting some critique because, as a general rule, geological epochs are backward looking, ie, they are named and dated when they have passed, always following prolonged observations of major changes in the fossil contents of rocks below

---

[28] The (still officially continuing) Holocene started approximately 12,000 years ago and is characterised by stable and temperate climatic and environmental conditions which have (mostly) allowed human development to flourish: E Swyngedouw, 'Whose Environment? The End of Nature, Climate Change and the Process of Post-Politicization' (2011) XIV *Ambiente & Sociedade Campinas* 69; and Rockström et al, 'A Safe Operating Space' (n 19) 472.

[29] J Zalasiewicz et al, 'Are we Now Living in the Anthropocene?' (2008) 18(2) *Geological Society of America Today* 4, 4.

[30] M Whitehead, *Environmental Transformations: A Geography of the Anthropocene*, Kindle edn (New York, Routledge, 2014) 398/5354.

[31] W Autin and L Holbrook, 'Is the Anthropocene an Issue of Stratigraphy or Pop Culture?' (2012) July *GSA Today* 60; E Crist, 'On the Poverty of our Nomenclature' (2013) 3 *Environmental Humanities* 129, 130. Waters et al explain that stratigraphy deals with the classification of geological time (geochronology) and material time-rock units (chronostratigraphy), which has historically defined geological units based upon significant, but temporally distant, events that are usually associated with major changes in the fossil contents of rocks and thus the temporal distribution of life forms. Scientists will probably use the appearance and increased abundance of anthropogenic deposits; biotic turnover; and geochemical evidence as potential stratigraphical tools and techniques that may be used to define the base of the Anthropocene: CN Waters et al, 'A Stratigraphical Basis for the Anthropocene' (2014) 395 *Geological Society of London Special Publications* 1, 1.

[32] F Oldfield et al, 'The Anthropocene Review: Its Significance, Implications and the Rationale for a New Transdisciplinary Journal' (2014) 1 *The Anthropocene Review* 1, 2.

[33] E Lövbrand, J Stripple and B Wiman, 'Earth System Governmentality: Reflections on Science in the Anthropocene' (2009) 19 *Global Environmental Change* 7, 11.

and above a particular horizon.[34] Thus in terms of normal geological convention, the Anthropocene (or the human impact) would be visible millions of years from now in the layer of sediment indicating the present time in our history, reflecting a distinct epoch marked by human-driven geological change.[35]

The Anthropocene, however, has already been informally named and dated well before the nature of the signature of this proposed stratigraphical unit has even been determined. One optimistic view on this dichotomy is that '[f]or the first time in geological history, humanity has been able to observe and be part of the processes that potentially may signal … a change from the preceding to succeeding epoch'.[36] Another is that proactive designation of the Anthropocene invites a temporal dimension to the global regulatory debate on environmental change: the Anthropocene 'is as much about the future as the past',[37] thus opening up a wider range of policy options to the regulatory community that are directed at future interventions. At the same time, the temporal dimension that the Anthropocene introduces challenges us to think more critically about our existing regulatory interventions and forces us to ask whether they are capable of responding to the events that are causing the Anthropocene.[38] If they are found lacking, we might still have the opportunity to change them accordingly.

Others argue more critically that any attempts at formal classification of the Anthropocene now are essentially useless 'because future generations will have plenty of information to classify and characterize [the current epoch] with great precision',[39] because it is and should be their task according to the conventions of stratigraphy. As Waters et al in a recent survey suggest:

> if there is a consensus that the main environmental changes lie ahead of us, it might be concluded that it is too early to judge the position of the base of the Anthropocene, even if there is sufficient material evidence that the stratigraphic change to date is significant.[40]

IV. Turning Rock into Air: A Brief History of the Anthropocene

Whether or not to formally designate the Anthropocene is not the only controversial issue. There seems to be considerable disagreement on assigning a specific date to the onset of the Anthropocene, with the many proposals that are advanced

---

[34] Waters et al, 'Stratigraphical Basis' (n 31) 1.
[35] S Baker, 'Adaptive Law in the Anthropocene' (2015) 90 *Chicago-Kent Law Review* 563, 566.
[36] Waters et al (n 31) 1–2.
[37] K Scott, 'International Law in the Anthropocene: Responding to the Geoengineering Challenge' (2013) 34 *Michigan Journal of International Law* 309, 316.
[38] ibid.
[39] G Visconti, 'Anthropocene: Another Academic Invention?' (2014) 25 *Rendiconti Lincei* 381, 387.
[40] Waters et al (n 31) 15.

either being culturally constructed in a subjective sense, or based on more objective scientific evidence emerging from a specific scientific field. Generally though, scientists seem to follow either the 'pre-industrial' or the 'industrial' approach. Some of the more prominent views that are situated in these two approaches are explored below.

On the basis of a rise in CO^2 and methane gasses as a result of land clearing, fires and rice cultivation, Ruddiman follows a pre-industrial approach and estimates the onset of a human-dominated geological epoch to be 6,000 years ago when humans abandoned hunter-gatherer lifestyles and embarked on the domestication of crops and livestock (the Neolithic revolution).[41] He postulates that these early agricultural practices have led to a situation where pre-industrial temperature changes caused by humans could even be more than double the anthropogenic warming caused by the more recent industrial era.[42]

Considering that the measure of onset is coupled to human intervention in the Earth system, Glikson argues that the Anthropocene has commenced even earlier during the mid-Pleistocene when humans developed the unique ability to ignite the carbon-rich biosphere with fire, which in turn considerably magnified entropy.[43] As a 'fire species', humans could modify extensive land surfaces of Earth with consequences for the composition of the atmosphere, a process that culminated in the Anthropocene and possibly a sixth mass extinction of species in the near future. (Although some indicate that a mass extinction in itself would not in stratigraphic terms necessarily be sufficient to label the Anthropocene as a formal geological epoch).[44] Notably though, while humans have not been around during the earlier five mass extinctions, it is humans, so the argument goes, that are now instigating a possible sixth mass extinction, not through natural processes that influence the Earth and all life on it, but through 'unnatural' processes such as genetic modification, the introduction of toxins not naturally occurring in the Earth system, and through the physical alteration of soil, water and air. The mastery of fire by humans also resulted in an increase in brain size and a drop in tooth size as it became easier to eat tough meat and as the brain obtained much more nourishment through increased protein intake,[45] allowing humans to become cleverer, leaner, taller and more dominating as a species.[46] The argument accordingly suggests that it was the discovery of fire and subsequent

---

[41] W Ruddiman, 'Orbital Insolation, Ice Volume, and Greenhouse Gases' (2003) 22 *Quaternary Science Reviews* 1597; W Ruddiman, 'The Anthropocene' (2013) *Annual Review of Earth and Planetary Sciences* 45.

[42] Ruddiman, 'The Anthropocene' (n 41) 65.

[43] AY Glikson, *Evolution of the Atmosphere, Fire and the Anthropocene Climate Event Horizon* (Heidelberg, Springer Verlag, 2014) 75–88.

[44] Waters et al (n 31) 16.

[45] The human brain nearly tripled in size up to an average volume of about 1,300 cm³, and gave humans the largest ratio between brain and body size of any species: W Steffen, PJ Crutzen and J McNeill, 'The Anthropocene: Are Humans Now Overwhelming the Great Forces of Nature?' (2007) 36 *Ambio* 614, 614.

[46] Glikson, *Evolution of the Atmosphere* (n 43) 82.

evolutionary developments that provided humans their dominating capabilities and allowed them to manipulate the Earth's systems in major ways from generation to generation in cataclysmic fashion.[47] Also in line with the pre-industrial view, Oldfield et al choose to designate more generally the period running throughout the Holocene, and increasingly since the transition to farming,[48] as the most likely onset date when human activities began to move crucial aspects of Earth system functions well outside the preceding envelope of variability.[49]

Following the mainstream industrial approach, Crutzen and Stoermer admit to the arbitrary nature of their own choice when they indicate the onset date of the Anthropocene to be the latter part of the eighteenth century with the start of the Industrial Revolution (and more specifically the invention of the steam engine in 1784 and later the internal combustion engine).[50] In a subsequent publication, Steffen, McNeill and Crutzen argue that pre-industrial humans did not possess the technological or organisational capability to match or dominate the great forces of nature.[51] It was only with the expansion in the use of fossil fuels as a result of the Industrial Revolution that the human imprint became a central marker for Earth system changes, with perhaps the single simplest indicator to track the progression of the Anthropocene being the tremendous spike in atmospheric CO^2 concentrations since the Industrial Revolution. The authors argue that as part of a three-staged historical continuum, the Industrial Era (1800–1945) (first stage) was followed by the Great Acceleration (1945–onwards) (second stage); a period that saw the global population doubling in size, the global economy increasing by more than 15-fold, as well as increased urbanisation and motorisation that led to unprecedented spikes in carbon dioxide, a rise in inorganic nitrogen in the oceans, and increases in atmospheric sulphur dioxide concentrations.[52] They believe that we are possibly now entering the third stage of the Anthropocene's development continuum, namely that of 'Earth System Stewardship' (more generally known as environmentalism). This stage is mainly characterised by growing awareness of human impacts on the Earth system and a desire to more fully respond to anthropogenic modifications of this system, while assuming greater responsibility and modicums of environmental care.

Clearly, determining a specific onset date for the Anthropocene has become a considerable academic enterprise in itself and debates around this issue are

---

[47] PJ Crutzen, 'The Anthropocene: Geology by Mankind' in HG Brauch et al (eds), *Coping with Global Environmental Change, Disasters and Security: Threats, Challenges, Vulnerabilities and Risks* (Heidelberg, Springer Verlag, 2011) 3.

[48] Although some question the hypothesis that the advent of agriculture thousands of years ago changed the course of glacial-interglacial dynamics: Steffen, Crutzen and McNeill, 'The Anthropocene' (n 45) 615.

[49] Oldfield et al, 'The Anthropocene Review' (n 32) 1.

[50] Crutzen and Stoermer, 'The "Anthropocene"' (n 13) 17. Grear, however, points out that this argument seems counter-intuitive, since it is odd to imagine that the invention of the steam engine would coincide precisely with its later effects: A Grear, 'Deconstructing Anthropos: A Critical Legal Reflection on "Anthropocentric" Law and Anthropocene "Humanity"' (2015) *Law and Critique* 1, 3.

[51] Steffen, Crutzen and McNeill (n 45) 614–21.

[52] ibid 617.

controversial, varied and likely to continue. It seems more probable, however, that the majority of commentators will follow the industrial approach, especially considering that we have significantly more first-hand knowledge and evidence about the causes and the consequences of global change for the period since the Industrial Revolution: after all, this period has been part of our living reality whereas the pre-industrial era has not been. Moreover, the pre-industrial approach could have the effect of entirely eliminating the Holocene, which has for long been the official geological designation of the past 10,000–12,000 years; because the Holocene is thought to be divided into three stages (early, mid and late), it does not leave the option of officially considering the Anthropocene as a Late Holocene stage.[53] Such an extension into the Holocene by the Anthropocene, as it were, could affect the Holocene's continued scientific legitimacy as a formal geological epoch; an undesirable scientific delegitimising eventuality which could put into question much of the scientific work that has been done on the Holocene.

For present purposes, it is probably less important to side with either of these opposing views (industrial vis-à-vis pre-industrial). Instead, the Anthropocene onset debate serves a useful purpose for this study to the extent that it accentuates human domination over the biosphere, while simultaneously beckoning a contemplation of how we should counter the countless infringements caused by anthropogenic impacts. Many of the landscapes upon which global change is occurring have a long history of human interference and modification,[54] resulting in complete human mastery over the biosphere with humans altering, shaping and reshaping the biosphere according to their own needs.[55] For example, humans' ability to alter natural conditions and to create their own controlled and controllable environments specifically suited to their needs, is clearly exemplified by the city and increased urbanisation, which has become a 'defining spatial characteristic'[56] of the Anthropocene.

This tendency of humans to dominate the living order is properly captured by the Anthropocene's imagery of human impacts that stretch as far back as the emergence of humans on Earth; impacts that have exponentially increased since the Industrial Revolution. Its imagery also projects a disembodied and dislocated Cartesian epistemic human mastery over the biosphere that atomistically prioritises the individual as the sole concern for all implications of social life,[57] including the many 'self–certainties of western capitalism and the epistemologies of mastery it underwrites' that 'condones multiple intolerable exploitations'.[58] Accepting that

---

[53] Waters et al (n 31) 3.
[54] Oldfield et al (n 32) 4.
[55] P Pattberg, 'Conquest, Domination and Control: Europe's Mastery of Nature in Historic Perspective' (2007) 14 *Journal of Political Ecology* 1, 1.
[56] Whitehead, *Environmental Transformations* (n 30) 2666/5354.
[57] A Grear, 'Human Bodies in Material Space: Lived Realities, Eco-crisis and the Search for Transformation' (2013) 4 *Journal of Human Rights and the Environment* 111, 113.
[58] L Code, *Ecological Thinking: The Politics of Epistemic Location* (Oxford, Oxford University Press, 2006) 4, 7.

the many inequalities and injustices in human relations are simultaneously reproduced in our relations with the environment,[59] these are exploitations of humans by humans, and of voiceless non-human, but living, entities by humans; a victorious human endeavour of conquest with all too predictable results in hindsight: 'history is written by the victors, and how much truer for the history of the planet's conquest against which no nonhuman can direct a flood of grievances that might strike a humbling note into the human soul'.[60] This imagery of human domination, exploitation and destruction that the Anthropocene seeks to project, inevitably leads to the realisation that '[t]he enslavement of nature and the subsequent enslavement of humans by other humans has led to a global state of affairs that is neither morally nor practically sustainable'.[61]

As well, the onset debate illustrates that the Anthropocene is not only about humans dominating and interfering with the biosphere; it is also about humans having become and becoming an integral part of the biosphere where the parochial separation between humans and 'nature' is becoming increasingly blurred as a result:

> Humanity is part of the flows of energy and materials within the biosphere, but we are adding novel factors into the arrangement of these flows; new chemicals, habitat changes, atmospheric change by literally turning rocks into air in the processes of carbon fuel combustion.[62]

In this way, the Anthropocene is responsible for the steady emergence of a new epistemic constellation where 'it is impossible to understand nature without society, and society without nature'.[63] Within this new understanding, humans have become more than removed observers of 'nature' as pristine landscapes and/or as resources to which we are entitled. In the Anthropocene we have instead become major contributors to and actors in biophysical and biochemical processes; a consideration that will likely have profound implications for how we view our position and responsibilities in the biosphere, how we view our regulatory institutions through which we legitimise and enable our self-proclaimed entitlements to nature, and how we evaluate and design regulatory interventions to deal with increasingly unstable and unpredictable biospherical conditions.[64]

The new epistemological space of the Anthropocene thus rejects an objectified, removed and simplified external nature that people are unable to understand or to

---

[59] R Baghel, 'Knowledge, Power and the Environment: Epistemologies of the Anthropocene' (2012) 3(1) *Transcience* 1, 3.

[60] Crist, 'On the Poverty of our Nomenclature' (n 31) 133.

[61] Pattberg, 'Conquest, Domination and Control' (n 55) 7.

[62] S Dalby, 'Anthropocene Ethics: Rethinking "The Political" after Environment' (Paper presented at the 45th International Studies Annual Convention, Montreal, Canada, 17–20 March 2004) www.yumpu.com/en/document/view/42485216/anthropocene-ethics-rethinking-the-political-after-environment/3.

[63] E Becker, 'Socio-ecological Systems as Epistemic Objects' (Institut für sozial-ökologische Forschung, 2010) www.isoe.de/ftp/publikationen/eb_socecsystem2010.pdf.

[64] M Hill, *Climate Change and Water Governance: Adaptive Capacity in Chile and Switzerland* (Dordrecht, Springer, 2013) 4.

care for, but able to exploit without limits.[65] It invites instead a more enlightened view of human-nature relations that requires a deliberate effort to shift the parochial human-dominant exploitative focus of our regulatory institutions to a more inclusive ecological one which does not only include responsibility for the self, but also for all other non-human entities. Bosselmann illustratively puts it thus:

> In the light of the fact that no species can survive without respecting its ecological conditions, an anthropocentric perception of human freedom [manifesting here as nature removed from humans] appears as an absurdity. It is the saw to cut the branch we are sitting on.[66]

At the same time, the Anthropocene's new constellation of greater responsibility challenges the notion of inter and intra-species hierarchies, working to transcend the divide that has for so long placed humans and nature on separate, yet interrelated, sides of a duality.[67] Such hierarchies are gradually disappearing as a result of a steady ontological shift that is being driven by the Anthropocene imagery, where nature and humans are seen to have become one in the Anthropocene:

> Nature as we know it is a concept that belongs to the past. No longer a force separate from and ambivalent to human activity, nature is not an obstacle nor a harmonious other. Humanity forms nature. Humanity and nature are one, embedded from within the recent geological record. This is the core premise of the Anthropocene thesis, heralding a potentially far-reaching paradigm shift in the natural sciences as well as providing new models for thinking about culture, politics, and everyday interactions.[68]

Or as Latour puts it:

> the Earth is no longer 'objective'; it cannot be put at a distance and emptied of all Its humans. Human action is visible everywhere—in the construction of knowledge *as well as* in the production of the phenomena those sciences are called to register.[69]

For the sake of our regulatory interventions that focus on the human-environment interface, the conventional human-nature dualism 'no longer provides an adequate basis for assessing the functional dimensions of human-environment interactions'.[70]

In sum, the overall utility and discursive importance of the Anthropocene and its history of human domination is that it points to our and the biosphere's vulnerability by allowing us to see that multiple forms of vulnerability are constructed, aggravated and perpetuated by human actions and by the power we exert over the

---

[65] On external and universal ideologies of nature, see N Smith, *Uneven Development: Nature, Capital and the Production of Space* (New York, Blackwell, 1984).
[66] K Bosselmann, 'In Search of Global Law: The Significance of the Earth Charter' (2004) 8 *Worldviews* 62, 63.
[67] Grear, 'Deconstructing Anthropos' (n 50) 1.
[68] Haus der Kulturen der Welt, 'The Anthropocene Project: An Opening' (10–13 January 2013) www.hkw.de/media/en/texte/pdf/2013_2/programm_6/anthropozaen/booklet_anthropozaen_eine_eroeffnung.pdf.
[69] B Latour, 'Agency at the Time of the Anthropocene' (2014) 45 *New Literary History* 1, 5.
[70] Oldfield et al (n 32) 4.

vulnerable biosphere and its many and varied components.[71] As vulnerable, but powerful, entities that live in an increasingly unpredictable geological epoch and as part of 'nature', we cannot afford to cross the planetary boundaries that are now looming closer than ever before, for these boundaries have the quality of both finitude and finality.[72] More pertinently, the Anthropocene's imagery of human mastery, vulnerability and Earth system decay redirects attention away from hitherto overpowering human demands on nature, to human responsibilities and duties to address the global socio-ecological crisis. As subsequent chapters in this book argue, these responsibilities and duties could be expressed, among others, through the idea of constitutionalism.

V. The Anthropocene: What Lies Behind a Word?

In her musings on the Anthropocene's etymology, Moore warns: 'we should use words cautiously. Words are powerful, magical, impossible to control. With a single misguided phrase, they can move a concept from one world into another, altering forever the landscape of our thinking'.[73] Traces of such occurrences are evident in the climate governance arena where, as Scott indicates, phrases such as 'climate catastrophe', 'securitization of climate change' and the 'declaration of war on climate change' have been used to bring climate change under more direct attention of world leaders (albeit not nearly sufficient to bring about any drastic regulatory changes yet).[74]

In addition to the foregoing insights surrounding the Anthropocene's onset date, what does the word 'Anthropocene' mean and is it capable of 'altering forever the landscape of our thinking' about human-environment relations? Because the Anthropocene has not been formally accepted as a geological epoch, it has no formal universally endorsed definition. This is perhaps because no deliberate paradigm-shifting scientific discovery or moment accompanied its creation; quite the opposite. An ecologist, Eugene Stoermer, has used the term informally since the 1980s, and in 1995 he sent an email to colleagues describing terrestrial and

---

[71] A Grear, 'The Vulnerable Living Order: Human Rights and the Environment in a Critical and Philosophical Perspective' (2011) 2 *Journal of Human Rights and the Environment* 23; E Grant, LJ Kotzé and K Morrow, 'Human Rights and the Environment: In Search of a New Relationship. Synergies and Common Themes' (2013) 3 *Oñati Socio-legal Series* 953. Hans Jonas refers in this context to the critical vulnerability (*kritische Verletzlichkeit*) of a nature that has been subjected by humans: H Jonas, *Das Prinzip Verantwortung: Versuch einer Ethik für die technologische Zivilisation* (Frankfurt am Mein, Suhrkamp, 1988) 26–27.

[72] LJ Kotzé, 'Crossing Boundaries: Water and the Rights Paradigm' (2014) 5 *Journal of Human Rights and the Environment* 1, 1–4.

[73] K Moore, 'Anthropocene is the Wrong Word' (*Earth Island Journal*, Spring 2013) www.earthisland. org/journal/index.php/eij/article/anthropocene_is_the_wrong_word/.

[74] Scott, 'International Law in the Anthropocene' (n 37) 312.

neritic oceanic production during 'the Anthropocene'.[75] Since then, popular use of the term caught on and in 2000 Stoermer and Crutzen published a more formal scientific account of the Anthropocene in the *Global Change Newsletter*.[76]

While a formal and universally endorsed definition is lacking, some commentators have ventured their own descriptions of the Anthropocene. For example, Steffen, Crutzen and McNeill state:

> The term *Anthropocene* … suggests that the Earth has now left its natural geological epoch, the present interglacial state called the Holocene. Human activities have become so pervasive and profound that they rival the great forces of Nature and are pushing the Earth into planetary *terra incognita*. The Earth is rapidly moving into a less biologically diverse, less forested, much warmer, and probably wetter and stormier state.[77]

In a later paper, the authors (with Grinevald) propose:

> The term Anthropocene suggests: (i) that the Earth is now moving out of its current geological epoch, called the Holocene and (ii) that human activity is largely responsible for this exit from the Holocene, that is, that humankind has become a global geological force in its own right.[78]

For Lövbrand, Stripple and Wiman, it is the human imprint that is now 'according to the Anthropocene logic, so pervasive and profound in its consequences that it is influencing the very dynamics and functioning of Earth itself';[79] an idea which is reiterated by Brauch, Dalby and Spring when they state that we are 'shaping the earth, literally producing nature, as a consequence of our industrial metabolism, a metabolism that has very uneven geographical results as development transforms our political spaces and natural circumstances simultaneously'.[80]

Globaïa, in its cartography of the Anthropocene, defines it thus:

> A period marked by a regime change in the activity of industrial societies which began at the turn of the nineteenth century and which has caused global disruptions in the Earth System on a scale unprecedented in human history [including]: climate change, biodiversity loss, pollution of the sea, land and air, resources depredation, land cover denudation, radical transformation of the ecumene, among others.[81]

In a paper exploring the history of scientific historiography, Robin and Steffen propose:

> The Anthropocene defines the momentous and historical change in circumstances whereby the biophysical systems of the world are now no longer independent of the

---

[75] J Syvitski, 'Anthropocene: An Epoch of our Making' (2012) 78 *Global Change* 11.
[76] Crutzen and Stoermer (n 13) 17.
[77] Steffen, Crutzen and McNeill (n 45) 614.
[78] Steffen et al (n 9) 843.
[79] Lövbrand, Stripple and Wiman, 'Earth System Governmentality' (n 33) 10.
[80] HG Brauch, S Dalby and Ú Oswald Spring, 'Political Geoecology for the Anthropocene' in HG Brauch et al (eds), *Coping with Global Environmental Change, Disasters and Security Threats, Challenges, Vulnerabilities and Risks* (Berlin, Springer, 2011) 1470.
[81] Globaïa, 'A Cartography of the Anthropocene: Mens Agitat Molem' (2013) globaia.org/portfolio/cartography-of-the-anthropocene/.

actions of people. It is the Epoch dominated by humans. People have officially and geologically changed the course of nature at a global scale.[82]

For me, Dalby captures most eloquently the essence of the Anthropocene when he states:

> we now inhabit a planet that has been remade by human activities and the technologies that power our social systems ... The need for a new term comes not from a single historical innovation or ecological change but from the recognition that the total amount of human activity in all its diversity is now on such a scale we are living in a qualitatively new era ... The larger context of our collective being isn't a matter of fate or divine design; increasingly we are constructing the context for our lives at the very biggest of scales that, at least so far, matter to humanity, that of the planetary biosphere itself.[83]

Yet, even before these descriptions have emerged, a variety of other terms were used to convey something similar to what the Anthropocene seeks to impart today. For example, the term Anthropozoic ('Anthropo' meaning 'human' and 'zoic' meaning 'life') was used in the 1870s by Stoppani to describe the increasing human impact on the Earth and its systems.[84] The early-1900s saw the emergence of terms and phrases such as 'anthroposphere'; 'anthropogenic transformation of the Earth system';[85] and Vernadsky's 'noösphere' (indicating the emergence of human cognition where people began to create resources through the transmutation of elements that also transform the biosphere).[86] In the 1970s, Lovelock suggested the Gaia hypothesis; a global conceptual framework for human influence on biogeochemical cycles that is concerned with 'the evolution of a tightly coupled system whose constituents are the biota and their material environment, which comprises the atmosphere, the oceans, and the surface rocks'.[87] More recently in 1992, in reference to a 'post-Holocene' period that he describes as a 'geological age of our own making', Revkin proposed the term 'Anthrocene'.[88]

How do the foregoing terms differ from the Anthropocene, and is there a reason why the Anthropocene stuck instead of any one of the other terms? Steffen et al propose that these related notions are not equivalent to the concept of the Anthropocene because the Anthropocene is the only term that accurately captures the more recent 'Great Acceleration' of human impacts since post-Second World

---

[82] L Robin and W Steffen, 'History for the Anthropocene' (2007) 5 *History Compass* 1694, 1699.
[83] Dalby, 'Anthropocene Ethics' (n 62).
[84] Steffen et al (n 9) 843–44.
[85] ibid 844.
[86] V Vernadsky, 'The Transition from the Biosphere to the Noösphere: Excerpts from Scientific Thought as a Planetary Phenomenon 1938' (2012) Summer-Spring *21st Century* 10 (trans W Jones). See also for a discussion B Guillaume, 'Vernadsky's Philosophical Legacy: A Perspective from the Anthropocene' (2014) *The Anthropocene Review* 1.
[87] JE Lovelock, 'Geophysiology, the Science of Gaia' (1989) 27 *Reviews of Geophysics* 215; JE Lovelock, 'Hands up for the Gaia Hypothesis' (1990) 344 *Nature* 100.
[88] A Revkin, *Global Warming: Understanding the Forecast* (New York, Abbeville Press, 1992) 55. See also Waters et al (n 31) 17.

War industrialisation, technological and scientific development, the nuclear arms race, the population explosion and economic expansion.[89] They seem to argue that the Anthropocene conceptually encompasses the same histories of human domination as the other concepts do, but that the Anthropocene significantly differs to the extent that it also includes within its conceptual remit a more accentuated reference to the recent unprecedented spike in the biospherical human imprint. Such an interpretation is perhaps slightly one-sided, since these scientists follow the view that the roots of the Anthropocene lie in the Industrial Revolution and not in some earlier period such as the mid-Pleistocene that significantly pre-dates the Industrial Revolution.[90] In my view there are neither any convincing indications that the term Anthropocene is more appropriate or should be more meaningful or descriptive than the other terms; nor that it carries any greater explanatory or conceptual gravitas that should emphasise human domination more than any of the other terms. If it is the Great Acceleration that justifies the use of the 'Anthropocene' for those who follow the 'industrial view', then there is equal justification for all the other terms that are not contingent on the Great Acceleration factor. Terms and their meanings are what people ascribe to them and it depends on how people interpret them in accordance with their own kaleidoscopic scientific orientations, cultural and ethical stances and the purpose for which they propagate scientific terms.

Therefore, the choice of the term Anthropocene and its ensuing popularity rather seem to be balancing on the tip of arbitrariness. The reasons for its terminological legitimacy, and ultimately discursive endurance, remain speculative. The fact that 'Anthropocene' prevailed and not 'Anthrocene', for example, could be merely accidental, or an occasion of timing where the term and its apocalyptic imagery that is reminiscent of end-of-the-world movies, became embedded in the imagination of a despondent scientific audience that has been eagerly awaiting a novel common conceptual paradigm to better understand and express the severity of global socio-ecological change. To be sure, the fact that the term Anthropocene has developed and has taken root in the spectacular way it has, probably emphasises our desperate attempts to understand the global socio-ecological crisis we are witnessing today and to collectively express, through one term, the surrounding epistemological challenges in this respect.

After all, it does not take much for a word, an idea or a concept to become enduringly engrained in popular and scientific imagination, and ultimately in legal and political reality. A United Nations report could suffice, as the Brundtland Commission's report *Our Common Future* of 1987 illustrates with respect to the term 'sustainable development'.[91] While not suggesting they are in any way similar

---

[89] Steffen et al (n 9) 845.
[90] See the discussion above.
[91] Brundtland GO, 'Report of the World Commission on Environment and Development: Our Common Future' (1987) www.un-documents.net/our-common-future.pdf.

in terms of their meaning or purpose,[92] the Anthropocene's popular rise as a term of art in the global legal and political domain is to some extent analogous to the rise of sustainable development as a framework. Since its creation in the 1970s, sustainable development has become the worldwide dominating leitmotif for shaping international environmental and developmental relations, and it has developed at the international, regional and national levels into 'a crucial political precept that governs virtually every sphere of activity aimed at balancing and integrating economic, social and environmental policies'.[93] Despite its many shortcomings, as a concept, sustainable development introduced a new way of thinking about the human-environment interface that was at least novel, if not paradigm shifting, at the time.[94] Considering that it is increasingly permeating scientific discourse and the popular media (if not yet policy and legal processes in the way that sustainable development does), the Anthropocene could very well walk the same route in terms of its terminological development trajectory.

A more constructive, if not entirely argumentatively satisfying etymological approach with respect to the Anthropocene, is arguably one which simply accepts that while the foregoing terms differ to a greater or lesser extent in their disciplinary origins, their scope and their depth, they do share a common denominator by collectively imparting the idea of an epoch of the natural history of the Earth that is being driven by humans. Etymologically, Anthropocene derives from the Greek 'anthropo' and 'cene', or 'kainos', which mean 'human' and 'new'/'recent' respectively.[95] In the geo-ecological context this denotes a new period when humans dominate the geological epoch by acting as major driving forces in modifying the biosphere with humans being very much aware of their unprecedented

---

[92] M Mahony, 'The Anthropocene: Reflections on a Concept—Part 1' (*Topograph: Contested Landscapes of Knowing: Blogspot*, 12 April 2013) thetopograph.blogspot.de/search?updated-min=2013-01-01T00:00:00-08:00&updated-max=2014-01-01T00:00:00-08:00&max-results=14.

[93] U Beyerlin and T Marauhn, *International Environmental Law* (Oxford, Hart Publishing, 2011) 76.

[94] An idea that was confirmed by the International Court of Justice in the *Gabčikovo-Nagymaros* case:

> Throughout the ages, mankind has, for economic and other reasons, constantly interfered with nature. In the past this was often done without consideration of the effects upon the environment. Owing to new scientific insights and to a growing awareness of the risks for mankind—for present and future generations—of pursuit of such interventions at an unconsidered and unabated pace, new norms and standards have been developed and set forth in a great number of instruments during the last two decades. Such new norms have to be taken into consideration, and such new standards given proper weight, not only when States contemplate new activities, but also when continuing with activities begun in the past. This need to reconcile economic development with protection of the environment is aptly expressed in the concept of sustainable development.

Gabčikovo-Nagymaros (1997) ICJ Reports 78 para 140.

[95] RA Slaughter, 'Welcome to the Anthropocene' (2012) 44 *Futures* 119; Dictionary.com, 'Anthropocene' (2016) dictionary.reference.com/browse/anthropocene.

impact on the Earth and its systems;[96] a central idea that is suggested by all other related terms. Collectively and from a descriptive point of view for the purpose of establishing a minimum definitional base line, all Anthropocene descriptions suggest the following: as a result of observable Earth systems changes such as climate change and biodiversity loss, informally and unofficially, there is a Holocene-Anthropocene boundary separating a more harmonious reality (Holocene) from an increasingly erratic, non-linear and non-static reality (Anthropocene); this boundary has been caused by humans who have become geological forces that are capable of changing the Earth and its systems in the same way that natural forces such as volcanoes are able to do; and the unprecedented global anthropogenic impacts that are exerted on the biosphere demand a shift in how humans understand and respond to global change.

Therefore, as with the onset debate, terminological exactitude seems ancillary to the broader consequences of the historically descriptive etymology debate: whether designated as 'the Anthropocene' or simply 'an historical era of novelty',[97] we now live in times of unprecedented socio-ecologic upheaval as a result of our own doing where we act as masters of the biosphere and are at once an integral part of the biosphere. This period has become popularly known as the Anthropocene, and unless this epoch of human domination is officially assigned another name, it is most likely that the Anthropocene will continue to be used in scientific and popular discourse, especially considering that it has become virtually inextricably embedded in global ecological change conversations.

Baskin correctly points out that the Anthropocene 'does not need to be an object of scientific inquiry by geologists and stratigraphers, or even a formally-recognised geological epoch, in order to have an impact'.[98] Arguably then, even if it is not formally established, the Anthropocene will remain useful as an informal term of art that expresses biospheric human domination; acting as a framework in all sectors of life that are concerned with mediating the human-environment interface. Informal endorsement and use of the term will mean that we can concentrate on developing a narrative and mapping 'a unit conceptually rather than conceptualizing a mappable stratigraphic unit',[99] that is based on a popular framework

---

[96] M Hodson and S Marvin, 'Urbanism in the Anthropocene: Ecological Urbanism or Premium Ecological Enclaves?' (2010) 14 *City* 299. The extent of human impacts on Earth has been extensively documented in many disciplines and contexts. In the context of the Anthropocene, see among others: R Wagler, 'The Anthropocene Mass Extinction: An Emerging Curriculum Theme for Science Educators' (2011) 73 *The American Biology Teacher* 78; JJ Armesto et al, 'From the Holocene to the Anthropocene: A Historical Framework for Land Cover Change in Southwestern South America in the Past 15,000 Years' (2010) 27 *Land Use Policy* 148; I Ayestaran, 'The Second Copernican Revolution in the Anthropocene: An Overview' (2008) 3 *Revista Internacional Sostenibilidad, Technologia y Humanismo* 146.

[97] Dalby (n 62).

[98] J Baskin, 'Paradigm Dressed as Epoch: The Ideology of the Anthropocene' (2015) 24 *Environmental Values* 9, 12.

[99] Autin and Holbrook, 'Is the Anthropocene an Issue of Stratigraphy or Pop Culture?' (n 31) 61.

that usefully and vividly expresses the extent of the global socio-ecological crisis. Baskin more recently has confirmed that the Anthropocene is 'paradigm dressed as epoch', that it has entered the *zeitgeist* in spectacular fashion, and that it has 'scientific respectability despite not yet being an accepted scientific term'.[100]

In sum then, I would estimate that Moore's earlier warnings about the Anthropocene's etymology are probably correct to the extent that the Anthropocene has been able, though an ongoing process, to alter the landscape of our thinking about our current reality, and the human role in changing the Earth and its systems. The Anthropocene is capturing the popular and scientific imagination of those who concern themselves with the global socio-ecological crisis, acting as it does, as a mindset that emphasises human responsibility for causing *and* responding to this crisis: '[I]t radically unsettles the philosophical, epistemological and ontological ground on which both the natural sciences and the social sciences/humanities have traditionally stood'.[101] To this end, the Anthropocene:

> is not simply a neutral characterisation of a new geological epoch, but it is also a particular way of understanding the world and a normative guide to action. It is ... more usefully understood as an ideology—in that it provides the ideational underpinning for a particular view of the world, which it, in turn, helps to legitimate.[102]

Because such a new world view or ideology 'heralds an opening of sorts, a clarion call for change',[103] as Baker argues, this change must also be reflected in, and carried through, our regulatory institutions as we shall see further in this book.

VI. The Anthropocene and Regulatory Institutions

Ironically, while humans are now arguably dominating the biosphere as ecological agents, we are simultaneously the only species capable of deliberately intervening in the human-environment interface to address the global socio-ecological crisis. As Kobayashi puts it:

> On the one hand mankind, as Hobbes, Voltaire and Schopenhauer stressed, is a foolish animal that has such ill morals as cruelty, greed, and arrogance, but on the other hand it has the potential for beautiful morals, creative imagination and a prosperous existence. Mankind is the only being in nature to enjoy a rational existence, and therefore to choose by itself the route of self-destruction is blasphemy against the self and the creator; such a foolish act must be avoided ... mankind must stop warfare and environmental destruction, and redirect the rudder towards a constructive future.[104]

---

[100] Baskin, 'Paradigm Dressed as Epoch' (n 98) 10.
[101] ibid.
[102] ibid 10–11.
[103] Baker, 'Adaptive Law in the Anthropocene' (n 35) 567.
[104] N Kobayashi, 'Constitutional Studies and World Problems: A Study of Japan's Constitutional History as a Starting Point' in T Fleiner (ed), *Five Decades of Constitutionalism: Reality and Perspectives (1945–1995)* (Bale, Helbing and Lichtenhahn, 1999) 14.

In an effort to 'redirect the rudder', it is clear that our social regulatory institutions must change if they are to better respond to the exigencies of the Anthropocene: the Anthropocene requires a fundamental reorientation and restructuring of our institutions towards more effective Earth system governance and planetary stewardship.[105] If it is true, as Dalby suggests, that '[t]he global political agenda for the twenty-first century will be about how to live in the Anthropocene',[106] and if we accept that law, order and regulation will always be required in any society, then we need to ask: what is the significance of the Anthropocene and its imagery for our regulatory institutions, and more specifically, for the institution of law?

As a powerful overarching trope expressing 'epochal manifestation of concrete socio- and bio-material conditions',[107] the Anthropocene could have myriad technological, regulatory, ethical, legal and broader social implications at many levels and in different spheres of life; 'command[ing] a major realignment of our consciousness and worldviews, and call[ing] for different ways to inhabit the Earth'.[108] Conceptually and as a term of art, the Anthropocene's significance lies in its recognition of human domination of Earth and its systems: it signifies that we are living in a period of Earth's geological history where our interactions with each other and with the non-human living and non-living world, the way we understand and practise science, and the way we create and maintain order, and design and implement social regulatory institutions such as law, economics, ethics and religion cannot continue to depart from the assumption that there is biospheric harmony, predictability and stasis as was the case in the Holocene, or that nature is something far removed from, yet available for the unrestricted use of, humans. Therefore, like Pallett, for me the significance and utility of the Anthropocene lies less in the empirical truth of the claim that we are in a new geological era, than in the Anthropocene acting as a system of thought that provides a framework and context for thinking about biospheric change, our responsibility for causing and mediating this change, and our regulatory responses to this change.[109]

To this end, the Anthropocene presents a new living reality characterised by the hitherto unacknowledged complexity of the Earth's systems, making it all but impossible to establish simple, clear, linear links between causes and effects, and making it crucially necessary, yet challenging, to craft and execute future regulatory interventions.[110] Our efforts to facilitate a sustainable future, to maximise equitable choices and to identify and enable those options that would keep us within safe operating spaces away from critical tipping points in the Earth

---

[105] F Biermann et al, 'Navigating the Anthropocene: Improving Earth System Governance' (2012) 335 *Science* 1306, 1306.
[106] S Dalby, 'Geographies of the International System: Globalization, Empire and the Anthropocene' in P Aalto, V Harle and S Moisio (eds), *International Studies: Interdisciplinary Approaches* (New York, Palgrave Macmillan, 2011) 143.
[107] Grear (n 50) 1.
[108] Globaïa, 'Cartography of the Anthropocene' (n 81).
[109] Mahony, 'The Anthropocene' (n 92); Lövbrand, Stripple and Wiman (n 33) 8.
[110] Oldfield et al (n 32) 3.

system, will require our better understanding, mediating and responding to human interference with an increasingly unpredictable and complex Earth system.[111] While the latter is probably the ultimate regulatory challenge of the Anthropocene, it simultaneously provides us with a framework to contemplate global Earth system change and to devise appropriate responses to such change.

Analogous to the influence that sustainable development has had on politics, law and governance generally (see the discussion above) and the extent to which it has become an object of governance, the Anthropocene could provide a current, far-reaching and consolidated conceptual objectification of a regulatory challenge or a governance problem, ie dramatic human-induced global environmental change that requires urgent regulatory intervention to ensure the continuation of life on Earth. Importantly, as a result of the severity of its imagery, the Anthropocene could possibly do this in a way that reaches further and deeper than any other framework has since been able to do. Acting as a collective term encapsulating the apocalyptical exigencies of many single issues through its expression of urgency, the Anthropocene 'is a concept which is perhaps big enough to urge transformation on the level of values and ontology in a way that could never have happened in response to one singular societal or environmental challenge, from globalisation to climate change'.[112]

Through its 'problem objectification' role, the Anthropocene could spur political action agitating for more effective environmental law and governance, because '[o]bjects can only be governed when they are represented and conceptualized in a way that can enter the sphere of conscious political calculation'.[113] Acting as a terminological collective that expresses both human mastery over the biosphere and regulatory urgency to counter the effects of human domination, the Anthropocene could arguably instigate more concerted and far-ranging global political and regulatory action to address ecological disaster by opening up an entire range of political rationalities;[114] thus working to instigate wholesale reforms of our regulatory interventions that are embedded in law, among others, as part of many alternative political rationalities.

As a counterpoint to the foregoing, while the Anthropocene imagery undoubtedly might spur some urgent and thorough interventions, some commentators caution that its reflexive dimension could have quite the opposite effect, ie one of ambivalence and inaction as a result of uncertainty, paralysis and humans' inability to control the future state of the world as a result:[115]

> The profound uncertainty generated within a globalized, indeterministic world erodes the basis for decision making, freezes action, and ultimately blocks the possibility of forward movement into the future. Indeed, the future no longer exists as something that

---

[111] ibid.
[112] Mahony (n 92).
[113] Lövbrand, Stripple and Wiman (n 33) 11.
[114] ibid.
[115] ibid.

is open to 'colonization' by confident, rational action, but rather as a site of anxiety, full of unknowns, that is not amenable to human intervention. This creates a quandary, for although the future may be radically contingent and unknowable, the individual must still engage with it. The problem that now faces them is—how to act.[116]

This is a cautionary tale of reality that has proven true for big ideas such as sustainable development and the many global environmental governance regimes which it informs: the ailing global climate change regime is probably most exemplary in this respect. Yet, for all the reasons mentioned above, there are also equally sufficient reasons to believe that the Anthropocene as a framework and everything that it seeks to convey, would be better able to spur the type of global regulatory interventions in a way that other grand ideas have not yet been able to do.

VII. Conclusion

This chapter has shown that the Anthropocene is a common denominator that facilitates our understanding of the human-dominated biosphere and the various challenges this creates. Bettini, Brandstedt and Thorén present us with a metaphor in which the Anthropocene is an inverted prism that 'combines into a single beam the numerous (apparently) divergent messages that signal the unprecedented impacts that humans exercise on the biosphere and gives them a common meaning'.[117] In doing so, the Anthropocene levels the scientific playing field, as it were; it creates a common understanding of the centrality of people in global Earth systems change; it refocuses the debate on ways to ameliorate this impact; it instils a common understanding of the global geographical, temporal and causal dimension of anthropogenic impacts and the resultant socio-ecological crisis; and it promotes a deeper appreciation of the divergent considerations relating to socio-legal institutional change and reforms because it helps us to recognise, understand and respond to the global socio-ecological crisis that we are witnessing.

Thus, as a framework, the Anthropocene could help us to better understand the global extent and effects of human impacts on the biosphere and resultant Earth system changes; it could guide us in rethinking our responses to these changes; it could offer a framework for re-imagined Earth system ethics, care and responsibility; and ultimately it could serve as a justification for interventionist action that can also be achieved through law as one of many regulatory institutional responses. With respect to the last point specifically, Baskin observes that the idea of the

---

[116] G Reith, 'Uncertain Times: The Notion of "Risk" and the Development of Modernity' (2004) 13 *Time Society* 383, 393.

[117] G Bettini, E Brandstedt and H Thorén, 'Sustainability Science and the Anthropocene: Re-negotiating the Role for Science in Society' (2010) edocs.fu-berlin.de/docs/servlets/MCRFile-NodeServlet/FUDOCS_derivate_000000001299/Bettini-Sustainability_Science_and_the_Anthropocene-305.pdf?hosts=.

Anthropocene clearly indicates that we are living amidst exceptional conditions and that such a 'framing through exceptionality can legitimate the need for exceptional rule'.[118] The remainder of this book reflects on constitutionalism as a form of 'exceptional rule', which it argues is essential for the type of urgent regulatory interventions that are required to more adequately confront the socio-ecological crisis of the Anthropocene.

[118] Baskin (n 98) 22.

3

Constitutionalism

I. Introduction

The notion of a constitution is an old one. Harking back to Roman times when *constitutiones* referred in a technical-legalistic sense to legislative acts of the sovereign, the term was later applied by the Church to ecclesiastical regulations in canonical law, and during the Middle Ages to secular administrative enactments.[1] In addition to its legalistic meaning, 'constitution' was also later considered during this early period to mean the body of a political organisation (*politeia*) in an Aristotelian sense.[2] But, as Almeida indicates, these conceptual usages remained separately applied to either the political or the legal domain.[3] 'Constitution' in modern parlance, as referring to the entire legal framework of a state in a political and legalistic sense, including the public aspects of the state and the law dealing therewith,[4] only emerged during the eighteenth century with the publication of De Vattel's *Le droit des gens ou principes de la loi naturelle appliqués à la conduite et aux affaires de Nations et des Souverains* ('The Law of Nations or the Principles of Natural Law Applied to the Conduct and to the Affairs off Nations and of Sovereigns').[5] Later, as a consequence of the American and French Revolutions, the term 'constitution' signified a crucial shift in the relationship between government and people, ie a rejection of status and hierarchy as a traditional means

---

[1] C McIlwain, *Constitutionalism: Ancient and Modern* (Amagi, Liberty Fund, 2007) 22–38; G Sartori, 'Constitutionalism: A Preliminary Discussion' (1962) 56 *American Political Science Review* 853.

[2] See for a comprehensive historical discussion, C Friedrich, *Der Verfassungsstaat der Neuzeit* (Berlin, Springer, 1953).

[3] F Almeida, 'The Emergence of Constitutionalism as an Evolutionary Adaptation' (*ExpressO*, 2014) works.bepress.com/fabio_almeida/3/.

[4] McIlwain, *Constitutionalism* (n 1) 22–38.

[5] E de Vattel, *Le droit des gens ou principes de la loi naturelle appliqués à la conduite et aux affaires de Nations et des Souverains* (Washington, Carnegie Institution of Washington, 1758, 1916 reprint). De Vattel stated, among others: 'The fundamental regulation that determines the manner in which the public authority is to be executed, is what forms the *constitution of the state*. In this is seen the form in which the nation acts in quality of a body politic,—how and by whom the people are to be governed,—and what are the rights and duties of the governors'. Quoted in F Venter, *Constitutional Comparison: Japan, Germany, Canada and South Africa as Constitutional States* (Cape Town, Juta, 2000) 23.

of ordering in favour of the creation of a government for the benefit of people established entirely by their majority consent.[6]

While constitutions and their associated terms such as democracy, rights, the rule of law and the separation of powers have since become an integral part of our political and legal systems, indeed of society itself, recent times have seen a remarkable revival of constitutional ideas in, what Dunhoff terms, an 'age of constitutionalism'.[7] This observably pronounced salience is attributed to, among others, post-Second World War reconstruction; decolonisation (mostly in Africa and South America); the radical constitutional changes in the former Eastern Bloc countries in the aftermath of the Cold War; the transitions made by post-fascist (Spain, Portugal) and post-apartheid (South Africa) regimes towards the formation of market-based economies and liberal democratic constitutional orders; as a response to globalisation with the emergence of regional governance entities such as the European Union and the constitutionalisation of EU law; and related calls for the constitutionalisation of some international organisations and their corresponding treaty regimes, such as the World Trade Organization.[8]

While the word 'constitution' is often used as a much more powerful trope than the word 'law' in legal arguments (possibly because lawyers have found the latter not sufficiently compelling when measured against constitutionalism to engender the authoritative binding and supreme nature of the institutions and rules they seek to convey),[9] the revival of constitutionalism is one which is also raising 'the intensity of interest in constitutions and constitutionalism considerably ... [creating] an opportunity for modern notions of constitutionalism to be expanded into new territories and to be tested under new circumstances'.[10]

II. About this Chapter

The previous chapter has indicated that the term Anthropocene suggests we are living in a new reality and circumstances calling for regulatory interventions, such as constitutionalism, to be expanded into new territories such as environmental law and governance. A pertinent central question that accordingly arises is: considering the centrality of constitutionalism as higher-order law that historically has

---

[6] M Loughlin, 'What is Constitutionalisation?' in P Dobner and M Loughlin (eds), *The Twilight of Constitutionalism* (Oxford, Oxford University Press, 2010) 47.

[7] J Dunhoff, 'Constitutional Conceits: The WTO's "Constitution" and the Discipline of International Law' (2006) 17 *European Journal of International Law* 647, 648.

[8] J Dunhoff, 'Why Constitutionalism Now? Text, Context and the Historical Contingency of Ideas' (2004/05) 1 *Journal of International Law and International Relations* 191, 192; M Frishman and S Muller (eds), *The Dynamics of Constitutionalism in the Age of Globalisation* (The Hague, Hague Academic Press, 2010); Loughlin, 'What is Constitutionalisation?' (n 6) 60.

[9] G Galindo, 'Constitutionalism Forever' (2010) 21 *Finnish Yearbook of International Law* 137, 138.

[10] Venter, *Constitutional Comparison* (n 5) 30.

shaped and changed societies (and continues to do so), is a constitutional form of law more suitable to respond to the Anthropocene's global socio-ecological crisis than 'ordinary' non-constitutional law and if so, how should this occur?

As a first step in answering this question, and acting as a foundational premise for the remainder of the book that seeks to investigate the expansion of modern notions of constitutionalism into the 'new territory' of global environmental law and governance beyond the state, this chapter explores the notion of constitutionalism in general terms. It does so by focusing on several guiding sub-questions: why have constitutions and constitutional ideas become such pivotal elements (basic necessities even) of society and of the world order that society constructs, without which we find it difficult to imagine the existence of a state, legal systems and polities? What is the meaning and rationale of constitutionalism; what are the drivers behind constitutionalism; and what are the advantages of constitutional modes of law and governance as opposed to non-constitutional modes, including critiques against constitutionalism? What are typical elements or features that characterise the constitutional state and against which one could measure the existence of a constitutional order?

In answering these questions and their related tracks, the discussion in Part 3 first traces the meaning of constitutionalism with reference to the terms 'constitution', 'constitutionalism', 'constitutionalisation' and 'constitutional state' from a generic and state-bound perspective. The state-bound perspective is an important point of analytical departure and interpretative foundation that is later expanded upon in Chapter 4 with a global perspective on constitutionalism that reaches beyond the state. Commencing from the domestic perspective is intuitive since '[c]onstitutionalism is a form of legal order that is tried and tested in domestic law, proven to indicate the final maturing of domestic governance and a faithful servant of legitimacy'.[11] That is, however, not to say that domestic constitutionalism is an open and shut case. Constitutionalism and constitutionalist thought remain in flux, also within domestic orders,[12] but it is true that domestic constitutions have completed the process of constitutionalisation to such an extent (although they have not completed it fully and perhaps never will), that they could provide a vehicle to usefully foresee what the constitutionalisation of a global (environmental) legal order that must respond to the Anthropocene will require.[13] While the purpose of defining constitutional terms and related phenomena can neither be to provide a comprehensive critical account of each within the restrictions of a single chapter, nor to propose some standard and universally accepted definitions, the heuristic value of such an analysis could be helpful to frame the general characteristics that are associated with constitutional terms and language, and to foster a deeper understanding of what lies behind constitutionalism, as it were.

---

[11] A O'Donoghue, *Constitutionalism in Global Constitutionalisation* (Cambridge, Cambridge University Press, 2014) 1.

[12] J Klabbers, 'Setting the Scene' in J Klabbers, A Peters and G Ulfstein (eds), *The Constitutionalization of International Law* (Oxford, Oxford University Press, 2009) 7.

[13] O'Donoghue, *Constitutionalism in Global Constitutionalisation* (n 11) 8.

Part 4 investigates the underlying reasons for the turn towards constitutionalism in a generic sense, thus providing an account of the motivations that underlie the constitutionalisation of polities and their legal regimes. In the interest of balanced critique, as a counter-narrative, this part also notes some arguments of sceptics and their reasons for being critical about constitutionalism.

Part 5 of this chapter turns to an analysis of the component parts or elements of constitutionalism as expressed by the constitutional state in an effort to provide a systematic conceptual account of the building blocks of constitutionalism within the context of the constitutional state. These elements include: the instrumental function and meaning of a constitution as a legal creation; the rule of law; the separation of powers doctrine; judicial independence and powers of judicial review; constitutional supremacy; democracy; and rights. This is not a closed list of course, and while there may be others, I focus on these features because they seem to be frequently recurring as elements of most domestic constitutional orders, as well as in the literature.[14] Whilst doing so, I am fully aware of potential criticism against such a reductionist and siloist approach. For example, Kleinlein states that constitutionalism is considered a holistic phenomenon; it is 'holistic insofar as it is more than the sum of its parts, and the various constitutional features take on a special normative significance in combination'.[15] While this is true, the heuristic value of 'breaking up' constitutionalism into component parts and trying to understand each within the broader context of constitutionalism is equally valuable when trying to understand such a complex phenomenon.

While the South African constitutional system will frequently appear as an example throughout the discussion,[16] I also refer to other jurisdictions where appropriate, notably the United Kingdom, German and United States Constitutions. For the sake of focused debate, the enquiry is also decidedly based on a Western liberal democratic conception of constitutionalism, and it excludes as a general rule references to non-Western constitutional approaches such as those prevailing in East Asia, for example.[17] As a further general caveat to the discussion that follows, constitutional language and the meaning attributed to constitutional concepts vary in response to different contexts and local histories, prevailing socio-economic and political circumstances, dominant ideologies and the composition of society. The reality is that dogmatic exactitude regarding the details of

---

[14] See for an approach similar to mine, CM Zoethout and P Boon, 'Defining Constitutionalism and Democracy: An Introduction' in CM Zoethout, ME Pietermaat-Kros and PWC Akkermans (eds), *Constitutionalism in Africa: A Quest for Autochthonous Principles* (Deventer, Gouda Quint, 1996) 5–7.

[15] T Kleinlein, 'Alfred Verdross as a Founding Father of International Constitutionalism?' (2012) 4 *Goettingen Journal of International Law* 385, 415.

[16] See for a concise discussion of South Africa's transition to a constitutional democracy (as measured against constitutional developments in the United States), MS Kende, *Constitutional Rights in Two Worlds: South Africa and the United States* (Cambridge, Cambridge University Press, 2009).

[17] See for an overview, E Caldwell and T Nardin, 'Methodological Approaches to Asian Constitutionalism: Introduction' (2012) 88 *Chicago-Kent Law Review* 3.

twenty-first-century constitutionalism is not at hand, and to pin down its meaning to the satisfaction of all is impossible.[18] One reason for this notional fluidity is that constitutions are the result of years and sometimes generations of customs, traditions and social structures that are anything but homogenous.[19] These notional and conceptual variances within constitutionalism notably do not reflect on the value of constitutionalism as a normative governance order, but rather on the diversity and plurality of the various domestic legal orders from which constitutionalism emerges, as well as on the multifarious critical discourse surrounding constitutionalism.[20] The concept of constitutionalism is thus an amorphous one, characterised as it is by 'innumerable nuances of constitutional ideals that can be (and are constantly being) expressed under the banner of constitutionalism'.[21] As a consequence, there are many other conceptual and analytical accounts and particular approaches that seek to flesh out constitutionalism's meaning, scope, purpose and features.[22] What follows, is only one of these.

III. Constitutional Concepts

At a very general level, Wiener et al distinguish between constitutions, constitutionalisation and constitutionalism as follows: while a constitution is established to keep politics and power in check; constitutionalisation is a phenomenon that evinces the need to put innovative regulatory or principled practices into place in a political and legal order. Because an unconstitutional political order is considered illegitimate and therefore devoid of a right to exist, constitutionalism is an ongoing project related to fostering greater legitimacy in law and of political orders,[23] acting as a 'normative pull' and as a mechanism that has the ability to bestow legitimacy on a political system.[24] In doing so, constitutionalism embodies the notion of progress in that it is perceived to foster progressive social orderings that are characterised by the 'creation and maintenance of a dichotomy between right and wrong, good and evil, civilized and uncivilized nations'.[25] Yet, there is much more to constitutionalism and its related (and overlapping) notions than the foregoing suggests, as we shall see below.

---

[18] See, generally, F Venter, 'Konstitusionalisme in Suid-Afrika' (2014) 11 *LitNet Akademies* 91.
[19] JR May and E Daly, *Global Environmental Constitutionalism*, Kindle edn (New York, Cambridge University Press, 2015) 326/11268.
[20] O'Donoghue (n 11) 15.
[21] Venter (n 5) 20.
[22] See, among others, the many diverse sources cited throughout this chapter.
[23] A Wiener et al, 'Global Constitutionalism: Human Rights, Democracy and the Rule of Law' (2012) 1 *Global Constitutionalism* 1, 4–6.
[24] J Klabbers, 'Constitutionalism Lite' (2004) 1 *International Organizations Law Review* 31, 48.
[25] Galindo, 'Constitutionalism Forever' (n 9) 144.

A. Constitution

From a pure formalistic point of view, a constitution is seen as the act and/or the norms that constitute a political body; and the structure and/or characteristics that define a constituted political body:[26] 'constitutions constitute a political entity as a legal entity, organize it, limit political power, offer political and moral guidelines, justify governance, and contribute to integration'.[27] Or as Peters states: a 'constitution (in a normative sense) is the sum of basic (materially most important) legal norms which comprehensively regulate the social and political life of a polity',[28] providing the foundation of a legal order, establishing the *trias politica* of the state and providing the basis and legitimacy for legality.[29]

In its formalistic guise, a constitution relates to the document (in most instances a constitution is a written document although there are exceptions as we shall see below) which legally constitutes a polity, and which creates the institutional architecture of the state. Formalistic constitutions memorialise and institutionalise political power that is limited by the territorial borders of a state.[30] The formalistic aspects of a constitution rarely specify what exactly a government must do and how it must perform its tasks; they usually only create the structures that enable governance. For example:

> The [American] Constitution, although it does set out the basic structure of government and delineates the procedural rules by which that government will operate, says remarkably little about what the government should do, and that is as it should be. By and large, such central substantive decisions about public policy should be made in more public, more representative, and more deliberative forums, whether those forums be the chambers of legislatures or the more important and more diffuse networks by which public opinion is formed, reformed, and implemented.[31]

As part of their formalistic constitutive functions, constitutions concern the results of the act of constituting authority and power. They derive their authority from the governed; they provide the principal authority for a state to make subsequent rules such as legislation; they regulate the allocation of powers, functions and duties among government agencies; and they define in a vertical sense the power relationship with the governed and often in a horizontal sense the power relations

---

[26] D Castiglione, 'The Political Theory of the Constitution' (1996) XLIV *Political Studies* 417, 418.
[27] K Milewicz, 'Emerging Patters of Global Constitutionalization: Toward a Conceptual Framework' (2009) 16 *Indiana Journal of Global Legal Studies* 413, 418.
[28] A Peters, 'Compensatory Constitutionalism: The Function and Potential of Fundamental International Norms and Structures' (2006) 19 *Leiden Journal of International Law* 579, 581.
[29] Loughlin (n 6) 50.
[30] LC Backer, 'From Constitution to Constitutionalism: A Global Framework for Legitimate Public Power Systems' (2008/2009) 113 *Penn State Law Review* 671, 674.
[31] F Shauer, 'Judicial Supremacy and the Modest Constitution' (2004) 92 *California Law Review* 1045, 1065.

between individuals.[32] To this end, the fundamental rationale and formalistic function of any constitution lies in the middle of two extremes: the prevention of tyranny on the one hand and the prevention of anarchy on the other:[33]

> The idea of a law of the state, that is, of a law to which the several branches of the government are subject and which they must obey in the exercise of their 'authority', is the bridge between an arbitrary despotic absolutism and a fully developed constitutionalism.[34]

Or, as Zoethout and Boon state '[a]rbitrary rule … is the very opposite of limited government. Predictability of state action is the basic rule of constitutionalism, while capriciousness or unpredictability is the mark of tyranny or dictatorship'.[35]

As part of their formalistic tasks, constitutions concretely perform a host of related strategic functions such as: establishing and maintaining order; providing long-term societal and political stability; and achieving integration and unification as far as a national identity is concerned, including consensus on matters of common public concern.[36] With respect to its integration and unification functions specifically, constitutions are seen 'to reconcile identity and difference sufficiently within the relevant polity so as to make self-government at once possible and (at least in principle) acceptable to all members of that polity as legitimate'.[37]

Some of the more esoteric functions of constitutions are that they could provide stability in functionally differentiated societies; they could provide psychological stability in morally pluralistic societies; and they could, and often do, replace morality and religion as sources of normative validity.[38] Constitutions could be said to also perform a symbolic function by transforming abstract ideas of political theory into concrete terms; by affirming and representing the identity of a polity; and, by denoting certain political conflicts as 'constitutional', actually elevate them as being of special value and interest, not only in law, but in other contexts as well: 'The symbolic power of constitutions accordingly lies in shaping and directing the debates through which political communities reinterpret their past, negotiate their present and plan their future'.[39] For example, the post-apartheid South African Constitution did not only require all South Africans to revisit their perceptions and understanding of the law as it applied to them, 'but it also sought to bring the divergent approaches to life characteristic of a pluralistic society under the discipline of one overarching set of entrenched legal norms'.[40]

---

[32] C Fombad, 'Challenges to Constitutionalism and Constitutional Rights in Africa and the Enabling Role of Political Parties: Lessons and Perspectives from Southern Africa' (2007) 55 *American Journal of Comparative Law* 1, 6.
[33] ibid.
[34] C Friedrich, *The Philosophy of Law in Historical Perspective* (Chicago, University of Chicago Press, 1953) 216.
[35] Zoethout and Boon, 'Defining Constitutionalism and Democracy' (n 14) 5.
[36] Venter (n 5) 27.
[37] M Rosenfeld, 'Is Global Constitutionalism Meaningful or Desirable?' (2014) 25 *European Journal of International Law* 177, 181.
[38] Almeida, 'Emergence of Constitutionalism' (n 3).
[39] GW Anderson, *Constitutional Rights after Globalization* (Oxford, Hart Publishing, 2005) 107–08.
[40] F Venter, 'South Africa: A Diceyan Rechtsstaat?' (2012) 57 *McGill Law Journal* 722, 733.

B. Constitutionalism

Constitutions do, however, not only constitute in a formalistic sense and it is possible to think about constitutions in a more substantive way as well. To avoid an ontological reality where a constitution is nothing but the formalisation of the existing location of political power where law entrenches and perpetuates power instead of constraining it, a constitution is and should be more than a mere observable fact or a shorthand term that describes the formalisation of the power structures of a state (in the sense that it is a symbol of the state and its power vis-à-vis the basis of the state and its power).[41] In other words, a constitution cannot only be purely constitutive in a formalistic sense, consisting only of constitutive and organisational norms; it must also contain some substantive norms from which the content and status of norms that limit power in a legal system could be derived.[42] As well, because a purely formalistic constitution cannot in itself offer the kind of coherent normative order that distinguishes it from 'ordinary' statutory or common law: '[A]s the source of legitimacy, it must possess a certain unity and an internal coherence, so that appeals to it may be meaningful and capable of carrying conviction'.[43]

Constitutions are thought to derive this special elevated status as a fundamental unified and representative norm of a polity from procedural safeguards such as the review functions of courts and the rule of law (among others); and from substantive meta-ethical preconceptions that are notionally embedded in, for example, natural law, rights, liberty and equality, that amalgamate to elevate a constitution to the status of superior law.[44] The latter collectively resort under the banner 'constitutionalism', and they work to imbue a pure formalistic constitution with substantive characteristics. To this end, the concept of constitutionalism goes beyond the simple articulation of formal rules and procedures of a constitution,[45] where it also instils the constitution with its own inherent dignity from which it derives its legitimacy and supreme normative authority.[46] As Klabbers states:

> when people think of ... constitutionalism, or any suchlike conjugation, the association is not only with something that is constituted in a technical sense, but also, and predominantly, with something that is constituted in a politically legitimate sense: a constitutional order is a legitimate order, deriving its legitimacy (in part at least) precisely from its constitutional nature.[47]

---

[41] Sartori, 'Constitutionalism' (n 1) 857.
[42] R Alexy, *A Theory of Constitutional Rights* (Oxford, Oxford University Press, 2002) 350.
[43] Castiglione, 'Political Theory of the Constitution' (n 26) 420.
[44] ibid.
[45] Milewicz, 'Emerging Patters of Global Constitutionalization' (n 27) 419.
[46] J Isensee, 'Staat und Verfassung' in J Isensee and P Kirchhof (eds), *Handbuch des Staatsrechts: Verfassungsstaat* (Heidelberg, Müller, 2014) 15.
[47] Klabbers, 'Setting the Scene' (n 12) 8.

Originally only used to describe a political and intellectual movement in the quest for a written constitution during the seventeenth and eighteenth centuries,[48] today constitutionalism, as a value laden rhetorical trope (elsewhere described as a 'normative thesis, a meta-legal doctrine and a political ideal'),[49] suggests the existence of elevated normative values or basic principles that protect against government overreach and that are epitomised through constitutional creatures such as rights and the rule of law, among others.[50] To this end, constitutionalism works through a constitution to provide the 'frame of political society, *organized through and by the law,* for the purpose of restraining arbitrary power'.[51] It is through its ability to limit political power that constitutionalism has gained much of its normative force and persistent authority,[52] by focusing on the core functions of the *trias politica*, ie the ability of the legislature to enact constitutional laws; the executive authority's ability to exercise limited power; and an independent judiciary's ability to oversee the power of the former two authorities.[53]

In this sense, constitutionalism implies, but significantly expands and reinforces, the values underlying the institutional-architectural provisions of a formalistic constitution, by exuding a prescriptive character that is associated with rights, the rule of law, judicial review and containment of power.[54] Part of constitutionalism's core value therefore also lies in its ability to prescribe that a limited government must be able to operate efficiently and effectively and that it can be compelled to act efficiently and effectively within certain constitutional limits.[55] Provisions on good governance are examples of such prescriptions that aim to improve a government's efficiency and efficacy.[56] The foregoing characteristics collectively, are what make a constitution constitutional, implying that constitutionalism is more than a constitution or that having a constitution is one thing, but that it is an entirely different matter to have a certain *type* of constitution: for a constitution to be considered a constitution in the fullest sense of constitutionalism's achievement, 'both [are] needed for a constitution to be a constitution'.[57]

---

[48] CM Zoethout, *Constitutionalisme: Een Vergelijkend Onderzoek naar het Beperken van Overheidsmacht door het Recht* (Arnhem, Gouda Quint, 1995) 2.
[49] J Murkens, 'The Quest for Constitutionalism in UK Public Law Discourse' (2009) 29 *Oxford Journal of Legal Studies* 427, 455.
[50] Dunhoff, 'Why Constitutionalism *Now?*' (n 8) 195.
[51] Sartori (n 1) 860.
[52] M Brandon, 'Constitutionalism and Constitutional Failure' (1999) 9(2) *The Good Society* 61, 61.
[53] Murkens, 'Quest for Constitutionalism' (n 49) 438.
[54] Peters, 'Compensatory Constitutionalism' (n 28) 583.
[55] Fombad, 'Challenges to Constitutionalism' (n 32) 7.
[56] See, eg, s 195 of the South African Constitution that sets out the basic values and principles governing the public administration. These include, among others, the following principles: a high standard of professional ethics must be promoted and maintained; efficient, economic and effective use of resources must be promoted; public administration must be development-oriented; services must be provided impartially, fairly, equitably and without bias; people's needs must be responded to, and the public must be encouraged to participate in policy-making; public administration must be accountable; and transparency must be fostered by providing the public with timely, accessible and accurate information.
[57] Sartori (n 1) 856.

Formalistic constitutions merely describe a system of limitless and unchecked power: 'They are not a dead letter. It is only that this letter is irrelevant to the *telos* of constitutionalism'.[58] To bridge this irrelevance, it is necessary that constitutions, in addition to constituting the state, must also regulate the highest powers in a state through formal and substantive means that are associated with the attributes and qualities that law should possess.[59] This is an intuitive truth that one readily accepts, if only to enable one to reject instinctively constitutions that are not characterised by constitutionalism. (Consider, for example, that the German National Socialist Constitution under Hitler was in every formalistic sense a constitution, but obviously not a substantively constitutional one that measured up to the standards of the rule of law or to rights protection.)[60]

In sum, constitutionalism seeks to provide a stable and legitimate framework for making possible interaction between a polity's citizens by means of restrictions on power[61] the provision of legal limits;[62] and the provision of certain guarantees which it facilitates through the recognition and protection of rights, the separation of powers doctrine, an independent judiciary that has the power of judicial review, the possibility to review the constitutionality of laws and actions (be they actions by the state or by non-state parties), strict control over amendments to the constitution, and the rule of law.[63]

C. Constitutionalisation

Conveying an action, constitutionalisation describes a legal and political process that is connected to, yet different from, the more static characteristics of a constitution and constitutionalism. As a process, it includes the emergence, creation and identification of constitution-like elements in a legal and political order, and more specifically involves attempts to subject governmental action to the structures, processes, principles and values of a constitution:[64]

> '*Constitutionalization*' is shorthand for the emergence of constitutional law within a given legal order. The concept of constitutionalization implies that a constitution ... can come into being in a process extended through time. It also implies that a legal text (or various legal texts) can acquire (or eventually lose) constitutional properties in a

---

[58] ibid 861.
[59] Murkens (n 49) 440.
[60] See, for a discussion of the totalitarian state of the Third Reich, R Weber-Fas, *Der Verfassungsstaat des Grundgesetzes: Entstehung, Prinzipien, Gestalt* (Tübingen, Mohr Siebeck, 2002) 17–30.
[61] Klabbers, 'Constitutionalism Lite' (n 24) 32.
[62] Restrictions on power are realised through constitutions by them establishing separate sets of distinctions, both hierarchically (right–good or law–religion/morality; federal–state–municipality; and citizen–state) and horizontally (law–politics or legislative–executive–judiciary): Almeida (n 3).
[63] See the discussion below.
[64] Loughlin (n 6) 47.

positive feedback process. A text can therefore be more (or less) constitution-like. It may be, in short, a constitution-in-the-making.[65]

Constitutionalisation thus refers to the traditional process of constitution-making; an action by which a constitution takes legal force; and the process which eventually ends up in a constitution through which the attributes of constitutionalism are imported into a legal system.[66] To this end, the process of constitutionalisation includes the process of legalisation (ie the act of creating legal norms through juridical processes); it includes the process of creating the architecture of a state that regulates the formalised power structure of a state; and it involves the creation of the many substantive higher-order aspects of constitutionalism such as rights and rule of law safeguards.

But the process of constitutionalisation reaches much wider than this formal juridical normative and institutional process to also include broader political and social practices that establish law-like rules and institutions.[67] Thus considered, the process of constitutionalisation is far more radical and encompassing than 'ordinary' processes of law reform, codification and juridification;[68] and it is more than merely establishing the institutional-architectural building blocks of the state or creating rights to protect the individual, for example. Constitutionalisation primarily includes these aspects, but reaches further into the social and the political domain, thus affecting the consciousness, the social fabric and very essence of a polity where it also seeks to legitimise a legal and political order through the entrenchment of moral or culturally derived higher values often encapsulated in rights, for example. This is so because constitutionalism 'reflects human nature, inseparable from human capacities, needs and deficiencies'.[69] Reflecting on constitutionalisation as a broader socio-legal process, Arts and Handmaker believe it includes:

> the processes that lead to codification- or other formal expression- of norms and values; the practices of claiming rights that emerge from, or are guaranteed by, such constitutional frameworks; and overall experiences at different levels of governance and from the perspective of all the main actors involved.[70]

As well, when one considers constitutionalisation as a method to create a constitutional order, which it is in part, constitutionalisation obviously goes

---

[65] Peters (n 28) 582. Peters' view of constitutionalisation is a narrow one. It is arguable that constitutionalisation rather refers to the emergence of constitutional features (instead of only constitutional law), in a legal order, and that it is not only legal texts that could acquire constitutional properties, but indeed also broader social and cultural practices of which the law is only one part.
[66] D Grimm, 'The Achievement of Constitutionalism and its Prospects in a Changed World' in Dobner and Loughlin (eds), *The Twilight of Constitutionalism?* (n 6) 4.
[67] Milewicz (n 27) 421.
[68] O'Donoghue (n 11) 5.
[69] May and Daly, *Global Environmental Constitutionalism* (n 19) 894/11268.
[70] K Arts and J Handmaker, 'Cultures of Constitutionalism: An Introduction' in M Frishman and S Muller (eds), *The Dynamics of Constitutionalism in the Age of Globalisation* (The Hague, Hague Academic Press, 2010) 50.

beyond legalisation because while lawyers are primarily involved in the legalisation process, ultimately, the constitution-making process is a much deeper and all-encompassing one that also involves political actors, courts in some instances, and the many civil and other public actors in any given society.[71] To this end, constitutionalisation as a process, when it also seeks to instil the elements of constitutionalism in a pure formalistic constitution, could do so beyond mere legalisation through socio-cultural processes that, from an anthropological point of view, includes 'a shared set of symbols, used to organize joint behavior for the solving of common problems, that is passed from generation to generation'.[72] Through this process of constitutionalisation, an institutional socio-cultural framework is thus created which evinces 'an evolutionary adaptation to specific historical and sociological circumstances' to accommodate diversity, pluralism and complexity in a society.[73]

D. The Constitutional State

The foregoing notional account of constitutions, constitutionalism and constitutionalisation culminates in what is considered to be a collective manifestation of contemporary constitutional thought in the realm of the nation state, ie the constitutional state. Expressing the complex of ideas, concepts and principles of constitutionalism, the constitutional state owes much of its conceptual development to German law and more particularly, to the German notion of *Verfassungsstaat* (constitutional state).[74] The *Verfassungsstaat* derives from the *Rechtsstaat*, a notionally more restricted concept which has its roots in nineteenth-century German constitutional law. The *Rechtsstaat* is often considered the German equivalent to the Anglo-Saxon rule of law (see the discussion below),[75] although Venter argues that the Anglo-Saxon or Diceyan notion of rule of law cannot necessarily be equated with the German concept of *Rechtsstaat*, since the

---

[71] A Arato, 'Forms of Constitution Making and Theories of Democracy' (1995) 17 *Cardozo Law Review* 191, 191–92.
[72] D Lutz, 'Thinking About Constitutionalism at the Start of the Twenty-First Century' (2000) 30(4) *Publius* 115, 128.
[73] Almeida (n 3).
[74] See for a comprehensive discussion, B Enzmann, *Der Demokratische Verfassungsstaat: Entstehung, Elemente, Herausforderungen* (Wiesbaden, Springer, 2005); and for a comprehensive historical overview of the development of the constitutional state, H Fenske, *Der Moderne Verfassungsstaat: Eine vergleichende Geschichte von der Entstehung bis zum 20. Jahrhundert* (Paderborn, Ferdinand Schöning, 2001).
[75] The rule of law is seen to overlap with the notion of the *Rechtsstaat* and the *Verfassungsstaat* in that it, among others, is characterised by effective constraints on power, whereas it fundamentally conflicts with the notion of the *Machtsstaat* (state of power or force), such as in Nazi Germany, which functions without restraints: I Flores, 'Law, Liberty and the Rule of Law (in a Constitutional Democracy)' in I Flores and K Himma (eds), *Law, Liberty and the Rule of Law* (Dordrecht, Springer, 2013) 84.

latter is much broader in its reach to the extent that it almost equates with the more encompassing notion of the constitutional state itself.[76]

The *Rechtsstaat* notion is historically understood to describe the collective counter-reaction by a liberal citizenry to power overreach by the state, including the citizenry's efforts to secure the protection of individual spheres of freedom and to restrict the free will of the sovereign.[77] With its intellectual roots firmly embedded in Kantian theory, in its earliest pre-Second World War guise, the *Rechtsstaat* stood for rational state rule, encompassing universal protection of institutional and procedural aspects of governance within the ambit of a unified legal order created by legislation, including a separate process of judicial checks and balances administered by independent courts. After the Second World War, the *Rechtsstaat* notion acquired, in addition to the early-Kantian procedural-institutional elements, a considerably greater substantive character that is grounded in fundamental rights, among others, and that is today fully reflected in, for example, the Basic Law of the Federal Republic of Germany and conceptually in the German idea of the *Verfassungsstaat*.[78] The *Rechtsstaat* accordingly provided the foundations for the contemporary *Verfassungsstaat*,[79] and both concepts have since become axiomatic to the German idea of constitutionalism, while at the same time managing to infiltrate other domestic constitutional regimes as well, to the point where the rule of law and the constitutional state are more or less considered today as being the cornerstones of contemporary liberal Western constitutionalism.[80]

Yet, as was hinted at above, the notion of the contemporary constitutional state is wider than the *Rechtsstaat* notion; the constitutional state is the sum of many elements of constitutionalism (including the *Rechtsstaat* idea) that have developed over centuries through diverse events and influences, culminating today into a historically rich amalgam under the banner 'constitutional state'. As Häberle states: 'The constitutional state ... is ... an aggregate arising from political philosophies, classical texts, party policies, experiential knowledge, as well as the "wounds", as

---

[76] With reference to the work of Klaus Stern, Venter points out that the German notion of *Rechtsstaat* includes various elements namely: the constitutional state; human dignity, liberty and equality; the separation and control of government authority; legality; judicial protection; a system of reparation; and a prohibition on the excessive use of government authority. This reading of the *Rechtsstaat*, so Venter argues, is more akin to the broader notion of constitutionalism, or the constitutional state, and is therefore much broader than the Diceyan notion of the rule of law (or the 'predominance of the legal spirit' in Dicey's words) which, taking its cue from the notion of parliamentary sovereignty, consists of three elements: no one is punishable or can be lawfully made to suffer in body or goods except for a breach of law established in the ordinary legal manner before the ordinary courts of the land; no one is above the law and everyone is subject to the ordinary law and to the jurisdiction of the courts; and the general principles of the constitution, such as the right to personal liberty, arise because of judicial decisions determining the rights of private persons in particular cases brought before the courts. Venter, 'South Africa: A Diceyan Rechtsstaat?' (n 40) 725–28.

[77] Zoethout, *Constitutionalisme* (n 48) 288.

[78] M Rosenfeld, 'The Rule of Law and the Legitimacy of Constitutional Democracy' (2001) 74 *Southern California Law Review* 1307, 1319.

[79] Fenske, *Der Moderne Verfassungsstaat* (n 74) 2.

[80] Venter (n 5) 26.

much as concrete utopias. It is an aggregate of revolutionary and evolutionary processes'.[81] Conceptually, Enzmann sees the modern, post-Second World War constitutional state as a form of ordering (*Ordnungsform*) that consists, among others, of the following building blocks or elements: the rule of law, the separation of powers, fundamental rights and constitutionalism.[82] She explains that as soon as a polity chooses to become a constitutional democracy amidst a 'constitutional moment' the character of the constitution changes from a political declaration to an actionable, supreme constitutional norm, and the constitution becomes the central source of legitimacy for and limitation of political authority. The position of the legislature subsequently changes to the extent that it loses its rank as the supreme lawgiver and its position as the most important body that articulates the will of the people, to now stand in the shadow of the constitution which binds it formally and substantively. There is also a significant shift in power in favour of the judiciary where it now assumes an important judicial review function to keep the executive and legislature in check. Related to the latter point, the relationship between law and politics changes significantly (as does the rank of politics in a country), to the extent that political actors in a constitutional state leave the interpretation of the constitution and its content to the courts. The relationship between the state and the citizen also significantly changes because of constitutionally entrenched fundamental rights that create a guaranteed space of freedom for the individual that are enforceable against the state and majority interests, thus enabling the individual to emancipate herself to a certain degree from state and societal paternalism.[83]

From this description, the minimum core of the constitutional state is evident: where the formal and substantive aspects of constitutionalism are entrenched by means of a constitution (be it written or unwritten—see below), one could speak of the existence of a constitutional state. As a normative concept, the contemporary constitutional state is therefore a state which, through its constitution, provides its people with a principled guarantee to establish the rightful and legitimate objectives of the political community; an organisational guarantee that the exercise of power is limited, controlled, effective, rational and proportionally corresponds to the proper ends of the political association; a representational guarantee providing equal participation and representation in political life;[84] and a substantive guarantee that fundamental rights are respected, protected and fulfilled. From a Western, liberal democratic point of view, the modern state can arguably only exist in a fully 'complete' and legitimate form if it is a constitutional state.[85]

---

[81] P Häberle, 'The Constitutional State and its Reform Requirements' (2000) 13 *Ratio Juris* 77, 78.
[82] Enzmann, *Der Demokratische Verfassungsstaat* (n 74) 3–4.
[83] ibid 4.
[84] Castiglione (n 26) 434.
[85] 'Der moderne Staat existiert in vollständiger und legitimer Form nur als Verfassungsstaat, er lässt sich heute nicht anders denken': U di Fabio, 'Verfassungsstaat und Weltrecht' (2008) 39 *Rechtstheorie* 399, 402.

IV. The Turn Towards Constitutionalism and Counter-constitutionalism Considerations

Chapter 1 of this book has already hinted at why constitutionalism is (re)gaining popularity as a focus of scholarship and as a political-juridical movement that seeks to create better legal orders: constitutionalism evokes positive emotive properties that are associated with regime change, stability, order and protection against abuse of power; it signifies progression and progressiveness; and as part of its elevated relative juridical position, it provides guarantees of individual freedoms, democracy, representation and participation, among others. Other positive attributes of constitutionalism are highlighted below to understand the motivation behind the turn to constitutionalism and ultimately, the rationale behind constitutionalism. Any such appraisal must, however, consider that constitutionalism is not all good and acceptable under all circumstances in an unqualified manner. The reasons that lie behind the turn towards constitutionalism and the advantages of constitutionalism must therefore be juxtaposed with the views of those that are considerably more sceptical about the nature and practical consequences of a constitutionalised order. The analysis commences with the advantages or the positive attributes of constitutionalism.

First, describing it as a political 'technology', Lutz captures the allure of constitutionalism as reflecting internal human goodness, or the deliberate will to be good (as expressed through juridical structures) when he states:

> Constitutional government is not a natural form of political organization, but a human artefact that is selected for use because of its beneficial tendencies. We choose to use this human-made tool, this technology, not for itself but for its relative advantage over other political technologies in the pursuit of fundamental human hopes. In a sense, one can view constitutionalism as resting on natural inclinations, but constitutionalism flows from the human psyche in an attempt to channel and improve human nature. A constitution rests on deeply shared human hopes, but not on behavior that, even when considered 'natural', is in any sense inevitable.[86]

Anastaplo argues in similar terms that '[i]n the background, if not even at the foundations, of any constitutional system are reflections upon the very notion of morality',[87] which galvanise the institutionalisation of prudence and that which we recognise as being 'good'. In this sense, constitutionalism transcends 'normal' politics and law, reaching deep into the moral fabric of a society that seeks to be good, as expressed through its constitutionalised political and legal order. Constitutionalism accordingly acts as a 'repository of the notions of the common good

---

[86] Lutz, 'Thinking About Constitutionalism' (n 72) 133.
[87] G Anastaplo, 'Constitutionalism and the Good: Explorations' (2003) 70 *Tennessee Law Review* 738, 738.

prevalent in a certain community'.[88] The almost universal contemporary recognition of constitutionalism as a model for the establishment, organisation and legitimation of political power is evident from the trend observed among some rulers who are notorious despots, but who feel compelled at least to pretend to act in accordance with a constitutional framework.[89] Yet, while this is no doubt one of constitutionalism's greatest advantages, it is at once its greatest potential drawback, acting as it sometimes does as a convenient smokescreen to window dress an essentially unconstitutional state (see the discussion below).

Second, constitutionalism notionally captures all the formal and substantive elements that are required to improve a legal and political order, acting as a collective rhetorical trope, promising 'all of these [constitutional elements] together, in a comprehensive package'.[90] Constitutionalism seeks to improve a pre-constitutional legal order by 'moving it away from a structure where the holders of power are entirely self-regulated and beyond review to a system encompassing scrutiny at its core'.[91] In doing so, constitutionalism seeks to fashion a balance that sacrifices arbitrary despotic absolutism in favour of limited government and predictability of state action where the rights and freedoms of people are entrenched and, together with constitutionally derived customs, mores and traditions, a society is better protected from evisceration.[92] Constitutionalism also allows people to better anticipate governmental behaviour, and thus the potential impact of this behaviour on them and their interests; it allows people to confront government without fear of retribution where they are threatened by power abuse; it provides a deliberative space and consensual basis for people to resolve disputes in an orderly and non-violent way; and it facilitates the peaceful periodic transitions of power in a society from one government to another.[93]

Third, related to the foregoing, a constitutionalised legal and governance order is seen to be considerably more coherent and able to instil legal certainty and predictability than non-constitutional orders. Such an order is also 'civilised to the extent that constitutionalism represents the epitome of efficient governance',[94] thus not only reflecting on the form of governance inherent to constitutional orders, but also on the quality of governance. To this end, constitutionalism is a precursor to good governance as was pointed out above.

Fourth, related to legal certainly, because constitutionalism elevates a constitution to the supreme law that is also difficult to amend, and because constitutionalism partly removes some elements of the legal order from the

---

[88] M Maduro, 'The Importance of Being Called a Constitution: Constitutional Authority and the Authority of Constitutionalism' (2005) 3 *International Journal of Constitutional Law* 332, 333.
[89] Grimm, 'Achievement of Constitutionalism' (n 66) 3.
[90] Klabbers (n 24) 45.
[91] O'Donoghue (n 11) 16.
[92] M Klarman, 'What's so Great about Constitutionalism?' (1998) 93 *Northwestern University Law Review* 145, 163.
[93] Grimm (n 66) 10.
[94] O'Donoghue (n 11) 17.

political arena, constitutionalism embeds a measure of continuity and longevity in a legal system that is absent in non-constitutional orders; the latter are often subjected to short-term political whims and fluctuations. This does not mean, however, that constitutions last forever. While constitutions strive to be perpetual, they do fail and end because they are essentially only human artefacts. Nevertheless, constitutionalism heralds an opposition to politics, as a 'necessary corrective to the pathologies of politics';[95] where good laws and scrutiny, following a process of constitutionalisation, replace bad politics. Constitutionalism is thus seen as an antidote to endemic 'bad' governance that exists as a result of bad politics. Klabbers explains that:

> constitutions are often thought to be of higher value: legislation is for the here and now, but a constitution is [relatively] forever. This taps into the promise of the end of politics, a promise inherent (if not always explicit) in all great ideologies. Constitutionalism is no exception: a constitutional polity is a polity where things are done according to the rule of law, not the rule of man. In much the same way as with human rights, one of the main attractions of constitutionalism is to suggest that there is a sphere beyond everyday politics, comprising values that cannot (or only with great difficulty) be affected or changed.[96]

So, constitutionalism legalises and regulates political decision-making processes (more broadly understood as governance); but it does not legalise politics itself: 'The constitution is a framework that enables political decisions, and a benchmark for their assessment. Thus, constitutionalism emerges as a standard of legitimacy'.[97] Neither does the confluence of law and politics in the constitutional domain suggest that law is necessarily politicised. It rather means that as a result of constitutionalisation, the law is more likely and better able to regulate political actions and political actors in terms of a consolidated constitutional basis, and to prevent undesirable short-term political externalities that negatively impact on society and its interests.[98]

As far as the sceptics of constitutionalism are concerned, as a first point, Nedelsky believes that (American) constitutionalism is founded on the tension between individual autonomy (which in turn is based on the defence of property), and democracy.[99] She sees the conception of individual autonomy, which she considers the basis of constitutionalism, as being flawed because of its association with property where an individual erects a 'wall of rights' between herself and others, with property being the 'ideal symbol for this vision of autonomy'.[100] The result of

---

[95] Dunhoff (n 8) 200.
[96] Klabbers (n 24) 47.
[97] Murkens (n 49) 440.
[98] O'Donoghue (n 11) 16.
[99] Historically, the constitutional link between property and the protection of the individual was a counter-reaction to feudalism and central state regulation of the economy where it was believed that freedom of property would be a better way of achieving justice and welfare for the individual. Grimm (n 66) 8.
[100] J Nedelsky, *Private Property and the Limits of American Constitutionalism: The Madisonian Framework and its Legacy* (Chicago, University of Chicago Press, 1990) 272.

this emphasis on individual autonomy and its consequent 'distancing' is evident from critique often levelled against human rights, namely that they are individualistic, thus countering efforts that seek to foster greater harmonious interdependence between humans *inter se* and between humans and non-human, but living Earth constituents.[101] Thus, while the individual autonomy that constitutionalism bestows is good in the sense that it protects the individual against power abuse, it could also autonomise the individual to such an extent that she is perversely alienated from other co-existing human bodies in material space, where the 'materialities of human embodied existence—in a lively world of beings and systems, scenes and contexts, environments and ecosystems',[102] are kept separate and prevented from harmonious co-existence.

Second, related to its being embedded in a conception of individual autonomy, the idea of constitutionalism could be too individualistic and too exclusively centred on humans, thus working to galvanise human mastery over a non-human world. The 'separateness' that constitutionalism could lead to in its pursuit of protecting individual freedoms (often through human rights), might also lead to the construction of inter and intra-species hierarchies and injustices. Examples of this are the primacy that is afforded to human dignity in the Basic Law of the Federal Republic of Germany,[103] and the Constitution of the Republic of South Africa,[104] where the human and its interests takes centre stage. Other examples are constitutions which contain environmental rights, but where almost all of these are anthropocentric.[105] While constitutionalism's anthropocentric focus is unavoidable, logical and understandable, by resisting to extend the scope of constitutionalism and its protective umbrella to include considerations for the non-human world (although there are exceptions such as the Constitution of Ecuador 2008 as we shall see in Chapter 7),[106] is seen by some commentators as a fundamental flaw in the constitutional agenda.[107]

---

[101] C Gearty, 'Do Human Rights Help or Hinder Environmental Protection?' (2010) 1 *Journal of Human Rights and the Environment* 7, 7–8.

[102] A Grear, 'Human Bodies in Material Space: Lived Realities, Eco-crisis and the Search for Transformation' (2013) 4 *Journal of Human Rights and the Environment* 111, 111.

[103] The very first article in the German Constitution, art 1(1), states that '[h]uman dignity shall be inviolable'.

[104] To this end it is instructive that s 1(a) of the Constitution of the Republic of South Africa, as part of the 'Founding Provisions' of the Constitution, no less, states: 'The Republic of South Africa is one, sovereign, democratic state founded on the following values: (a) Human dignity, the achievement of equality and the advancement of human rights and freedoms'. S 10 of the Bill of Rights reinforces the predominance of human dignity by providing: 'Everyone has inherent dignity and the right to have their dignity respected and protected'.

[105] See for a detailed comparative analysis, DR Boyd, *The Environmental Rights Revolution: A Global Study of Constitutions, Human Rights, and the Environment* (Vancouver, UBC Press, 2012).

[106] Art 71 of the Constitution of the Republic of Ecuador 2008 provides: 'Nature, or Pacha Mama, where life is reproduced and occurs, has the right to integral respect for its existence and for the maintenance and regeneration of its life cycles, structure, functions and evolutionary processes'.

[107] K Bosselmann, *Im Namen der Natur: Der Weg zum ökologischen Rechtsstaat* (Bern, Scherz, 1992); K Bosselmann, *Ökologische Grundrechte: Zum Verhältnis zwischen individueller Freiheit und Natur* (Baden-Baden, Nomos Verlagsgesellschaft, 1998).

Third, in more general terms, as was intimated above, constitutionalism is often derided for being a mere symbolic exercise in the regulatory scheme of things because constitutional provisions, as a result of them usually being formulated in the abstract and in broad terms, could be weakly enforced and vaguely specified.[108] Constitutionalism has also been criticised for being too Western-oriented; for being too dependent on the contested notion of democracy; for the disproportional power that is afforded to courts to strengthen judicial review functions that could result in a countermajoritarian dilemma; for its hesitance to acknowledge the role of non-state actors as important contributors to work towards a common (constitutional) governance goal; and for often being disingenuous by attempting to window dress.[109]

Nevertheless, given the premium that is placed on constitutions the world over, and the many positive advances that have been made in terms of creating constitutional democracies with all that goes with that impulse, it would appear on balance as if constitutionalism has been and continues to be a generally positive evolution in law and governance, despite the many criticisms levelled against it.

V. General Elements of the Contemporary Constitutional State

A constitution, the rule of law, the separation of powers doctrine, judicial independence and review, constitutional supremacy, democracy and rights are generally representative of the (often overlapping) elements of the contemporary constitutional state. They fulfil a useful analytical function in that they are also broadly representative of the core characteristics of constitutionalism. Obviously these features cannot constitute a complete checklist to state the existence of a constitutional state, or offer a final typology and topography of constitutionalism that is easily translatable to the global arena or to a specific focus area of law such as environmental law. The utility of describing these features rather lies in that they could be used as a framework to inform an evaluation that determines in broad terms the emergence of a constitutional and, for present purposes, a global environmental constitutional order. Naturally, because there is no example of a perfectly constitutionalised domestic legal order, all the elements need not be present to state the existence of some 'complete' constitutional order; some could be absent or present in a less forceful way, while others may overlap or compensate for another's absence.

---

[108] DA Kysar, *Regulating from Nowhere: Environmental Law and the Search for Objectivity* (New Haven, Yale University Press, 2010) 229, 231.
[109] Boyd *Environmental Rights Revolution* (n 105) 5–6.

A. A Constitution

An earlier part of this chapter has already considered the meaning and broad objectives of constitutions. A constitution is the foundation of the constitutional state to the extent that the state is fully dependent on a constitution for its existence; a constitution is the original existential source of a state and determines a state's particular historical-political existence.[110] It was indicated that a constitution regulates the socio-political life of a polity; it provides the architecture for the state and its institutions, which in turn, enables governance; and it mediates power and relations between the state and its organs, the state and its citizens, and citizens *inter se*. In short, a constitution provides a master plan and a unitary centre from which the entire political-legal order of a state originates, including the guidelines for the future manifestation of the state and of a polity.[111] In this sense, a constitution is not a philosophical abstraction, but rather a set of legal norms that emanate from a political decision,[112] creating the possibility to specify in advance specific rules of state conduct that have been designed to minimise the extent to which the state asserts and exercises its power in relation to its citizens.[113] Constitutions achieve the latter task by means of substantive rules (such as rights), and procedural and institutional rules (such as provisions on access to courts and the independence of the judiciary and powers of judicial review).

It was also indicated that the word constitution has traditionally always been connected to the nation state, since it is considered a foundational element of the state: in terms of the state, a constitution constitutes a political entity; it establishes its fundamental structure; and it defines the limits within which the state's political powers can be exercised.[114] The state is the object of a constitution;[115] every state has and must have a constitution, otherwise the state is merely a non-entity, an abstraction of political theory; an idealistic notion (*ein Idealtypus, eine Kunstschöpfung der Theorie, eine Abstraktion der Allgemeinen Staatslehre*).[116] To this end, the constitution is the essence of statehood; it is not a goal in itself, but becomes an instrument as the only form of law that is able to authorise, bind and limit the political authority of a community to such an extent that those ideal fundamental principles that are dear to a community are complied with.[117] Whether it would

---

[110] Enzmann (n 74) 84.
[111] ibid 89.
[112] Grimm (n 66) 9.
[113] R Kay, 'Constitutional Chrononomy' (2000) 13 *Ratio Juris* 31, 32.
[114] 'The state' for present purposes could be understood as 'a community of people legally forming a sovereign unit for the purposes of the creation and maintenance of a legal order within a determined territory': Venter (n 5) 9.
[115] U Preuss, 'Disconnecting Constitutions from Statehood: Is Global Constitutionalism a Viable Concept?' in Dobner and Loughlin (n 6) 24–46.
[116] Isensee, 'Staat und Verfassung' (n 46) 4.
[117] Di Fabio, 'Verfassungsstaat und Weltrecht' (n 85) 402.

be possible to separate the idea of a constitution from the idea of the nation state in the sense that a constitution could exist without a state, or that it moves beyond the state in a global setting as a global constitution, is determined in Chapter 4.

Following some five different families of constitutions (including the British dominions; the presidential-cum-federal systems of Latin America; the constitutional monarchy-cum-cabinet systems in France; the German-Austrian-Hungarian systems; and the unique Swiss federal system),[118] with reference to its formal characteristics, a constitution is mostly a single codified or written document; it is something observable and often tangible. 'Writtenness' is, however, by no means a requirement for a constitution to be a constitution. This is evident from the unwritten 'living' constitution of New Zealand, where a written constitution is not a prerequisite for the existence of constitutionalism in a legal order. As well, the United Kingdom's long-standing adherence to the ideals and requirements of constitutionalism without a formally written constitution suggests that a constitution need not exist in a single codified format for constitutionalism to be proclaimed.[119]

In addition to being either written or unwritten, constitutions are characterised as having precedence over 'normal' laws, or being superior, by being either rigid or flexible in terms of the possibility to amend them;[120] and having come about as a result of a political revolution as opposed to a more protracted evolutionary process of continuous legislative developments.[121]

The creation of constitutions can be understood in terms of the notion of 'constitutional moments'. In a generic sense a constitutional moment 'is distinguished by lasting constitutional arrangements that result from specific, emotionally shared responses to shared fundamental political experiences'.[122] In this sense, most constitutions will have come about as result of a constitutional moment. Others ascribe to it a time factor where a constitutional moment is associated with a fairly sudden or rapid transformation such as the case of Nelson Mandela's South Africa, post-Second World War Germany or the United Nations Charter of 1945 that created a new world order.[123] This view, however, does not acknowledge constitutions such as that of the United Kingdom that have not come about as a result of a sudden event. Although originally developed for the purpose of

---

[118] Venter (n 5) 26.

[119] ibid 21.

[120] Whereas the Constitution of the Republic of South Africa is an example of a rigid constitution which is very difficult to amend, the United Kingdom Constitution is more flexible, to the extent that the British Parliament has, by virtue of its parliamentary sovereignty, the power to affect constitutional changes through the ordinary legislative procedure.

[121] The South African Constitution is an example of a constitution that came about as a result of an instantaneous constitutional moment, as opposed to, for example, the unwritten constitution of the United Kingdom which followed a far more protracted development trajectory over a longer period of time.

[122] A Sajó, 'Constitution without the Constitutional Moment: A View from the New Member States' (2005) 3 *International Journal of Constitutional Law* 243, 243.

[123] A Slaughter and W Burke-White, 'An International Constitutional Moment' (2002) 43 *Harvard International Law Journal* 1.

describing American constitutional developments in particular, a more inclusive and mainstream view is the one famously propounded by Ackerman, stating that constitutional moments, or 'moments of constitutional creation', are 'rare periods of heightened political consciousness' with long periods between them when 'normal politics' prevail and manipulate the constitutional forms of political life to pursue specific collective interests.[124]

The foregoing opposites in the debate around constitutional moments usefully illustrate that there are no generally accepted criteria for describing a constitutional moment,[125] and that constitutional moments are probably more important for what they signify than how they occur. Whether rare or frequent, sudden or prolonged, constitutional moments signal a wholesale transition in an existing political and legal order. As well, constitutional moments highlight discontent with an existing constitutional arrangement; an urge to change the status quo, and they set in motion an entire range of reforms with respect to those governance, political and juridical aspects of a country that a constitution would typically determine and regulate (even though some constitutional moments do not necessarily lead to an order where constitutionalism prevails, as the former National Socialist German Constitution suggests). Finally, although some constitutional moments such as the demise of the Weimar Constitution in the 1930s that led to the totalitarian Nazi state could obviously be dangerous,[126] as promises of possibilities, constitutional moments mostly evince hope for a future that is somehow better than the past or present:

> a constitutional moment is best seen as one in which each of us has some knowledge of our fortunes and circumstances, and are seeking to establish the rules and understandings that will regulate the way in which we can constitutionally govern ourselves.[127]

In addition to these general characteristics, and mindful of the risk of generalisation, the contemporary written constitution typically would include several components. First, a preamble that sets out the context within which the constitution was adopted, the reasons for its adoption, the grounds of its legitimation, the right to self-determination of a society and its sovereign power to create a constitution; and a proclamation of the type of order, in broad ideal terms, that a society seeks to achieve through the constitution and the subsequent legal and political order

---

[124] B Ackerman, 'The Storrs Lectures: Discovering the Constitution' (1984) 93 *Yale Law Journal* 1013, 1022.

[125] M McConnell, 'The Forgotten Constitutional Moment' (1994) 11 *Constitutional Commentary* 115, 120.

[126] See, more generally, G Quinn, 'Dangerous Constitutional Moments: The "Tactic of Legality" in Nazi Germany and the Irish Free State Compared' in J Morison, K McEvoy and G Anthony (eds), *Judges, Transition, and Human Rights* (Oxford, Oxford University Press, 2007) 223–49.

[127] J Ferejohn, 'Independent Judges, Dependent Judiciary: Explaining Judicial Independence' (1999) 72 *Southern California Law Review* 353, 367–68.

that it establishes.[128] Second, a part setting out rights and other protective guarantees in a substantive sense (usually a bill of rights)[129] and, third, an extensive formal part providing for the organisation of the state, including the establishment and functions of its institutions, their tasks and their powers,[130] are most commonly found in written constitutions all over the world. The worth of such a generic delimitation lies in its pointing to the general practice of constitutions containing both formal and substantive aspects; a distinction that is also clearly reflected by the rule of law discussed below.

B. The Rule of Law

Despite its almost universal endorsement, including by institutions such as the United Nations,[131] like its notional root constitutionalism, the rule of law as a concept, its rationale, meaning and purpose, are all but universally clear and agreed.[132] Adding to its abstruseness, there seems to be a tendency to employ the rule of law as a shorthand description for all the positive aspects of any given political or legal system,[133] or generally, where the rule of law is lacking, as a reference to

---

[128] eg the Preamble of the South African Constitution states:

> We, the people of South Africa, recognise the injustices of our past; honour those who suffered for justice and freedom in our land; respect those who have worked to build and develop our country; and believe that South Africa belongs to all who live in it, united in our diversity. We therefore, through our freely elected representatives, adopt this Constitution as the supreme law of the Republic so as to: heal the divisions of the past and establish a society based on democratic values, social justice and fundamental human rights; lay the foundations for a democratic and open society in which government is based on the will of the people and every citizen is equally protected by law; improve the quality of life of all citizens and free the potential of each person; and build a united and democratic South Africa able to take its rightful place as a sovereign state in the family of nations. May God protect our people.

[129] eg ch 2 of the South African Constitution that provides for a bill of rights.

[130] eg chs 3–14 of the South African Constitution provide for procedural/operational matters such as cooperative governance; and matters related to parliament, the presidency and national executive, provinces, local government, courts and the administration of justice, state institutions supporting constitutional democracy, principles of public administration, the security services, traditional leaders and financial matters.

[131] United Nations General Assembly Resolution on the Rule of Law (A/RES/67/1), 30 November 2012.

[132] Analytically as well, scholars seem to employ the rule of law in various guises: as a condition to determine if a legal system exists or not; as a practical constraint on a legal system; as a procedural principle to identify legal systems, to prescribe the practices of a legal system, or to evaluate the moral worth of a legal system; and as an object-level practice whereby laws are enforced and enforcement is justified through the rule of law: B Burge-Hendrix, 'Plato and the Rule of Law' in Flores and Himma (eds), *Law, Liberty and the Rule of Law* (n 75) 34.

[133] C Hamara, 'The Concept of the Rule of Law' in Flores and Himma (eds) (n 75) 11–12. See as an example of such an expanded view, S Baykal, 'The Rule of Law in the European Union Context and Turkey's Accession Process' in P Müller-Graff and H Kabaalioglu (eds), *Turkey and the European Union: Different Dimensions* (Baden-Baden, Nomos Verlag, 2011) 37–51.

chaotic states such as Syria that have fallen into an ungovernable downward spiral of failed governance.[134] While it is mostly true that '[e]veryone except anarchists extols the "rule of law"',[135] such generalisations extend far beyond the rule of law's traditional juridical meaning as an element of constitutionalism. These generalisations thus work to almost fully equate the rule of law to the broader notion of constitutionalism itself,[136] and potentially result in political and 'ideological abuse and general over-use'.[137] As we shall see later in this section, while the rule of law is obviously a (if not *the*) central element of constitutionalism, it is possible to delimit and describe several of its specific features that render it unique when compared to its parent concept, constitutionalism.

The rule of law's historical roots lie scattered over the jurisdictional landscape. Termed rule of law in the Anglo-American world;[138] *Rechtsstaat* in Germany (see the discussion above);[139] *regsstaat* in South Africa,[140] and *Etat de Droit* in France,[141] these notions impart one key idea, namely that the lack of insight, fallibility and gullibility that often characterise people, and thus the governments that they form, require and allow a substantial containment of their freedom of choice and decision through fixed general rules that they have devised and adopted themselves and that they remain subject to under all circumstances.[142] Based on the Aristotelian, and to a certain extent the Diceyan, idea that the rule of law is better than the rule of man, it is from here that the popular expressions of this doctrine developed, namely: that the rule of law and not the rule of man prevails; that no one is above the law; and the rule of law is a state of order created by law.[143]

---

[134] See, on Syria and the rule of law, among others, United Nations, 'Syria Calls for Application of Rule of Law in "Unimaginable" Situation Facing Country, as Sixth Committee Concludes Rule of Law Debate' (Sixty-seventh General Assembly, 11 October 2012) www.un.org/press/en/2012/gal3437.doc.htm.

[135] D Magraw, 'Rule of Law and the Environment' (2014) 44 *Environmental Policy and Law* 201, 201.

[136] See for an example of such a conflation, J Tully, 'The Unfreedom of the Moderns in Comparison to their Ideals of Constitutional Democracy' (2002) 65 *Modern Law Review* 204.

[137] Lord Bingham, 'The Rule of Law' (2007) 66 *Cambridge Law Journal* 67, 68.

[138] In the American legal system the rule of law is grounded in a written constitution and designed to provide legal expression to pre-existing, inalienable fundamental rights and liberties that belong to the individual. It envisions a minimal state almost exclusively concerned with securing pre-existing natural rights that it would seek to protect through a variety of procedural rights: Rosenfeld, 'Rule of Law' (n 78) 1334–35.

[139] See, Weber-Fas, *Verfassungsstaat des Grundgesetzes* (n 60) 154–71.

[140] The South African understanding of *regsstaat* (Afrikaans) is more or less similar to the German notion of *Rechtsstaat*, although it is more limited than the more encompassing notion of constitutional state or *Verfassungsstaat* in South Africa and Germany respectively: Venter, 'Konstitusionalisme in Suid-Afrika' (n 18) 94.

[141] As a literal translation of *Rechtsstaat*, the French notion imparts the idea of a state-backed legal regime that is shaped by fundamental liberal rights that constrain the democratic state rule through law: Rosenfeld (n 78) 1330–31.

[142] As Enzmann states: 'Ihnen allen liegt die Idee zugrunde, dass die mangelnde Erkenntnisfähigkeit, Fehlbarkeit und Verführbarkeit. des Menschen eine weitgehende Einhegung ihrer Entscheidungsfreiheit durch feststehende allgemeine Regeln erforderlich machen': Enzmann (n 74) 1.

[143] I Flores and K Himma, 'Introduction' in Flores and Himma (eds) (n 75) 2.

Collectively, these turn on a similar notion: the broader the governance discretion is, the greater the scope for subjectivity and arbitrariness, which is considered the antithesis of the rule of law.[144]

What then is the essential meaning of the rule of law in extant terms as measured against its historical cosmopolitan development? A contemporary vision of the rule of law is that it provides certainty in a legal order, it prevents the entrenchment of power, and it plays a more-than-symbolic role in the constitutional state in that it offers a normative justification and foundation for the entrenchment of procedural and substantive mechanisms to prescribe and proscribe power.[145] In broader terms then, being related to other constitutional considerations such as the separation of powers and constitutional supremacy, the rule of law works to protect a legal order from the arbitrary manipulation of power that is exercised in the political realm.[146]

In his famous list of essential elements of legality (or in this context the rule of law), Fuller determined that the law must be general and publicly promulgated, clear, not demand something impossible, be prospective in effect (as opposed to being retrospective), understandable, consistent and constant by applying equally to all cases, non-contradictory, and relatively stable and congruent.[147] Additions to these, or slight variations on the theme, include those proposed by Bingham: the law must be accessible, intelligible, clear and predictable; questions of legal right and liability should be resolved by application of the law and not the exercise of discretion; the law should provide everyone unimpeded access to a court or tribunal to have a dispute resolved, including affordable legal redress that must be fair and available without excessive delay; and compliance by the state with its obligations under international law.[148] For Flores, the rule of law revolves around the conception of obedience to law; the conception of the judge as a law that speaks; the conception of a duty to obey the law; and the conception of a due process of law including principles such as *audi alteram partem* and *nemo iudex in causa sua* (collectively denoting the idea of administrative justice).[149]

These are not categories that always apply in an absolute sense, however. For example, there are instances where justice can only be done in private where the

---

[144] Lord Bingham, 'Rule of Law' (n 137) 72.

[145] I believe it is sufficient to classify the rule of law as being procedural; and/or substantive. But there are other versions such as that of Merkel who believes that the rule of law could either be: (a) minimalist (or rule by law as power executed by positive law); (b) mid-range (a liberal democratic version which includes rule by law plus notions of equality, democracy, an independent judiciary and human rights, among others); and (c) maximalist (or social democratic rule of law which includes all the foregoing plus social universal rights institutionalised in a welfare state and legal regulation to reduce socio-economic inequality to a minimum): W Merkel, 'Measuring the Quality of the Rule of Law: Virtues, Perils, Results' in M Zürn, A Nollkaemper and R Peerenboom (eds), *Rule of Law Dynamics in an Era of International and Transnational Governance* (Cambridge, Cambridge University Press, 2012) 22.

[146] O'Donoghue (n 11) 27.

[147] LL Fuller, *The Morality of Law* (New Haven, Yale University Press, 1964) 33–94.

[148] Lord Bingham (n 137) 67–85.

[149] Flores, 'Law, Liberty and the Rule of Law' (n 75) 86.

public is excluded, such as judicial hearings involving minors; but derogation always calls for close consideration and clear justification.[150] Also, these characteristics are mostly procedural in nature; they do not relate to the substance of the law, but rather provide procedural dictates for the exercise of power specifically, and more generally, dictates for governance. This strictly procedural view on the rule of law:

> appears to be neutral as to content. It does not require there to be one ideological system or another, but what procedural rule of law, at the very least, does seem to necessitate is a system where law cannot be exercised, created or acted upon in an arbitrary fashion. It thus maintains a sphere within which the law must operate, though in this characterization without any particular substantive element to this law.[151]

A procedural conception of the rule of law therefore does not necessarily mean the rule of good law that is premised, among others, on rights and democracy. As Goldsworthy states, a procedural rule of law simply endeavours to 'ensure that the law is capable of guiding the behaviour of its subjects'.[152] To use South Africa as an example, its apartheid constitutions upheld the rule of 'bad' law in a procedural sense, and not the rule of 'good' law in a substantive sense as its new constitution currently does.

It is accordingly necessary that the outcome of compliance with the law must meet a substantive standard.[153] For the rule of law to also ensure the rule of good law, some degree of substantive elements, such as those provided by human rights, need to be included within the remit of the rule of law. While there may be others, respect for the rule of law as a means to establishing a measure of moral constraint of power as overseen by the courts (or judicial oversight), could be considered a substantive element of the rule of law. While the legislative and executive authorities must ensure observance of and compliance with the procedural dictates of the rule of law, the courts, through their powers of review, provide checks and balances and continuous scrutiny within which the legislative and executive authorities must operate (see the discussion below). In other words, the rule of law provides the democratic space where the 'opposing' powers of the judiciary vis-à-vis that of the legislative and the executive authorities equalise to prevent power abuse on the one hand (through judicial review) and the countermajoritarian dilemma from taking root on the other hand.[154]

Another substantive aspect of the rule of law lies in the belief that the law should apply equally to all, 'save to the extent that objective differences justify

---

[150] Lord Bingham (n 137) 69.
[151] O'Donoghue (n 11) 29–30.
[152] J Goldsworthy, 'Legislative Sovereignty and the Rule of Law' in T Campbell, KD Ewing and A Tomkins (eds), *Sceptical Essays on Human Rights* (Oxford, Oxford University Press, 2001) 66.
[153] Magraw, 'Rule of Law and the Environment' (n 135) 202.
[154] O'Donoghue (n 11) 30.

differentiation'.[155] Equality in this sense is a substantive element of the rule of law that is most often entrenched in a right. An example of an objective difference where unequal treatment could be justified is the deep socio-economic inequalities that characterise South African society as a result of past discriminatory laws that marginalised the majority of people in the country. In terms of the fundamental right to equality in South Africa:

1. Everyone is equal before the law and has the right to equal protection and benefit of the law.

...

3. The state may not unfairly discriminate directly or indirectly against anyone on one or more grounds, including race, gender, sex, pregnancy, marital status, ethnic or social origin, colour, sexual orientation, age, disability, religion, conscience, belief, culture, language and birth.
4. ... Discrimination on one or more of the grounds listed in subsection (3) is unfair unless it is established that the discrimination is fair.[156]

To this end, the practice of affirmative action in the country where socio-economic opportunities are provided to marginalised or previously disadvantaged groups instead of previously advantaged groups, can be justified as a means of benefiting one group at the expense of another with a view of creating a more equal society. Such a practice would be entirely in line with the substantive aspect of equality that the rule of law aspires to.[157]

A third substantive element of the rule of law is that the law must afford adequate protection of rights; a suggestion that Bingham fully acknowledges may be controversial to rule of law proceduralists.[158] He notes the explicit link between rights and the rule of law in the Universal Declaration of Human Rights 1948 which states in its Preamble: 'it is essential, if man is not to be compelled to have recourse, as a last resort, to rebellion against tyranny and oppression, that human rights should be protected by the rule of law'. By way of example, in the South African context, the rule of law, in addition to its formal dimension, also has a substantive element firmly embedded in rights that must be understood in terms of the country's post-apartheid constitutional dispensation. Whereas the procedural elements of the rule of law have always been part of South African law, (ironically in the past to uphold the rule of apartheid law), substantive aspects related to the rule of constitutional law specifically relate to the protection of rights and advancement of freedom and democracy. As Dyzenhaus points out:

> The commitment in new-order South Africa to the supremacy of the constitution and the rule of law does not, in itself, mark a departure from the past. The apartheid legal

---

[155] Lord Bingham (n 137) 73.
[156] S 9 of the Constitution of the Republic of South Africa. Emphasis added.
[157] O Dupper, 'In Defence of Affirmative Action in South Africa' (2004) 121 *South African Law Journal* 187.
[158] Lord Bingham (n 137) 75.

order implemented a racist ideology through law but was formally no less committed than the new order to both the supremacy of the constitution [sic] and the rule of law.[159]

What makes the new-order rule of law different from the apartheid era rule of law, is that the Constitution and its provisions collectively seek to break from a past political and legal dispensation by entrenching fundamental rights (among others): 'what marks the difference is the fact that the Constitution also guarantees a list of rights and liberties, and utterly rejects the discriminatory ideology of the previous order'.[160]

The South African example suggests a particular aspect of the rule of law, namely that a purely procedural manifestation of the rule of law does not necessarily advance the broader substantive ideals and objectives of constitutionalism. This could be an untenable situation since the constitutional state demands a vision of the rule of law that is both procedural and substantive; or what could be stated as the 'constitutional rule of law': 'the rule of law requires the creation and application of norms to be limited not only by adjective-formal procedures but also by substantive-material principles and a balanced application'.[161] An account that accordingly understands the rule of law for the purpose of the contemporary constitutional state as including both the procedural aspects to restrict power and the substantive elements that work in tandem with procedural dictates and other constitutional elements such as rights towards realising the larger ideal of constitutionalism, seems to be the most acceptable contemporary vision of the rule of law.[162]

In summary, I find Enzmann's systematic approach to the rule of law and division of its elements concisely descriptive and representative. In her view, the rule of law consists of formal/procedural and substantive/material aspects. Whereas the formal/procedural aspects of the rule of law provide for and determine those procedural elements that are necessary to establish and maintain a state order purely on the basis of positive law, the material/substantive aspects of the rule of law bind the state to substantive standards that aim to achieve substantive justice. The formal elements have three objectives: legality, limited allocation of powers, and judicial oversight. The elements of legality include: laws that are valid in a formal and material sense, legality of the administration, legal certainty and protection of citizens' trust in the stability and continuity of the law (*Vertrauensschutz*).

---

[159] D Dyzenhaus, 'The Pasts and Future of the Rule of Law in South Africa' (2008) 124 *South African Law Journal* 734, 735. Venter, in similar vein argues that:

> Apartheid 'constitutionalism' was therefore highly formal with little principled substance. It was based upon a highly positivist application of notions such as parliamentary sovereignty sourced from the common law and often perverted to serve sectional political purposes.

Venter (n 40) 732.

[160] Dyzenhaus, 'Pasts and Future of the Rule of Law' (n 159) 736.
[161] Flores (n 75) 90.
[162] See further on the procedural vis-à-vis substantive aspects of the rule of law, P Craig, 'Constitutional Foundations, the Rule of Law and Supremacy' (2003) Spring *Public Law* 92.

Limited allocation of powers includes: the subsidiarity principle along with clear governance competencies; responsibility, accountability and liability; prohibition of arbitrary exercise of authority (*Willkürverbot*); and proportionality (*Verhältnismäßigkeit*). Judicial oversight as an objective of the formal aspects includes: independent courts, guaranteed access to courts, a fair trial and compensation by the state and citizens for damage that they cause. The primary objective of the material aspects is to ensure justice and morality through, among others: fundamental rights for the individual; solidarity and public welfare rights for society as a whole; as well as the general principles of justice.[163]

C. Separation of Powers

Less ambiguous than the rule of law, but intimately coupled therewith and no less ambitious, the separation of powers doctrine essentially entails that the authority to govern in any state should be divided among different institutional nodes responsible for governance; ie the executive, the legislature and the judiciary (otherwise known as the *trias politica*):

> The classic formulation of the doctrine of separation of powers in its 'pure' form is based on the fundamental idea that there are three separate, distinct, and independent functions of government-the legislative, the executive, and the judicial-which should be discharged by three separate and distinct organs-the legislature, the executive (or government), and the judiciary (or the courts).[164]

While there is some dispute as to the precise origins of this doctrine, many agree that its modern conception can be traced to Aristotle, Locke and Hobbes, but most definitively, to Montesquieu who, by indicating the doctrine's centrality to civil liberty, managed to substantially influence the French and American Revolutions with this notion.[165]

The separation of powers doctrine, which is representative of a formal/procedural element of the rule of law, concerns itself with power relations in a polity, the institutional architecture to prevent power abuse and the establishment of checks and balances by means of which the three nodes of governmental power co-exist as three separate, but collective entities. To this extent, the separation of powers is fully linked with democracy and the rule of law, deriving its normative appeal from this intimate interdependence. As Conway correctly indicates: 'Both democracy and the rule of law require a division between the legislature

---

[163] Enzmann (n 74) 43–163.

[164] C Fombad, 'The Separation of Powers and Constitutionalism in Africa: The Case of Botswana' (2005) 25 *Boston College Third World Law Journal* 301, 306.

[165] H Mansfield, 'Separation of Powers in the American Constitution' in B Wilson and P Schramm (eds), *Separation of Powers and Good Government* (Lanham, Rowman and Littlefiel, 1994) 4–10; W Gwyn, *The Meaning of the Separation of Powers: An Analysis of the Doctrine from its Origin to the Adoption of the United States Constitution* (The Hague, Martinus Nijhoff, 1965).

and judiciary, so that laws are not constituted only when adjudicated'.[166] In addition to being a means to a constitutional end (ie countering the centralisation of power in tandem with the other elements of the constitutional state such as the substantive aspects of the rule of law), separation of powers also relates to the formalistic constitutive functions of constitutions more generally in that it seeks to achieve, by constitutionally delimiting the institutional architecture of the state, three separate tracks of government power. To this end the separation of powers doctrine fulfils a descriptive role (stating the separate power tracks of government), as well as an idealistic role that envisions, as an aspirational notion, how relations between government institutions and between government and its people should be conducted (ie independently and not subject to interference from other spheres).[167] Its embeddedness in the rule of law paradigm that seeks to counter a centralisation and abuse of authority, is powerfully illustrated by Bondy's prosaic description of the situation which the separation of doctrine seeks to mediate:

> The earliest dawn of civilization discloses, as the most primitive form of political organization, a warfaring society grouped about a victorious chief. This powerful personage is supposed to represent the fittest product of the period of barbaric liberty and self-help, which immediately preceded the period of governmental organization. The chieftain's superiority in valor convinces his superstitious admirers, as well as himself, that he is of divine descent. This superstition invests him with a halo of glory and clothes him with sovereign power. The religious sanction secures reverence for his person and obedience for his laws. He experiences no opposition in immediately exercising all governmental powers. He is priest, war chief, judge and legislator.[168]

Even though it is clear which three types of state powers should be kept separate, it is less clear why and to what extent they should be separated. Regarding the 'why', there are at least three justifications that have been advanced for keeping nodes of government power separate, ie: rule of law considerations, the promotion of accountability and enhancement of government efficiency.[169] With respect to the rule of law, the idea is that those who make the law should not also be able to judge or punish violations of the law; neither should those who judge or punish be able to make law; a notion which is aptly expressed through the common law notion of *nemo iudex in causa sua* (no one should be a judge in his own case). Clearly the idea behind the rule of law understanding of the separation of powers doctrine is to prevent the concentration of power in any single group of people or a person from entirely controlling the governance machinery of the state.

Closely related to the rule of law, the creation of accountability through the separation of government powers is an obvious requirement for a limited

---

[166] G Conway, 'Recovering a Separation of Powers in the European Union' (2011) 17 *European Law Journal* 304, 308.

[167] R Masterman, *The Separation of Powers in the Contemporary Constitution: Judicial Competence and Independence in the United Kingdom* (Cambridge, Cambridge University Press, 2011) 4–5.

[168] W Bondy, *The Separation of Governmental Powers in History, in Theory, and in the Constitutions* (New York, Columbia College, 1896) 7–8.

[169] Fombad, 'Separation of Powers and Constitutionalism in Africa' (n 164) 307.

government that must be able to justify its decisions and actions and to act responsibly externally towards its people and internally vis-à-vis other state institutions. Accountable and responsible governance can only be maintained in a legitimate way if those who are being scrutinised and held to account for their governance actions and decisions are not also those performing the oversight role.

The notion of governance efficiency means that some state institutions in different nodes of state power are better placed to perform certain governance functions than others. The judiciary, after all, is ill equipped to promulgate laws; so is the legislature not in a position (nor should it be in terms of the rule of law) to adjudicate the conflicts that arise from the laws that it creates. The judiciary will also hardly have provision within its ranks for a secret service that is required to gather intelligence for certain executive functions that must be performed. The very fact of them being separated could work to instil among the three powers numerous qualities usually associated with good governance such as deliberation, collaboration, steady administration and judgement qualities that are required to achieve common governance objectives: 'the legislative, executive, and judicial branches play distinct but potentially complementary roles in performing basic government functions, and it is the very separation (with overlap) of these institutions that often produces salutary effects for governance'.[170] In other words, a constitutionally imposed separation of the three different nodes of power actually creates the need for deliberate cooperation if a collective (good) governance effort is to be achieved at all.

Naturally, the degree to which there will be a separation between the legislative, executive and judicial authorities will vary across jurisdictions; there is no standard formula that applies universally.[171] As a general rule, however, it is common that there should not (and from a practical point of view to the extent that governance functions sometimes must overlap, probably cannot), be an absolute disjunction between the various authorities of a state government where the separation of powers doctrine works as a 'rigid rule that completely prevents one organ of power from performing any of the functions normally performed by the other'.[172] Any rigid separation may also adversely impact the potency of checks and balances if it does not allow the three branches of government to actively check the actions of one another (the important function of judicial review, for example, would be impossible in a pure form of separation of powers—see the discussion below). Indeed, the very fact of separation cannot be sufficient to uphold constitutionalism.[173] A form of absolute separation of powers which

---

[170] B Peabody and J Nugent, 'Toward a Unifying Theory of the Separation of Powers' (2003) 53 *American University Law Review* 1, 24.

[171] See, for an overview of various European states and their experiences with the separation of powers doctrine as interpreted by their respective constitutional courts, P Paczolay and B Bitskey (eds), *Separation of Powers Regarding the Jurisdiction of the Constitutional Court: The 10th Conference of the European Constitutional Courts, Budapest, 6–9 May, 1996* (Budapest, Hungarian Constitutional Court, 1997).

[172] Fombad (n 164) 309.

[173] Masterman, *Separation of Powers* (n 167) 11.

embraces a complete disjunction between the three branches of government is also untenable for its being un-accommodative of constitutional models such as the United Kingdom where certain members of the legislature are also members of the executive in terms of the Westminster model.[174] Moreover, the absolute approach to the separation of powers presupposes that all government functions can be neatly placed in one of three categories without the possibility of these even minimally overlapping, as the case might very well increasingly be in modern governance practices and approaches that are based on models of networked governance.[175] Clearly, because a rigid separation of powers could prevent government from functioning at all, what is required instead is 'sufficient separation to forestall the dangers that are inherent in the concentration of powers'.[176] The extent of sufficiency will depend on the broader legal, the political, and more specifically the constitutional customs, histories, contexts, cultures and traditions of countries.

D. Judicial Independence and Powers of Review

While it has been expressed as a manifestation of the separation of powers doctrine,[177] judicial independence (and implicitly therewith the review functions of courts) is clearly related also to the rule of law. There are many views on this doctrine. Rosenn, for example, states that judicial independence is 'the degree to which judges actually decide cases in accordance with their own determinations of the evidence, the law and justice, free from the coercion, blandishments, interference, or threats of governmental authorities or private citizens'.[178] Larkins' broader explanation is that:

> Judicial independence refers to the existence of judges who are not manipulated for political gain, who are impartial towards the parties of a dispute, and who form a judicial branch which has the power as an institution to regulate the legality of government behavior, enact 'neutral' justice, and determine significant constitutional and legal values.[179]

The foregoing suggests that at its core, judicial independence originates from the notion of conflict resolution by a neutral third party who can be trusted to settle conflicts after considering only the facts and their relation to relevant laws.[180] This is one of the minimum necessities for the rule of law and it has been recognised

---

[174] ibid. Witteveen refers to this approach as a 'balance of powers': W Witteveen, 'Doctrinal Stories' (1993) 6 *International Journal for the Semiotics of Law* 179, 195.
[175] Masterman (n 167) 11.
[176] Fombad (n 164) 341.
[177] Masterman (n 167) 16.
[178] K Rosenn, 'The Protection of Judicial Independence in Latin America' (1987) 19 *University of Miami Inter-American Law Review* 1, 7.
[179] C Larkins, 'Judicial Independence and Democratization: A Theoretical and Conceptual Analysis' (1996) 44 *American Journal of Comparative Law* 605, 611.
[180] ibid at 608.

General Elements

by the United Nations in its Basic Principles on the Independence of the Judiciary of 1985,[181] which provide, among others:

(1) The independence of the judiciary shall be guaranteed by the State and enshrined in the Constitution or the law of the country. It is the duty of all governmental and other institutions to respect and observe the independence of the judiciary.

(2) The judiciary shall decide matters before them impartially, on the basis of facts and in accordance with the law, without any restrictions, improper influences, inducements, pressures, threats or interferences, direct or indirect, from any quarter or for any reason.[182]

In any society, there is always a need for a neutral third party that ensures at least (a) the principled, and unbiased enactment of justice; and (b) the enforcement of constitutional constraints on government power. To this end, Ferejohn helpfully explains that judicial independence has an internal and external dimension.[183] Internally, and correlating with (a), judges are required to be independent, autonomous moral agents who are required to exercise objectivity and impartiality as part of their character in a manner congruent to the values that underlie a constitutional democracy (elsewhere referred to as personal independence or impartiality).[184] The external dimension of judicial independence correlates with (b) but is more easily controllable in that it relates to judges being able to be manifestly free and protected from politics, ideological considerations and influence from the executive, the legislature and the public at large (the judiciary's political insularity).[185] External judicial independence is thus 'a feature of the institutional setting within which judging takes place,' and which is 'instrumental to the pursuit of other values, such as the rule of law or constitutional values';[186] it is not an end in itself, but an important means to a constitutional goal that seeks to uphold the procedural ideals of the rule of law (especially to the extent that separation of powers establishes a system of checks and balances on legislative and executive authority); and the substantive aspects of the rule of law such as the protection of rights.

It is possible for both internal and external judicial independence to be guaranteed, if not completely, then at least to a significant extent through a range of safeguards. For example, to ensure internal judicial independence, judges are usually appointed subject to a stringent selection process and their actions are directed by some code of conduct that is either entrenched in a constitution, and/or in a specific statute dealing with the judiciary. External judicial independence is achieved

---

[181] As adopted by the Seventh United Nations Congress on the Prevention of Crime and the Treatment of Offenders held at Milan from 26 August to 6 September 1985 and endorsed by General Assembly Resolutions 40/32 of 29 November 1985 and 40/146 of 13 December 1985.
[182] Principles 1 and 2.
[183] Ferejohn, 'Independent Judges' (n 127) 353.
[184] A Nollkaemper, 'The Independence of the Domestic Judiciary in International Law' (2006) XVII *Finnish Yearbook of International Law* 261, 299.
[185] O Fiss, 'The Limits of Judicial Independence' (1993) 25 *Inter-American Law Review* 57, 59.
[186] Ferejohn (n 127) 353.

through separation of powers provisions in a constitution, and/or by deliberate explicit proclamations stating the independent status of the judiciary.[187] As a minimum, internal and external judicial independence should work to facilitate:

> the provision of a certain kind of public or collective good ... the collective good takes the form of creating a capacity of the political system to commit to a future course of action- that is, to commit not to interfere with judicial decisions, no matter what their content. Independent judging makes it possible that substantive rules adopted now will be reliably upheld in the future, even in the face of strong temptations to do otherwise.[188]

While the rationale behind judicial independence is evident from the foregoing, it is less clear to what extent judges should be able to act independently to uphold the rule of law and at the same time not assume too much power that would enable them to rule without constitutional restraints themselves by usurping the functions of the executive and legislature. On the one hand it seems logical to afford the judiciary sufficient powers to enable it to fulfil its basic functions, ie interpreting laws, mediating conflicts and thus contributing to a constitutional state that seeks to uphold the procedural and the substantive aspects of the rule of law; by preventing the arbitrariness of power; by pronouncing on the constitutionality of decisions, acts and laws; and by protecting rights.[189] On the other hand, the judiciary's power (embedded in minority institutions of courts to which judges are not necessarily democratically elected by the majority of citizens) cannot be so comprehensive or overwhelming that it culminates in a countermajoritarian dilemma; a situation where virtually unlimited powers are afforded to courts to review, amend and/or annul legislative, executive and administrative actions of a government that is popularly representative of a citizen majority. The state of affairs that the countermajoritarian dilemma projects is problematic for several reasons: it describes a situation wherein the separation of powers is transgressed; courts do not garner their judicial authority from a general democratic process as the legislative and executive branches of a government and could easily become an illegitimate supreme power onto themselves; and courts should not be allowed to become involved in political controversies inherent in the actions they seek to review.[190]

While there is no universal formula or best practice, what is clear is the need for a fine balance to be struck that must ensure the constitutional state prevails through judicial independence and the review functions of courts. Importantly, '[j]udicial independence is a relative rather than absolute concept. All judiciaries are [only] to some extent independent and to some extent subservient'.[191] The courts need to

---

[187] eg ch 8 of the South African Constitution sets out in detail all matters related to the judiciary, including the appointment of judges, their competencies and procedures for their removal.
[188] Ferejohn (n 127) 367.
[189] Larkins, 'Judicial Independence and Democratization' (n 179) 606.
[190] Venter (n 5) 81.
[191] Rosenn, 'Protection of Judicial Independence' (n 178) 3.

General Elements

co-operate with the executive and legislative authorities, and are affected by their policies and actions. So too are:

> courts naturally embedded in an environment with their own distinct values that will influence the outlook and approach of courts and that in particular cases may colour their decisions ... it is unrealistic and undesirable to separate courts from the society of which they are a part.[192]

Yet, it remains important for the sake of upholding the rule of law in any constitutional state, that the courts are seen to be the final arbiters of conflicts in law and in society, thus enabling the judiciary to act as the guardians of constitutionalism in a state. To this end, greater judicial independence and constitutional oversight authority that is vested in the courts is probably more preferable than less.

E. Constitutional Supremacy

Of all the features of the constitutional state, constitutional supremacy seems the least complex. In literal terms, by conferring the highest authority in a legal system on a constitution, the doctrine of constitutional supremacy assumes that there is no higher juridical norm in the state than the constitution. A clearly articulated example is found in the South African Constitution which states: 'This Constitution is the supreme law of the Republic; law or conduct inconsistent with it is invalid, and the duties imposed by it must be performed'.[193] Article 6 of the Constitution of the United States, more famously declares:

> This Constitution, and the laws of the United States which shall be made in pursuance thereof; and all treaties made, or which shall be made, under the authority of the United States, shall be the supreme law of the land; and the judges in every state shall be bound thereby, anything in the Constitution or laws of any State to the contrary notwithstanding.[194]

Linking with the notion of separation of powers, statements such as these indicate the existence of a particular legal/normative and institutional hierarchy:

> Stating this principle does not mean just giving a rank order of legal norms. The point is not solely a conflict of norms of differing dignity. The principle of the supremacy of the constitution also concerns the institutional structure of the organs of State. The scope of the principle becomes clear if we reformulate it: the supremacy of the constitution means the *lower ranking* of statute; and that at the same time implies the *lower ranking* of the legislator.[195]

---

[192] Nollkaemper, 'Independence of the Domestic Judiciary' (n 184) 300.
[193] S 2.
[194] This provision is generally regarded as the origin of the constitutional supremacy clause, which also later managed to substantially influence other constitutional developments across the world. See C Drahozal, *The Supremacy Clause: A Reference Guide to the United States Constitution* (Westport, Praeger, 2004).
[195] J Limbach, 'The Concept of the Supremacy of the Constitution' (2001) 64 *Modern Law Review* 1, 1.

The consequence of this juridical-normative and institutional hierarchy is that all laws in a country, including all decisions and acts of government, are subject to the constitution and that laws, decisions and acts could, for example, be declared unconstitutional and invalid, as the South African example above illustrates. It will mostly be up to the courts to review and pronounce on the constitutionality of laws, decisions and acts, and it will consequently mostly remain within the purview of the courts to safeguard constitutional supremacy, as was pointed out above.

The intuitive opposite to constitutional supremacy in this literal sense (ie the constitution as the highest law of the land) would be parliamentary sovereignty (as is the case in the United Kingdom and the previous South African apartheid legal order), which has been famously described by Dicey as follows:

> Parliament ... has, under the English constitution, the right to make or unmake any law whatever; ... no person or body is recognised by the law of England as having a right to override or set aside the legislation of Parliament.[196]

Importantly though, parliamentary sovereignty in the British context is not an absolute term that necessarily indicates a turn away from constitutionalism, as was the case in South Africa. The United Kingdom is widely considered to be a constitutional democracy (apartheid South Africa was not), in which case parliamentary sovereignty operates within the context of a constitutional democracy by invoking democratic positivism instead of liberal constitutionalism.[197] Therefore, depending on the constitutional arrangement of a particular country and its political goals, parliamentary sovereignty could either work to uphold constitutional democracy in a state, or it could have the complete opposite effect and be used perversely to legitimise and entrench the power of an oppressive regime.[198]

Mindful of the possible perverse effects of the countermajoritarian dilemma, it will mostly be up to the judiciary to ensure that the supremacy of the constitution is upheld. In this sense, constitutional supremacy is a reaction to the countermajoritarian dilemma (acting at once also as a legitimisation of judicial independence through which a minority of judges can overturn the decisions and acts of democratically elected majoritarian institutions such as the executive and the legislature). Because the constitution is supreme and because the constitution's supremacy must be protected, the courts are entitled to oversee the acts and decisions of the other spheres of authority, especially where executive and legislative actions and decisions could threaten constitutional democracy. Constitutional

---

[196] AV Dicey, *Introduction to the Study of the Law of the Constitution*, 8th edn (London, Macmillan, 1915; reprinted Indianapolis, Liberty Fund, 1982) 3–4.

[197] M Hunt, 'Reshaping Constitutionalism' in J Morison, K McEvoy and G Anthony (eds), *Judges, Transition, and Human Rights* (Oxford, Oxford University Press, 2007) 469.

[198] See, for an illuminating constitutional comparison between the British concept of parliamentary sovereignty and the American system, L Claus, 'Separation of Powers and Parliamentary Government' in V Amar and M Tushnet (eds), *Global Perspectives on Constitutional Law* (New York, Oxford University Press, 2009) 48–58.

supremacy thus in effect entrenches the independence of the courts and to some extent, the separation of powers (see the discussion above). In some jurisdictions this view finds practical expression, such as the German and South African Constitutional Courts which are specifically empowered to uphold constitutional supremacy.[199] Acting as guardians of constitutional supremacy, the Courts bolster the sanctity of the rule of law generally, counter the centralisation and concentration of power and ensure respect for rights. Effectively then, constitutional supremacy acts as a safeguard that provides critical stability of the source of power from which the government derives its authority and within which higher values such as the rule of law and rights are embedded and protected from external influences.

F. Democracy

For a constitution to be higher law it needs to be backed by a special, distinct and original constituent power (*pouvoir constituant originaire*),[200] which is located in the popular sovereignty of the people of the state. The latter is predicated on the social contract theory and best expressed as 'We the people',[201] where a constitution is not an act of government but an act of the people who, through a democratic process, constitute a government (the constituent power thus supersedes the constituted power in a sense):

> In order to be effective, a constitution, like any other legal norm, must be adopted and put into operation with authority. For the authority to be effective, it is necessary also to be legitimate in the sense of enjoying a sufficient degree of acceptance by the citizenry in that it is not subject to serious challenge. In the constitutional state authority is characterized by democratic legitimization to which also the democratic minority acquiesces … it has become axiomatic in the context of the modern constitutional state that the legitimate constitutional author will endow the Constitution with superior normative effect.[202]

This suggests that a constitution hails from a constituted legitimate public power located in the people.[203] The legitimating principle of a constitution is therefore popular sovereignty whereby legitimacy is solely dependent on the consent of the governed ('We the People'). The ability of 'the People', or the polity, to determine the conditions in terms of which they subject themselves to political power, is intricately linked with the issue of democracy.

Democracy is important to create constitutional orders in that it facilitates the implementation of the will of the majority of a polity through law; it is thus

---

[199] See s 167 of the South African Constitution and art 93 of the German Basic Law.
[200] P Eleftheriadis, 'Parliamentary Sovereignty and the Constitution' (2009) 22 *Canadian Journal of Law and Jurisprudence* 1, 1.
[201] See, among others, the Preamble of the Constitution of the United States.
[202] Venter (n 5) 57–58.
[203] Grimm (n 66) 7.

central to the legitimisation process described above and could thus be considered a precondition for constitutional and broader government, governance and juridical legitimacy. With reference to the constitutional moment that gives birth to a constitutional democracy, Kumm explains that:

> the moment of constitutional foundings, often institutionalised in constitutional conventions, can play something close to a mythical role in constitutional democracies. These are moments in which 'We the People' has willed into existence a new legal order. Such an account is *voluntarist* in that it focuses on the *will* of a collective subject. And it is structurally *nationalist* in that the relevant subject deemed to have the moral authority to establish an ultimate legal authority is the particular *demos* of a territorially circumscribed state.[204]

Thus, without the supreme moral authority deriving from the sovereignty of a *demos* that expresses the majority will of that particular collective subject (ie without a democratic process carried by a majority of 'We the People'), a constitutional state cannot legitimately come into existence:

> The democratic justification for the legal order is underpinned by the principle of popular sovereignty. A body of free and equal citizens comes together ... to enact rules to promote the general welfare. The business of government must be conducted within the framework of these rules (hence the idea of government under law) and officers of government are accountable to the people through their representatives and as a consequence of periodic popular elections. This democratic form of accountability of governors to citizens ensures the laws reflect the will of the people. The legal order ... is thus justified on the ground that, to all intents and purposes, it is a set of laws which the people have given themselves.[205]

While it is clearly connected with law and legal processes, democracy is also a deeply political concept (not unlike popular visions of the rule of law described above), and it is subject to criticism. For example, some argue that democracy generally is not always desirable in all societies. In contrast to heterogeneous societies where democracy works well, in close-knit homogeneous and deeply religious societies that are ruled by religious leaders, a theocracy would arguably be more suitable. Another criticism is that democracy entrenches the will of the majority, thereby paradoxically working in a regressive manner against its own rationale where it 'coerces political minorities to contribute to the realization of majority objectives with which minorities may strongly disagree',[206] and which may themselves not be constitutional in any substantive sense. Democracy is also sometimes derided for its being culturally imperialist and for its overwhelming orientation towards Western ideologies which consequently shut out alternative possibilities of governance and co-existence such as those found in some indigenous African or Middle

---

[204] M Kumm, 'The Jurisprudence of Constitutional Conflict: Constitutional Supremacy in Europe before and after the Constitutional Treaty' (2005) 11 *European Law Journal* 262, 275.

[205] M Loughlin, 'Rights, Democracy, and Law' in T Campbell, KD Ewing and A Tomkins (eds), *Sceptical Essays on Human Rights* (Oxford, Oxford University Press, 2001) 42.

[206] Rosenfeld (n 78) 1310, 1312.

Eastern societies.[207] Yet, despite these criticisms, realistically considered, democracy seems to be and will continue to be the prevailing form of government for the foreseeable future in the majority of (Western) countries around the world.

From a pure constitutional point of view, democracy can arguably best be understood as an enabler of constitutionalism, or as a necessary condition for the establishment and legitimacy of a constitutional state. After all, no state and its government would be legitimately considered a state or a government in liberal Western terms (neither a constitutional state for that matter), if a minority has constituted them. As a case in point: throughout the apartheid regime's entire rule, the majority of the South African population (and the international community for that matter) never considered the white minority government, nor its apartheid state, as legitimate creations fully representative of the entire population that answered to the dictates of formal and substantive constitutionalism.[208]

Yet, even if the apartheid government were elected by a majority of South Africa's people, which was not the case, that fact in itself would not have been sufficient to state that democracy was at play. Democracy signifies more than majority rule; it also relates to the need for elected officials to adhere to fundamental constitutional dictates such as the rule of law and rights:

> Majority rule does not by itself constitute the essence of Western-style democracy. Democracy means not just that State power derives from the people and politics is determined by their elected representatives. Another part of democracy comprises particular fundamental values [encapsulated in rights for example], to which all organs of state are committed.[209]

Democracy alone therefore does not equal constitutionalism and while democratic processes are necessary to constitute a structured polity as an expression of a people's sovereign self-determination, it must also work in tandem with the other elements of the constitutional state to restrict the power structures emanating from sovereign self-determination:

> According to the classical conception, the laws of a republic express the *unrestricted* will of the united citizens. Regardless of how the laws reflect the existing ethos of the shared political life, this ethos presents no limitation insofar as it achieves its validity only through the citizens' own process of will-formation. The principle of the constitutional exercise of power, on the other hand, appears to set limits on the people's sovereign self-determination.[210]

---

[207] See, among the many publications in this respect, J Walker, 'A Critique of the Elitist Theory of Democracy' (1966) 60 *American Political Science Review* 285; G Farred, 'Disorderly Democracy: An Axiomatic Politics' (2008) 8(2) *New Centennial Review* 43.

[208] In fact, the international community, through United Nations resolutions, explicitly rejected the apartheid South African state's creation of so-called black homelands or *Bantustans* as individual international states that exclusively accommodated non-whites: HJ Richardson, 'Self-determination, International Law and the South African Bantustan Policy' (1978) 17 *Columbia Journal of Transnational Law* 185.

[209] Limbach, 'Concept of the Supremacy of the Constitution' (n 195) 3.

[210] J Habermas and W Rehg, 'Constitutional Democracy: A Paradox Union of Contradictory Principles?' (2001) 29 *Political Theory* 766, 766.

In the same way that a constitution or the rule of law does not necessarily guarantee constitutionalism (see the discussion above), democracy, if it is purely considered as a means of ensuring majority rule, also cannot guarantee constitutionalism. As Robert Mugabe's Zimbabwe suggests, a democratic majority of people conceivably could unwillingly elect a dictator and keep him in power if they are sufficiently threatened to do so, or if they are effectively constrained to demand accountability or deprived of their power to terminate or control the exercise of the despotic power.[211] It is possible even that citizens could, by valid democratic majority vote, overturn a constitution for their own dark intentions. This suggests that where democracy enables the establishment of a constitutional state, it should then work in tandem with other constitutional features such as the rule of law and rights protection to uphold constitutionalism by preventing the government that has been elected by the majority, to do as it pleases.[212] For example, constitutional provisions related to constitutional supremacy in the German Basic Law which state that the Constitution's 'basic rights shall bind the legislature, the executive and the judiciary as directly applicable law',[213] do just that. Or section 8(1) of the South African Constitution which provides: 'The Bill of Rights applies to all law, and binds the legislature, the executive, the judiciary and all organs of state'. It is from this expanded view of democracy that the frequently invoked term 'constitutional democracy' emerges.[214] Constitutional democracies are democratic because democratically elected representative institutions are ultimately majoritarian. They are constitutional because the authority of the democratically elected majoritarian institutions is regulated and limited and subject to the rule of law, constitutional supremacy, judicial independence and so forth.

G. Rights

As exemplified by Anderson's reference to 'rights constitutionalism',[215] it has become virtually impossible to think about constitutionalism without also invoking the notion of rights. This is because rights (most often expressed as *human* rights as a result of their historically international law roots), more than any other juridical expression of constitutionalism, properly postulate the idea that people have certain universal (belonging to everyone everywhere); inborn (the fact of being human bestows a right); inalienable and imprescriptible claims (rights cannot be transferred, forfeited, waived or lost due to them not being claimed); that may not

---

[211] See, generally, P du Toit, *State-building and Democracy in Southern Africa: A Comparative Study of Botswana, Zimbabwe and South Africa* (Pretoria, HSRC Publishers, 1995).
[212] Limbach (n 195) 4.
[213] Art 1(3).
[214] See, among others, M McConnell, 'A Moral Realist Defense of Constitutional Democracy' (1998) 64 *Chicago-Kent Law Review* 89.
[215] He believes that the 'global spread of rights constitutionalism exemplifies the ideal that the liberal legalist promise of freedom through law is best secured by entrenching individual rights as higher law guarantees enforceable against the state': Anderson, *Constitutional Rights* (n 39) 5–6.

be infringed upon by governments or by other persons.[216] Deriving from early natural law and rights theories, the claims of rights relate to benefits essential for freedom, liberty, well-being, dignity and fulfilment, thus epitomising a core impetus of constitutionalism itself, ie protection of the individual from abuse of power and the full realisation of being human. These claims 'as of right', and indeed the idea of rights imply:

> entitlements on the part of the holder in some order under some applicable norm; the idea of human rights implies entitlement in a moral order under a moral law, to be translated into and confirmed as legal entitlement in the legal order of a political society. When a society recognizes that a person has a right, it affirms, legitimizes, and justifies that entitlement, and incorporates and establishes it in the society's system of values, giving it important weight in competition with other societal values.[217]

Rights thus lie at the very core of constitutionalism and are at the heart of the constitutional state itself. Borne by the ideals of equality, humanism and liberalism and deriving their special status from the dignity that is inherent in every human being (*dignitas humana*), rights are considered to be the foundation of every society, the source of regimen legitimisation and the point of departure of social ordering.[218] In the words of Weinrib:

> The primary feature of the modern constitutional state is its conceptual foundation. The foundation is substantive: it regards the free and equal person as the basic building block of the political order. This basis generates the values, aspirations and institutional roles of the modern constitutional state.[219]

To this end, rights are even considered 'primary, anchoring principles' that are morally and normatively superior to other constitutional elements such as democracy, 'due to the inadequacy of the other constitutional principles to the challenge of governing the multicultural, diverse, pluralistic, egalitarian and secular characteristics of the post-war state'.[220] The primacy of rights in the constitutionalism agenda is particularly evident from the fact that criticism levelled against governments that do encroach on constitutional limits, is often cast in human rights terms. Thus, while the civil war, and arguably related acts of genocide, that are occurring in Syria are just that, it is often framed as grave human rights abuses committed by the al-Assad regime.[221]

As further testimony to their prominence, rights have become the central existential justification of a new world order embodied through the United Nations and its Universal Declaration of Human Rights in 1948 (resulting in what

---

[216] Venter (n 5) 127.
[217] L Henkin, *The Age of Rights* (New York, Columbia University Press, 1990) 3.
[218] Di Fabio (n 85) 408.
[219] L Weinrib, 'Constitutionalism in the Age of Rights: A Prolegomenon' (2004) 121 *South African Law Journal* 278, 285.
[220] ibid 285.
[221] Amnesty International describes it as a 'human rights' crisis. Amnesty International, 'Syria', (2013) www.amnestyusa.org/our-work/countries/middle-east-and-north-africa/syria.

Loughlin refers to as a post-Second World War 'rights revolution'),[222] with the overwhelming majority of domestic constitutions providing for basic rights, and with the bulk of constitutional theory and critique dedicated to the issue of rights. To be sure, as Henkin famously suggested:

> Ours is the age of rights. Human rights is the idea of our time, the only political-moral idea that has received universal acceptance ... It is significant that all states and societies have been prepared to accept human rights as the norm, rendering deviations abnormal, and requiring governments to conceal and deny, or show cause, lest they stand condemned ... the suspension of rights is the touchstone and measure of abnormality.[223]

The most common doctrinal ideas that feature in the burgeoning rights discourse that also relate to the characteristics of rights generally include, among others: rights are part of a higher law (derived from natural law, religious traditions, universal morality and/or the ethical values of a society) that is elevated above the positive law where their embodiment in positive law gives their enforcement a legitimating basis in political consent because they also reflect non-legal principles that have normative force independent of their embodiment in positive law. The individual's dignity, freedom and equality are impregnable and are expressed through rights, thus also lending rights their universal character that seeks to counter differentiation and hierarchy based on human characteristics; respect for rights is a critical necessity for justice; and government, if it abuses its powers, is potentially the single greatest threat to rights, whereby rights then serve to counter this encroachment by providing higher-order guarantees to a person.[224] To this latter end, in the realm of the rule of law, rights typically work to establish procedural and substantive obstacles to legislative and executive overreach 'depending on the extent to which the action departs from the presumptions of political morality expressed in the constitutional rights catalogue'.[225]

While I employ the non-specific term 'rights' for the purpose of this book, they are also referred to as 'constitutional rights', 'fundamental rights' and 'human rights'. The distinction between these categories is not immediately apparent. One plausible explanation is that *human* rights usually refer to classic natural law demands for liberty, equality and dignity in the international context such as in the Universal Declaration of Human Rights 1948. Where this international vision of human rights is entrenched in a domestic constitution, the term *fundamental* rights (and less so, *constitutional* rights), is employed. Domestic constitutional

---

[222] Loughlin (n 6) 62.
[223] Henkin, *Age of Rights* (n 217) vii–x.
[224] K Boyle, 'Linking Human Rights and Other Goals' in J Morison, K McEvoy and G Anthony (eds), *Judges, Transition, and Human Rights* (Oxford, Oxford University Press, 2007) 407; Venter (n 5) 127–28; GL Neuman, 'Human Rights and Constitutional Rights: Harmony and Dissonance' (2003) 55 *Stanford Law Review* 1863, 1866.
[225] J Rivers, 'A Theory of Constitutional Rights and the British Constitution: Translator's Introduction' in Alexy, *A Theory of Constitutional Rights* (n 42) xxi.

incorporation of human rights therefore transforms these human rights into constitutionally enforceable fundamental or constitutionally created public subjective rights.[226]

Notably, rights in the constitutional context are not fundamental because they are absolute. Constitutional rights are only designated as being fundamental to engrain the idea that they are indispensable for life, dignity, well-being, liberty, freedom and so forth,[227] and 'because they incorporate decisions about the basic normative structure of state and society'.[228] Rights can, and often are, subject to limitation. In pursuit of the idea that all rights are not necessarily absolute, in some jurisdictions such as South Africa, all rights in the Constitution's Bill of Rights can be limited under exceptional circumstances such as under a public emergency that threatens the lives of people.[229] Affirming the idea that rights are not absolute, (but also conversely that rights should not be unduly limited), article 29(2) of the Universal Declaration of Human Rights 1948 states in similar terms:

> In the exercise of his rights and freedoms, everyone shall be subject only to such limitations as are determined by law solely for the purpose of securing due recognition and respect for the rights and freedoms of others and of meeting the just requirements of morality, public order and the general welfare in a democratic society.[230]

While there is no universally accepted classification of rights, the one most often followed (although this division is not absolute), divides rights into civil and political rights such as the right to vote (or first generation rights); economic, social and cultural rights such as the right to water or housing (or second generation rights); and solidarity or group rights such as labour rights (so-called third generation rights). Another approach is to divide rights into normative rights (rights providing a principled foundation for the interpretation of a constitution, or legal order more generally, such as the rights to human dignity, liberty and equality); subjectively enforceable defensive rights to protect the individual against state power (such as the rights to privacy, property and freedom of expression); procedural rights such as the rights to information, administrative justice and access to courts that broadly aim to give effect to the procedural aspects of the rule of law;

---

[226] Venter (n 5) 129.
[227] Henkin (n 217) 4.
[228] Alexy (n 42) 350.
[229] S 36 of the South African Constitution provides:

> 36. (1) The rights in the Bill of Rights may be limited only in terms of law of general application to the extent that the limitation is reasonable and justifiable in an open and democratic society based on human dignity, equality and freedom, taking into account all relevant factors, including—
>
> (a) the nature of the right;
> (b) the importance of the purpose of the limitation;
> (c) the nature and extent of the limitation;
> (d) the relation between the limitation and its purpose; and
> (e) less restrictive means to achieve the purpose.

[230] See, more generally on the theory of the limits of constitutional rights, Alexy (n 42) 178–222.

community-oriented rights that facilitate participation in community life (such as the right to freedom of religion and cultural and linguistic rights); and rights on state performance, or socio-economic rights, such as the right to housing or water, that force the state to do (provide or realise) or refrain from doing something.[231] Notably, environmental rights have recently emerged in constitutions the world over, and as one of the latest additions to the rights catalogue, they often do not fall in any one of these categories, instead exuding characteristics that render them at once normative, subjective and enforceable, procedural, community oriented and socio-economic (see the discussion in Chapters 5 and 6).

The foregoing mostly reflects on the positive attributes of and virtuous perceptions associated with rights, but considerable criticism has been levelled against rights such as: they are often negatively perceived to be couched in a masculinist ontology because they are based on the male as the basis for their normativity;[232] rights are criticised because of their predominantly Western characteristics, thus excluding indigenous non-Western cultures and concerns.[233] The promotion and protection of human dignity through material well-being is seen as the core of rights, which is mostly achieved through increased economic security and, hence, increased consumption activities.[234] Rights therefore act to provide the justificatory basis for human mastery over the world that lies outside the human being; as creating entitlements instead of duties and responsibilities; and as being individualistic, thus countering efforts that seek to foster harmonious inter-dependence not only between humans, but also between humans and non-human entities.[235] Sometimes the origin of rights is understood to have religious roots, such that they are used in a perverse way to justify unjustifiable encroachments on the rights and interests of others.[236] Because the socio-economic, political and legal change that rights seek to achieve in constitutional orders is not always immediately apparent, rights have also understandably been described as 'all rhetoric and exhortation',[237] often leading to insignificant concrete improvements of the myriad vulnerabilities they have been designed to address in the first place. It is also true that some countries enshrine fundamental rights in their constitutions, but merely do so

---

[231] Neuman, 'Human Rights and Constitutional Rights' (n 224) 1863–900.

[232] eg art 29(2) of the Universal Declaration of Human Rights alluded to above includes the following phrase: 'In the exercise of *his* rights and freedoms'. Emphasis added.

[233] P Spike, 'Whose Rights? A Critique of the "Givens" in Human Rights Discourse' (1990) XV *Alternatives* 303, 305, 308. Although Henkin, correctly in my view, points out that criticism related to rights being Western constructs are overdrawn. He argues that rights as a political idea prescribing relations between individuals and society may have Western roots, but it is not more suitable or appropriate to Western societies than to others. Moreover, many other political ideas such as democracy, statehood and sovereignty are Western and have become universal in the same way as rights have, and they are widely endorsed in non-Western societies as well: Henkin (n 217) 28.

[234] Spike, 'Whose Rights?' (n 233) 310.

[235] Gearty, 'Do Human Rights Help' (n 101) 8.

[236] S Jerome, 'The Philosophical Foundations of Human Rights' (1998) 20 *Human Rights Quarterly* 201, 205–06.

[237] Henkin (n 217) 27.

to window dress and to conceal rights abuses from the outside world,[238] as the Zimbabwean example alluded to above suggests. Their commitment to rights is decidedly 'less than authentic and whole hearted'.[239] Yet, as Henkin points out:

> the fact of the commitment, that it is enshrined in a constitution ... are not to be dismissed lightly. Even hypocrisy may sometimes deserve one cheer for it confirms the value of the idea, and limits the scope and blatancy of violations ... A constitution is at least a promise to the people at home and an assertion to the world at large, it responds to and generates forces that induce compliance, and it cannot long be maintained in the face of blatant noncompliance.[240]

From this emerges the appeal of rights which lies in them being ethical demands that extend beyond law, while at once also being based on law and operating at an elevated juridical level.[241] Their attraction to social movement energies and energetic global solidarities evinces their increasing popularity as legal constructs that supplement the traditional instrumentalist functions of law.[242] More generally, the appeal of rights is evident in the 'significant move in constitutional democracies toward a "rights consciousness"'.[243] Despite their many limitations and the legitimate criticism often levelled against rights generally, as 'a language of the human good', rights remain enduringly valuable juridical constructs in a normative and political sense:

> Rights talk does have notorious limitations as a language of the human good. Who does not suppose, for example, that love is an essential human good, but who believes we all have a 'right to love'? These problems with rights as a language of the good are well known, but no better language is likely to be found ... Rights talk will remain an essential component of any global ethic, precisely because the protections it affords can be demanded by actual individuals.[244]

Considering the foregoing, it is highly likely that rights will continue to form a crucial element of domestic constitutional systems and more generally of the idea of constitutionalism itself.

VI. Conclusion

Constitutionalism is not a perfect form of law that magically corrects all governance wrongs, protects every citizen from the abuse of all state power and from one another, and somehow enables an idyllic vision of a perfect world yet to

---

[238] See, also Häberle, 'The Constitutional State' (n 81) 86.
[239] Henkin (n 217) 28.
[240] ibid 28–29.
[241] A Sen, 'Elements of a Theory of Human Rights' (2004) 32 *Philosophy and Public Affairs* 315, 319.
[242] See, among others, Gearty (n 101) 7–22.
[243] Lutz (n 72) 125.
[244] M Ignatieff, 'Reimagining a Global Ethic' (2012) 26 *Ethics and International Affairs* 7, 7.

be created through a normative order that has been established democratically by the consent of all to the benefit of everyone. But from a juridical-regulatory point of view, 'it is [arguably] the only, and unavoidable, moral imperative possible'.[245]

In many countries the steady progression from pure formalistic constitutions to substantive ones, the entrenchment of catalogues of rights and other procedural and substantive rule of law safeguards that have been democratically sanctioned by majoritarian will, evince not only the human longing for a good legal order, but also the ability of humans to create juridical institutions, however imperfect, that must promote the collective good.

As such, constitutionalism has much going for it as a normative programme of progressive, superior and good law and governance. In addition to highlighting the reasons behind and benefits and shortcomings of constitutionalism, this chapter has also shown that it is possible to state the existence of a constitutional order if all or some of the following elements are present: a constitution, the rule of law, separation of powers, judicial independence, constitutional supremacy, democracy and rights. While the constitutionalisation of domestic legal orders is not complete, constitutionalism, as it manifests domestically, could provide a blueprint for a normative and analytical effort that seeks to situate constitutionalism beyond the state. Resorting under the banner of 'global constitutionalism', the steady progression of constitutionalism and its features into the global sphere are the central focus of enquiry of Chapter 4.

---

[245] Galindo (n 9) 154.

4

Global Aspects of Constitutionalism

I. Introduction

Our current understanding of contemporary constitutionalism is inherently state bound, tied as it is to state sovereignty, physical borders, a *demos* and a government. This point was elaborated in Chapter 3. Today, however, mainly as a result of globalisation, hitherto closed epistemic spaces, especially in juridical discourse, are gradually opening up to invite alternative conversations that search for constitutionalism in the global sphere, or beyond the state, as it were. Having commenced with Verdross in the early-1900s (notably a German scholar, which might explain the present discourse being predominantly grounded in German scholarship),[1] these conversations are neither complete, nor are they always satisfyingly convincing as a result of the difficulty to think about constitutionalism in global terms. There is a view that global constitutionalism, 'if not totally dormant, at best lacks momentum or confidence'.[2]

Yet, by my reading the majority of commentators consider such an apprehensive estimation (dismissal even) of the phenomenon of global constitutionalism to be overdrawn and pessimistic, and they have consistently been arguing for the extension of constitutionalism into the global realm, not only in an analytical sense, but also normatively.[3] In fact, global constitutionalism has become a flourishing academic enterprise with multifarious debates as to its occurrence happening specifically in the domain of rights (acting as apex global constitutional norms); the European Union (in the sense of the Union's founding treaties being a constitution, its support for rights protection, and the direct effect and supremacy

---

[1] A Verdross, *Die Verfassung der Völkerrechtsgemeinschaft* (Vienna, Springer, 1926); A Verdross, 'Zur Konstruktion des Völkerrechts' (1914) 8 *Zeitschrift für Völkerrecht* 329. See, for a discussion, T Kleinlein, 'Alfred Verdross as a Founding Father of International Constitutionalism?' (2012) 4 *Goettingen Journal of International Law* 385.

[2] N Tsagourias, 'Introduction—Constitutionalism: A Theoretical Roadmap' in N Tsagourias (ed), *Transnational Constitutionalism: International and European Models* (Cambridge, Cambridge University Press, 2007) 3.

[3] See, among the many authorities and views, P Kjaer, *Constitutionalism in the Global Realm: A Sociological Approach* (New York, Routledge, 2014); and the numerous publications cited throughout this chapter.

of its laws with respect to Member States); and the World Trade Organization (mostly with reference to its shift from a power to a rule-oriented system and its quasi-obligatory dispute settlement system).[4]

II. About this Chapter

In order to explore the potential of constitutionalism for global environmental law and governance later in this book, this chapter seeks to understand what global constitutionalism is, what its rationale is, what its relationship with domestic constitutionalism is, its different descriptive approaches, and how the various elements of domestic constitutionalism could possibly manifest globally. As a prelude, the chapter commences by critically explaining how and why it is possible to think about constitutionalism in a global context, and it includes a discussion on the extent to which one could use domestic constitutionalism, as described in Chapter 3, as the principal referent for global constitutionalism. This is followed by an investigation of the reasons why scholars pursue the global constitutionalism agenda with a view to sketching the appeal of global constitutionalism including, as a counter-narrative, points of criticism that are often levelled against global constitutionalism. This discussion will show that, despite valid criticisms, there are convincing reasons to keep pursuing the global constitutionalism agenda.

The enquiry then traces the main discursive tracks of the global constitutionalism debate, its many manifestations and the different meanings various scholars ascribe to global constitutionalism. This, admittedly descriptive latter part, serves as a point of departure for the more exploratory concluding analysis that critically seeks to locate and briefly to describe in the context of the global domain the generic elements of constitutionalism that have been distilled in Chapter 3, namely: a constitution, the rule of law, separation of powers, the judiciary and its review functions, constitutional supremacy, democracy and rights. Collectively the analysis in this chapter contributes to the conceptual framework for understanding and systematically describing in the remaining chapters of this book, the contours and content of global environmental constitutionalism and the various ways in which it manifests.

---

[4] See, among others, respectively: E de Wet, 'The International Constitutional Order' (2006) 55 *International and Comparative Law Quarterly* 51; N Walker, 'Reframing EU Constitutionalism' in J Dunhoff and J Trachtman (eds), *Ruling the World: Constitutionalism, International Law, and Global Governance* (Cambridge, Cambridge University Press, 2009) 149–76; J Dunhoff, 'The Politics of International Constitutions: The Curious Case of the World Trade Organization' in J Dunhoff and J Trachtman (eds), *Ruling the World: Constitutionalism, International Law, and Global Governance* (Cambridge, Cambridge University Press, 2009) 178–205.

III. From the Local to the Global

Our geographically limited and epistemologically constrained domestic focus on and experience of constitutionalism is a consequence of long-held conceptions of the state in the context of the axiomatic Westphalian paradigm, which has been reinvigorated as a result of a fragmented Europe after the Second World War, the emergence of newly de-colonised states in Africa and South America and the emergence of new liberal countries in the Eastern Bloc. These countries all sought to reaffirm their independence and claim their rightful place in the international community through triumphant liberations and affirmations of state-bound sovereignty coupled with a strong state-bound constitutional centre, intentionally bound only by a system of international law that seeks to preserve state sovereignty.

Today, however, this insular perception is being altered by the forces of globalisation; by significant advances in communication technology and social media that are literally connecting the world; by modes of travel that enable unprecedented physical global connectivity; by systems of free trade; by the creation of regional and international superstructures of governance such as the European Union; by dissolving state boundaries to create transfrontier conservation areas such as in Southern Africa; by the rise of non-state actors such as epistemic networks and non-governmental organisations including non-state, but law-like, rules in the global realm; by the emergence of treaty regimes and international norm-producing functional organisations such as the World Bank that enable inter-state cooperation in specific areas; the steady growth of multinational corporations that function in an intermeshed transnational setting; and by the emergence of global environmental problems such as climate change that are affecting everyone everywhere with scant regard to physical borders or to the sanctity of state sovereignty.[5] As we shall see below, these globalisation-related considerations increasingly agitate for notions of constitutionalism to be applied beyond the nation state, thereby extending domestic constitutionalism's relevance, application and currency to the global sphere.

A. The Inappropriateness of Domestic Constitutionalism for the Global Sphere

Yet, as Walker points out, there are various conceptual difficulties presenting themselves as plausible reasons why domestic constitutionalism cannot and/or should not be transplanted to the global sphere.[6] The first is that the features of

---

[5] These non-traditional state entities have all become 'autonomous forms of social orderings which constitutes [sic] their own cognitive spaces on a global scale': Kjaer, *Constitutionalism in the Global Realm* (n 3) 4.

[6] N Walker, 'Taking Constitutionalism Beyond the State' (2008) 56 *Political Studies* 519, 520–25.

domestic constitutionalism are inappropriate for the global sphere, having been designed to fulfil specific roles that are very peculiar to the type and extent of power situated in the nation state. States, after all, have their own unique version of normative ethos which would be difficult to change.[7] For example, as we will see later in this chapter, the separation of powers doctrine as it is understood in a domestic context sits oddly in the global domain because the power that this doctrine seeks to separate globally is not the same as the power it would traditionally separate in a domestic setting: there is neither a clearly discernable global government, nor a clear *trias politica* in the global sphere. While the constituted powers at the domestic and global levels differ quite significantly; so too do the constituent powers: whereas the domestic constituted power is evident in a government, the global governance order notoriously lacks a central government and whereas the citizens of a state are the constituent power domestically, it is far more difficult to discern a constituent power globally. At a more practical level, there is no universal global mechanism to resolve all disputes that might arise around a global constitution as there usually is domestically; and while material divergences within society are minimised domestically and moulded into a commonly shared national constitutional identity, this is and probably can never be the case in the cosmopolitan global sphere.[8] Because spaces beyond states do not perfectly replicate all constitutional attributes found within states, it is therefore easy to see why constitutionalism is approached with scepticism and considered to be inappropriate in the global space beyond the state.[9]

The second related reason for being sceptical about translating domestic constitutionalism to the global sphere lies in epistemological closures that restrict such a translation: for some it is difficult to imagine constitutionalism as a global phenomenon because of long-held and restrictive 'truths' such as the notion of the state, state sovereignty and the idea of self-contained and integrated domestic legal and political orders. Walker indicates that 'if these background ideas … are not in place, as arguably they are not unless in the presence of the modern state, then we cannot meaningfully characterise any candidate normative and institutional design as constitutional'.[10] Epistemic inflexibility towards a deeply historical and parochially constructed paradigm such as constitutionalism in domestic state terms, and a reluctance to open up epistemic spaces in the constitutional discourse to the realities of globalisation, engenders the implausibility of constitutionalism taking root in the global space.

Thirdly, and again relatedly, Walker argues that it is improbable that domestic constitutionalism will ever be meaningfully translated to the global sphere

---

[7] Tsagourias, 'Introduction—Constitutionalism' (n 2) 4.
[8] M Rosenfeld, 'Is Global Constitutionalism Meaningful or Desirable?' (2014) 25 *European Journal of International Law* 177, 190.
[9] Tsagourias (n 2) 4.
[10] Walker, 'Taking Constitutionalism Beyond the State' (n 6) 521.

considering the primacy and deep entrenchment of sovereignty and the prevailing Westphalian configuration of autonomous and mutually-exclusive states that are in essence only connected through a 'state-parasitic framework of international law'.[11] Countering anything that threatens its configuration and integrity, this framework preserves and maintains the independence and primacy of the sovereign state and will probably prevent any attempt, arguably including a global constitutionalist one, from upsetting it. As Von Bogdandy reminds us, the international system cannot adopt the blueprint provided by comparative (municipal) constitutional law as a result of the continuing significance of state sovereignty.[12]

Finally, considering it might be inappropriate, likely inconceivable, and improbable, if constitutionalism could only then be a matter for the nation state, any attempt to translate it to the global sphere would be illegitimate:

> If a claim of constitutional status is made on behalf of an entity or a set of regulatory practices in circumstances where the tools are inappropriate to the problem, or where the requisite underlying belief system is not in place, or where the necessary *de facto* authority is absent, then that claim becomes an empty or misleading one.[13]

If we consider this apprehensive counter-narrative cautioning against a wholesale transplantation of domestic constitutionalism to the global sphere, what are the possibilities and prospects, at least conceptually, of its global emergence? As a point of departure, it seems unlikely that a domestic constitutional order could be replicated in full and as is in the global sphere and be required to fulfil a typecast role in exactly the same way as it normally would domestically:

> The emergence of new forms of transnational legal and political structures are not ... likely to imply a simple transfer of nation-state forms of law and politics ... through the constitution of a world state or any other form of structure which merely copies the form and function of nation states.[14]

Following Walker's views above, an exact and complete translation of domestic constitutionalism to the global sphere will in all likelihood be inappropriate, inconceivable and improbable.

B. The Appropriateness of Domestic Constitutionalism for the Global Sphere

Yet, while no direct transplantation of domestic constitutionalism to the global sphere is possible, at least not in any unqualified way, it is more likely that core

---

[11] ibid 522.
[12] A von Bogdandy, 'Constitutionalism in International Law: Comment on a Proposal from Germany' (2006) 47 *Harvard International Law Journal* 223, 230.
[13] Walker (n 6) 522.
[14] Kjaer (n 3) 3.

constitutional ideas, norms and/or features could be more or less replicated in the global sphere:

> [I]t is quite possible to separate State and constitution and to transfer the notion of constitution into non-State contexts. The point is, that the concept of constitution changes its meaning when it is transferred and this change of meaning is reinforced by the current structural changes of the international system: the disaggregation of the State on the one hand, and the process of sectoralization within international law.[15]

Because the totality of the state is not absolute any longer, the modernist idea that constitutionalism can and should only manifest in domestic, state-bound terms is gradually giving way to alternative understandings of constitutionalism's potential relevance and application that reaches beyond the state.[16] The shift between the world as we knew it and the considerably more complex globalised world we know today, has manifold implications for constitutionalism, not least because state-bound constitutional endeavours 'were operational answers to their times and societies and cannot claim eternal truth'.[17] This realisation indicates that the term constitution, while historically state-bound, cannot continue to operate only within the exclusive purview of the nation state; it should and in fact is now loosing up in ways that are going beyond the state, as it were:[18] 'an exclusive focus of constitutionalism on the Nation State cannot be maintained. It needs to give way to a graduated approach which views constitutionalism as a process, extending constitutional structures to fora and layers of governance other than nations'.[19]

This process is already occurring, as is clear from the emergence of constitutionalism in several global spaces beyond the state (see the discussion below). Notably, however, the application of constitutionalism in the global sphere and discussions about its application can only be worthwhile if they are attuned to the particular idiosyncrasies of the global order, such as the fact that there is no clear global *demos* in the sense that we understand it domestically.[20] Whereas domestic constitutionalism's is a familiar narrative, made up as it is by foundational concepts such as a clearly defined *demos, trias politica* and the rule of law that are not easily translatable beyond the conceptually comfortable imagery of the state, constitutionalism in the global sphere will instead demand an opening of discursive and analytical closures and different questions to be asked that may lead to

---

[15] C Walter, 'International Law in a Process of Constitutionalization' in J Nijman and A Nollkaemper (eds), *New Perspectives on the Divide between National and International Law* (Oxford, Oxford University Press, 2007) 193–94.

[16] Walker (n 6) 519.

[17] T Cottier and M Hertig, 'The Prospects of 21st Century Constitutionalism' (2003) 7 *Max Planck Yearbook of United Nations Law* 261, 263.

[18] A Peters, 'Compensatory Constitutionalism: The Function and Potential of Fundamental International Norms and Structures' (2006) 19 *Leiden Journal of International Law* 579, 581.

[19] Cottier and Hertig, 'Prospects of 21st Century Constitutionalism' (n 17) 264.

[20] Tsagourias (n 2) 5–6.

counter-intuitive answers somehow relating to, but not always fully replicating, the domestic constitutionalism referent. A 'black and white' approach to global constitutionalism is therefore likely to fail.[21]

Another counter-argument to the inappropriateness-inconceivability-improbability critique against global constitutionalism is that debates about global constitutionalism are sometimes overdrawn to the extent that they seem to envisage some idealistic, fully comprehensive and perfect global constitutional order; it is an 'all-or-nothing' approach.[22] However, considering that there is no domestic example of a perfect, fully constitutionalised legal order, the global order probably also cannot ever be perfectly constitutionalised. In other words, considering the limits of constitutionalism as they clearly emerge from the domestic order (see Chapter 3), the domestic reference point for the global constitutionalisation project is equally incomplete and imperfect. Arguably the project of constitutionalism can and never will be complete. There is no agreement on what a perfectly constitutionalised legal order should look like; only some shared common understanding of a law and governance system that is somehow and to some extent constitutional currently exists.[23] The fact that global law and governance cannot and arguably never will be fully transformed into a perfectly constitutionalised order does, however, not mean that the global order is not susceptible to, and steadily in search of, at least some minimal form of constitutionalisation. Expectations of constitutionalism in the global sphere must remain realistic, as they continue to in the domestic sphere (although the latter are admittedly more ambitious) and the often 'limited and limiting presuppositions of the constitutional imaginary'[24] will have to give way, or at least open up, to an expanded understanding and application of constitutionalism beyond the state that reflects a 'more-or-less' approach, unless we wish to run the risk of closing down debate.

Finally, to argue that it is unlikely or undesirable for domestic constitutionalism to contribute to the global constitutionalist paradigm, is to ignore the fact that many states, as members of the international community, are constitutional states whose global actions (including their relations with other states, the global commons and environmental resources, for example), are in most instances influenced by their own unique internal domestic constitutional impulses. Surely this would require less evolutionary efforts to shift from an unconstitutionalised global order to one where there is at least some minimal global agreement on and observance of core (if not exactly similar) constitutional principles that infiltrate the global realm in a bottom-up way.[25]

---

[21] Cottier and Hertig (n 17) 287.
[22] Walker (n 6) 523.
[23] A O'Donoghue, *Constitutionalism in Global Constitutionalisation* (Cambridge, Cambridge University Press, 2014) 50.
[24] Walker (n 6) 523.
[25] Von Bogdandy, 'Constitutionalism in International Law' (n 12) 240.

IV. Why (Not) Constitutionalise the Global Order?

Various considerations contribute, mostly in a collective and interrelated way, to the appeal of global constitutionalism. While these considerations are often the reasons why constitutionalism is sought beyond the state, they simultaneously act as reasons why some commentators are critical of global constitutionalism.

A. Globalisation

The most evident consideration related to the rise of global constitutionalism is globalisation which essentially is a process describing the intensification of global interdependence and, as a result, a concomitant increase in vulnerability among global actors and constituents. Understood to mean the exponential increase in the flow of people, capital, goods, services and ideas across the globe, globalisation increases the number, reach and intensity of global institutions and law to regulate the foregoing aspects, while increased (although insufficient) legal and institutional arrangements, such as those apparent in trade law, conversely support and further expand the processes of globalisation.[26] To this end globalisation is a reciprocal and mutually re-enforcing process of regulatory growth that feeds itself (often also as a result of liberalisation and regionalisation),[27] where specialised legal and institutional arrangements are created as a response to global regulatory problems that, in turn, are themselves created by the processes of globalisation.

In a globalised world, regulatory problems demand a global response and a body of regulatory arrangements, which is particularly evident in the environmental context where the exponential growth of international environmental law (evidenced by the hundreds of multilateral environmental agreements and their related governance regimes) is seen as a reaction to the many global environmental problems that are created by, among others, the drivers and consequences of globalisation.[28] While globalisation is forcing us to take a global regulatory focus, the effects of globalisation on our traditional socio-legal and other systems of order have been and continue to be immense. This is because globalisation and its processes and consequences are putting the state and state constitutions under strain, compelling states to cooperate globally and to provide for normative arrangements and governance institutions in spaces beyond the state.[29]

---

[26] J Dunhoff and J Trachtman, 'A Functional Approach to International Constitutionalization' in J Dunhoff and J Trachtman (eds), *Ruling the World: Constitutionalism, International Law, and Global Governance* (Cambridge, Cambridge University Press, 2009) 5–6.

[27] C Fombad, 'Internationalization of Constitutional Law and Constitutionalism in Africa' (2012) 6 *American Journal of Comparative Law* 439, 440.

[28] See, more generally, LJ Kotzé, *Global Environmental Governance: Law and Regulation for the 21st Century* (Cheltenham, Edward Elgar, 2012).

[29] A Peters, 'Global Constitutionalism in a Nutshell' in K Dicke et al (eds), *Weltinnenrecht: Liber Amicorum Jost Delbrück* (Kiel, Walther Schücking Institut für Internationales Recht, 2005) 536.

Because of globalisation's reciprocal and interrelated nature and its domestic rooted origins, the value of global constitutionalism as a response to the forces of globalisation does not only lie in the global domain. Peters believes that global constitutionalism could usefully serve as a means to compensate globally for regulatory deficits that arise within domestic jurisdictions as a result of globalisation (otherwise understood as the 'deconstitutionalisation' of the nation state).[30] By this reading, deconstitutionalisation of the state could be countered through a process of compensatory global constitutionalisation that provides the institutions, means and procedures for states to enhance cooperation, co-existence and the collective governance of regulatory problems that have their origin in globalisation.

Globalisation therefore is essentially challenging age-old truths about the state, law and governance, visions of global order and anarchy, and ways to sustainably and peacefully co-exist. While we are by no means on the brink of a 'new global human community'[31] as some believe, it has been suggested in this context that:

> globalization produces a serious challenge to conventional premises: the axiomatic notion of the nation-state as the cornerstone of the territorial sovereignty of the almost 200 states of the world as it developed over centuries, is rapidly losing definition; the state's perceived dominance as provider of the framework within which law is made, administered, adjudicated and enforced is increasingly being challenged; the potential for integration of legal norms across conventional national and international jurisdictions, is growing exponentially.[32]

In addition, globalisation is questioning the continued prevalence of geographically defined territorial dictates as a crucial consideration in the design and focus of global law and governance, and it 'appears indeed characterized by a shift from territorial borders to functional boundaries'.[33] The world, our current social reality, and our perceptions of reality are evidently changing and lawyers especially require 'a fresh vocabulary, and expanded set of concepts, [and] alternative ways of framing the challenge [to govern and maintain order]'.[34] Global constitutionalism is seen as one of the 'fresh' and 'expanded' ways of framing prevailing global challenges and as a global normative response to these challenges. As Cottier and Hertig poignantly put it:

> The moment has come to live up to these challenges in legal theory and constitutionalism. The goals of liberty, justice and dignity, of equity but also efficiency and security

---

[30] Peters, 'Compensatory Constitutionalism' (n 18) 579–610.
[31] R Domingo, 'The New Global Human Community' (2012) 12 *Chicago Journal of International Law* 563.
[32] F Venter, *Global Features of Constitutional Law* (Nijmegen, Wolf Legal Publishers, 2010) 20.
[33] A Paulus, 'Commentary to Andreas Fischer-Lescano and Gunther Teubner: The Legitimacy of International Law and the Role of the State' (2004) 25 *Michigan Journal of International Law* 1047, 1048.
[34] W Boyd, 'Climate Change, Fragmentation, and the Challenges of Global Environmental Law: Elements of a Post-Copenhagen Assemblage' (2010) 32 *University of Pennsylvania Journal of International Law* 457, 466.

all remain unimpaired. But ways and means to secure them in coming decades and perhaps centuries need to be developed in the context of an increasingly globalized society.[35]

At the same time constitutionalisation of the global regulatory domain has the potential of legitimising global law and governance, especially to the extent that this global regime is considered to be illegitimate as a result of its not having a democratically elected centralised government and a uniform, universally applicable, and systematic legal framework. As Chapter 3 explained, 'the very notions of constitution, constitutionalism, and constitutionalization carry with them an element of legitimacy'.[36] To this end, a flexible and open-minded approach to the possibility of constitutionalism in the global domain, and global constitutionalism itself, 'is not a vain intellectual exercise, but ... a necessary step to secure the values of constitutionalism in an era of globalization and interdependence'.[37]

B. Fragmentation

A second consideration is the popular, albeit in no way uncontroversial, belief that global constitutionalism could be a normative response to the many challenges posed by the fragmentation of international law and governance.[38] In short, international law is considered to be fragmented as a result of a highly decentralised process of international law and governance development that essentially responds to specific global problems through a normative and institutional framework that exists in silos as it is centred on separate functional areas such as environment, trade, human rights and humanitarian law. In most instances these functional areas are themselves highly fragmented inherently as well, as international environmental law with its separate tracks of climate law and governance, global biodiversity law and governance and global oceans law and governance illustrate. Various governance institutions such as treaty secretariats (for example, the United Nations Framework Convention on Climate Change Secretariat), and international institutions such as the United Nations Environment Programme, are created to coordinate and enforce the fragmented, yet burgeoning body of global normative arrangements that must address numerous global environmental problems.[39]

Fragmentation in this sense is a threat to what many lawyers perceive to be effective law as it leads to conflicts which some believe may hamper regulatory

---

[35] Cottier and Hertig (n 17) 262.
[36] Kleinlein, 'Alfred Verdross as a Founding Father' (n 1) 413.
[37] Cottier and Hertig (n 17) 297.
[38] See, for a discussion of fragmentation of global environmental law and governance, LJ Kotzé, 'Fragmentation Revisited in the Context of Global Environmental Law and Governance' (2014) 131 *South African Law Journal* 548.
[39] See, generally, U Beyerlin and T Marauhn, *International Environmental Law* (Oxford, Hart Publishing, 2011).

effectiveness.[40] From a constitutional point of view, effective law is considered to be law that is based on strong control emanating from a homogenous, unified and hierarchical order or authority. Where this is not the case, lawyers are not at ease since a fragmented dispensation works counter-intuitively to the expectations they would have had under a unified/homogenous/single source of normative validity and authority.[41] Martineau suggests in this respect that:

> to invoke fragmentation is to evoke an image of chaos, explosion. As performatives, all such references raise a particular sensibility—that is, a fear of anarchy, a feeling of lack of direction, a worry over the end of an international order.[42]

Fragmentation is therefore considered a 'perilous division'[43] and a threat to the consistency, stability, credibility, reliability and, ultimately, the authority and legitimacy of the international legal order.[44]

Constitutionalisation of the fragmented global order, on the other hand, is seen as a way to introduce hierarchy and order into an otherwise unstable, inconsistent, unreliable and incoherent system whereby 'hierarchically superior norms and coordinating mechanisms can manage or resolve conflicts and thereby produce greater predictability and certainty for actors subject to the rules'.[45] In short, a constitutionalised global order is perceived to be more stable, predictable and effective, with global constitutionalism acting as 'a tool for allocating power and tracing accountability hierarchies within a framework that may otherwise seem chaotic'.[46]

C. Enhanced Regulation for Global Problems

Third, Schwöbel argues that 'any changes in global social reality are believed to call for new or enhanced regulation',[47] essentially because such changes lead to anxiety about the lack of law in the global regulatory space and the prevalence of disorder as a result. To this end, global constitutionalism seeks to identify and advocate for the application of constitutional principles in the international domain with a view to improving the effectiveness and fairness of the international law and

---

[40] eg, in the environmental context, '[e]very unnecessary diversification of the law detracts from the primary aim of the most effective global environmental protection possible': U Beyerlin and T Marauhn, *Law Making and Law-Enforcement in International Environmental Law after the 1992 Rio Conference* (Berlin, Erich Schmidt Verlag, 1997) 19.

[41] M Koskenniemi and P Leino, 'Fragmentation of Internal Law? Postmodern Anxieties' (2002) 15 *Leiden Journal of International Law* 553, 556–57.

[42] A Martineau, 'The Rhetoric of Fragmentation: Fear and Faith in International Law' (2009) 22 *Leiden Journal of International Law* 1, 4–5.

[43] ibid 2.

[44] Koskenniemi and Leino, 'Fragmentation of Internal Law?' (n 41) 560.

[45] Dunhoff and Trachtman, 'Functional Approach to International Constitutionalization' (n 26) 8.

[46] C Schwöbel, 'The Appeal of the Project of Global Constitutionalism to Public International Lawyers' (2012) 13 *German Law Journal* 1, 9.

[47] ibid 10.

governance order.[48] If we accept that the Anthropocene's imagery evinces such changes, as was suggested in Chapter 2, it then becomes possible to appreciate the appeal of global constitutionalism as a useful framework to better regulate social life in a changed global social reality that is currently being dislodged by a global socio-ecological crisis and where existing global legal arrangements may be lacking as an institutional mechanism to address this crisis. In this sense, global constitutionalism is considered a potent remedy to provide an appropriate framework that could regulate social life in the global domain: 'the use of global constitutional language provides international lawyers with a legal tool that they regard as a tool for regulating a better global social reality'.[49]

D. Critiquing Global Constitutionalism

The main criticism often levelled against global constitutionalism, especially as a normative project, is that it is and will remain a mere symbolic exercise, especially when one considers the reality of the deeply entrenched, ultimately resilient, and self-centred global political powers that are at play.[50] Interests such as state security, economic well-being and military power could and often do trump and actively resist global constitutional impulses that might not be conducive to such state-centric, hegemonic, neo-liberal interests. Global constitutionalism is thus considered 'too idealist and does not adequately reflect the realist view of governments'.[51] The difficulties that marred the long road to finally reach a global agreement in Paris 2015 that more or less seeks to tackle climate change after the Kyoto Protocol, the raging climate misinformation campaign by the global petroleum sector (and the fact that it is allowed by governments to continue) and the reticence of states to forego unlimited economic growth in favour of climate protection, are only some examples in this respect.[52] In other words, from a realist point of view, not even constitutionalism is considered sufficiently resilient or powerful to withstand global political pressures and neo-liberal economic interests that might run counter to its core rationale and what it seeks to achieve.

To this end, Rosenfeld indicates that the recent economic crisis in Europe (especially the Greek financial meltdown); the rise of right-wing extremists in Europe such as Germany's 'Patriotic Europeans Against the Islamization of the Occident' (PAGIDA) movement; the threats of some influential European countries such as the United Kingdom to withdraw from the European Union; the mounting refugee crisis in Europe; and the increasing non-interventionist practice of states today

---

[48] A Peters, 'The Merits of Global Constitutionalism' (2009) 16 *Indiana Journal of Global Legal Studies* 397, 397.
[49] Schwöbel, 'Appeal of the Project of Global Constitutionalism' (n 46) 11.
[50] As discussed and refuted in Peters, 'Global Constitutionalism in a Nutshell' (n 29) 549.
[51] Peters, 'Merits of Global Constitutionalism' (n 48) 401.
[52] See for a discussion of these issues, A Giddens, *The Politics of Climate Change*, 2nd edn (Cambridge, Polity, 2011).

to turn a blind eye to grave human rights abuses elsewhere in the world, collectively evince a counter-constitutionalist trend in the global regulatory domain.[53] It seems that 'the nexus between constitutions and the ideal of constitutionalism is more fragile than may have seemed at the dawn of the new century', effectively rendering global constitutionalism 'not only a hotly contested concept but also one that may be incoherent or purely utopian'.[54] Other commentators point to the idea that to use constitutionalism in the global regulatory domain might be considered a misnomer and a disingenuous exercise that creates false and unrealisable expectations. In these instances '[c]onstitutionalist language … abuses the highly value-laden term "constitutionalism" in order to reap profit from its positive connotations and to dignify the international legal order'.[55]

A further point of critique that is worth mentioning, and indeed one which could also be levelled against this book's analytical approach, is that global constitutionalism is primarily a Euro-centric notion that is being driven by a particular ideology that is cast in modern Western liberal constitutionalism terms.[56] It is seen as a monolithic programme that shuts out indigenous juridical experiences and that ignores the multiple cosmopolitan approaches to what is often considered constitutionalism's core rationale, namely, 'a reaction to the universal experience of domination by humans of other humans',[57] that are all differently situated across the globe where multiple socio-economic, cultural and political conditions prevail.

While these are all valid points of criticism against global constitutionalism, there are counterclaims auguring for the continuance of the global constitutionalism project. First, in response to the last criticism concerning Euro-centrism, there is no singular vision of constitutionalism, as was already pointed out in Chapter 3. Constitutionalism, especially in the context of the global domain which is much more complex, polycentric and multi-levelled when compared to domestic spaces, is a notion representing many ways to counter domination of humans by other humans, regardless of its socio-cultural-juridical orientation. The idea behind constitutionalism, despite its inevitably being viewed through a specific analytical lens, is arguably sufficiently universal to counter claims of cultural hegemony and bias.

As well, the criticisms detailed above are as true for domestic constitutionalism as they are for global constitutionalism. Yet, the relative successes and advantages of domestic legal orders that have been constitutionalised as compared to nonconstitutional systems (see Chapter 3), suggest that constitutionalism, on balance, remains a powerful trope and higher-order normative approach in any regulatory space, including the post-nation state space. The fact that global constitutionalism

---

[53] Rosenfeld, 'Is Global Constitutionalism Meaningful or Desirable?' (n 8) 179.
[54] ibid.
[55] Peters (n 48) 400.
[56] ibid 404.
[57] ibid.

is not manifesting or happening in the way that we expect it to (an expectation that is based on our long-standing experience with domestic constitutionalism), is mainly as a result of the difficulties outlined above with translating constitutionalism to the global domain and as a result of the unique characteristics and idiosyncrasies of the global law and governance order. If global constitutionalism does not perform to the fullest satisfaction of our expectations, it is arguably mainly as a result of us not being sensitive to the uniqueness of the global domain where we seek it.

Finally, the criticisms are, at least in part, countered by the fact that there is not a perfect vision of constitutionalism, or of a completely constitutionalised order domestically or globally. Constitutionalism is also not an instant solution to all regulatory problems everywhere. To this end, it is unlikely that the entire global regulatory sphere will ever be completely constitutionalised. More dramatically stated, 'if all (international) law is somehow constitutionalized, then nothing is constitutional. The explicative power of the concept would be reduced to zero'.[58] While it does have a decisive normative role to play, the idea of constitutionalism in the global regulatory domain only remains a perspective that forces us to ask questions concerning fairness, justice, effectiveness, legitimacy and good governance, as well as a normative option to achieve the foregoing.[59] Global constitutionalism will continue to be critically viewed as a result of its indeterminacy and its often abstractly constructed and esoteric manifestations and grand ideals. But as an imperfect, continuously evolving phenomenon, global constitutionalism remains 'symbolically productive as a counterfactual ideal'.[60]

V. Approaches to and Meaning of Global Constitutionalism: A Devil with Many Faces

Few will disagree that there is little consensus about the meaning of global constitutionalism. The sustained and increasingly urgent search for global constitutionalism continues and it is evident from, among others, the robust intellectual movement surrounding it that has gained considerable momentum in the last decade, with numerous (mostly political science, constitutional law and international law) scholars convening under the banner of global constitutionalism to explore, in an endless pursuit, the possibilities of constitutionalisation beyond the state.[61] The complexity and controversy that permeate the global constitutionalism

---

[58] Peters (n 48) 403.
[59] ibid 400.
[60] Rosenfeld (n 8) 179.
[61] eg, the establishment of a journal exclusively dedicated to global constitutionalism is testimony to both the extent and the importance of the debate in this particular legal and discursive domain. See Cambridge Journals Online, 'Global Constitutionalism' (2015) journals.cambridge.org/action/displayJournal?jid=GCN.

debate are immense, with the different approaches to global constitutionalism already having been identified and systemised by other commentators.[62] A detailed replication here serves no purpose other than repetition. This part instead seeks to briefly map the different tracks that pervade global constitutionalism debates with a view to providing a systemised classification of the different manifestations and understandings of global constitutionalism.

There are several methodologies to classify global constitutionalism into specific approaches or tracks. One such methodology is offered by Schwöbel who differentiates between social constitutionalism (focusing on concerns to co-exist in a global society including the constitutionalisation of global civil society structures and practices); institutional constitutionalism (focusing on the existence, legitimisation and constraint of a global institutional power such as the United Nations); normative constitutionalism (focusing on the existence of universally applicable global norms such as human rights); and analogical constitutionalism (focusing on comparative analogies between domestic, regional and international law and governance).[63] Yet by her own admission, this division allows for considerable overlap between the different classifications, resulting in a less than clear, logical and systematic separation for the purpose of the present enquiry.[64] I suspect that, considering global constitutionalism's complexity, these concerns would be equally true for many other methodologies that seek to classify and explain global constitutionalism. Following from and expanding on Walker's approach,[65] I prefer to classify and summarise (realising full well the injustice and possible lack of nuance of such a concise summary), the different tracks of global constitutionalism as follows:

A. The Internationalist Approach

First, efforts that seek constitutionalism in the corridors of the global law and governance maze manifest most clearly, and certainly most intuitively, in the arguments of those suggesting that international law and its governance institutions have become, or are becoming, constitutionalised. Commentators belonging to this predominantly European and mostly German influenced school of thought (which one could term the internationalist approach), include Peters, Habermas, Fassbender, Simma, Tomuschat, Von Bogdandy and De Wet, among others.[66]

---

[62] See, among others, C Schwöbel, *Global Constitutionalism in International Legal Perspective* (Leiden, Martinus Nijhoff, 2011).
[63] Schwöbel (n 46) 1–22.
[64] ibid 5.
[65] Walker (n 6) 533–36.
[66] See Peters (n 29) 535–50; J Habermas, *The Divided West* (Cambridge, Polity, 2006); De Wet, 'International Constitutional Order' (n 4) 51–76; B Fassbender, 'The United Nations Charter as the Constitution of the International Community' (1998) 36 *Columbia Journal of International Law* 529; B Simma, 'From Bilateralism to Community Interest in International Law' (1994) 250 *Recueil des Cours de l'Académie de Droit International* 6; C Tomuschat, 'International Law: Ensuring the Survival of Mankind on the Eve of a New Century' (1999) 281 *Recueil des Cours de l'Académie de Droit International* 63; Von Bogdandy (n 12) 223–42.

Some general claims by the internationalist school around which they fashion their respective visions of global constitutionalism include:[67] there is a global authority organised around the United Nations and its organs with the Charter of the United Nations 1945 as its global constitution; there is a discernable international community acting as a constituent power; and a normative hierarchy exists which is similar to a domestic bill of rights that contains elevated norms such as *jus cogens* and *erga omnes* obligations, indicating some universal values that supersede multilateral and bilateral normative arrangements and other 'inferior' norms.[68]

What all these different manifestations within the internationalist approach have more or less in common is that they are focused on establishing the autonomy of international law vis-à-vis state sovereignty and state consent.[69] At a more practical level it is also about establishing international legal unity as a response to fragmentation, and perhaps more deliberately, albeit less likely, a global legal integration of states and the creation of a fully representative and comprehensive body of international law.[70] The internationalist approach also describes a global constitutional phenomenon both in terms of structure (allocation of competencies and the delineation of spheres of jurisdiction in the international community); and substance (the existence of higher-order norms that must be respected because as apex norms they are considered constitutional).[71] Especially in terms of the 'new' substance of law that the internationalist track foresee, international law, and by implication global governance, 'can no longer be understood as a neutral, value-free inter-state order, a mere emanation of State interest'.[72] Through global constitutionalism, material constraints are placed on state consent while sovereign interests that run counter to the higher-order substance of international law are diluted to some extent, especially through human rights.

B. The Regionalist Approach

A second equally prominent, but more recent, approach is what could be termed the regionalist school of global constitutionalists. This approach (also predominantly European) seeks constitutionalism in regional governance orders, most notably the European Union which is considered by global constitutionalists neither a super-state, nor a classic international organisation, but rather what Pernice calls a regional constitutional federation (*Verfassungsverbund*).[73] Proponents of this

---

[67] For a broad overview of this approach, see R Macdonald, 'Fundamental Norms in Contemporary International Law' (1987) 25 *Canadian Yearbook of International Law* 115.
[68] Walker (n 6) 535–36.
[69] Kleinlein (n 1) 388.
[70] K Milewicz, 'Emerging Patterns of Global Constitutionalization: Toward a Conceptual Framework' (2009) 16 *Indiana Journal of Global Legal Studies* 413, 424.
[71] Kleinlein (n 1) 391–92.
[72] ibid 399.
[73] I Pernice, 'Multilevel Constitutionalism in the European Union' (2002) 27 *European Law Review* 511.

approach argue that some form of softer multilevel constitutionalism (as opposed to Constitutionalism with a capital 'C')[74] exists in the European Union. While the Union does not have a single constitution carrying that name (despite failed attempts that started in 2001 to negotiate a Treaty Establishing a Constitution for Europe),[75] it is argued that its treaty system, including among others the Treaty on European Union of 1992 (TEU) and the Treaty on the Functioning of the European Union of 1958 (TFEU), could be regarded as forming some type of collective constitutional set-up that supersedes the national constitutional orders of the Member States,[76] while also determining, constraining and regulating the exercise of power by the European Union's institutions and the relations between the European Union and other international organisations.

The constitutionalism debate is bolstered by the central role of the European Convention on Human Rights 1950, which is a basic legal instrument of the Council of Europe, an international organisation that predates the European Union.[77] The European Court of Human Rights is also an institution of the Council of Europe and continues to play a crucial role in the development of rights jurisprudence based on the Convention.[78] In addition to the European Convention on Human Rights, the European Union, which is in the contentious process of acceding to the Convention on Human Rights,[79] has its own Charter of Fundamental Rights of 2000, which has been binding on the Union's Member States since 2009 by virtue of article 6(1) of the TEU. The Charter broadly seeks to entrench all rights that have crystallised from the case law of the European Union Court of Justice, the rights in the European Convention on Human Rights and other rights emanating from common constitutional traditions of European Union countries and other international instruments.[80]

The possibility of thinking about the European Union, its institutions and normative set-up in constitutional terms, has been amplified (even before formal negotiations with respect to establishing a constitution for Europe began),

---

[74] The burgeoning literature on constitutionalisation in the European Union is too expansive to list here. See for a summary of the debate, Walker, 'Reframing EU Constitutionalism' (n 4) 149–76.

[75] See http://europa.eu/eu-law/decision-making/treaties/pdf/treaty_establishing_a_constitution_for_europe/treaty_establishing_a_constitution_for_europe_en.pdf.

[76] The supremacy of European Union law over Member States' law was already confirmed in 1964 by the European Court of Justice in *Flaminio Costa v ENEL* [1964] ECR 585 (6/64).

[77] The Council of Europe has 47 Member States, including Russia, Azerbaijan, Turkey and Georgia and 6 observer states, such as Japan and the United States.

[78] See further, J Verschuuren, 'Contribution of the Case Law of the European Court of Human Rights to Sustainable Development in Europe' in W Scholtz and J Verschuuren (eds), *Regional Environmental Law: Transnational Comparative Lessons in Pursuit of Sustainable Development* (Cheltenham, Edward Elgar, 2015) 363–84.

[79] See for an abbreviated discussion, J Nergelius, *The Accession of the EU to the European Convention on Human Rights: A Critical Analysis of the Opinion of the European Court of Justice* (Stockholm, Swedish Institute for European Policy Studies, 2015).

[80] European Union Charter of Fundamental Rights: http://ec.europa.eu/justice/fundamental-rights/charter/index_en.htm.

by the European Court of Justice's characterisation of the founding treaties of the European Union as the 'constitutional Charter of a Community based on the rule of law'.[81] Such deliberate judicial phraseology seems to suggest that constitutionalisation of the European Union is anything but an empty exercise.

C. The International Regulatory Regime Approach

The third approach (mostly a mix between European and North-American scholars), is one which traces constitutionalism in increasingly autonomous clustered regimes of international law that are organised around a specific issue area such as global trade, ocean governance and climate change.[82] A prominent example of where the global constitutionalism debate occurs in this respect is in the area of global trade which consists of a specific regime that is clustered to the extent that it consists of an international organisation, a set of enforceable norms, administrative institutions and enforcement machinery; in this case the World Trade Organization and the many trade-related agreements that have been signed under the auspices of this organisation.[83]

With reference to international organisations and their regimes, these constitution-like agreements create a new subject of international law with some law-making autonomy, whereby the international organisation is mandated by states to realise certain common goals within a specific regulatory domain such as global trade, while its power is constrained and required to be exercised within the limited dictates of its constituting treaty and within the limits set out by general provisions of international law.[84] The constitutional debate arises in this context from the general practice to call the founding agreements of international organisations 'constitutions',[85] focusing on the extent to which these 'constitutions' regulate the establishment and internal functions of the international organisation itself and its relationship with its Member States. Relatedly, because these international organisations are sometimes non-state actors, the constitutionalism narrative is also used to legitimise their actions and the increasingly invasive state-like role that they play in global governance vis-à-vis the state.

---

[81] Opinion 1/91, Referring to the Draft Treaty on a European Economic Area [1991] ECR I-6079, 6084; Case 294/83, *Parti écologiste 'Les Verts' v European Parliament* [1986] ECR 1339.

[82] See for a general discussion, A Stone Sweet, 'Constitutionalism, Legal Pluralism, and International Regimes' (2009) 16 *Indiana Journal of Global Legal Studies* 621.

[83] See, for an overview of these agreements and other legal texts, World Trade Organization, 'WTO Legal Texts' (2016) www.wto.org/english/docs_e/legal_e/legal_e.htm.

[84] De Wet (n 4) 53.

[85] See, eg, Constitution of the Food and Agricultural Organization of the United Nations, 16 October 1945; Constitution of the United Nations Educational, Scientific and Cultural Organization, 16 November 1945; Constitution of the World Health Organization, 22 July 1946; Constitution of the International Labour Organization, 9 October 1946. See further, Kleinlein (n 1) 403.

But constitutional rhetoric is much more tenuous and tentative in this area than is the case in the internationalist and regionalist tracks since, unlike the United Nations and the European Union,

> at the WTO there has not been- and is not currently- an ongoing political process of crafting a constitutional instrument, nor is there any likelihood of such a process in the foreseeable future ... There is no ... readily identifiable constitutional moment.[86]

The World Trade Organization also does not possess any strong form of enabling constitutional norms that would allow it to produce ordinary international law. Yet, while it lacks legislative capacity, the World Trade Organization does have a strong judicial arm through its Appellate Body and dispute panels, which also contribute to judicial law-making, but their potential for enabling constitutionalism remains 'highly constrained'.[87] Whatever the merits and the prospects are for the constitutionalisation of the World Trade Organization and other international regulatory regimes (it is not the purpose of this book to discuss these in detail), the constitutional turn in the international institutional domain is generally suggestive of constitutionalism's allure to globalists in those areas beyond the state where a post-state regulatory regime is better suited to govern an issue that increasingly falls beyond the ability of single states to govern on their own.

D. Global Civil Society Constitutionalism

Reminiscent of Schwöbel's notion of social constitutionalism (see above), a fourth approach that is mostly European, is that of global civil society constitutionalism,[88] which specifically focuses on the emergence of civil 'constitutions' in a global society including non-state entities such as non-governmental organisations and epistemic communities. These non-state entities are seen to contribute to global law beyond the state where law has 'in line with the logic of functional differentiation, established itself globally as a unitary social system'.[89] Whereas the internationalist school might regard this as somewhat improbable, the global civil society constitutionalist school does not situate global law-making capacity exclusively in the nation state or in public authority-wielding entities, arguing instead that global law also derives its validity, appeal and legitimacy from processes of non-state law-making processes. Teubner and Fischer-Lescano explain that:

> '"Transnational communities," or autonomous fragments of society, such as the globalized economy, science, technology, the mass media, medicine, education and transportation, are

---

[86] Dunhoff, 'Politics of International Constitutions' (n 4) 180.
[87] ibid 182.
[88] See, for a general overview, G Teubner, 'Societal Constitutionalism: Alternatives to State-Centred Constitutional Theory?' in C Joerges, I Sand and G Teubner (eds), *Transnational Governance and Constitutionalism* (Oxford, Hart Publishing, 2004) 3–28.
[89] G Teubner and A Fischer-Lescano, 'Regime-Collisions: The Vain Search for Legal Unity in the Fragmentation of Global Law' (2004) 25 *Michigan Journal of International Law* 999, 1007.

developing an enormous demand for regulating norms which cannot, however, be satisfied by national or international institutions. Instead, such autonomous societal fragments satisfy their own demands through a direct recourse to law. Increasingly, global private regimes are creating their own substantive law. They have recourse to their own sources of law, which lie outside spheres of national law-making and international treaties.[90]

The emerging *lex mercatoria* of the international economy, the *lex constructionis* of the global building sector and the *lex digitalis* of the information technology sector are examples of private legal regimes in which non-state, law-like norms are created. Other examples are standardised contracts, agreements of professional associations, routines of formal organisations and rules for technical and scientific standardisation such as those issued by the International Organization for Standardization (ISO).[91]

In all these examples, global civil society constitutionalism is evident in increased modes of co-governance in the global domain where the hitherto strict divide between public and private forms of authority are gradually making way for non-state or private actors to take part in those global governance tasks traditionally reserved for state actors, and to play an increasingly assertive role as 'subjects' of international law. For example, private parties can now trigger the compliance mechanism under the Aarhus Convention on Access to Information, Public Participation in Decision-making and Access to Justice in Environmental Matters 1998;[92] and individuals are allowed to lodge complaints directly with the European Court of Human Rights when they believe their human rights under the European Convention on Human Rights 1950 have been violated.[93]

The constitutionalism debate in the global civil society space focuses therefore not on the energies of political power in nation states as such, but on the social regulatory energies and accompanying forms of power emanating from global civil society, ways to regulate global civil society power, and the potentially tenuous interactions between global civil society power and political state power. Accepting that there are many 'law-free spaces of globality',[94] as the uncontrollable dynamics of global capital markets, the power and practices of multinational corporations and the unregulated activities of epistemic communities suggest, the global civil society constitutionalism approach highlights the potential of constitutionalism

---

[90] ibid 1010.
[91] ibid 1013.
[92] See for a detailed discussion, E Hey, 'The Interaction between Human Rights and the Environment in the European "Aarhus Space"' in A Grear and LJ Kotzé (eds), *Research Handbook on Human Rights and the Environment* (Cheltenham, Edward Elgar, 2015) 353–75.
[93] Art 34 of the Convention states:

> The Court may receive applications from any person, nongovernmental organisation or group of individuals claiming to be the victim of a violation by one of the High Contracting Parties of the rights set forth in the Convention or the Protocols thereto. The High Contracting Parties undertake not to hinder in any way the effective exercise of this right.

[94] G Teubner, 'Constitutionalising Polycontexturality' (2010) www.jura.uni-frankfurt.de/42852930/ConstitutionalisingPolycontexturality_eng.pdf.

to react not only to the expansionist tendencies of state-based global law and governance, but also to other global social subsystems when they impact individual or institutional autonomy. To this end, global civil society constitutionalism as a normative programme 'occurs to the degree that reflexive social processes, which determine social rationalities through their self-application, are juridified in such a way that they are linked with reflexive legal processes'.[95]

E. Transnational Comparative Constitutionalism

A fifth approach is that of transnational comparative constitutionalism (elsewhere referred to as 'multi-level constitutionalism')[96] which is particularly popular among North-American scholars. Contrary to the internationalist or regionalist approaches, 'global' in this context has a weaker international or regional character, but a very strong comparative, cross-jurisdictional and/or transnational focus that is collectively seen as a global amalgamation of variously situated domestic norms around the globe that are less isolated within their domestic jurisdictions than one might intuitively believe at first glance. 'Global' in this sense is therefore the sum of many individual parts (domestic norms) that are often closely intertwined through processes of cross-jurisdictional learning, comparison and legal transplantation, including processes of transnational migration, interdependence, crosspollination and sharing of constitutional ideas between countries. 'Global' means 'comparative' or 'transnational' to the extent that it focuses on universalism and convergence of domestic norms that are at once also significantly influenced and in tune with international and regional law, especially to the extent that domestic law in most jurisdictions is partly dependent for their substance and form on these supra-national norms.[97] This approach is clearly exemplified by authors such as Law and Versteeg who, in their article, *The Ideology and Evolution of Global Constitutionalism*, investigate the rights-related content of national constitutions all over the world during the last six decades. They find that 'global constitutionalism ... is characterized by striking patterns of both similarity and dissimilarity' and confirm that 'a core set of constitutional rights ... [is] generic to the vast majority of national constitutions'.[98]

Importantly then, while the focus of transnational comparative constitutionalism is mostly on domestic states, it does not see the interaction between the legal systems of these states as being isolated from regional and international law

---

[95] Teubner and Fischer-Lescano, 'Regime-Collisions' (n 89) 1016.
[96] Kleinlein (n 1) 410.
[97] LC Backer, 'From Constitution to Constitutionalism: A Global Framework for Legitimate Public Power Systems' (2008/2009) 113 *Penn State Law Review* 671, 687. Another case in point is, K Kersch, 'The New Legal Transnationalism, the Globalized Judiciary, and the Rule of Law' (2005) 4 *Washington University Global Studies Law Review* 345.
[98] D Law and M Versteeg, 'The Ideology and Evolution of Global Constitutionalism' (2011) 99 *California Law Review* 1163, 1170.

developments. 'Transnational', while predominantly focusing on inter-state developments in an inter-national sense, also has a distinct international and (often regional) dimension to it, especially to the extent that national jurisdictions are influenced by supra-national and foreign law and vice versa,[99] including the internationalisation of domestic constitutional obligations (for example, 'outsourcing' human rights protection to supra-national bodies where the domestic order is found lacking), and the constitutionalisation of international law (such as the emergence of higher-order peremptory norms and *erga omnes* obligations).[100] It is a process that sees, among other things, international law norms supplementing domestic constitutions, especially where they fill gaps in relation to human rights when domestic constitutions do not provide for human rights protection and, to a lesser extent, the regulation of the democratic origin of governments through measures such as sanctions and war.[101] In its broadest sense then, the transnational comparative constitutional approach includes the internationalisation of domestic laws; the nationalisation of international law; the inter-jurisdictional transplantation of laws (or the inter-nationalisation of laws); the regionalisation of domestic laws; and the nationalisation of regional laws.[102]

F. Towards a Singular Vision?

What we see from all the related foregoing accounts of global constitutionalism's various manifestations, is that it is not only a descriptive exercise that seeks to explain what the law in the global space is, how the forces of globalisation have

---

[99] See for a comprehensive discussion on the role of foreign and international law in global constitutionalism, G Halmai, *Perspectives on Global Constitutionalism: The Use of Foreign and International Law* (The Hague, Eleven International Publishing, 2014), and more generally on transnational constitutional law, Rosenfeld (n 8) 177–99. Two examples of domestic constitutions that are receptive to international constitutional and broader juridical influences are those of Japan and South Africa. The Constitution of Japan 1946 proclaims in its Preamble:

> We believe that no nation is responsible to itself alone, but that laws of political morality are universal; and that obedience to such laws is incumbent upon all nations who would sustain their own sovereignty and justify their sovereign relationship with other nations.

S 233 of the Constitution of the Republic of South Africa provides:

> When interpreting any legislation, every court must prefer any reasonable interpretation of the legislation that is consistent with international law over any alternative interpretation that is inconsistent with international law.

See also s 39 which obliges courts to use rely on international law when interpreting the Bill of Rights and the discretion to rely on foreign law. These provisions mean that the further development of domestic constitutionalism is inherently tied to a vision of international law as it is being developed through the consensus of nations across the globe, thus allowing international law and associated constitutional developments to very directly influence domestic constitutional law.

[100] Cottier and Hertig (n 17) 269–75.
[101] Kleinlein (n 1) 410.
[102] Kotzé, *Global Environmental Governance* (n 28) ch 8.

shaped law and how law should respond to global regulatory challenges.[103] Importantly, global constitutionalism has a distinct normative character to the extent that it seeks to achieve in a 'chaotic' global regulatory space beyond the state what constitutionalism typically would seek to achieve within the borders of a state; ie a predictable, responsive, resilient, coherent, reliable, structured, comprehensive, protective or simply 'good' global legal order. To this end, global constitutionalism acts as an analytical and normative framework to devise solutions to the challenges of globalisation, fragmentation and complex global problems such as climate change, including the exponentially expanding regulatory problems that appear increasingly to fall beyond the control of states' domestic constitutional and broader juridical apparatus. All five of the approaches outlined above are more or less geared towards these goals, and they are all equally valid and legitimate tracks that endeavour to seek constitutionalism beyond the state, even though the goals apply variously in terms of five different approaches.

From a liberal constitutionalism point of view, these approaches emphasise the potential of constitutionalism to achieve a good global law and governance order in that it aims 'to guarantee a political [and socio-juridical] process that brings about sustainable and fair compromises between diverging interests'.[104] It could do so by restricting arbitrary rule of global powers through a global-type constitution containing a set of higher-order norms; in a related sense to 'softening' the sovereignty of states and restricting their unilateral actions through the limits imposed by rights that are encapsulated in treaties or captured as *jus cogens* norms; enhancing participative governance by non-state actors through the process of global civil society constitutionalism; demanding transparency and accountability from those who govern in the global domain; where these arrangements are absent, constituting normative and other institutional arrangements related to specific issue areas such as the environment; and providing the possibility for transnational, cross-jurisdictional juridical transplantation to occur.

VI. In Search of Constitutionalism's Features in the Global Sphere

If we accept the merit of the argument above that broadly explains and justifies the transplantation of constitutionalism to the global sphere, how do the basic elements of constitutionalism distilled in Chapter 3 find expression globally when measured against the different manifestations of global constitutionalism explained in the foregoing part?

---

[103] C Volk, 'Why Global Constitutionalism does not Live up to its Promises' (2012) 4 *Goettingen Journal of International Law* 551, 551.
[104] ibid 560.

A. A Global Constitution

Finding (a) global constitution(s) is a focus of the internationalist, regionalist and regulatory regime approaches to global constitutionalism discussed above. As a point of departure, Peters believes it is difficult to state the existence of a global constitution in a formal or substantive sense.[105] The Charter of the United Nations of 1945 with its almost universal membership and stringent requirements for amendment, while it constitutes the institutional architecture and describes the powers and functions of United Nations bodies and to some extent limits the unilateral powers and actions of states through its article 103 provision on normative superiority (see below), it still stops short of fully delimiting and effectively limiting the powers of whatever could be perceived as a global government. The existence of a global constitution must therefore be considered in the very real context of the absence of a global government and the incomplete desire to afford existing United Nations bodies, such as the Security Council, the type and measure of power that a unitary global government should presumably have.[106]

The majority of commentators accordingly agree with the view that the Charter is a *sui generis* treaty. The Charter is said to have a *sui generis* character since it remains a treaty, but it does have a somewhat elevated status above those treaties that constitute and regulate international regimes, such as the World Trade Organization.[107] To this end, it constitutes and regulates an international organisation with particularly elevated authority, but it does not constitute the basis of a global government or world order in a formal sense, nor does it impose significant limitations on states or global governance power in a comprehensive substantive and/or formal way.[108] Yet, while the Charter is not at present a global constitution, some commentators believe it does have the potential (however minimal) to become a global constitution in time:

> The extent to which it will succeed in developing into a full constitution ultimately will depend on the priority it is accorded and its capacity to develop more fully and effectively the law creation, application, and enforcement machinery, and to make concrete the values that international society deems fundamental.[109]

Equally, the foundational treaties of treaty regimes and international organisations, such as the World Trade Organization, are considered not to properly fulfil

---

[105] Peters (n 18) 46.

[106] Binding decisions of the Security Council are considered to have supreme force over any conflicting obligations of UN Member States, but no court has the power to review any decisions of the Security Council and permanent members can veto any decision rendering this high level political construct not so much constitutional as deeply political: Rosenfeld (n 8) 196.

[107] The elevated status of the United Nations Charter is derived from its art 103. See the discussion below. There is a view that the United Nations and its Charter, 'by virtue of the scope and significance of its responsibilities and the extent of its membership, is the de facto cornerstone of the existing world order': Macdonald, 'Fundamental Norms in Contemporary International Law' (n 67) 119

[108] Macdonald (n 67) 120.

[109] ibid.

the role of a formalistic or substantive global constitution since they only pertain to very specific niche areas and not to the regulation of a global power in its totality. The same goes for regional governance bodies and their normative arrangements such as those evident in the European Union. At present, these are not sufficiently representative geographically and of all regulatory concerns in the global domain that would allow one to characterise any one of them as a global constitution. The treaties of international and regional organisations and regimes therefore rather act as sub-'constitutions' that, under the collective banner of the United Nations, make up global governance. Their constitutional-like character is exemplified by the foundational documents of some of these organisations that are explicitly described as 'constitutions'. For example, the 'basic texts' of the United Nations Food and Agriculture Organization explicitly refer to (at least part of) these texts as the 'constitution' of the Organization.[110]

Considering the slim possibility for the eventual emergence of a single, written global constitution, at present it seems more likely that a global constitution might exist or eventually come about in the sense that the United Kingdom or New Zealand has a constitution, ie not a single codified one, but one which consists of various 'constitutions' which also have the potential to influence domestic legal orders, including for example, multilateral treaties;[111] the Charter of the United Nations; and the establishing treaties of regional and international organisations such as the World Trade Organization and the European Union. Such a fragmented, aggregated approach to a global constitutional regime is reminiscent of De Wet's 'constitutional conglomerate' or 'constitutional co-existence' (*Verfassungskonglomerat*) which describes an 'increasingly integrated international legal order in which the exercise of control over the political decision-making process would only be possible in a system where national and post-national (ie regional and functional) constitutional orders complemented each other'.[112] This conglomerate consists of variously situated individual regimes that function as complementary elements of a larger whole to create an 'embryonic international constitutional order with the United Nations Charter system as the main connecting factor'.[113] Such a view is also accommodative of a globalised, cosmopolitan and hugely diverse notion of 'international community', which is 'made up of different, sometimes overlapping communities each with its own normative (value) system, which can be of a

---

[110] Food and Agricultural Organization, 'Basic Texts of the Food and Agricultural Organization of the United Nations: Volumes I and II' (2013) www.fao.org/docrep/meeting/022/k8024e.pdf.

[111] Although some, correctly so, find it difficult to envisage treaties ever performing some higher-order and universally applicable substantive constitutional role, as opposed to their more likely general formal constituting and descriptive constitutional role. In other words, treaties are arguably more suitable for constituting and regulating power, but they might not be able to act as higher-order protective guarantees since they 'remain primarily agreements among sovereigns rather than constitutions plausibly construed as social contracts among equal citizens who cohere as a single people': Rosenfeld (n 8) 191.

[112] De Wet (n 4) 53.

[113] ibid 56.

national, regional or a functional (sectoral) nature'.[114] As such, the global constitutional conglomerate, because it would be more diverse, could also aptly counter criticism levelled against global constitutionalism's perceived Euro-centrism and singular cultural and ideological hegemony highlighted above.

B. Global Rule of Law

As a result of the global regulatory domain's abstractness, its complex power structures and relationships that are situated at different levels, and its amorphous nature, coupled with the difficulty to find elements of constitutionalism in these spaces, the potential for overlap between the generic constituent parts or features of the constitutional state is far greater in the global domain than it is in the domestic context. This is especially true for the rule of law.

The corresponding discussion in Chapter 3 has pointed out that there are both formal and substantive dimensions to a contemporary vision of the rule of law. With reference to the discussion immediately above, the most likely candidates to satisfy the formalistic requirements of the rule of law globally are the Charter of the United Nations 1945; the founding treaties of international treaty regimes such as the climate regime and international organisations such as the World Trade Organization; and the founding treaties of regional organisations such as the European Union, among others. As such, the formalistic aspects of the global rule of law are generally to be found in the internationalist, regionalism and regulatory regime approaches to global constitutionalism.

While this is by no means a closed list, it illustrates that several constitution-like instruments in the global sphere contain provisions that seek to provide for and determine the constitutive or formalistic elements that are necessary to establish a global governance order and it is an approach that is mainly based on positive law. With reference to Enzmann's rule of law typology set out in Chapter 3,[115] these formal elements provided by global constitutional instruments should work to more or less constitute elements of the global governance order, ensure legality, a description of competencies, limited allocation of powers and separation of powers within the global order insofar as this is possible in this idiosyncratic order. It is likely that with increased globalisation and everything that goes with that impulse, there will be a concomitant growth of international bodies through which states will seek to respond to the many challenges of globalisation. This in turn will significantly add to the exponential growth of those instruments that feed the formalistic component of the global rule of law.

Yet, a formal vision of the global rule of law alone is insufficient to fulfil the minimum requirements of (global) constitutionalism. For the global rule of law to

---

[114] ibid.
[115] B Enzmann, *Der Demokratische Verfassungsstaat: Entstehung, Elemente, Herausforderungen* (Wiesbaden, Springer, 2014) 43–163.

also ensure the rule of *good* global law, in addition to its formalistic functions, certain substantive elements must be included within the remit of a comprehensive conception of the global rule of law. Domestically, this is typically done by, among others, the often mutually contingent aspects of establishing a measure of moral constraint of power as overseen by the judiciary; the equal application of law to equally situated entities; and the provision and protection of rights. Globally, these substantive rules could play a similar role as they do domestically to the extent that they seek to protect people against human rights abuses; and circumscribe and limit the power of the state by means of human rights and universal higher-order peremptory norms which states are not competent to derogate from, and which may be changed only by another rule of the same character.[116] We already see these substantive rules emerging, specifically when viewed through the internationalist approach to global constitutionalism lens, in global human rights instruments such as the Universal Declaration of Human Rights 1948 and numerous non-derogable *jus cogens* norms that are also embedded in human rights (see the discussion below).[117]

One major concern with respect to the substantive aspects of the global rule of law is the lack of a powerful global judiciary with universal jurisdiction that is able to provide checks and balances and continuous scrutiny within which the legislative and executive organs of the global governance regime (insofar as they exist) and nation states *inter se* and vis-à-vis their individual citizens, must operate.[118] As the discussion below shows, while there is a more or less elaborate global judicial system, these courts exist in a piecemeal fashion and are focused on specific issue areas mostly in specific geographical regions such as the European Court of Human Rights or the African Commission on Human and Peoples' Rights. Moreover, despite remarkable progress in terms of holding states and individuals accountable for human rights abuses over the years, state sovereignty and state interests remain major inhibiting factors that prevent the global judiciary from fully constraining state consent and sovereign interests that run counter to the higher-order substance of international law. Alston confirms that the prevailing *realpolitik* evinces the 'deep reluctance of states to create new institutions endowed with any significant capacity to restrict their freedom of maneuver in relation to human rights-related policies'.[119] A more current example of this anti-global rule of law attitude is the South African Government's refusal to arrest Sudan's President Omar al-Bashir during the 2015 African Union Summit in Johannesburg against whom an international arrest warrant for alleged war crimes in Sudan has

---

[116] United Nations, 'Documents of the Second Part of the Seventeenth Session and of the Eighteenth Session Including the Reports of the Commission to the General Assembly (UN Doc A/CN.4/SER.A/1966/Add.1)' (1966) 2 *Yearbook of the International Law Commission* 1, 247.

[117] See for the definitive account, De Wet (n 4) 51–76.

[118] Despite recent efforts in support of the establishment of a World Court for Human Rights, such an institution remains a pipe dream, and as some point out, correctly so. See PG Alston, 'Against a World Court for Human Rights' (2014) papers.ssrn.com/sol3/papers.cfm?abstract_id=2344333.

[119] ibid 7.

been issued. This is despite South Africa being a signatory to the Rome Statute of the International Criminal Court 1998; a court order issued by its own High Court directing the Government not to allow al-Bashir to leave the country; and far-reaching domestic constitutional provisions obliging the Government to observe international human rights law, including prevailing *jus cogens* norms such as the rule prohibiting genocide.[120]

C. Global Separation of Powers

It is difficult to see how the traditional horizontal approach to separation of powers, ie the *trias politica* as it manifests in domestic legal orders, could be fully replicated in the global sphere. The improbability of such a complete replication is evident from the fact that there is no unitary global government based on a unified constituted power with a clearly defined judiciary, executive and legislature that derive their powers from a single constituent power. Some measure of separation of global governance power in a purely formalistic sense that seeks to delineate three separate institutional tracks of power can, however, vaguely be discerned to the extent that the International Court of Justice, the International Criminal Court and treaty tribunals, could form the global judicial power; the United Nations General Assembly and Security Council the executive; and as the legislature, the many international organisations that are responsible for treaty-making and compliance control.

Regionally, global separation of powers is clearer from the construction of the European Union. Often described as some sort of federal system similar to the United States,[121] and although the distinction is not watertight since the nature of some of its governance functions overlaps, the European Union has an executive authority in the form of the European Commission and European Union Council (also called the Council of Ministers) that act closely with the European Parliament which is the primary legislative authority. The European Court of Justice serves as its main judicial body, and it is assisted by the European Court of Human Rights which is the primary adjudicatory organ in relation to disputes arising from the European Convention on Human Rights 1950.[122]

What emerges from the examples is that these global power constructions are probably not sufficiently connected or crystallised in the first place to warrant any absolute separation in a constitutional sense that would aim to achieve a prevention of global power abuse through the establishment of checks and balances

---

[120] See the Constitution of the Republic of South Africa, ss 39 and 231–33. See for a discussion, E de Wet, 'The Implications of President Al-Bashir's Visit to South Africa for International and Domestic Law' (2015) 13 *Journal of International Criminal Justice* 1.

[121] G Conway, 'Recovering a Separation of Powers in the European Union' (2011) 17 *European Law Journal* 304–22.

[122] A Rosas, 'Separation of Powers in the European Union' (2007) 41 *The International Lawyer* 1033, 1034.

(ie the traditional function of the separation of powers doctrine domestically). However, because of the need to apply domestic constitutionalism in a nuanced way to the global domain, such a close connection between three distinct separate global powers arguably need not really exist, as long as the separation of powers doctrine achieves more or less globally what it seeks to ultimately achieve domestically, namely: preventing the concentration of power in any single state, group of states or supra-national organisation (in a counter-hegemonic sense); creating accountability by requiring (a) limited global government(s) to justify decisions and actions and to act responsibly towards the international community; and increasing global governance efficiency where some global governance institutions are better placed to perform certain governance functions than others.

If we accept that 'a "pure theory" of the separation of [domestic] powers is not reflected in any political system [and that] [s]ome interaction between the branches is inevitable',[123] the global regulatory domain would arguably call for an even less rigid separation of powers than its domestic counterpart. What is arguably required is only 'sufficient separation to forestall the dangers that are inherent in the concentration of powers'.[124] Considering this 'imperfect' vision of the separation of powers, coupled with the inevitable unique idiosyncrasies of the global law and governance space, it is possible to follow O'Donoghue and to think about the global separation of powers in geographical terms, which is akin to the vertical form of separation of powers in a federal system described in Chapter 3.[125]

Based on devolution or subsidiarity, vertical global separation of powers would result in a clear distinction being drawn between local or municipal, federal (provincial or state), national, regional (such as the European Union) and international (the United Nations and other international organisations) centres of power.[126] Because it includes the national sphere of powers and that sphere's unique horizontal division of powers as well, by necessary implication, geographical division of powers would include the traditional horizontal division of powers within a state, while integrating the national horizontal division of powers within the regional and international 'territorial centres'.[127] At the same time, the geographical separation of powers would include whatever minimal form of separation of powers is evident in the United Nations and European Union context as well.

While geographical or vertical separation of powers beyond, but including, the state cannot function in exactly the same way as the horizontal separation of powers within a state, it does provide a means to limit the concentration of powers at any single geographical level by divesting each sphere of some power through the

---

[123] Conway, 'Recovering a Separation of Powers' (n 121) 308.
[124] C Fombad, 'The Separation of Powers and Constitutionalism in Africa: The Case of Botswana' (2005) 25 *Boston College Third World Law Journal* 301, 341.
[125] Recognising that constitutionalism needs to encompass different layers because of the multi-layered nature of global governance, Cottier and Hertig follow a similar approach, describing federalism in this sense as a 'Five storey house': Cottier and Hertig (n 17) 299.
[126] O'Donoghue, *Constitutionalism in Global Constitutionalisation* (n 23) 34–35.
[127] ibid 35.

multi-levelled geographical arrangement. While the national sphere will always have the majority of power as a result of state sovereignty, national governments are subject to regional and international law that constrains their behaviour, at least to some extent. *Jus cogens* rules and customary international law more generally, as well as the binding provisions of the treaties states have signed, serve to divest them from such absolute power. To a limited extent, the International Court of Justice, or the European Court of Justice in the case of European Union Member States, could act as some form of check on the abuse of these rules, however minimal or insufficient this measure of checks and balances is perceived to be within the larger debate concerning state accountability and enforcement of international law. Clearly the foregoing approach is predominantly reminiscent of a mixture between transnational comparative constitutionalism and the internationalist approach to global constitutionalism.

D. The Global Judiciary

While there are numerous international and regional courts and tribunals, Howse and Teitel indicate that the only institution that could truly replicate the role of a domestic court in the global sphere, especially insofar as it could secure the place of higher law above politics in the sense that constitutional supremacy does, is the International Court of Justice.[128] This view seems to find at least some measure of recognition by the Court itself. In a separate opinion in the *Oil Platforms* case, Justice Bruno Simma made it clear that the International Court of Justice 'is not an isolated arbitral tribunal or some regional institution but the principal organ of the United Nations';[129] arguably suggesting that it is the principal global institution that is mandated and capable of protecting the integrity and authoritativeness of the international legal order.

Yet, the International Court of Justice is by no means an 'international constitutional court';[130] it does not have the type of jurisdiction and competencies to hear all matters in a global law and governance context in the same way that say, a supreme or constitutional court in a specific country does; nor does it have any explicit powers for judicial review during contentious proceedings. Its advisory opinions are also non-binding and decisions on contentious proceedings between parties are only binding *inter partes*. Inevitably, despite the International Court of Justice's potential, 'the establishment of an international constitutional court with compulsory jurisdiction over constitutional matters is unlikely'.[131]

---

[128] R Howse and R Teitel, 'Global Judicial Activism, Fragmentation, and the Limits of Constitutionalism in International Law' in U Fastenrath et al (eds), *From Bilateralism to Community Interest: Essays in Honour of Judge Bruno Simma* (Oxford, Oxford University Press, 2011) 961–74.

[129] *Oil Platforms (Iran v United States of America)* (Separate Opinion of Justice Simma) [2003] ICJ Rep 324 para 6.

[130] De Wet (n 4) 65.

[131] Peters (n 48) 408.

The fact that there is not a supreme global constitutional court does not, however, mean that there is no global aggregated judiciary in any expanded sense. In tandem with appreciating the uniqueness of the global regulatory order and especially the lack of fully separated global executive, legislative and judicial nodes of power, it is easier to think of the global judiciary as a non-hierarchical amalgamation of various courts, each designed for a specific purpose and to deal with a specific regulatory domain and/or region. This global judicial amalgamation is clear through the lens of the internationalist, regionalism, regulatory regime and transnational comparative global constitutionalism approaches discussed above.

In terms of an internationalist approach to global constitutionalism, it includes as the most 'universal' of all global judicial bodies, the International Court of Justice as the principal judicial organ of the United Nations, which is there to settle 'in accordance with international law, legal disputes submitted to it by States and to give advisory opinions on legal questions referred to it by authorised United Nations organs and specialized agencies'.[132] The International Court of Justice is available to adjudicate inter-state disputes that arise from time to time, but it will be an inappropriate forum to deal with pure criminal matters, which is within the purview of the International Criminal Court.[133] Acting complementary to domestic criminal systems, the International Criminal Court is not part of the United Nations system, but a treaty-based regime that aims to help end impunity for the perpetrators of serious crimes.[134] To this end, it focuses specifically on adjudicating 'the most serious crimes of concern to the international community as a whole', including genocide, crimes against humanity, war crimes and acts of aggression.[135]

As far as the regionalist approach to global constitutionalism is concerned, in addition to these judicial bodies with almost universal jurisdiction, there are numerous regional courts that are situated within regional governance regimes. This is by no means a closed list and include, among others: the European Court of Justice and the European Court on Human Rights; the African Commission on Human and Peoples' Rights and the Court of Justice of the African Union; and the Inter-American Commission on Human Rights and the Inter-American Court of Human Rights.[136] Most of these adjudicatory institutions have a strong human

---

[132] International Court of Justice, 'The Court' (2015) www.icj-cij.org/court/index.php?p1=1.

[133] Other related but ad hoc international criminal tribunals situated in the UN framework include the former International Criminal Tribunal for Yugoslavia and the International Criminal Tribunal for Rwanda.

[134] International Criminal Court, 'About the Court' (2015) www.icc-cpi.int/en_menus/icc/about%20the%20court/Pages/about%20the%20court.aspx. The Court was established by the adoption of the Rome Statute of the International Criminal Court 1998.

[135] Rome Statute of the International Criminal Court 1998, art 5.

[136] See among others, D Shelton, 'Human Rights and the Environment: Substantive Rights' in M Fitzmaurice, D Ong and P Merkouris (eds), *Research Handbook on International Environmental Law* (Cheltenham, Edward Elgar, 2010) 266–67; LJ Kotzé, 'Human Rights, the Environment and the Global South' in S Alam et al (eds), *International Environmental Law and the Global South* (New York, Cambridge University Press, 2015) 171–90.

rights focus and have been created in terms of regional treaties that set out elaborate details with respect to their composition, functions, jurisdictions and so forth. While some are more effective than others, notably those situated in Europe and the Americas, they only have geographical jurisdiction over the Member States of a particular regional grouping.[137]

A broadly encompassing definition of the global judiciary from a regulatory regime approach to global constitutionalism would also see the inclusion within its remit of quasi-judicial institutions such as the Permanent Court of Arbitration; the World Trade Organizations' dispute settlement and Appellate body; the World Bank's International Center for the Settlement of Investment Disputes; Inspection Panels at various multilateral development banks; and related Administrative Tribunals.[138] The International Tribunal for the Law of the Sea also belongs to this category. It is an independent judicial body established by the United Nations Convention on the Law of the Sea 1982 and hears disputes arising from the interpretation and application of the Convention.[139]

Finally, from a transnational comparative constitutionalism perspective, there is an evident emergence of transnational judicial conversations or dialogues between courts around the globe whereby they either voluntarily or obligatorily borrow from foreign jurisdictions and regional courts, as well as from international courts, when performing their adjudicative functions.[140] Such transnational judicial borrowing and cross-pollination has the added advantage that it does not only enrich domestic law, but it could also influence in a bottom-up way the creation of regional and international law norms, however minimally. Domestic courts do so through:

> informal networks of domestic courts worldwide, interacting with and engaging each other in a rich and complex dialogue on a wide range of issues. Transnational judicial dialogue is the engine by which domestic courts collectively engage in the co-constitutive process of creating and shaping international legal norms and, in turn, ensuring that those norms shape and inform domestic norms.[141]

For example, the Constitution of the Republic of South Africa states that when interpreting the Bill of Rights, a court 'must consider international law' and 'may consider foreign law'.[142] The South African judiciary, and notably the Constitutional Court, have done so on various occasions.[143]

---

[137] See, more generally, K Nyman Metcalf and I Papageorgiou, *Regional Integration and Courts of Justice* (Antwerp, Intersentia, 2005).

[138] See further, R Mackenzie and P Sands, 'International Courts and Tribunals and the Independence of the International Judge' (2003) 44 *Harvard International Law Journal* 271.

[139] See, more generally, S Rosenne, 'Establishing the International Tribunal for the Law of the Sea' (1995) 89 *American Journal of International Law* 806–14.

[140] See among the many publications on this issue, M Waters, 'Mediating Norms and Identity: The Role of Transnational Judicial Dialogue in Creating and Enforcing International Law' (2005) 93 *Georgetown Law Journal* 487.

[141] ibid 490.

[142] S 39.

[143] See for a general discussion and examples of specific cases, I Currie and J de Waal, *The Bill of Rights Handbook*, 6th edn (Cape Town, Juta, 2013).

As far as establishing and strengthening the independence of these courts and its officers are concerned, each contains fairly elaborate provisions in their founding treaties and rules of the court to assert and protect judicial independence and impartiality.[144] Nevertheless, ensuring the impartiality and independence of judges of supra-national adjudicatory bodies is far more difficult than it is at the domestic level, especially considering that these global courts and tribunals specifically aim to be as representative and cosmopolitan as possible, which means that they are subject to many more influences and political pressures than would normally be the case domestically. They also do not operate under one specific legal culture and one set of domestic laws like a national judiciary typically does.

While impartiality of a global judge would have the same meaning as it does for a domestic judge, the issue of independence from external influences takes on a more nuanced meaning in the global domain. Here it is considered that judges 'must enjoy independence from the parties to cases before them, their own states of nationality or residence, the host countries in which they serve, and the international organisations sponsoring their court or tribunal'.[145] Considering these challenges, it is encouraging that the International Law Association's Study Group on the Practice and Procedure of International Courts and Tribunals developed the Burgh House Principles on the Independence of the International Judiciary in 2004 which, although non-binding, is a useful set of guidelines that could contribute to judicial independence and impartiality of the global judiciary.[146] What the impact of these guidelines has been on strengthening impartiality and independence of the global judiciary remains unclear.

E. Global Constitutional Supremacy

Determining global constitutional supremacy is an important, if difficult, venture. A useful way to do so is through the lens of 'normative hierarchy in international law', which is part and parcel of the internationalist approach to global constitutionalism.[147] The obvious first place to look for such hierarchy is in the norms encapsulated in a global constitution. Through a narrow domestic constitutionalism lens it is, however, impossible to determine the supremacy of a global constitution, because as the previous parts have shown, a single global instrument does not exist at present, although it may develop over time. If there currently is some form of a global constitution, at best it is probably an aggregate of various

---

[144] See, eg, arts 2 and 3 of the Statute of the International Court of Justice 1945.
[145] Preamble of the Burgh House Principles (International Law Association, 'Burgh House Principles on the Independence of the International Judiciary' (2004) www.ucl.ac.uk/laws/cict/docs/burgh_280604.pdf.
[146] International Law Association, 'Burgh House Principles on the Independence of the International Judiciary' (2004) http://www.ucl.ac.uk/laws/cict/docs/burgh_280604.pdf.
[147] E de Wet and J Vidmar (eds), *Hierarchy in International Law: The Place of Human Rights* (Oxford, Oxford University Press, 2012).

individual global instruments with constitution-like properties, or a constitutional conglomerate as was argued above.

Within this conglomerate it is possible that the Charter of the United Nations, while it is not a global constitution, does have some elevated status as a supreme norm under certain circumstances, which would mean that the obligations under the Charter could in theory claim a hierarchically superior normative status in the global legal order. This much is evident from its article 103, which states:

> In the event of a conflict between the obligations of the Members of the United Nations under the present Charter and their obligations under any other international agreement, their obligations under the present Charter shall prevail.

By ratifying the Charter, states accept that all obligations under the Charter, including binding United Nations Security Council decisions, have precedence over any other conflicting treaty obligation and therefore would be superior to them.[148] Yet, while this provision explicitly relates to the relationship between the superior Charter and 'any other [subordinate] international agreement' in the event of treaty conflict, it remains uncertain whether it also establishes the supremacy of the Charter vis-à-vis general international law other than treaties.[149] One can therefore not derive a general notion of global constitutional supremacy in terms of the Charter from this provision alone that would apply universally.

In addition to the Charter, various other apex norms exist that have an elevated, and in some instances non-derogable, status in international law. These norms are exemplified by higher-order universal values such as human rights that are contained in regional human rights treaties and the Universal Declaration of Human Rights 1948 (see the discussion below),[150] as well as in *jus cogens* norms, customary international law and *erga omnes* obligations.[151] Collectively they 'represent the fundamental values underpinning the international legal order'.[152]

Jus cogens norms are compelling to the extent that they are mandatory, do not permit derogation and can be modified only by general international norms of equivalent authority (ie other *jus cogens* norms).[153] They are universal in that they are seen to have *erga omnes* effect, meaning that they apply to all members of the

---

[148] E de Wet, 'Sources and the Hierarchy of International Law' in S Besson and J D'Aspremont (eds), *Oxford Handbook on the Sources of International Law* (Oxford, Oxford University Press, forthcoming).

[149] See, among others, R Kolb, 'Does Article 103 of the Charter of the United Nations Apply only to Decisions or also to Authorizations Adopted by the Security Council?' (2004) 64 *Zeitschrift für ausländisches öffentliches Recht und Völkerrecht* 21.

[150] Regional human rights treaties include: the European Convention for the Protection of Human Rights and Fundamental Freedoms of 1950; the American Convention on Human Rights, 1969 and its San Salvador Protocol of 1988; Asian Human Rights Charter 1998; the Arab Charter on Human Rights 2004; and the African (Banjul) Charter on Human and Peoples' Rights (African Charter) 1981.

[151] See for a definitive account on these issues, De Wet (n 4) 51–76.

[152] De Wet, 'Sources and the Hierarchy of International Law' (n 148).

[153] EJ Criddle and E Fox-Decent, 'A Fiduciary Theory of *Jus Cogens*' (2009) 34 *Yale Journal of International Law* 331, 332.

international community of states, even if a state does not consent to a *jus cogens* norm's mandatory application.[154] *Jus cogens* norms are obligatory to the extent that they create obligations on states to refrain from doing something; ie they create so-called negative obligations.[155] Although there is no universal agreement on this, the rules of international law that are currently accepted as having *jus cogens* status include, among others: the prohibition of the threat or use of force against the territorial integrity or political independence of any state; the prohibition of genocide; the prohibition of torture; crimes against humanity; the prohibition of slavery and slave trade; the prohibition of piracy; the prohibition of racial discrimination and apartheid; and the prohibition of hostilities or force directed at a civilian population.[156] Notably, the majority of these norms are directly or indirectly related to human rights concerns (some commentators even suggest they are pure human rights norms).[157]

Collectively, these characteristics confirm that there is something inherently constitutional about *jus cogens* norms.[158] It is, after all, now generally accepted that the international law order has a 'layered texture';[159] a feature which could render it constitutional to some extent by instilling some degree of normative hierarchy in international law.[160] To this end, *jus cogens* is situated at the apex of the hierarchy of international law norms, even surpassing 'ordinary' customary international law norms and *erga omnes* obligations.[161] In the words of the International Criminal Tribunal for the former Yugoslavia, *jus cogens*,

> enjoys a higher rank in the international hierarchy than treaty law and even 'ordinary' customary rules. The most conspicuous consequence of this higher rank is that the

---

[154] A point that was confirmed by the ICJ in *Barcelona Traction, Light and Power Company Ltd* (Second Phase) [1970] ICJ Rep 32. See De Wet (n 4) 61. The author, however, at the same time correctly points out that not all *erga omnes* obligations necessarily have *jus cogens* status which means that not all *erga omnes* human rights norms are peremptory norms.

[155] *Jus cogens* does not create positive obligations that compel states to do something, eg, to make good human rights abuses. They only compel states not to commit some human rights abuses. This is often seen as one of the greatest drawback of *jus cogens* rules: J Vidmar, 'Norm Conflicts and Hierarchy in International Law: Towards a Vertical International Legal System?' in de Wet and Vidmar (eds), *Hierarchy in International Law: The Place of Human Rights* (n 147) 33.

[156] E de Wet, '*Jus Cogens* and Obligations *Erga Omnes*' in D Shelton (ed), *The Oxford Handbook on International Human Rights Law* (Oxford, Oxford University Press, 2015) 543. As a consequence, 'a strong argument can be made that at least certain human rights could be put at the top of the pyramid of international legal norms'; in other words, that certain human rights have *jus cogens* status: E de Wet and J Vidmar, 'Introduction' in de Wet and Vidmar (n 147) 8.

[157] De Wet (n 4) 58–59.

[158] Criddle and Fox-Decent, 'Fiduciary Theory of *Jus Cogens*' (n 153) 332.

[159] De Wet (n 4) 62.

[160] D Shelton, 'Normative Hierarchy in International Law' (2006) 100 *American Journal of International Law* 291.

[161] To be sure, some point out that arguments have been made that *jus cogens* norms are so hierarchically superior, that they trump Ch VII resolutions made by the Security Council under the Charter of the United Nations: Vidmar, 'Norm Conflicts and Hierarchy in International Law' (n 155) 20.

principle at issue cannot be derogated from by States through international treaties or local or special customs or even general customary rules not endowed with the same normative force.[162]

Other universally shared values that may in time acquire an elevated status in international law's normative hierarchy are also gradually emerging. To this end, De Wet suggests that article 53 of the Vienna Convention on the Law of Treaties (VCLT) provides states sufficient freedom to determine themselves what are peremptory norms and what are not.[163] In practice, this would occur through a process that first identifies a norm as customary international law and then an agreement on whether derogation is permitted from that customary norm or not. This form of 'double acceptance' thus not only requires proof of *usus* and *opinio juris* (the first stage of acceptance); but also acceptance of the special character of the norm in question (the second stage) that is seen to be embedded in the 'universally accepted strong ethical underpinning of these norms'[164] that affords them their peremptory character.

Global constitutional supremacy in the global regulatory domain expressed as normative hierarchy, could lead to greater accountability among those (particularly state actors) who are subject to certain higher-order norms to the extent that they are not allowed to violate these norms. When they do violate such higher-order 'constitutional' norms, political, legal and/or economic sanctions might ensue that are meant to strengthen accountability and redress. The existence of a normative hierarchy in international law should, however, not be overstressed, since the development of global apex universal shared values and norms remains hesitant. The hierarchical divisions between the various norms are not clear and the norms themselves including *jus cogens*, *erga omnes* obligations, customary international law and more generally human rights, are still evolving. While their incremental development evinces some form of substantive constitutionalism emerging in the global regulatory domain, the reality is that it remains difficult for the pluralistic international community to reach agreement on the basic values that must underlie a hierarchy of norms, as well their specific content. International law is rather developing as a regional enterprise instead of a universal one, as the strong regional governance centres such as the European Union suggests, and universalism is somewhat countered by the fragmentary growth of international law along separate problem-oriented tracks such as 'environment', 'trade' and 'armed conflict'.[165]

---

[162] *Prosecutor v Anto Furundžija*, Judgment of 10 December 1998, Case No IT-95-17/1, Trial Chamber II.
[163] De Wet, '*Jus Cogens* and Obligations *Erga Omnes*' (n 156) 542.
[164] Vidmar (n 155) 26.
[165] Macdonald (n 67) 146–47.

F. Global Democracy

Of all constitutionalism's features, democracy is the most difficult to discern in the global sphere, requiring considerable epistemological flexibility when thinking about it in global terms. This is because of the nation state's tenacious hold on and ownership of the idea of democracy: state boundaries delimit a country geographically, but they also constitute the boundaries of democratic governance to the extent that they encircle a nation, thereby depicting a relatively homogenous social entity, which through a majority vote, politically constitutes a legitimate government that is bound by a constitution.[166] Such a single encircled homogenous social entity is absent in the global sphere where the necessary political process whereby states and their people (as an original constituent power) can vote for a hitherto non-existent global government that makes and enforces global laws, is also not immediately evident.

The forces of globalisation further complicate constructing an understanding of global democracy. Of all of constitutionalism's features, democracy is arguably the closest related to politics. The nature of global politics and the impact of state sovereignty on global politics in a globalised world is such that it significantly complicates any well-meaning and clear vision of what democracy could mean in the global regulatory domain. According to Cohen and Sabel, global politics 'is marked by a proliferation of political settings beyond domestic boundaries',[167] as it is typically characterised by increased economic integration that has distinct political consequences, as well as by persistent diversity in all respects. As a response to these two realities, there is increased global rule-making in which state and notably non-state actors are involved which, in turn, has consequences for the conduct and welfare of individuals, corporations, states and global civil society.

Within the globalisation paradigm, especially non-state rule-making is set to expand and to become increasingly influential (if not entirely authoritative) with the result that global norm creation 'is taking place, undemocratically but not entirely unaccountably, in global settings created by the world's nations but no longer under their effective control'.[168] In a globalised world therefore, state majoritarianism will become more ambiguous from a global democracy point of view because of the involvement in global governance of a broad range of different non-state actors such as transnational corporations, non-governmental organisations and epistemic networks, with strategic interactions among these entities that are not necessarily arranged in formal hierarchies.[169] To the extent that states are 'contracting out' their norm-creating activities to international organisations such

---

[166] Cottier and Hertig (n 17) 289.
[167] J Cohen and C Sabel, 'Global Democracy?' (2005) 35 *International Law and Politics* 763, 763.
[168] ibid 765.
[169] Peters (n 48) 399.

as the World Trade Organization, the 'demise' of the state in global governance potentially gives rise to significant concerns relating to the legitimacy of norm creation, adjudication, enforcement, accountability and participation in global governance. This in turn will only increasingly highlight the need for and discussions surrounding the emergence of global democracy specifically and global constitutionalism more generally.

Considering the difficulties that the absence of the 'state boundary-social entity' continuum in the global domain presents, and in light of the legitimacy issues that globalisation raises, how could democracy be construed in a way that fits the global regulatory domain while more or less fulfilling the trite objectives of domestic conceptions of democracy? The latter was summarised in Chapter 3 as including legitimisation of government and its laws and governance through majority will; and to the extent that democracy signifies more than majority rule, to guarantee adherence to fundamental constitutional elements such as the rule of law, rights and prohibition of power abuse with the view to strengthening accountability.

As is the case in domestic legal systems, legitimacy is crucial in the global sphere since questions of legitimacy relate to questions of obedience '[o]nly if and to the extent that international law is legitimate is there a moral duty to obey international law'.[170] Yet, this fact in and of itself does not explain why legitimacy is a concern in the global regulatory arena. The more complete answer to this is related to the issue of obedience and to the fact that contemporary law in the global regulatory space increasingly serves 'if not as an iron cage—[then] certainly as a firmly structured normative web that makes an increasingly plausible claim to authority'.[171] In other words, as the entire body of supra-national law (including non-state law) asserts greater normative significance, questions related to legitimacy will arise for the same reasons they arise in the domestic sphere.

With respect to the need for democracy as a legitimising factor in and among the broad range of global governance institutions and in their relations with states and with global civil society,[172] it is useful to know that there is 'a substantial spectrum of meaning hidden within [the notion of democracy]'.[173] This means that democracy's meaning could be expanded to better suit the idiosyncrasies of the global regulatory domain. Such a conceptual shift could be facilitated through the increasingly popular reference to an 'international community' in global law and governance discourse;[174] ie states *and* global civil society acting as 'We the People' of the global regulatory domain. Such an approach accords with efforts to take a broader view of the relationship between legitimacy, global democracy, an

---

[170] M Kumm, 'The Legitimacy of International Law: A Constitutionalist Framework of Analysis' (2004) 15 *European Journal of International Law* 907, 908.

[171] ibid 912.

[172] Understood here in the generally accepted sense as used in, eg, M Bexell, J Tallberg and A Uhlin, 'Democracy in Global Governance: The Promises and Pitfalls of Transnational Actors' (2010) 16 *Global Governance* 81.

[173] Backer, 'From Constitution to Constitutionalism' (n 97) 691.

[174] Von Bogdandy (n 12) 234.

expanded view of 'international community' and, ultimately, a broadening of the sociological concept of 'people'. The idea of a pluralistic and multi-actor 'international community' that is situated at various levels and in different spheres of influence fully aligns with the ideals and agenda of global civil society constitutionalism discussed above.

As well, at a less abstract level, realising that 'there is no single actualised form of liberal democracy which could easily be identified as the ideal model of governance',[175] opens up the possibility of thinking about global democracy in expanded terms that include measures to enhance participation, transparency and ultimately, accountability in global law and governance. Thus, the legitimacy of the global law and governance order and of international and regional law themselves is not so much contingent on their institutional structures being democratically created by an enabling original constituent power, but rather on the type of processes that have led to their creation; ie are they at least transparent, representative, participative and inclusive, if not fully democratic in the more apparent domestic sense? Considered together, a broadly construed 'international community' as an aggregated global constituent power should ideally be enabled to drive participative, representative, inclusive and transparent modes of global governance in the spaces where states and their citizens, international organisations as global representatives or agents of states, and global civil society actors operate. Yet, the depth and quality of democracy that could emerge in relation to the international community will significantly depend on the extent to which states do not allow sovereign interests to neutralise global democracy's potential.[176]

The global civil society constitutionalism approach usefully refocuses attention in the domain of global democracy to consider means to promote the procedural aspects of global governance with a view to increasing its legitimacy. There is no single global framework instrument that generally and comprehensively seeks to regulate and improve participation, transparency and accountability in global governance generally. These provisions are instead scattered across the global governance and legal landscape and can typically be found in, among others, the 'constitutions' of international organisations such as the United Nations, the constituting treaties of regional governance entities such as the European Union, and related procedural provisions in the many treaties that exist today. In the environmental domain, however, the Convention on Access to Information, Public Participation in Decision-Making and Access to Justice in Environmental Matters 1998 extensively provides for these matters (see Chapters 6 and 7).

Outside of the more formal state-driven global law and governance agenda, global civil society is also able to assert itself as an observer during global conferences and cooperate more closely with states to achieve global governance

---

[175] De Wet (n 4) 72.
[176] F Venter, 'Re-imagining the Role of the Sovereign State and Individual Rights in Mitigating the Effects of the Deterioration of the Environment' in A Grear and LJ Kotzé (eds), *Research Handbook on Human Rights and the Environment* (Cheltenham, Edward Elgar, 2015) 121–40.

objectives. As well, multi-actor transnational networks are increasingly created that contribute to realising some of the goals of global governance in a bottom-up way. One often-cited example is the United Nations Global Compact, which is a global corporate sustainability initiative that provides a platform that engages corporations, governments and other stakeholders to work collectively towards sustainability goals.[177] Finally, from a transnational comparative constitutional perspective it is likely that the world's many domestic constitutional democracies, simply because they are democratic and constitutional, could work in a compensatory and bottom-up way to engender globally some appreciation of and adherence to the core rationale of democracy. It is arguably more likely that the many actors in global governance will themselves be more democratic and inclined to observe the minimal dictates of democracy and constitutionalism in the global regulatory realm when these actors hail from domestic constitutional democracies.

Although the foregoing arrangements are probably (still) insufficient to offer any comprehensive vision of democracy in terms of the global law and governance order, they collectively suggest that the notion of democracy is not entirely foreign to the global realm. More importantly, they augur for the gradual and more deliberate emergence of democracy in the global regulatory order and are at once testimony to the potential of global democracy to legitimise and strengthen global law and governance.

G. Global Rights

Because rights are considered constitutionally superior norms that manifest at the global level, they are a significant part, and they strengthen claims, of global constitutional supremacy in the light of the normative hierarchy paradigm discussed above. By constraining state conduct, sovereignty and unilateral action, rights, regardless of whether they are contained in domestic, regional and/or international legal instruments or exist as *jus cogens* norms or *erga omnes* obligations, are part and parcel of the substantive elements of the global rule of law, as we have seen. To this end rights, perhaps more than any other feature of constitutionalism, have transcended their parochial domestic boundaries to manifest globally as 'core elements of the international value system',[178] which squarely positions them at the higher end of international law's normative hierarchy:

> [W]e need not think of human rights as part of a specifically liberal political outlook so deeply implicated in the mix of individualism, states, and courts. In the first place, human rights claims can be presented as elements of a global standard—a global public reason, itself part of the world of global politics—that sets out conditions of acceptable

---

[177] See for a comprehensive discussion, generally, B Richardson, *Socially Responsible Investment Law: Regulating the Unseen Polluters* (New York, Oxford University Press, 2008).
[178] De Wet (n 4) 57.

treatment, requiring in particular that political societies assure conditions of membership for those who live in their territory.[179]

Being firmly ensconced in all the approaches to global constitutionalism discussed above, rights arguably are the most evident globally universal feature, as it were, of global constitutionalism.

There are several reasons for the emergence and continued prevalence of rights in the global regulatory sphere. First, mainly as a response to the ravages of two world wars, rights have formally gained global acceptance and endearing appeal since 1945, with the United Nations Charter proclaiming that the purpose of the United Nations is to promote and encourage 'respect for human rights and for fundamental freedoms for all without distinction as to race, sex, language, or religion'.[180] In full complement of the Charter, considering their global application and virtually universal endorsement, the Universal Declaration of Human Rights 1948; the Covenant on Civil and Political Rights (ICCPR) of 1966; and the Covenant on Economic, Social and Cultural Rights (ICESCR) of 1966, are the most obvious contenders for a 'global bill of rights'.[181] It has been estimated that the:

> treaty systems sponsored by the United Nations provide the backbone to the international human rights regime. They have codified and legitimated human rights ideas, served as inspiration for regional human rights treaty systems, and have given leverage to nongovernmental activists in promoting human rights and publicizing violations. In the last 4 decades, both the number of U.N. international human rights treaties and that of states parties to these treaties have increased dramatically. This growing commitment to global human rights by national governments is remarkable considering that these human rights treaties essentially constrain their sovereign rights while providing few tangible short-term benefits for them.[182]

Second, the United Nations human rights regime has also provided the all-important foundation for the eventual development of regional human rights instruments.[183] One of the most prominent regional human instruments is the European Convention on Human Rights 1950 with the European Court of Human Rights which ensures rights protection in terms of this instrument.[184]

---

[179] Cohen and Sabel, 'Global Democracy?' (n 167) 788.
[180] Art 1(3) and supported by arts 55, 56, 62 and 68.
[181] Other human rights treaties that belong to the UN system but which are not necessarily perceived as being part of the 'global bill of rights' include: International Convention on the Elimination of all Forms of Racial Discrimination 1965; International Convention on the Suppression and Punishment of the Crime of Apartheid 1973; Convention on the Elimination of all Forms of Discrimination against Women 1979; Convention against Torture and other Cruel, Inhuman or Degrading Treatment of Punishment 1984; and Convention on the Rights of the Child 1989.
[182] CM Wotipka and K Tsutsui, 'Global Human Rights and State Sovereignty: State Ratification of International Human Rights Treaties, 1965–2001' (2008) 23 *Sociological Forum* 724, 725.
[183] See the discussion above.
[184] See among the many publications in this respect, A Mowbray, 'The Creativity of the European Court of Human Rights' (2005) 5 *Human Rights Law Review* 57–79; SC Greer, *The European Convention on Human Rights: Achievements, Problems and Prospects* (Cambridge, Cambridge University Press, 2006).

The Convention does not apply universally; it remains a geographically delimited transnational regime, but one which could nevertheless be 'persuasively characterized as constitutional and consistent with the ideal of constitutionalism',[185] most notably because it entrenches rights protection and rights values at the higher constitutional level in Europe. Similarly, but far less effective in comparison, the African Charter on Human and Peoples' Rights 1981 sets out a broad range of rights that should be respected, protected and fulfilled in Africa and the African Commission on Human and Peoples' Rights has delivered several (unfortunately non-binding) judgments in cases that have been brought before it.[186]

An important third consideration, and one that is situated in global civil society constitutionalism driving the globalisation of rights, their appeal, and to some extent their observance and vindication globally, is the increasingly strong energies that are emerging from global civil society networks and in particular from non-governmental organisations. From an environmental perspective Gearty explains that:

> Shed of its layers of philosophical and legal mystification, human rights advocacy emerges as a social movement of the very first importance. In their commitment to change, their attitude to power and in their mode of organizing, human rights groups resemble the green and environmental activists who have done so much to bring the need for environmental protection to public attention.[187]

While global civil society and the many energetic global social movements that seek to promote rights observance and protection cannot compete at the same political or normative level as the state, they are significantly contributing to the global visibility of rights; they informally influence and shape the global rights agenda; and they provide a visible (often through the media) moral check on state accountability in relation to rights protection.[188]

From a transnational comparative constitutionalism perspective, a fourth consideration in rights acting as important components of global constitutionalism is the cross-pollinating effect of domestic rights experiences across the world. This issue has already been extensively canvassed above and is best exemplified in the work of comparative constitutionalists such as May and Daly, and Boyd.[189]

The criticism that is levelled against rights in domestic constitutions will equally apply to rights in the global sphere. There are also legitimate concerns about the practical effect of rights, their enforcement and the actual extent to which they

---

[185] Rosenfeld (n 8) 193.
[186] See for a general discussion pt III of the seminal work, F Viljoen, *International Human Rights Law in Africa*, 2nd edn (Oxford, Oxford University Press, 2012).
[187] C Gearty, 'Do Human Rights Help or Hinder Environmental Protection?' (2010) 1 *Journal of Human Eights and the Environment* 7, 11.
[188] Wotipka and Tsutsui, 'Global Human Rights and State Sovereignty' (n 182) 587–620.
[189] JR May and E Daly, *Global Environmental Constitutionalism*, Kindle edn (New York, Cambridge University Press, 2015) 2; DR Boyd, *The Environmental Rights Revolution: A Global Study of Constitutions, Human Rights, and the Environment* (Vancouver, UBC Press, 2012).

are able to restrict state sovereignty. Yet, in the absence of any similar juridical construct with equal historical legitimacy, providence and almost universal moral appeal, there is sufficient reason to believe that rights will continue to act as the cornerstone foundation of global constitutionalism.

VII. Conclusion

While it did not offer any comprehensive treatise on global constitutionalism, this chapter's more focused aim was to flesh out a concise meaning of global constitutionalism with a view to providing a basis for explaining, in Chapter 7, how global constitutionalism is relevant to and important for addressing the global socio-ecological crisis of the Anthropocene. It was established that global constitutionalism is an analytical perspective and/or a normative programme that departs from, and is oriented by, the idea of constitutionalism as it manifests domestically. While there are others, for the purpose of this enquiry, the approaches to global constitutionalism could be described as internationalist, regionalist, the regulatory regime approach, the global civil society approach and the transnational comparative approach to global constitutionalism. In these five approaches it is possible to identify, to a greater or lesser extent, the existence of many of the elements that are present in domestic constitutionalism, namely: a constitution, the rule of law, a judiciary that has the powers of review, constitutional supremacy, democracy and rights.

Importantly, those who expect to find a vision of domestic constitutionalism that is perfectly replicated in the global domain will be disappointed. A major insight stemming from the analysis is that global constitutionalism requires a different mindset and analytical approach altogether. By virtue of the global regulatory domain's unique characteristics, its complex prevailing political realities, and its historical baggage, the question of global constitutionalism is one that rather begs for a nuanced and graduated approach to constitutionalism that is able to venture beyond a traditionalist mindset: 'static thinking will not assist in solving practical problems of modern governance'.[190] The analysis suggests that, despite there being no single and clearly discernable global government, constitution or constituent power, there is sufficient evidence of the existence and gradual emergence of constitutional-like characteristics and elements in the global regulatory space to be able to confirm global constitutionalism's normative prevalence and potential for future development in that space.

The analytical and normative project of global constitutionalism is therefore a useful, but incomplete, one that remains current. This project will arguably increase in appeal as globalisation gathers pace and new threats to a sense of global order

---

[190] Cottier and Hertig (n 17) 283.

and socio-ecological security, such as those posed by the Anthropocene, become increasingly apparent and urgent. There is accordingly every reason to believe that global constitutionalism will become critically relevant, if it is not already thus, to global environmental issues as well. The next chapter returns this book's focus to the environment by analysing and systematically describing the notion of environmental constitutionalism in generic terms. This discussion serves as the theoretically grounded pretext for the final systematic description of global environmental constitutionalism in Chapter 7.

5
The Fundamentals of Environmental Constitutionalism

I. Introduction

With reference to the role of science in the environmental constitutionalism paradigm, Jasanoff asks what it would take to bring about a radical change in the way people have constructed unsustainable preferences; a change in the rationalisation of these preferences; and a change in the underlying normative presumptions that steadfastly resist radical ideas of change that must ultimately be able to 'ratchet open the closed discourse of welfare economics and completely reframe the discussion, using new terms with new normative implications?'[1] Neither narratives constructed around a global natural threat such as climate change (despite evidence of its emergence and life-threatening implications), nor a political leitmotif such as sustainable development,[2] have been able to instil the type of radical new regulatory thinking, let alone actual reforms, that are capable of changing human behaviour vis-à-vis the environment.

Chapter 2 has argued that the Anthropocene is a radical new idea that has the potential to provide a new framework within which to resituate the discussion on the global socio-ecological crisis and within which to reframe the requisite global normative interventions to address this crisis. With reference to this book's central hypothesis, part of the normative interventions to cope with the Anthropocene should be constitutional, since constitutionalism is an apex juridical construct that aims to establish order where there is none, and to improve a legal order and its regulatory effects, while countering forms of domination (in this case human domination of the Earth system and its constituents, as it is perpetuated through states and socio-institutional legal systems).

There seems to be growing recognition of the need for constitutional institutions, structures and processes to embrace environmental care and to extend constitutionalism into the environmental domain and to invite environmentalism into the constitutionalism domain. While some have called for 'a wider range of

---

[1] S Jasanoff, 'A World of Experts: Science and Global Environmental Constitutionalism' (2013) 40 *Boston College Environmental Affairs Law Review* 439, 443.
[2] U Beyerlin and T Marauhn, *International Environmental Law* (Oxford, Hart Publishing, 2011) 76.

options [and] a new paradigm'[3] in this respect, others suggest that in addition to legitimacy, constitutional review, democracy, accountable government and respect for human rights, 'the constitutionalism of the future' must as a result of contemporary threats and challenges, embrace notions such as human solidarity for the preservation of the planet and its resources and equitable principles in the allocation of scarce resources within and among people and countries.[4]

Kobayashi illustratively frames the convergence between environmentalism and constitutionalism in terms of 'open world problems' which he identifies to include: global environmental degradation, unprecedented population growth, natural resource scarcity, armed conflict (often as a result of the foregoing) and the development of science and technology. He believes that:

> the contemporary nation-state has changed from previously being passive about a variety of domestic problems to taking a positive role in global problems ... one can say that the time has come for constitutional studies to take an open stance regarding this position.[5]

Because the Anthropocene and its global socio-ecological crisis is evidently present in all of these 'open world problems', this geological epoch will arguably demand nothing less than an apex constitutional approach to address the causes and consequences of, and ways to mediate, this crisis.

II. About this Chapter

This chapter seeks to understand the notional content of environmental constitutionalism and to show that environmental constitutionalism, as an apex juridical construct, has the potential to provide the type of regulatory options for environmental law and governance to mediate the human-environment interface in the Anthropocene. This argument is premised on the hypothesis that the Anthropocene's global socio-ecological crisis is such that, alongside traditional regulatory issues such as reduction of unemployment, state security and social welfare, this crisis arguably has become a 'reform question'[6] or requirement of the modern constitutional state, demanding regulatory intervention at the highest level.

With reference to constitutionalism's suitability as a form of law to mediate the human-environment interface in the Anthropocene, environmental

---

[3] BJ Gareau, 'Global Environmental Constitutionalism' (2013) 40 *Boston College Environmental Affairs Law Review* 403, 408.

[4] B Ramcharan, 'Constitutionalism in an Age of Globalisation and Global Threats' in M Frishman and S Muller (eds), *The Dynamics of Constitutionalism in the Age of Globalisation* (The Hague, Hague Academic Press, 2010) 18–19.

[5] N Kobayashi, 'Constitutional Studies and World Problems: A Study of Japan's Constitutional History as a Starting Point' in T Fleiner (ed), *Five Decades of Constitutionalism: Reality and Perspectives (1945–1995)* (Bale, Helbing and Lichtenhahn, 1999) 10–13, 15.

[6] P Häberle, 'The Constitutional State and its Reform Requirements' (2000) 13 *Ratio Juris* 77, 84.

constitutionalism has the potential to refocus attention on pertinent questions such as (and this is not a closed list): are there legal limits that could be placed on the freedom of the state and by implication its people to encroach on a vulnerable environment; to what extent could sovereignty, rights and freedoms be limited by ecological considerations; to what extent and how could people and nature have equal recognition and protection in a constitutional democracy; in the face of increased uncertainty and unpredictability of an erratic Earth system, which higher-order juridical measures are available to counter anthropogenic impacts; and under which conditions does irreversible Earth system harm lead to accountability and liability and how is it possible to nurture accountability and best impose liability? Questions like these go to the heart of the relationship between law, constitutionalism and the environment because they refocus attention on re-imagined and expanded ways through which the state and other stakeholders must fulfil their traditional constitutional duties to guarantee a safe, just and free society in the Anthropocene.

At the same time an opportunity arises to rethink the creation of new constitutional forms of responsibility; to contemplate the proper division of environmental governance tasks between regulatory entities and between the different geographical levels of governance; to question the traditional representative democratic order and the place of humans and of living non-human entities in this order, including the extent to which democratic governance processes could work to enhance environmental protection; to interrogate the future role of a constitution, as the basic juridical order (*Grundordnung*) of a polity, to create a reality where ecological concerns rank at least as paramount as traditional axiomatic constitutional goals such as peace and security; and ultimately to determine the extent to which constitutional features such as rights and the rule of law could be invoked to ensure better environmental care.[7]

This chapter pursues these diverse, but interrelated, discursive tracks with a view to fleshing out the meaning of environmental constitutionalism and to providing a comprehensive and systematic account of this unfledged concept that seems to be steadily gaining in analytical and normative importance. The analysis commences in Part 3 with a retrospective survey that sheds light on the gradual convergence between environmental protection, on the one hand, and constitutionalism on the other. The discussion in this part shows that while constitutional environmental protection measures are nothing new, and while scholars have been debating the environment-constitutionalism relationship for several years now, environmental constitutionalism, as a concept, has only been denoted as such since 2012. Part 3 therefore also elaborates the contemporary conceptual state of the art by tracing the meaning that various scholars have attributed to environmental constitutionalism over the years. This is followed by a conclusion in Part 4 that seeks to formulate a current definition of environmental constitutionalism that embraces

---

[7] R Steinberg, *Der ökologische Verfassungsstaat* (Frankfurt am Main, Suhrkamp, 1998) 20, 28.

its historical roots and that is representative of a contemporary understanding of the concept.

Moving from the foregoing conceptual account to a more concrete understanding of environmental constitutionalism as it manifests in domestic constitutional systems, Part 5 seeks domestic examples of environmental constitutionalism as measured against the generic constitutionalism framework distilled in Chapter 3 and briefly describes them in an effort to providing a more comprehensive conceptual map of environmental constitutionalism and its varied manifestations. With reference to the elements of constitutionalism described in Chapter 3, the discussion takes the view that environmental constitutionalism is much more than the issue of rights that many confine it to. Premised as it is on a constitution, environmental constitutionalism is a more holistically encompassing concept that also embraces constitutional issues related to the rule of law, separation of powers, the judiciary and its functions, constitutional supremacy and democracy.

III. A Historical-conceptual Account of the Convergence Between Environmentalism and Constitutionalism

Environmental protection has been part of the law and of domestic legal systems for many years. While there are several historical accounts, Benhör finds traces of juridical environmental protection going as far back as the Roman and early common law systems (for example, in the *actio negatoria* of property owners).[8] While it is difficult to determine exactly when the first environmental provision of any kind was incorporated into a constitution (one estimation is that this occurred in 1866 in the Romanian Constitution),[9] Gellers indicates that the first environmental right to have found its way into a constitution was in 1974 when Yugoslavia adopted an environmental right.[10] Significantly, this date corresponds with the United Nations Conference on the Human Environment held in Stockholm in 1972, which is widely considered to be the global impetus that sparked the exponential growth of international, regional and national environmental law regimes, including their rights-related aspects. The Stockholm Declaration states, among others:

> In the long and tortuous evolution of the human race on this planet a stage has been reached when, through the rapid acceleration of science and technology, man has

---

[8] H Benhör, '1. Arbeitsbereich: Umweltrecht in Deutschland im 19. Jahrhundert' in M Kloepfer (ed), *Umweltstaat als Zukunft: juristische, ökonomische und philosophische Aspekte* (Bonn, Economica Verlag, 1994) 108.

[9] Z Elkins, T Ginsburg and J Melton, 'Comparative Constitutions Project: Characteristics of National Constitutions' (2014, version 2.0) comparativeconstitutionsproject.org/ccp2015/download-data/.

[10] J Gellers, 'Explaining the Emergence of Constitutional Environmental Rights: A Global Quantitative Analysis' (2015) 6 *Journal of Human Rights and the Environment* 75.

acquired the power to transform his environment in countless ways and on an unprecedented scale. Both aspects of man's environment, the natural and the man-made, are essential to his well-being and to the enjoyment of basic human rights the right to life itself.[11]

While this mostly concerns the rights-related aspects associated with environmental constitutionalism, a more generic question arises: what is the historical path of convergence between environmental issues and constitutionalism more generally, and how did this convergence collectively contribute to the way we understand environmental constitutionalism today?

A. Should Trees have Standing?

Around the time that substantive constitutional environmental provisions such as environmental rights emerged in the early-1970s, one of the earliest and most influential scholarly reflections on the potential of constitutions to promote environmental care also came to light. Published in 1972, Stone's iconic *Should Trees have Standing?* proffered a radical possibility of rights, as constitutionalism's most representative and arguably most sacred elements, to extend their application to non-human living entities.[12] Stone believed that:

> It is not inevitable, nor is it wise, that natural objects should have no rights to seek redress in their own behalf. It is no answer to say that streams and forests cannot have standing because streams and forests cannot speak. Corporations cannot speak either; nor can states, estates, infants, incompetents, municipalities or universities. Lawyers speak for them, as they customarily do for the ordinary citizen with legal problems.[13]

This view was then, and remains to this day, a daring and paradigm-shifting proposition that has been met with widely divergent degrees of sincerity and embrace.[14] While constitutions that do afford non-human entities rights entitlements still remain absolutely minimal (see the discussion below), Stone's proposition managed to open the steadfast epistemological closures that have been working effortlessly, and decidedly successfully, to safeguarding the anthropocentric individualism of rights:

> [*Should Trees have Standing?*] has caused a great many of its readers to begin to reflect in an ecological manner, by imagining what it means to conceive of the interests of a natural object from a non-human perspective. It has established a space between the legal order that *is*, and the one that *might be*, a space within which our imaginations can reflect on

---

[11] Declaration of the United Nations Conference on the Human Environment 1972, Preamble, para 1. See also its Principle 1.
[12] C Stone, 'Should Trees have Standing? Towards Legal Rights for Natural Objects' (1972) 45 *California Law Review* 450.
[13] ibid 464.
[14] See for a critical general overview, A Grear (ed), *Should Trees have Standing? 40 Years on* (Cheltenham, Edward Elgar, 2012).

alternative approaches to conserving nature for the sake of nature—radical perhaps- but certainly a necessary contribution.[15]

Stone's provocative thesis also ignited and laid some of the foundations for the current debate on constitutional environmental care by aligning conventional constitutional discourse on rights with not-so-conventional ecological concerns that, until that point in the 1970s, remained well outside the parameters of what was considered acceptable or comfortable in law and constitutional conversations. Thus, Stone's thesis could be considered an important first indication of the critical relationship between an ecological ethic and constitutional law that provided the foundations for future scholars (if not for states themselves) propagating the incorporation of environmental protection into a state's set of constitutional obligations, functions and regulatory objectives.[16]

B. Jonas and the Imperative of Responsibility

Departing from radical constitutional ideas such as those offered by Stone, the bulk of environmental constitutionalism's conceptual roots could be traced to late-twentieth-century European and mostly German, scholarship. In 1988, Jonas presented a comprehensive treatise on the 'imperative of responsibility' (*Das Prinzip Verantwortung*).[17] It would become a classic text that has managed to influence later German thinking on the relationship between the environment and constitutionalism (notably Bosselmann below). Jonas postulated, among others, that humans (and per implication their social institutions such as the state) have an important future-oriented moral responsibility towards nature and future generations. This responsibility must (also) find expression in the broader legal, constitutional and political institutions of a state that create, order and continuously maintain the state and society.[18]

C. Kloepfer's Environmental State

In 1989, Kloepfer proposed that for it to be able to exit in any legitimate way, the modern state requires an environment that supports its existence as a fourth element in addition to the three classical elements states usually require to exist

---

[15] P Sands, 'On Being 40: A Celebration of "Should Trees have Standing?"' (2012) 3 *Journal of Human Rights and the Environment* 2, 3.

[16] eg, in 1975 James Buchanan, also an American scholar, by setting forth a social contract theory, made the case that environmental protection should become part and parcel of the constitutional state's objectives: J Buchanan, *The Collected Works of James Buchanan: Volume 7—The Limits of Liberty: Between Anarchy and Leviathan* (Indianapolis, Liberty Fund, 1999–2002).

[17] H Jonas, *Das Prinzip Verantwortung: Versuch einer Ethik für die technologische Zivilisation* (Frankfurt am Main, Suhrkamp, 1988).

[18] See for a concise, critical treatment of Jonas' thesis, P Taylor, '"The Imperative of Responsibility" in a Legal Context: Reconciling Responsibilities and Rights' in R Engel, L Westra and K Bosselmann (eds), *Democracy, Ecological Integrity and International Law* (Newcastle upon Tyne, Cambridge Scholars Publishing, 2010) 198–225.

(ie a *demos*, state authority and a territory).[19] This would be in response to the deepening socio-ecological crisis, as a result of people becoming increasingly aware of the socio-ecological crisis, and as a result of people demanding in increasingly urgent terms that the state does something about this crisis. Upon incorporation of the environment as its fourth existential element, the state becomes an environmental state (*Umweltstaat*) which is a state with a legal and political system that renders environmental integrity its primary objective, standard and the central orientation of all its decisions and acts.[20] The environmental state is also a type of state in which protection of the natural foundations of life becomes a central task of the entire polity; environmental protection is not an ancillary or incidental consideration but a foundational one in which everyone (including specifically future generations and nature itself) has an interest. Because of its monopoly on power and the extensive regulatory machinery available to it, Kloepfer considers that it is only the state that is able to create the necessary constitutional, statutory and institutional arrangements to protect the natural foundations of life: the state is the deciding caretaker for the future (*Der Staat ist der enthscheidende Patron für die Zukunft*).[21]

Kloepfer's 1994 *Umweltstaat als Zukunft* (Environmental State as the Future),[22] presented a collection of ideas around the central theme of an environmental state where ecological concerns are both an objective and primary regulatory standard of all decision-making and governance processes in the modern constitutional state. Kloepfer believes that the environmental state, as a concept and practical matter of governance, raises several pertinent constitutional questions including: to what extent should environmental protection be entrenched in a state's constitution; how could state-driven environmental protection be improved through the constitutionalisation of environmental protection; to what extent is there a danger that traditional constitutionally protected individual freedoms such as the right to life could be negatively impacted through the state's newly-acquired environmental objectives; relatedly, how much power should the environmental state have without becoming an ecological dictatorship (*Öko-Diktatur*);[23] and which existing regulatory instruments could the state use to achieve its constitutional objectives of environmental protection, or should it design and adopt new instruments?[24]

Kloepfer also indicates that the primary objectives of the constitutional state have changed over time in response to specific types of problems it had to

---

[19] M Kloepfer, 'Auf dem Weg zum Umweltstaat' in M Kloepfer (ed), *Umweltstaat: Ladenburger Diskurs* (Berlin, Springer Verlag, 1989) 39–78.
[20] ibid 42.
[21] ibid 45.
[22] M Kloepfer (ed), *Umweltstaat als Zukunft: juristische, ökonomische und philosophische Aspekte* (Bonn, Economica Verlag, 1994).
[23] While he addresses this issue in his collected volume, Kloepfer also reflected on it more extensively in M Kloepfer, 'Droht der autoritäre ökologische Staat?' in H Baumeister (ed), *Wege zum ökologischen Rechtsstaat: Umweltschutz ohne Öko-Diktatur* (Taunusstein, Eberhard Blottner Verlag, 1994) 42–50.
[24] M Kloepfer, 'Eröffnungsvortrag: Das Ladenburger Kolleg Umweltstaat: Resultate und Perspektiven' in Kloepfer (ed), *Umweltstaat als Zukunft: juristische, ökonomische und philosophische Aspekte* (n 22) 4.

mediate. For example, the end of the Second World War led to the creation of very protective sovereign states and institutions with a noticeable monopoly on power. Later, as a response to globalisation, states surrendered some of their monopoly on power to international organisations such as the World Trade Organization to help it govern beyond its borders. Later still, when the state was confronted by myriad socio-economic tensions, it changed its constitutional make-up to respond to these challenges through the construction of the social-welfare state.[25] With the increased realisation that the environment is centrally woven into these more 'traditional' security, globalisation and social welfare concerns, environmental protection has arguably become the most recent, if still not the dominant, objective of governance, where a destroyed environment destroys the constitutional consensus of a polity, and a destroyed constitutional consensus in turn destroys the constitutional state. The future state must therefore also become and, is becoming, an environmental state.[26]

Kloepfer believes that the environmental state will have as its main objective to prioritise environmental protection, even if it entails limiting individual freedoms. As well, an ideal vision of the perfect constitutional state is not a vision where environmental protection is only one of many aspects, objectives and functions. Environmental protection becomes the most prominent foundation and objective of the entire state, its politics and of society;[27] or the *Grundnorm* of the *politik*. In such a construction, environmental protection thus becomes the primary objective of all organs of state and of society, and where the obligation to protect the environment is not respected, the legitimacy of the state is equally dislodged and affected.[28] To this end, and in trite terms, the ability of the state and of society to protect the environment is arguably as important for the legitimacy of the state, its laws, constitution and existence, as democracy is.

D. Bosselmann's Ecological *Rechtsstaat*

In his 1992 book *Im Namen der Natur* ('In the Name of Nature'), Bosselmann fervently makes a case for the creation of an ecological *Rechtsstaat* as a countermeasure to the anthropocentrism that pervades our legal, economic, social, political and ethical systems.[29] He argues that the practice of environmental damage is much older than that of environmental protection, and even where environmental protection was incorporated into the earliest of legal systems, it was done for the

---

[25] ibid 8–9.
[26] ibid 37.
[27] Kloepfer (n 22) 105.
[28] D Murswiek, '2. Arbeitsgruppe: Staatliche Umweltverantwortung' in Kloepfer (n 22) 111.
[29] K Bosselmann, *Im Namen der Natur: Der Weg zum ökologischen Rechtsstaat* (Bern, Scherz, 1992). See also the later publications that focused in greater detail on ecological fundamental rights and ecological justice: K Bosselmann, *Ökologische Grundrechte: Zum Verhältnis zwischen individueller Freiheit und Natur* (Baden-Baden, Nomos Verlagsgesellschaft, 1998); K Bosselmann and M Schröter, *Umwelt und Gerechtigkeit: Leitlinien einer ökologischen Gesetzgebung* (Baden-Baden, Nomos Verlagsgesellschaft, 2001).

exclusive benefit of people to promote their well-being and/or to safeguard and multiply their property.[30] This mostly remains the situation today. As a result, the design and orientation of laws, the state and state constitutions have always been geared towards promoting unlimited human development with little respect for ecological limits. The constitutional significance of this fact is that state and legal traditions indicate the closely intertwined relationship between environmental destruction and the extent to which the state has been willing and able to secure and expand the neo-liberal exploitation of Earth and its resources through the best-known regulatory instruments at its disposal: the constitution and broader legal-political system that is embedded in and justified and legitimised by that constitutional foundation. He argues that from the earliest feudal systems through to the present territorial state model, constitutions and the type of state organisation and societal order they sought to imbue have never been neutral; they have been used as institutional regulatory instruments to promote individualism and materialism with predictably dire ecological consequences.[31] Examples are property rights and classic individualistic political rights such as the rights to life, personal freedom, and equality that have historically been the backbone of many constitutions and that have been used (and continue to be used) as a legitimising basis for unlimited human development.[32]

It is in this context that Bosselmann makes the case for a wholesale ecologically reoriented constitutional, political, ethical, legal and state system alongside the principle of the ecological *Rechtsstaat*. Reflecting on the importance of constitutionalism for environmental care, he seems to argue that a constitutional reordering is first and foremost necessary, acting as an inevitable precursor as it were, to provide the foundation upon which politics, ethics, laws and governance could be reformed; the type and magnitude of social reordering that he envisages is only possible if it departs from and is guided by constitutional reforms.

His conception of the ecological *Rechtsstaat* builds on other German ideas such as the environmental state (*Umweltstaat*) where the state entrenches environmental protection as a central goal in its constitution; and the more esoteric nature state (*Naturstaat*) where the constitutional text is not of overriding importance, but rather the general conviction it engenders, i.e., that society and the state must follow a non-anthropocentric ethic.[33] As a metamorphosis or continuation of these, Bosselmann's ecological *Rechtsstaat* is one where: human rights and the rights of nature are equal; any assessment of potential conflicts between human and ecological interests must consider that humans and nature are a dialectical unit in terms of which the one is part of the other; the inherent worth of nature demands that ecological interests be represented by people in all decision-making in the same way as human interests would be; the inherent value of nature depends on

---

[30] Bosselmann, *Im Namen der Natur* (n 29) 97–107.
[31] ibid 115.
[32] See, generally, D Grinlinton and P Taylor (eds), *Property Rights and Sustainability: The Evolution of Property Rights to meet Ecological Challenges* (Boston, Martinus Nijhoff, 2011).
[33] Bosselmann, *Im Namen der Natur* (n 29) 190.

knowledge about the interaction between ecosystems and their relationship with other ecosystems, while legal norms must fortify such interaction; decisions about the permissibility of development must be based on neutral science and knowledge as opposed to interest-dependent knowledge that is subject to the influence of particular lobby groups; and lack of scientific knowledge should not negatively impact nature and where there is such a risk, this risk must be fully justifiable when measured against the inherent value of nature.[34] In a later book, Bosselmann adds that the ecological *Rechtsstaat* is one that guarantees an ecological balance which requires that the constitution and the organisation of the state are modernised to recognise the inherent worth of nature and where individual freedoms could even be limited as a result of the state's ecological responsibilities.[35]

Bosselmann's ecological *Rechtsstaat* does not only require gradual reforms, but also more immediate and fundamental transformations that could change the entire polity from one that is based on an industrial society to one that becomes a sustainable society (*nachhaltige Gesellschaft*).[36] While the law, and per implication the constitution, are unable on their own to make the change to an ecological *Rechtsstaat* happen, as it were, constitutions will play a decidedly important role in creating the necessary apex ecological juridical framework within which the ecological transformation of a polity is possible.[37] Bosselmann concludes that no constitutional order is static and unchangeable, despite the supreme status of the constitution which renders it difficult to amend, and foresees that there will be an increased shift within constitutional orders towards greater ecological care as societies become more aware of the global socio-ecological crisis.

E. Verschuuren's Environmental Constitutional Democracy

Verschuuren, a Dutch environmental law scholar, sought to describe the meaning of environmental law's constitutional foundation in 1994.[38] He proposed the

---

[34] ibid 373–74. Bosselmann's 'pure' ecocentric approach has been supported by fellow German environmental lawyers such as Kloepfer, who believe that from a constitutional law perspective, any radical ecocentric constitutional construction that aims to give rights to nature which would take precedence above all other rights in the event of conflict, even if it is difficult to imagine such a construction juridically, could increasingly be possible and even desirable in the modern constitutional state: Kloepfer, 'Eröffnungsvortrag: Das Ladenburger Kolleg Umweltstaat' (n 24) 12. Yet, there are alternative views that propose a more limited form of 'responsible anthropocentrism' (*verantworteter Anthropozentrismus*) where even though nature does not have rights, humans have a greater responsibility of care and no right themselves to cause environmental damage: CF Gethmann, '3. Arbeitsgruppe: Freiheit und Rechtsstaatlichkeit im Umweltstaat' in Kloepfer (n 22) 114.
[35] Bosselmann, *Ökologische Grundrechte* (n 29) 20–21.
[36] K Bosselmann, 'Der Ökologische Rechtsstaat: Versuch einer Standortbestimmung' in H Baumeister (ed), *Wege zum ökologischen Rechtsstaat: Umweltschutz ohne Öko-Diktatur* (Taunusstein, Eberhard Blottner Verlag, 1994) 53–54.
[37] ibid 57.
[38] J Verschuuren, 'The Constitutional Right to Environmental Protection' (1994) 12(2) *Current Legal Theory* 23.

concept 'environmental constitutional democracy' which in his words is a form of the environmental *Rechtsstaat*; an imaginary state where environmental care is one of the foundations of the modern constitutional state. In this environmental *Rechtsstaat*, protection of substantive fundamental environmental rights is the first and most important task of the state; procedural constitutional and statutory rules play an important role in achieving this primary objective to the extent that they satisfy the formal aspects of the rule of law (including participation, representation and democracy); and constitutional environmental provisions, together with environmental statutes, must be ecocentrically oriented to the extent that they recognise the intrinsic value of nature and seek to protect nature's inherent integrity.[39]

F. Steinberg and the Ecological Constitutional State

Interestingly, all the foregoing scholars preferred to describe the ecological state in *Rechtsstaat* terms, which they seem to equate with the more broadly constructed constitutional state (*Verfassungsstaat*). It was, however, shown in Chapter 3 that strictly speaking, the *Rechtsstaat* is closer to the narrower concept of the rule of law, which is only an element of the terminologically more encompassing constitutional state.[40] Thus, if one were to be fully truthful to terminological accuracy, Steinberg's 1988 publication on the ecological constitutional state (*ökologische Verfassungsstaat*) is the more preferred conceptually encompassing term.[41]

Semantics aside, similar to Kloepfer, Steinberg proposes a useful historical development trajectory of the state-environment-constitutionalism relationship, ie the 'five sequential stages of the constitutional state' (*fünf Stufen des Verfassungsstaates*). In generalised terms, he believes that historically the most elementary and first stage of the constitutional state was designed around its principal aim to guarantee security, safety and peace. This stage was followed by the inclusion of rule of law-based measures in constitutions (both formal such as judicial review, and substantive such as freedom and equality rights), to limit government authority and to ensure accountability. The third stage was the influence of democracy; and fourthly, the caring, guiding, redistributing and serving social-welfare state (of which Germany is a prime example). Most recently, perceptions of the global socio-ecological crisis and acknowledgement of the need to maintain ecological integrity in tandem with, and as a prerequisite for, preserving the other four elements of the constitutional state, are giving rise to the fifth stage of the constitutional state which provides the means to secure socio-ecological security. Expressing its possible simultaneous anthropocentric and ecocentric duality, the

---

[39] ibid 33–35.
[40] See for an extensive discussion in addition to what has been stated in Ch 3, F Venter, 'South Africa: A Diceyan *Rechtsstaat*?' (2012) 57 *McGill Law Journal* 722.
[41] Steinberg, *Der ökologische Verfassungsstaat* (n 7).

ecological state, says Steinberg, aims to protect natural living conditions in their own right as an end in itself,[42] and as a means to an end to the extent that the constitutional state and the social order it seeks to maintain is dependent on a mutually supportive Earth system.[43]

G. Green Constitutionalism

One of the most recent related terms to emerge from the state-constitutionalism-environment debate is Ekeli's 'green constitutionalism'. In a 2007 work, Ekeli lays out his vision of a new constitutional provision (or the 'posterity provision') that has substantive and procedural elements and that is specifically geared towards protecting the vital needs of future generations.[44] His is the first among the approaches surveyed above that extensively focuses on the ways in which constitutionalism could be used as an apex regulatory intervention to protect the interests of future generations as well. In terms of green constitutionalism's posterity provision:

> [T]he state has a duty to avoid and prevent decisions and activities that can cause avoidable damage to critical natural resources that are necessary to provide for the basic physiological (biological and physical) needs of future generations ... [and] courts should have the competence to appoint guardians for future people, and these guardians should be empowered to initiate legal proceedings on behalf of posterity on the basis of the posterity provision.[45]

Reflecting the procedural and substantive elements of the rule of law as described in Chapter 3, the constitutional posterity provision must have as its two basic elements substantive and procedural guarantees, where the substantive provisions set out the larger strategic objective, and the procedural provisions the way in which to achieve the substantive objective. Typically the substantive aspects would guarantee a right to a healthy environment for present and future generations that is vague and indeterminate, while the procedural aspects relate to more detailed and concrete measures for public participation, access to justice and access to environmental information, among others, to enable the realisation of the vague substantive objectives. By enforcing constitutional law, and because they are mandated

---

[42] For Bosselmann, likewise, this means that: 'Natur ist nicht mehr das Andere, die bloße Lebensgrundlage des Menschen. Sie wird zur Natur aus eigenem Recht, zur eigenen Bestimmungsgröße, an der die Bedürfnisse des Menschen auszurichten haben': Bosselmann, *Im Namen der Natur* (n 29) 14.

[43] Steinberg (n 7) 45. Bosselmann agrees that the ecological constitutional state (although he uses the more limited term *Rechtsstaat*) is a natural extension of the social-welfare state in terms of which the state's governance duties do not exclusively revolve around its obligation to regulate the social interaction between people, but also the responsibility of people towards nature: 'the social dimension has been extended to the ecological dimension'. Bosselmann, *Im Namen der Natur* (n 29) 189.

[44] K Ekeli, 'Green Constitutionalism: The Constitutional Protection of Future Generations' (2007) 20 *Ratio Juris* 378.

[45] ibid 379.

by the constitution to do so, courts are deemed to be the apex guardians of the posterity provision and, hence, of the interests of future generations.

Focusing more extensively on the notional content, meaning and advantages of green constitutionalism, Barry argues that:

> constitutional provisions are among the most basic political structures of any society, the greening of the constitution is a potentially powerful mechanism for any transition away from unsustainability. Hence any change in the constitution in a green or sustainable direction could signal a profound shift in the political order.[46]

To this end a green approach to constitutionalism, as it were, offers a way of adjoining a 'green commitment' to substantive and procedural human rights protection and socio-economic regulation, which could work collectively to increase the democratic credentials of environmental decision-making procedures, facilitate environmental justice and foster an ethic of ecological stewardship.[47] Barry summarises the rationale behind and the advantages of entrenching ecological care constitutionally as including: it sets the socio-political-juridico scene for and therefore mandates, justifies and enables far-reaching strategic institutional transformation at the highest political level; it is universally binding within the borders of a state and applies to everyone in equal measure; it secures the regulation of economic actors that impact on the environment, such as corporations and it stands critically towards notions that entrench corporate economic powers, such as property rights; it could work in a bottom-up and compensatory way in that it contributes to global environmental justice through the diffusion of domestic norms in a transnational sense, as well as through the creation of an international legal infrastructure which drives the global environmental justice agenda; and because it alters and redistributes political and economic power within and between societies, issues of environmental and distributional injustice and inequalities could more easily be addressed at the constitutional level.[48]

H. Boyd's Environmental Rights Revolution

Jumping almost five years into the future from the time of Ekeli and Barry's green constitutionalism, Boyd's seminal work, *The Environmental Rights Revolution*,[49] arguably provided the critical foundation in 2012 for the contemporary conceptual development of environmental constitutionalism. The book is a global

---

[46] J Barry, 'Towards a Green Republicanism: Constitutionalism, Political Economy, and the Green State' (2008) 17(2) *The Good Society* 3, 4. See also, A Gosseries, 'Constitutions and Future Generations' (2008) 17(2) *The Good Society* 32.
[47] Barry, 'Towards a Green Republicanism' (n 46) 4–5.
[48] ibid 5.
[49] DR Boyd, *The Environmental Rights Revolution: A Global Study of Constitutions, Human Rights, and the Environment* (Vancouver, UBC Press, 2012); and more recently, DR Boyd, 'Constitutions, Human Rights, and the Environment: National Approaches' in A Grear and LJ Kotzé (eds), *Research Handbook on Human Rights and the Environment* (Cheltenham, Edward Elgar, 2015) 170–99.

comparative study of constitutions, human rights and the environment and was the first comprehensive mapping of environmental human rights in constitutions the world over, including an innovative appraisal and description of the impact of these rights, their successes and failures. While it does not offer a conceptual treatment of environmental constitutionalism as such, the book does reflect on the advantages of a constitutional approach to environmental protection (with a specific focus on rights) which approach it deems to include: constitutions as the supreme law direct and constrain government powers; protect individual rights; allocate and regulate power between different authorities; implement the rule of law; and express the 'deepest, most cherished values of a society', which collectively work to provide a range of environmental benefits, including stronger laws, enhanced public participation and improved environmental performance.[50]

Following an almost exhaustive empirical analysis, Boyd concludes that there is a consistent correlation between constitutional environmental protection and superior environmental performance which might explain why 150 national constitutions today include environmental protection provisions such as a government duty to protect the environment; an individual right to a healthy environment; an individual duty to protect the environment; and procedural environmental rights.[51] While this 'rights revolution' is not a panacea for the global socio-ecological crisis, it does suggest that '[c]onstitutional protection for the environment ... has the legal and symbolic power to both change the rules of the game and alter our vision of the world, bringing us closer to the elusive goal of achieving sustainability'.[52] In other words, there is sufficient empirical evidence that environmental constitutionalism improves environmental governance outcomes.

I. 'Thin' and 'Thick' Environmental Constitutionalism

In that same year my own tentative efforts to understand global environmental constitutionalism required me to look for the essence of environmental constitutionalism from a conceptual point of view.[53] It seemed appropriate at the time to distinguish environmental constitutionalism's evaluative, formal or descriptive functions (or its 'thin' characteristics), from its (arguably) more important functional, prescriptive or substantively constitutional functions (otherwise called its 'thick' characteristics). Whereas thin environmental constitutionalism relates to constitutional law establishing, defining and organising the main organs of government, its constitution and its powers, thick environmental constitutionalism relates to constitutions being substantively constitutional, ie superior law that is justiciable, entrenched and that expresses a common ideology such

---

[50] Boyd, *Environmental Rights Revolution* (n 49) 4–5.
[51] ibid 279.
[52] ibid 291.
[53] LJ Kotzé, 'Arguing Global Environmental Constitutionalism' (2012) 1 *Transnational Environmental Law* 199.

as through rights. I concluded that constitutionalism is important for environmental protection because it provides the means to defend environment-related rights and interests, to restrict authority and private encroachment on these rights and interests, and to compel the state and non-state actors to act affirmatively to ensure better environmental protection.[54]

A more recent account suggested that environmental constitutionalism is mostly employed to denote a regulatory transformation, specifically as a mode of environmental governance that seeks to enhance environmental protection by elevating it to the constitutional level.[55] It probably originated from the failures of 'ordinary' (mostly pollution- and conservation-oriented) statutory laws to provide the requisite level of environmental protection initially envisaged by the fathers of environmental law. If history is anything to go by, regulators and legislators, in uncertain times such as the present, seem to seek refuge in the familiar, the constant and the trusted. Constitutions have been an influential component of political history, thus providing a familiar language and a logical 'go to' solution for environmental regulators in times of ecological upheaval and regulatory uncertainty. I thought that environmental regulators' turn towards constitutionalism was therefore not surprising.

J. Environmental Constitutionalism as a Discursive-contemplative Framework

In 2014, Fisher delivered a keynote address at the Resource Management Law Association of New Zealand, wherein she shed some light on the meaning and nature of environmental constitutionalism.[56] Her point of departure was that 'environmental protection is a normative choice',[57] which, while it is influenced by politics, science and societal perceptions, among others, will then naturally also be facilitated through law. With reference to the New Zealand Resource Management Act of 1991, she suggests that environmental statutes should not merely be seen as statutory tools, but rather as 'constitutions' that 'set in motion ongoing debates about the role of law in contributing to environmental protection'.[58] Seeing environmental statutes through a constitutional lens transforms them into continuously evolving and contested juridical frameworks that allow a more

---

[54] ibid 211.
[55] LJ Kotzé, 'Human Rights and the Environment through an Environmental Constitutionalism Lens' in Grear and Kotzé (eds), *Research Handbook on Human Rights and the Environment* (n 49) 145–69; LJ Kotzé, 'The Conceptual Contours of Environmental Constitutionalism' (2015) 21 *Widener Law Review* 187; LJ Kotzé, 'The Anthropocene's Global Environmental Constitutional Moment' (2015) *Yearbook of International Environmental Law* (forthcoming).
[56] E Fisher, 'Towards Environmental Constitutionalism: A Different Vision of the Resource Management Act 1991?' (Resource Management Law Association of New Zealand Inc, 2014) www.rmla.org.nz/upload/files/annual_conference/2014_papers/lfisher.pdf.
[57] ibid 2.
[58] ibid 1.

fruitful engagement with the regulatory complexity of environmental problems, while opening up the possibility of taking the law seriously, as it were. As well, because of the nature of environmental problems (for example, they are uncertain, wide-spread, transboundary and complex), environmental statutes should be considered constitutional to the extent that they could provide a more foundational engagement with environmental *problematique* through constitutionalism's ability to provide a 'power map' that enables regulatory institutions, allocates powers, and frames legal discourses.[59] Fisher says:

> Talking in terms of constitutions is often an excuse to talk in high minded normative terms about rights and abstract principle, but I use the term to reflect the functional role that environmental legislation is playing ... where the constitution is 'constitutive' of the legal and political structure. In being so it is expected that that structure is stable, canonical (written), superior, justiciable, entrenched, and reflects the 'common ideology' of that culture.[60]

Clearly, environmental constitutionalism to Fisher is not exclusively restricted to issues such as rights or democracy. Environmental constitutionalism is also valuable for its formalistic or structural functions (see below) in relation to the role of law in constituting and limiting environmental decision-making, as well as for its practical function to enable an entire panoply of state machinery, including laws and institutions, to achieve better environmental outcomes alongside the dictates of constitutionalism such as those encapsulated by the rule of law.

K. Global Comparative Environmental Constitutionalism

In further pursuit of Boyd's comparative analysis of constitutional environmental rights, May and Daly brought together their own long-standing expertise on comparative environmental constitutionalism in a recent publication entitled, *Global Environmental Constitutionalism*.[61] This is one of the most comprehensive accounts of environmental constitutionalism to date. While it does not aim to offer a conceptual analysis of environmental constitutionalism, it provides a comprehensive inquiry into current trends in environmental constitutionalism in many of the world's constitutions by predominantly focusing (like Boyd) on their environmental human rights provisions and judicial interpretative trends. Thus, their rights-based conception of environmental constitutionalism includes as its basic elements: substantive individual environmental rights to a quality environment (such as section 24 of the South African Constitution); other substantive environmental rights (such as South Africa's right of access to water in section 27 of the Constitution); mostly state, but often also individual, environmental duties

---

[59] ibid 5–6.
[60] ibid 6.
[61] J May and E Daly, *Global Environmental Constitutionalism*, Kindle edn (New York, Cambridge University Press, 2015).

and responsibilities (such as article 16 of the Constitution of Guinea 2010);[62] and procedural constitutional environmental rights (such as the rights of access to information and administrative justice in South Africa's Constitution).[63]

Implicitly acknowledging the juridical superiority and perceived regulatory advantages of constitutionalism, their thesis is that the environment has become a proper subject that warrants protection by constitutions all over the world. This phenomenon is called environmental constitutionalism, which 'represents the confluence of constitutional law, international law, human rights, and environmental law'.[64] Importantly, May and Daly recognise that environmental constitutionalism is only one among various potential juridical approaches to achieve better environmental protection; it is not and can never be the complete answer to all regulatory deficits and to all efforts aimed at augmenting environmental care.

That said, '[e]nvironmental constitutionalism offers one way to engage environmental challenges that fall beyond the grasp of other legal constructs … [it] offers a way forward when other legal mechanisms fall short'.[65] In addition to reaching into virtually all aspects of life such as health, peace, food and culture and covering human and non-human phenomena; another one of its characteristics is that environmental constitutionalism is highly contemporary and non-static and that it often changes rapidly and extensively. They cite the adoption of environmental human rights during the past 10 years in countries such as Armenia, Bolivia, Dominican Republic, Ecuador, Egypt, France, Guinea, Hungary, Jamaica, Kenya, Madagascar and South Sudan as examples.[66] While their approach to environmental constitutionalism is distinctly comparative, the authors do admit that 'global' environmental constitutionalism includes an element of transnational law-making to the extent that domestic constitutional orders are influenced by regional and international instruments, and vice versa.[67] In summary, May and Daly suggest that:

> [E]nvironmental constitutionalism suggests a *new way of thinking* about the relationship among individuals, sovereign governments, and the environment with the overall goal of prompting governments to more aggressively protect environmental resources for the benefit both of humans, present and future, and of the environment itself.[68]

Environmental constitutionalism provides the premise for a holistic regulatory approach; ideally it speaks for everyone and represents everyone; it has the power of politics behind it as well as claims of justice supporting it; it 'occupies all the spaces in which law exists'; and because it is an apex juridical construct, it usefully 'speaks with all the authority and legitimacy of the sovereign'.[69]

---

[62] Art 16 provides: 'Every person has the right to a healthy and lasting environment and the duty to defend it. The State sees to the protection of the environment'.
[63] See ss 32 and 33 respectively.
[64] May and Daly, *Global Environmental Constitutionalism* (n 61) 3/11268.
[65] ibid 535/11268.
[66] ibid 375/11268.
[67] ibid 790/11268.
[68] ibid 1139/11268.
[69] ibid 1154/11268.

L. Structural and Fundamental Environmental Constitutionalism

More recently in 2015, Hudson shared his understanding of environmental constitutionalism as reflecting ways of 'addressing the question of how constitutional provisions impact environmental quality and the environmental rights of citizens'.[70] This mostly occurs through fundamental textual provisions aimed at protecting substantive and/or procedural citizen rights to a quality environment. In a generic sense, fundamental environmental constitutional provisions (especially as expressed through rights) tend to set some future-oriented generic goal in broad, idealistic and aspirational terms. For example, the South African environmental right states: 'Everyone has the right to an environment that is not harmful to their health or well-being; and to have the environment protected, for the benefit of present and future generations'.[71] The potential functions of such fundamental environmental constitutional provisions include to: alter the operational rules of government; prohibit specified government action; create and reaffirm rights; and express aspirational goals. Hudson argues that these provisions typically target intra- and intergovernmental relations; relations between a government and citizens; relations between citizens; and one might add, relations between citizens and the environment; as well as relations between the present generation and future generations (to follow Ekeli's constitutional posterity provision above). In addition to being fundamental, environmental constitutionalism is also structural to the extent that it allocates environmental regulatory authority across levels of government within a specific jurisdiction.

Hudson's approach to environmental constitutionalism is clearly similar, albeit differently termed, to the thick-thin approach to environmental constitutionalism described above. Like the thin-thick approach, his fundamental-structural approach to environmental constitutionalism usefully aligns with the dualist conception of the rule of law as including formal and substantive aspects (see Chapter 3). Whereas the thick or fundamental elements of environmental constitutionalism such as rights are usually put on a pedestal as environmental constitutionalism's most prominent features, Hudson argues that structural (thin) environmental constitutionalism is as important as fundamental (thick) constitutionalism is:

> Ultimately, constitutional design related to regulatory authority within national and subnational jurisdictions can be a structural form of environmental constitutionalism that may have as much, or more, impact than the protection of fundamental environmental rights within [a] constitutional text.[72]

This is because structural environmental constitutionalism concerns the proper allocation of governance authority to specific governance levels and

---

[70] B Hudson, 'Structural Environmental Constitutionalism' (2015) 21 *Widener Law Review* 201.
[71] Constitution of the Republic of South Africa, s 24.
[72] Hudson, 'Structural Environmental Constitutionalism' (n 70) 202.

functionaries with a view to better achieving the objectives of fundamental environmental constitutionalism. He believes where the structural environmental constitutional design is not optimal in jurisdictions (a strong possibility especially in multi-levelled federal set-ups such as the United States), then there is significant potential for regulatory deficits and anomalies to occur in what is often a fragmented, inadequate, duplicative and inefficient governance architecture.

In addition to being a political matter, environmental governance authority is also a constitutional matter, and it requires constitutional intervention to create governance institutions that promote environmental care. The extent to which constitutions are able to divide, properly allocate, and regulate the powers that relate to environmental governance, directly correlates with the quality of environmental governance to the extent that these structural environmental constitutional arrangements must support the achievement of the fundamental objectives of environmental constitutionalism. Herein also lies structural environmental constitutionalism's potentially greater impact when compared to fundamental environmental constitutionalism: it concerns practical matters of governance that are more easily addressed than trying to enforce broadly phrased and idealistic rights; it could facilitate political will that induces action with respect to certain environmental issues; and it provides much clearer and tangible mandates and objectives for environmental governance when compared to the more esoteric ideals of fundamental environmental constitutionalism.[73]

IV. A Contemporary Description of Environmental Constitutionalism

The foregoing survey suggests that constitutional environmental protection is not a new phenomenon. Since the 1970s there has been an increased scholarly appreciation of the value of constitutionalism for the purpose of environmental protection where the constitutional order of a polity is seen as an important strategy to transform unsustainable societies to sustainable ones. Environmental protection has been part of constitutional regimes for more than a hundred years, and of the environmental and constitutional law discourse for at least 40 years, where environmental protection has been connected with constitutional ideas such as rights, democracy, the rule of law and the constitutional state, among others.

While somewhat generalised, the scholars surveyed above have vested their strategies for environmental protection and sustainability in the constitutionalism paradigm because they believe: constitutional transformations have proven advantageous for improving regulatory outcomes in other domains such as armed conflict and human rights protection and that it could do the same for the

---

[73] ibid 213–16.

environment; because the state is the main actor in upholding constitutionalism and because it is empowered by a constitution to do so, the state must play the predominant role in safeguarding the natural foundations of life; and politics, laws and societal behaviour generally speaking are not geared towards ecological sustainability as a governance objective and because a constitution has the power to change a polity, its legal system and politics, there is a reasonable prospect that constitutionalism would be able to do the same in the environmental domain. Other themes that emerge include: the present socio-ecological crisis is so severe that it warrants nothing less than constitutional intervention as an apex form of law; and because the envisaged changes to law, politics and societal behaviour might be so drastic in order to ensure more sustainable outcomes for society, constitutionalism is an alternative juridical modicum that is legitimately able to initiate, carry and complete these paradigm-shifting regulatory, political and societal changes.

The environmental constitutionalism narrative is clearly also forward-looking and sets an idealistic vision of a potentially more contemporary, notionally enlarged, ecologically-oriented constitutional state that has progressed beyond the social-welfare state and that, through its constitution, has to redefine its traditional role in the larger scheme of governance matters; re-envisage its functions and the role and rule of the law in achieving better environmental care; and rethink the role of traditional constitutional constructs such as rights, democracy and the individualistic nature of liberal constitutionalism for environmental protection. Such a progression would allow the state to fulfil its ecological obligations which have become the most recent and pressing challenge for the state. Arguably, consequent upon the inclusion of ecological concerns as the fifth and latest stage in the historical constitutional development continuum described above, the hierarchal order of these stages has been turned upside down where ecological concerns, considering their centrality to life, now form the basic element upon which the other four stages of the constitutional state must rest.

In sum, the following conclusions can be drawn:

— Environmental constitutionalism is part of the larger constitutional paradigm, both as an evolving scholarly discipline and analytical perspective and as a socio-political and legal transformation project in a normative sense.
— Environmental constitutionalism recognises the importance of environmental care and expresses this juridically at the highest possible level that law is able to offer, thus working to bring the environment under the protective umbrella of a constitution and enabling the application of all constitutionalism's virtues to the environment.
— In doing so, environmental constitutionalism renders the issue of environmental care a matter of justice, especially to the extent that it couches environmental care in intra- and inter-species and inter-and intra-generational terms of equity, dignity and integrity.
— Environmental constitutionalism embodies a transformative approach that relies on formal constitutions to provide for the architecture of environmental

governance, whereupon it then acts to improve environmental protection through various substantive constitutional features such as fundamental rights and duties, the rule of law and enduring aspirational values such as ecological sustainability.
— Environmental constitutionalism redefines the relationship between the environment, the state and the people in a state and provides a legitimisation and justificatory foundation for environmental care in a society and its law and governance system.
— In doing so, environmental constitutionalism sets environmental care as a condition for all other functions of the state, the law and of society, and renders environmental care a primary obligation and function of the state, thereby broadening the scope of traditional state governance functions to deliberately include environmental concerns.
— Environmental constitutionalism opens up the trite arsenal of constitutional remedies to environmental care.
— Environmental constitutionalism engenders a sense of government and societal responsibility for the environment in the same way as it does responsibilities towards respect for life and human dignity, and it introduces the possibility to think about environmental care in the same way as one would think of the need to respect dignity and life, among others.
— Relatedly, environmental constitutionalism helps to achieve a societal paradigm shift that is more deliberately oriented towards the environment in terms of cultural, political, social and legal experiences and practices, while deeply entrenching within the political, social and juridical spheres environmental care as a common ideology and moral/ethical obligation.
— There is a sense of urgency to the environmental constitutionalism project that requires the world to embark on constitutionalising environmental care and to expand, deepen and refine existing processes of environmental constitutionalism.

V. Environmental Constitutionalism in Domestic Constitutional Orders

It would be difficult to provide a comprehensive and fully representative account of all aspects of environmental constitutionalism as they manifest in all domestic constitutional systems the world over in the limited scope of this book. Even though they predominantly focus on environmental human rights, the two works that come closest to such an ambitious undertaking are Boyd's *The Environmental Rights Revolution* and May and Daly's *Global Environmental Constitutionalism* referred to above. Fully realising the risk of its being perceived as too superficial, in keeping with this book's primary focus on the conceptual contours of environmental constitutionalism, the following section's three-fold aim instead is to extrapolate the generic elements of the constitutional state that were developed in Chapter 3 to the environmental domain. Where appropriate, the discussion is supported by examples of these constitutional elements as they appear in some domestic constitutional orders (and mostly the South African legal order, which has a revered constitution that is representative of a modern democratic constitutional state and the elements of constitutionalism).[74]

In doing so, the discussion primarily seeks to illustrate how environmental constitutionalism as a concept, an analytical perspective and a normative reform programme, could encapsulate all of the features of the broadly conceived constitutional state. A secondary aim of the discussion below is to provide a reference framework that could be applied in the search for the elements of environmental constitutionalism in the global domain in Chapter 7. The subsequent discussion illustrates that this reference framework cannot be confined to rights, as is the case in some of the approaches to environmental constitutionalism discussed above. A more comprehensive, holistic and inclusive vision of environmental constitutionalism arguably should see it manifesting not only as rights, but also in terms of the other aspects of constitutionalism discussed in Chapter 3.

A. Formal and Substantive Environmental Constitutions

It has been explained in Chapter 3 that 'constitution', in the simplest of terms, can generally be taken to mean two things. First, the term refers to a higher law in a country (mostly, although not always, in written form) that has the purpose of steering and constraining the state, its governance processes (including law-making, conflict resolution and law enforcement), and its agents of governance. In this sense a constitution provides for certain basic constitutive rules that determine how other rules are created, interpreted, changed and enforced.[75] A constitution also seeks to regulate the vertical interaction between the state and its subjects and the horizontal interaction between the subjects *inter se*. By organising and setting out the order and organisation of the state and of political life, a constitution thus establishes, defines and organises the main organs of government, how they

---

[74] To this end, an important caveat applies throughout the subsequent analysis: while the generic objectives of environmental constitutionalism would be similar for all the countries and regions of the world, the specific content, design, elements and reach of environmental constitutionalism will differ from country to country and in different regions because of the different histories, and prevailing socio-political, environmental and economic conditions; reflecting the immensely divergent legal cultures of a kaleidoscopic world. The predominantly generic analysis that follows cannot fully represent the rich diversity of environmental constitutional provisions in all of the world's constitutions. A more representative and detailed account will be a crucial aspect of the future research agenda, which might also focus on empirical issues.

[75] D Bodansky, 'Is There an International Environmental Constitution?' (2009) 16 *Indiana Journal of Global Legal Studies* 565, 567.

are constituted and the remit of their power.[76] This first general understanding could be described as delineating the concept of a constitution in the 'thin', structural or formal sense to the extent that the constitution constitutes and regulates the state.[77]

The second meaning attributed to constitutions is based on the expressive and symbolic, rather than on the architectural or formal characteristics of constitutions. This understanding delineates constitutions in the higher-order substantively 'thick' sense to the extent that constitutions are conceived of as being self-confident assertions of the collective will;[78] value-laden, and exuding numerous characteristics that could legitimise,[79] dignify and improve a legal order.[80] Constitutions in the substantive sense relate to a constitution being substantively (not merely formalistically) constitutional, ie substantive constitutions provide certain higher-order, protective guarantees.[81] They offer the highest possible level and means in law of demonstrating the shared values and guiding principles of a social order to which the majority of people are taken to democratically consent to,[82] including conceptions of fairness, justice and legitimacy and the provision of legal stability and predictability (notably, all aspects of the rule of law). Constitutions do so through fundamental substantive rules such as those on rights; a hierarchical structure where some rules are superior to others; rules that are mandatorily applicable and of a non-consensual nature; rules that reflect process values regarding participation, transparency and the separation of powers; and rules that are entrenched and thus difficult to amend.[83]

When applied to the environmental domain and in further pursuit of the formal-substantive metaphor, it is possible to understand a formal environmental constitution in a functional, structural or descriptive way as a means to determine, at the highest possible level, the ordering, composition and architecture of environmental governance. This would include, among other things, the means and procedures to establish environmental governance powers and environmental

---

[76] M Allen, 'Globalization and Peremptory Norms in International Law: From Westphalian to Global Constitutionalism' (2004) 41 *International Politics* 341, 342; A Wiener, 'Editorial: Evolving Norms of Constitutionalism' (2003) 9 *European Law Journal* 1, 1–2, 5.

[77] Wiener, 'Editorial: Evolving Norms of Constitutionalism' (n 76) 5.

[78] Wiener (n 76) 5; B Bryde, 'International Democratic Constitutionalism' in R St John Macdonald and D Johnston (eds), *Towards World Constitutionalism: Issues in the Legal Ordering of the World Community* (Leiden, Martinus Nijhoff, 2005) 105.

[79] Neuman believes that '[n]ational constitutions in the liberal tradition are understood as originating in direct or indirect exercises of popular sovereignty that provide one source of legitimation for the enforcement of the rights they contain': GL Neuman, 'Human Rights and Constitutional Rights: Harmony and Dissonance' (2003) 55 *Stanford Law Review* 1863, 1866.

[80] A Peters, 'The Constitutionalist Reconstruction of International Law: Pros and Cons' (2006) NCCR International Trade Working Paper No 11(07-2006) 5.

[81] G Sartori, 'Constitutionalism: A Preliminary Discussion' (1962) 56 *American Political Science Review* 853, 855.

[82] Bosselmann, *Im Namen der Natur* (n 29) 190.

[83] Bodansky, 'Is There an International Environmental Constitution?' (n 75) 568, 571.

governance institutions, including the power of environmental authorities themselves when they make decisions that affect the environment (for example, their power to evaluate and decide on a licence to mine); for establishing and steering law-making, conflict resolution and law enforcement processes of the state insofar as they relate to environmental matters; for determining the roles and responsibilities of all the public and private actors involved in environmental governance; and for regulating the vertical interaction between the state and its subjects and the horizontal interaction between the subjects in respect of environmental matters.

There are many domestic examples of constitutions with formal environment-related elements. One is the Constitution of the Republic of South Africa. Its formal elements are evident from, among others, the Founding Provisions in Chapter 1 providing that South Africa is 'one, sovereign democratic state'.[84] Chapter 3 sets out procedures that must facilitate good, cooperative (environmental) governance between the national, provincial and local spheres of government and all the line-function departments in each sphere. The functions and responsibilities, as well as the powers of the president, parliament, the national executive, the provinces and local authorities, are clearly regulated in Chapters 4 to 7. Chapter 8 provides the all-important provisions related to the role of the courts, their functions and independence, as well as to the broader issues related to the administration of justice. Schedule 4 specifically designates the environment as a functional area of concurrent national and provincial legislative competence, while Schedule 5 sets out a range of environmental services that are the functional area of local legislative competence. Clearly, all of these are provisions that constitute, establish, legitimise and guide the day-to-day governance of environmental matters in South Africa, and whereas the country (like countries elsewhere in the world) has no single all-encompassing *environmental* constitution that establishes and regulates environmental governance authority, its national Constitution contains various elements that aim to do what a formal environmental constitution would typically set out to achieve.

An environmental constitution in the substantive sense could provide, among other things, for a rights-based approach to environmental governance, including a right to a healthy environment and for the rights of nature, as well as incidental political and socio-economic rights and rights that facilitate participative, representative and transparent environmental governance. Other than rights, substantive environmental constitutions could provide for directive principles or principles of state policy that work to galvanise, though not compel, legislative, judicial and executive activities to protect the environment.[85] These could include the many state and non-state duties with respect to environmental protection such as: to ensure inter- and intra-generational equity; to conserve resources; to ensure equitable access to and use of resources; to avoid adverse environmental impacts;

---

[84] S 1.
[85] E Daly, 'Constitutional Protection for Environmental Rights: The Benefits of Environmental Process' (2012) 17(2) *International Journal of Peace Studies* 71, 71.

to prevent environmental disasters, minimise damage and provide emergency assistance; to compensate for environmental harm; to ensure environmental justice; to ensure access to justice; and to ensure sufficient civil society representation and participation.[86] The 1949 Basic Law of the Federal Republic of Germany's, provision on the environment is an example in this respect. Article 20a provides:

> Mindful also of its responsibility toward future generations, the state shall protect the natural foundations of life and animals by legislation and, in accordance with law and justice, by executive and judicial action, all within the framework of the constitutional order.

Constitutions and laws of countries also frequently prescribe the manner in which such duties must be performed by a government and its agencies, with the minimum threshold usually being the dictates of good governance (transparent, inclusive, participative, ethical, non-corrupt governance).[87] In other words, environmental constitutionalism is not only about the duty to realise substantive environmental obligations, but also about the manner in which these obligations are fulfilled, because its sets a standard for, and could even be used to enforce, good environmental governance, mostly through procedural guarantees.

Substantive environmental constitutionalism could further include comprehensive provisions for judicial review, the separation of powers, as well as provisions that explicitly uphold the supremacy of a constitution. In addition, it could provide for aspirational values that should permeate a society, such as human dignity, equality and possibly even ecological sustainability which are usually expressed through rights or the broadly formulated preambular provisions of a constitution.

While there are many others, the South African Constitution is an example of a broadly conceived substantive domestic environmental constitutionalist approach that incorporates, through its environmental right, the specific objectives of intergenerational equity and sustainable development. The right clearly elevates environmental protection to the constitutional level, and it sets out various obligations on government (and the private sector to the extent that the right applies horizontally)[88] to achieve the objectives of the right through legislative and other measures. Section 24 of the Bill of Rights provides:

Everyone has the right:

(a)   To an environment that is not harmful to their health or well-being; and

---

[86] E Brown Weiss, *In Fairness to Future Generations: International Law, Common Patrimony; and Intergenerational Equity* (Dobbs Ferry, Transnational Publishers, 1989) 50–86.

[87] See, eg, s 195 of the Constitution of the Republic of South Africa.

[88] S 7(2) of the Constitution explicitly provides that the duty to respect, protect, promote and fulfil the Bill of Rights applies to the state. This is confirmed by s 8(1), which states: 'The Bill of Rights applies to all law, and binds the legislature, the executive, the judiciary and all organs of state'. However, s 8(2) then extends this application to non-state parties as well in that '[a] provision of the Bill of Rights binds a *natural or a juristic person* if, and to the extent that, it is applicable, taking into account the nature of the right and the nature of any duty imposed by the right'. (Emphasis added.) For a more recent discussion on the horizontal application of the Bill of Rights, see N Friedman, 'The South African Common Law and the Constitution: Revisiting Horizontality' (2014) 30 *South African Journal of Human Rights* 69.

(b) To have the environment protected, for the benefit of present and future generations, through reasonable legislative and other measures that:
  (i) Prevent pollution and ecological degradation;
  (ii) Promote conservation; and
  (iii) Secure ecologically-sustainable development and use of natural resources while promoting justifiable economic and social development.[89]

The idea that substantive environmental constitutionalism is primarily based on, but could potentially stretch beyond, a pure environmental rights-based approach is also exemplified by the South African Constitution, which asserts its own supremacy and that of the rule of law by declaring that the Constitution is 'the supreme law of the Republic; law or conduct inconsistent with it is invalid, and the obligations imposed by it must be fulfilled'.[90] The ambit of the Constitution's supremacy also covers environmental matters by virtue of the latter concerns being included in the Bill of Rights. As well, the Constitution, and indeed the country as a whole, is founded on a set of aspirational but fundamental values that should permeate all of society.[91] While these do not include values that directly or explicitly relate to the environment (such as ecological integrity or ecological sustainable development, for example), they do include related values such as human dignity, the achievement of equality and the advancement of human rights and freedoms, non-racialism and non-sexism, as well as the rule of law.[92] Owing to their interdependence, adhering to these traditional human rights values, and/or stating them as aspirational objectives that any governance effort should strive towards, could conceivably contribute to promoting environmental protection as well. Conversely, a sound environment conducive to health and well-being is crucial for fostering conditions where these values could be realised, enhanced and protected. In the words of the United Nations Special Rapporteur on Human Rights and the Environment (former Independent Expert): 'Human rights are grounded in respect for fundamental human attributes such as dignity, equality and liberty. The realization of these attributes depends on an environment that allows them to flourish'.[93] This interconnectivity is evident from the various environment-related rights that the South African Constitution provides in addition to the environmental right itself. For example, the right to equality prohibits unfair discrimination and provides that '[e]veryone is equal before the law and has the right to equal protection and benefit of the law'.[94] Section 10 recognises that

---

[89] ibid, s 24.
[90] ibid, s 2.
[91] ibid, s 1.
[92] ibid, s 1.
[93] United Nations Human Rights Council, 'Report of the Independent Expert on the Issue of Human Rights Obligations Relating to the Enjoyment of a Safe, Clean, Healthy and Sustainable Environment, John H Knox' (2012) www.ohchr.org/Documents/HRBodies/HRCouncil/RegularSession/Session22/A-HRC-22-43_en.pdf, para 10.
[94] S 9 of the Constitution.

'[e]veryone has inherent dignity and the right to have their dignity respected and protected', while section 11 succinctly states '[e]veryone has the right to life'. Section 27 also provides that '[e]veryone has the right of access to … sufficient food and water'. These political and socio-economic rights have a direct bearing on the environment, including on all sustainability considerations by virtue of their being linked with environmental justice.

In addition, alongside these substantive constitutional rights, a number of procedural rights form part of the broader rights-based approach to environmental governance in South Africa, and they must be used where appropriate to enforce substantive rights-based claims.[95] These include the right to just administrative action; the right of access to information; and clauses relating to access to courts and the enforcement of rights.[96] These provisions that relate to the formal aspects and thus the quality of environmental governance, are reinforced by section 195 which provides for an elaborated set of basic values and principles governing the public administration that must be considered by government, including environmental authorities, when exercising authority.

B. Environmental Rule of Law

In the main, the formal and substantive elements of environmental constitutionalism co-exist and they are often difficult to tell apart. As a general rule, the environment-related provisions of a constitution should ideally not only create the architecture of the state and of environmental governance, but must also be constitutional in the more substantive sense that they seek to improve and 'make good' a legal and political order that also encapsulates environmental matters. The South African Constitution described above is a case in point and is a clear example of a formal and substantive constitution that comprehensively provides for the architecture of environmental governance, as well as for a range of substantive constitutional elements that elevate environmental protection to a higher and more normatively authoritative juridical level. This intermeshed nature of substantive and formal environmental constitutionalism aligns with the point made in Chapter 3, namely that the rule of law, as a feature of constitutionalism, includes both formal and substantive aspects that are to a greater or a lesser extent linked with one another.

Rule of law considerations, while reflective of the broader constitutionalism paradigm, are increasingly touted as critical considerations for environmental

---

[95] LJ Kotzé, 'The Application of Just Administrative Action in the South African Environmental Governance Sphere: An Analysis of Some Contemporary Thoughts and Recent Jurisprudence' (2004) 7(2) *Potchefstroom Electronic Law Journal* 58.
[96] Ss 32, 33 and 34 and 38 respectively.

protection and sustainability. This is occurring in tandem with the emergence of terms such as 'rule of law for nature',[97] and the more common 'environmental rule of law'. In a May 2015 Issue Brief, the United Nations Environment Programme declared:

> Environmental rule of law is central to sustainable development ... Natural resources that are managed sustainably, transparently, and on the basis of the rule of law can be the engine for sustainable development as well as a platform for peace and justice.[98]

UNEP's understanding of the rule of law accords with that of its parent institution, the United Nations, ie the rule of law is a principle of governance in which all persons and public and private institutions are accountable to laws that are publicly promulgated, equally enforced and independently adjudicated, and which are consistent with international human rights norms and standards.[99] UNEP believes that the environmental rule of law must play a central role to 'reduce violations of environmental law and to achieve sustainable development overall', including through good governance practices (access to information and justice, public participation and transparency), enhanced compliance and enforcement, and a deliberate role for independent and impartial courts as constitutional guardians:

> Environmental rule of law integrates the critical environmental needs with the essential elements of the rule of law, and provides the basis for reforming environmental governance. It prioritizes environmental sustainability by connecting it with fundamental rights and obligations. It implicitly reflects universal moral values and ethical norms of behaviour, and it provides a foundation for environmental rights and obligations. Without environmental rule of law and the enforcement of legal rights and obligations, environmental governance may be arbitrary, that is, discretionary, subjective, and unpredictable.[100]

In support of UNEP's position, the United Nations recognises that:

> the rule of law and development are strongly interrelated and mutually reinforcing, [and] that the advancement of the rule of law at the national and international levels is essential for sustained and inclusive economic growth, sustainable development, the eradication of poverty and hunger and the full realization of all human rights and fundamental freedoms.[101]

This position is reiterated in the Rio+20 outcome document, 'The Future we Want';[102] while Goal 16 of the recently proclaimed Sustainable Development

---

[97] See for a recent scholarly account, C Voigt (ed), *Rule of Law for Nature: New Dimensions and Ideas in Environmental Law* (Cambridge, Cambridge University Press, 2013).
[98] United Nations Environment Programme (UNEP), 'Issue Brief—Environmental Rule of Law: Critical to Sustainable Development' (May 2015) www.unep.org/delc/Portals/24151/Documents/issue-brief-environmental-justice-sdgs.pdf.
[99] See, generally, United Nations General Assembly Resolution on the Rule of Law (A/RES/67/1), 30 November 2012.
[100] UNEP, 'Issue Brief' (n 98).
[101] United Nations General Assembly Resolution on the Rule of Law (A/RES/67/1), 30 November 2012, para 7.
[102] United Nations Conference on Sustainable Development (Rio+20), 'The Future We Want' (2012) www.uncsd2012.org/content/documents/727The%20Future%20We%20Want%2019%20June%201230pm.pdf, paras 8, 10, 252.

Goals implicitly references the rule of law requirement to '[p]romote peaceful and inclusive societies for sustainable development, provide access to justice for all and build effective, accountable and inclusive institutions at all levels'.[103]

Significant as it is that there seems to be a gradual convergence between sustainability as a goal and the rule of law as a means towards achieving that goal, the foregoing broad statements also reflect a concern that was highlighted in Chapter 3 that is clearly evident in the environmental governance domain: the environmental rule of law is used, at least at the higher strategic political level (and thus understandably so), as a catch-all phrase that envelopes all things that are constitutional and good and that might improve environmental protection where the rule of law is perceived to be able, and must endeavour, to improve all environmental outcomes.[104] While its practical significance is less obvious, the valuable historically embedded meaning and distinct character, as well as a more qualified understanding of the environmental rule of law, could consequently be lost through such a generalisation.

A slightly more focused and detailed approach to the environmental rule of law that traces its separate procedural and substantive tracks more clearly is found in academic circles. Ristroph, for example, defines environmental rule of law as meaning:

> (1) there is a system of laws in place that regulate, to the extent practicable, all human-induced actions that by themselves or collectively have significant impacts on the environment; (2) these laws will be consistently applied over time and across the jurisdiction; and (3) effective and fair enforcement action, initiated by a government entity or citizen suit/complaint, will be taken against one who breaks the law, regardless of the offender's socioeconomic or political status.[105]

While Nemesio believes environmental rule of law is 'a system of environmental laws that are consistently and equally applied to everyone and are effectively and fairly enforced against violators',[106] Magraw argues that the environmental aspects of the rule of law include: environmental law must be available; environmental law must be enforceable and enforced; environmental law applies to anyone, including the state and non-state parties; and environmental law must have sufficient authority to be observed. In addition, the regulatory environment must allow full non-state stakeholder participation, and observance of the environmental rule of law is the primary task of the courts.[107]

---

[103] United Nations Division for Sustainable Development, 'Transforming Our World: The 2030 Agenda for Sustainable Development' (2015) sustainabledevelopment.un.org/post2015/transformingourworld.

[104] Another example of such a very expansive politically laden, policy level approach is T Greiber (ed), *Judges and the Rule of Law: Creating the Links—Environment, Human Rights and Poverty* (Gland, IUCN, 2006).

[105] E Ristroph, 'The Role of Philippine Courts in Establishing the Environmental Rule of Law' (2012) 42 *Environmental Law Reporter* 10866, 10867.

[106] I Nemesio, 'Strengthening Environmental Rule of Law: Enforcement, Combatting Corruption, and Encouraging Citizen Suits' (2015) 27 *Georgetown International Environmental Law Review* 321, 322.

[107] D Magraw, 'Rule of Law and the Environment' (2014) 44 *Environmental Policy and Law* 201, 202.

The broader populist political view on the one hand and more doctrinally circumscribed academic views on the other, collectively suggest that the environmental rule of law must improve the effectiveness of environmental laws; increase compliance and enforcement; promote participatory environmental governance; and increase government accountability through checks and balances such as strengthened judicial control, citizen suits, and protection of rights-related environmental entitlements (both procedural and substantive). To achieve these broad objectives, a domestic legal system that is based on the environmental rule of law will typically provide a comprehensive collection of constitutionally sanctioned environmental laws that must be clear, publicly promulgated and that apply to everyone; constitutionally established institutional governance machinery that provides, separates and regulates environmental authority alongside measures to strengthen accountability; higher-order environmental guarantees encapsulated in rights; independent and impartial courts that have the power of review and that are able to resolve conflicts of sustainability, conflicts of law and conflicts of authority in environmental governance; and a strong compliance and enforcement machinery that is situated not only with public authorities, but also with private entities such as corporations and the broader public.

Thus the environmental rule of law would arguably mostly be evident in a legal order as a collection of formalistic and substantive constitutional and subsequent statutory and institutional elements that are scattered across the legal landscape, instead of one explicit constitutional provision that provides for the environmental rule of law. Such a broad typology of the environmental rule of law corresponds with Enzmann's approach to the rule of law described in Chapter 3 in that it consists of aspects that respectively aim to provide for and determine the procedural elements that are necessary to establish and regulate a state order purely on the basis of positive law; and the material/substantive aspects of the rule of law that bind the state to substantive standards.[108] There seems to be a more realistic possibility of preserving historical conceptual authenticity if this two-pronged division is maintained in environmental rule of law conversations.

C. Separation of Environmental Governance Powers

The discussion in Chapter 3 has shown that the separation of powers doctrine is intimately coupled with the rule of law, especially to the extent that this doctrine seeks to establish checks and balances, foster accountability in government and increase governance efficiency. While provisions that entrench and maintain the separation of powers in a state are most usually provided for in a constitution, few constitutions contain an express provision that separates the *trias politica* as such. For example, separation of powers can be derived from the structure

[108] B Enzmann, *Der Demokratische Verfassungsstaat: Entstehung, Elemente, Herausforderungen* (Wiesbaden, Springer, 2014) 43–163.

(or the thin constitutional aspects) of the Constitution of the United States of America where article I deals with the Legislative Department; article II with the Executive Department; and article III with the Judicial Department. The South African Constitution likewise does not contain an explicit provision on the separation of powers. Section 8(1) of the Constitution instead hints at such a separation, stating: 'The Bill of Rights applies to all law, and binds the legislature, the executive, the judiciary and all organs of state'. This provision relates to substantive environmental constitutionalism to the extent that it asserts constitutional supremacy. The degree of separation is deepened by specific chapters in the Constitution containing formal constitutional aspects that deal with Parliament (Chapter 4), the President and National Executive (Chapter 5), the Courts and Administration of Justice (Chapter 8).[109]

The separation of powers provisions in a constitution could pertain to environmental law and governance to the extent that they establish and regulate the judicial, legislative and executive environmental functions of the state. More specifically, it is concerned with the delineation and subsequent regulation of environmental governance authority in a state and the establishment of checks and balances by means of which the three nodes of governmental power co-exist as a three-pronged collective entity in the broader environmental governance paradigm (for example, through measures for cooperative governance)[110] in a formal sense. It could also include substantive measures for the prevention of power abuse and measures to increase accountability (such as judicial oversight); and measures to facilitate governance efficiency (such as through procedural rights).

The separation of powers doctrine is important for environmental governance because it could counter the centralisation of powers and decision-making competence with respect to environmental matters. In doing so, it will determine and distinguish the power relations of and among environmental authorities, while determining how relations between government institutions and between a government and people should be conducted (ie independently and not subject to interference from other spheres). It could also enhance environmental governance efficiency to the extent that state institutions situated in the three power spheres

---

[109] See, for a detailed discussion, F Venter, *Constitutional Comparison: Japan, Germany, Canada and South Africa as Constitutional States* (Cape Town, Juta, 2000) 212, 220–23.

[110] See, eg, Ch 3 of the South African Constitution which provides detailed provisions on cooperative governance including, among others that:

> All spheres of government and all organs of state within each sphere must –
> ...
> (h) co-operate with one another in mutual trust and good faith by –
> (i) fostering friendly relations;
> (ii) assisting and supporting one another;
> (iii) informing one another of, and consulting one another on, matters of common interest;
> (iv) co-ordinating their actions and legislation with one another;
> (v) adhering to agreed procedures; and
> (vi) avoiding legal proceedings against one another.
> S 41(1)(h).

are identified, mandated and empowered to perform specific environmental governance functions that they are best equipped to perform. The courts, for example, are arguably best suited to mediate conflicts that arise in environmental law and governance and conflicts arising from the opposing social, economic and environmental concerns of sustainable development, among others. The legislature and executive are better placed to respectively enact environmental laws and to enforce them.

The result of the foregoing formal architectural arrangement should have substantive benefits in the sense that the separation of powers doctrine prevents the concentration of environment-related decision-making power in any single group of people or a person. This could work to counter any efforts in a government to monopolise environmental decision-making powers; to entrench measures facilitating a dictatorial or autocratic regime (the admittedly unlikely Öko-Diktatur);[111] or to enrich itself through endemic corruption that could occur through, for example, the authorisation of mining licences.[112]

In line with the observations made in Chapter 3 concerning the degree to which separation of powers must be maintained, it seems preferable, also in the environmental governance domain, that there cannot and should not be an absolute disjunction between the various authorities of a state that concern themselves with environmental governance. The environment, after all, is an integrated phenomenon that requires a balanced, integrated, holistic, deliberative, collaborative and cooperative regulatory approach. That the separation of powers doctrine should not apply in an absolute sense in the environmental governance domain is also evident from the notion of Earth systems governance, which requires environmental governance to be sensitive towards, among others, inter-generational dependencies, functional interdependence of Earth system transformation and of potential responses, and spatial Earth system interdependence in a social and ecosystem sense.[113] An ideal form of separation of environmental governance powers is therefore one which keeps the three nodes of government powers sufficiently apart to achieve the broader objectives of constitutionalism and everything that goes with that impulse, but that does allow some form of convergence, within the confines of constitutionalism more generally, where this is necessary and permissible to ensure optimal environmental governance of a complex and integrated phenomenon in a balanced manner.

---

[111] See specifically, Kloepfer, 'Droht der autoritäre ökologische Staat?' (n 23) 42–50. See more generally on the differences between environmental democracy and environmental autocracy, P Fredriksson and J Wollscheid, 'Democratic Institutions versus Autocratic Regimes: The Case of Environmental Policy' (2007) 130 *Public Choice* 381.

[112] The potential for corruption in a regulatory system that does not observe the rule of law and important constitutional ideas such as the separation of powers is vividly illustrated by Nemesio, 'Strengthening Environmental Rule of Law' (n 106) 321–42. See also, A Standing, *Corruption and the Extractive Industries in Africa: Can Combatting Corruption Cure the Resource Curse?—ISS Paper 153* (Pretoria, Institute for Security Studies, 2007).

[113] F Biermann, '"Earth System Governance" as a Cross-cutting Theme of Global Change Research' (2007) 17 *Global Environmental Change* 326.

D. Judicial Independence and Powers of Review

Chapter 3 has indicated that courts are considered crucial institutions of the constitutional state that must uphold constitutionalism more generally and aspects of the rule of law more specifically. To properly fulfil their role in a constitutional democracy, courts and their judicial officers need to be impartial and independent, separated as they should be from the executive and legislature and endowed with the authority and competence to resolve conflicts in law, ensure accountability in the other branches of state power and protect the constitution as the foundation of the constitutional state. All of this must be accomplished without assuming too much power that might create a countermajoritarian dilemma.

Measures to entrench the independence, impartiality and review functions of courts are usually associated with the separation of powers doctrine and are also found in a constitution. By way of example, the South African Constitution provides:

> 165. (1) The judicial authority of the Republic is vested in the courts.
>
> (2) The courts are independent and subject only to the Constitution and the law, which they must apply impartially and without fear, favour or prejudice.
>
> (3) No person or organ of state may interfere with the functioning of the courts.
>
> (4) Organs of state, through legislative and other measures, must assist and protect
>
> the courts to ensure the independence, impartiality, dignity, accessibility and effectiveness of the courts.
>
> (5) An order or decision issued by a court binds all persons to whom and organs of state to which it applies.[114]

Independent and impartial courts will also focus their attention on environmental matters, as they do on other issues and conflicts that arise at any given time in society. To be sure, mainly as a response to the Rio Declaration's directive in 1992 to states to provide '[e]ffective access to judicial and administrative proceedings, including redress and remedy',[115] states have set up elaborate judicial mechanisms through which domestic courts have been producing numerous decisions to balance environmental and economic considerations, promote conservation, achieve environmental justice and implement the goals of sustainability, among others.[116]

Because of the nature of environmental conflicts, their public nature and the exceptionally broad public interest in these conflicts, questions around the judiciary in environmental law and governance usually turn on the issue of access to courts and judicial redress.[117] To this end, the contribution of the judiciary to the

---

[114] Constitution of the Republic of South Africa, s 165.
[115] Rio Declaration on Environment and Development 1992, Principle 10.
[116] Nemesio (n 106) 325.
[117] The role of the judiciary in environmental law and governance has occupied many environmental scholars for several years. One example is LJ Kotzé and AR Paterson (eds), *The Role of the Judiciary in Environmental Governance: Comparative Perspectives* (Alphen aan den Rijn, Kluwer, 2009).

environmental constitutionalism project should not be measured only in relation to the constitutional measures that exist to endow courts with their impartial and independent status, but also in relation to constitutional and secondary statutory laws that provide members of the public with access to courts, including wide *locus standi* measures for public interest environmental litigation, citizens' suits and class actions. It is in this context that constitutional and subsequent statutory provisions on access to justice, *locus standi*, access to information and the right to just administrative action are crucial elements to empower people to fully utilise avenues of judicial environmental governance.[118]

Another task of the judiciary in addition to those falling under the traditional remit of constitutionalism is its increasingly valuable function to innovatively develop, expand and create environmental obligations, especially where they do not exist in a constitution. The Supreme Court of India is an oft-cited example in this respect. While it might be argued that it could be violating the separation of powers doctrine, the Court has been intimately involved in laying down new principles of environmental law, creating new environmental governance institutions and structures, and even conferring additional powers on existing authorities in the absence of a constitutional environmental right.[119]

In most jurisdictions general courts hear environmental matters. In tandem with the growing realisation that environmental matters often require highly specialised expertise and judicial skills, many countries have and are, however, in the process of creating specialised environmental courts and tribunals. A leading 2009 study estimates that over 350 specialised environmental courts and tribunals have been established in 41 countries (a figure which could very well be more today).[120] Two prominent examples are the Green Bench of the Supreme Court of India and Australia's Land and Environment Court in New South Wales. It is generally believed that such specialised courts are often better placed in certain circumstances to engage with the highly complex, often technical and specialised nature of environmental related conflicts to the extent that they: have greater expertise; are more efficient and visible; provide more affordable procedures that are not as drawn out as the general judicial process; follow more uniform approaches which increases predictability and legal certainty; could provide specialised conditions for wider standing; foster greater commitment and creativity among judges; provide a more integrated approach to sustainability conflicts; and increase public confidence in environmental adjudication in general terms.[121]

---

[118] See, ss 32, 33, 34 and 38 of the South African Constitution, which provide for the rights to access to information, just administrative action, access to courts and *locus standi* respectively. These domestic provisions mirror similar provisions of international soft law (eg, Principle 10 of the Rio Declaration on Environment and Development); and treaty law, the most notable being the Aarhus Convention on Access to Information, Public Participation in Decision-making and Access to Justice in Environmental Matters 1998.
[119] G Sahu, 'Implications of Indian Supreme Court's Innovations for Environmental Jurisprudence' (2008) 4 *Law, Environment and Development Journal* 1, 3.
[120] G Pring and C Pring, *Greening Justice: Creating and Improving Environmental Courts and Tribunals* (The Access Initiative, 2009) www.eufje.org/images/DocDivers/Rapport%20Pring.pdf.
[121] ibid 14–16.

While the advances in judicial environmental governance are too many to list here, there is general agreement that judicial power can be used creatively in the environmental context: to energise participative environmental democracy and to make it more deliberative; to animate vague and often indeterminate environmental constitutional provisions such as rights; to recognise and protect environmental rights; to judicialise political processes, bring fairness into political processes, and ensure accountability in environment-related political matters; to judicialise environmental law and governance more generally and bring it into the regulatory scope of constitutionalism; to highlight environment-related matters that would otherwise go unnoticed in society and politics; to identify, elaborate and develop precise rules of conduct and more general principles of environmental law; and to strengthen private actor involvement in environmental governance and especially in compliance and enforcement procedures.[122] To this end, Stephens estimates that courts have a unique opportunity to act beyond the trite confines of traditional judicial functions in the adjudication of environmental matters:

> The institution of adjudication (in its independence), the process of argumentation (according to criteria of rationality), and the decision-making process (according to law) mean that courts ... are uniquely placed to speak beyond the confines of the dispute at hand and confront the major environmental challenges of our time.[123]

Although the variability of judicial processes around the world makes it difficult to state common trends, courts are increasingly fulfilling their traditional roles in safeguarding constitutionalism more generally while achieving tangible environmental outcomes and providing enhanced environmental protection. There is accordingly also an evident move towards fulfilling the broad aspirations set out by judges from across the globe in the Johannesburg Principles on the Role of Law and Sustainable Development, which was adopted at the Global Judges Symposium during the World Summit on Sustainable Development in 2002. These include, among others: recognition that an independent judiciary and judicial process is vital for the implementation, development and enforcement of environmental law; the rapid evolution of environmental law requires courts to interpret and apply new legal instruments in keeping with the principles of sustainable development; the fragile state of the environment requires the judiciary, as the guardian of the rule of law, to boldly and fearlessly implement and enforce applicable environmental laws; and the judiciary plays a critical role in the enhancement of the public interest in environmental matters.[124] International declarations such as these are also increasingly finding application in domestic jurisdictions.

---

[122] Boyd, *Environmental Rights Revolution* (n 49) 6–7; May and Daly (n 61) 2651/11268.
[123] T Stephens, *International Courts and Environmental Protection* (Cambridge, Cambridge University Press, 2009) 116.
[124] United Nations Environment Programme (UNEP), 'Senior Judges Adopt Ground-Breaking Action Plan to Strengthen World's Environment-Related Laws' (2002) www.unep.org/Documents. Multilingual/Default.asp?ArticleID=3115&DocumentID=259.

With reference to the Johannesburg Principles, the South African Constitutional Court, for example, recently confirmed that:

> The role of the courts is especially important in the context of the protection of the environment and giving effect to the principle of sustainable development. The importance of the protection of the environment cannot be gainsaid. Its protection is vital to the enjoyment of the other rights contained in the Bill of Rights; indeed, it is vital to life itself. It must therefore be protected for the benefit of the present and future generations. The present generation holds the earth in trust for the next generation. This trusteeship position carries with it the responsibility to look after the environment. *It is the duty of the Court to ensure that this responsibility is carried out.*[125]

In tandem with the judiciary's increased assertion of its crucial role in environmental governance, judges also recognise that in a globalised world, domestic courts cannot remain isolated, but are increasingly required to become part of the process of transnational environmental constitutionalism that requires courts in different countries and regions of the world to collaborate with the view to improving compliance with, implementation, development and enforcement of environmental law.[126] The extent to which this is contributing to globalising environmental constitutionalism is investigated in Chapter 7.

E. Constitutional Supremacy

Constitutional supremacy does not manifest in any specific way in the environmental domain; it does so more generally in the context of the environmental rule of law, the separation of powers and through rights provisions. Following on from the generic analysis in Chapter 3, constitutional supremacy in the environmental domain is nevertheless particularly advantageous because it establishes a normative hierarchy which elevates the environment within that normative hierarchy as an ethical concern and an object of governance to the highest juridical norm in a polity where the environment has been incorporated as part of the formal and, more particularly, the substantive elements of a constitution. In addition to this legal superiority that works to instil a normative hierarchy in a legal order, constitutional supremacy also indirectly establishes an institutional hierarchy in environmental governance, especially to the extent that all environment-related decisions and acts of government are subject to the constitution where laws, decisions and acts of state and non-state entities could be declared unconstitutional and invalid by the courts. An ancillary result of constitutional supremacy is therefore that it also entrenches the independence of the judiciary and its powers of review in environmental matters.

---

[125] *Fuel Retailers Association of Southern Africa v Director General: Environmental Management, Department of Agriculture, Conservation and Environment, Mpumalanga Province* 2007 (6) SA 4 (CC) at paras H–I at p 39. Emphasis added.

[126] UNEP, 'Senior Judges Adopt Ground-Breaking Action Plan' (n 124).

One example of environmental constitutional supremacy is provisions found in the South African Constitution that state South Africa 'is one, sovereign, democratic state founded on the [value of inter alia] Supremacy of the constitution and the rule of law';[127] and that the 'Constitution is the supreme law of the Republic; law or conduct inconsistent with it is invalid, and the obligations imposed by it must be fulfilled'.[128] Section 7(1) provides that the 'Bill of Rights is a cornerstone of democracy ... It enshrines the rights of all people in our country and affirms the democratic values of human dignity, equality and freedom'. While the state must 'respect, protect, promote and fulfil the rights in the Bill of Rights'; the Bill of Rights applies 'to all law, and binds the legislature, the executive, the judiciary and all organs of state'; as well as in some instances a natural and/or juristic person.[129] By virtue of its entrenchment as a right in the Bill of Rights through section 24, environmental care in South Africa is afforded a superior juridical status as part of the Constitution's, and more specifically, the Bill of Rights' supreme provisions. This would mean that all law or conduct inconsistent with the environmental right is invalid, and that the obligations imposed by it must be fulfilled; that rights-based environmental care provisions are part of the foundations of South Africa's democratic society; that these provisions impose duties on government and non-state entities; and that they bind all spheres of power in the country.

F. Democracy

The discussion in Chapter 3 highlighted that democracy is a crucial element of, and a precursor to, constitutionalism. The interrelated reciprocal relationship between democracy and constitutionalism is evident from the fact that a constitutional order comes about through democratic processes, while the continued solidification of democracy is entrenched through constitutional institutions, instruments and processes. Democracy alone (in the sense of majority rule) does not equal constitutionalism though, and while majoritarian democratic processes are necessary to constitute a structured polity as an expression of a people's sovereign self-determination, democracy must also work in tandem with the other elements of constitutionalism to restrict the power structures emanating from sovereign self-determination. How could democracy be understood in the environmental context?

One connection between democracy and the environment lies in the fact that environmental sources are public goods. Public goods can generally not be purchased on the market, so environmental protection is mostly left to the state and its governance institutions.[130] Because the state is ultimately the custodian or

---

[127] South African Constitution, s 1.
[128] ibid, s 2.
[129] ibid, s 8.
[130] M Winslow, 'Is Democracy Good for the Environment?' (2005) 4 *Journal of Environmental Planning and Management* 771, 771.

public trustee of public environmental goods,[131] the regime type of government (autocratic or democratic, for example) is an important consideration in environmental governance because it will determine the state's environmental governance approach and its effectiveness; the legitimacy of its environmental governance institutions, decisions and processes; and the extent to which people are represented in and support the overall environmental governance effort.

While some commentators have argued that democracy is unable to cope with resource scarcity and that as a consequence, authoritarian or dictatorial regimes are necessary to prevent unsustainable ecological destruction (a view that is reminiscent of the *Öko-Diktatur*),[132] the majority view today is that while democracy is no *panacea* for environmental protection, the greater the degree to which democracy is entrenched in a polity, the better the environmental quality is likely to be in that state.[133] Reasons for this are that environmental harm and costs tend to be more equally distributed in a democratic society; political leaders and environmental government officials are usually more accountable in a democracy; democratically elected environmental authorities and legislatures are seen to be more legitimate which could promote compliance with their directives and the laws they make; the public is better represented in and involved with environmental decisions that affect them; access to environmental information is more readily available; non-governmental organisations that promote environmental interests (especially those of marginalised groups) are tolerated and can flourish; access to justice and judicial recourse is more readily available to enforce environmental laws and assert environmental rights claims; and democracies more readily participate in a global society with other states and non-state actors that collectively aim to improve global environmental protection and justice.[134]

Democracy in the environmental context is usually used in the sense of community participation in environmental-related decision-making and governance processes. The general view is that while environmentalism generally speaking is probably (still) not a primary driving factor for democracy as such, it remains a critical consideration in any constitutional democracy, especially to the extent that it invites issues related to participatory and representative environmental

---

[131] See among others, PH Sand, 'The Concept of Public Trusteeship in the Transboundary Governance of Biodiversity' in LJ Kotzé and T Marauhn, *Transboundary Governance of Biodiversity* (Boston, Brill, 2014).

[132] A famous account is W Ophuls, *Ecology and the Politics of Scarcity* (San Francisco, WH Freeman Press, 1977).

[133] Although the empirical results of studies on this issue is somewhat mixed. See Winslow, 'Is Democracy Good for the Environment?' (n 130) 772.

[134] ibid. Another possible empirical metric that indicates a strong correlation between democracy and environmental protection is the Yale Environmental Performance Index. The countries with the strongest environmental performance are those that are generally known for the quality of their deliberative democratic constitutional systems (ie Finland, Iceland, Sweden and Denmark, among others). See http://epi.yale.edu/.

governance, deliberate public involvement and bottom-up measures to ensure government accountability, into the environmental constitutionalism domain.[135]

Democracy will also play a crucial role in legitimising environmental authorities and their decisions, since these authorities are seen to have been constituted through democratic processes in line with the majority will of a polity. This could contribute to improving environmental enforcement and compliance to the extent that people are more likely to adhere to environmental laws and the enforcement commands of institutions they perceive to be legitimately constituted by themselves through a choice of their own. In doing so, democracy could also increase the extent and quality of environmental protection measures in a country on the one hand, while on the other hand it would be able to counter an (unlikely) ecological dictatorship (*Öko-Diktatur*).

In addition to enhancing participation, inclusion and legitimisation, democracy is also seen to create substantive and formal equality among people, which in turn could promote equal access and use of scarce natural resources and prevent conflict over these resources: 'if democracy and environmental protection are not mutually supportive, especially under conditions of economic scarcity, then there may ultimately exist the choice between environmental protection and civil conflict'.[136] Or put more famously in the words of Maathai on the 'unbreakable link' between peace, environment and democracy: 'Peace cannot exist without equitable development, just as development requires sustainable management of the environment in a democratic and peaceful space. In order to advance peace, we must promote its underlying democratic institutions and ideals'.[137]

Mindful of democracy's pitfalls that will also apply to the environmental domain (as described in Chapter 3), and its being presented here very generally as a monolithic undifferentiated idea, Midlarsky argues that environmental governance that is also democratic holds out several advantages over a non-democratic environmental governance regime including: environmental rights are generally better protected in democracies than in autocracies; democracies are inherently more responsive to the environmental and other needs of their people because governors depend on majority votes to keep them in power; technical environmental information flows more freely in democracies which empowers people and increases opportunities for political learning; democracies are more likely to cooperate with one another and support each other with respect to internal domestic, regional and international environmental problems while at the same time being more receptive to the pressures of global environmental lobbies and interest

---

[135] One example among the many publications dealing with this issue is J Jacobs, 'Community Participation, the Environment, and Democracy: Brazil in Comparative Perspective' (2002) 44(4) *Latin American Politics and Society* 59, 59.

[136] M Midlarsky, 'Democracy and the Environment: An Empirical Assessment' (1998) 35 *Journal of Peace Research* 341, 342.

[137] W Maathai, 'An Unbreakable Link: Peace, Environment, and Democracy' (2008) Winter *Harvard International Review* 24.

groups; and democracies with free market economies tend to more stringently subject private actors such as corporations that are prone to causing environmental harm to fiscal incentives and disincentives.[138]

G. Environmental Rights

Rights are conceived as 'reflections of nonlegal principles that have normative force independent of their embodiment in law, or even superior to the positive legal system'.[139] The idea of rights as apex norms derive from natural law, religious traditions, universal morality and/or ethical values, which opens up the possibility of including concerns such as environmental care into the protective realm of constitutions through the entrenchment of such care in rights. There is justifiable criticism levelled against rights more generally (see Chapter 3), and environmental rights specifically, such as: they are vague, absolute, redundant, sometimes undemocratic, non-enforceable and non-justiciable; too culturally imperialist, too focused on individuals; and they are disingenuous by creating false hopes.[140] As well, despite the predominance that rights assume within the larger environmental constitutionalism project, they remain only one of the aspects of substantive environmental constitutionalism, suggesting that a more encompassing understanding of environmental constitutionalism would be in order. Reflecting on the potential of rights as part of the broader environmental constitutionalism agenda, Saward suggests:

> Debates about constitutionalising environmental rights will, rightly, continue. But there is another thread of work which is centred upon constituting sustainability as an avowedly procedural and political project, the elements of which are only beginning to come more into focus. This thread does not so much deal with constitutions for politics, as the creative constituting of politics, in politics. And it does not require a single revolutionary founding, but rather a series of creative re-foundings using political tools both familiar and innovative.[141]

Yet, as legal mechanisms possessing unique characteristics, rights are uniquely elevated within the juridical order as meta-values and thus able to perform a singular mediating role in the human-environment interface.[142]

The continued contribution of rights to the environmental constitutionalism movement is evident from the fact that the environment was not a concern whatsoever during the first significant global constitutional moment that saw the almost universal adoption of rights following the Universal Declaration of Human

---

[138] Midlarsky, 'Democracy and the Environment' (n 136) 344.
[139] Neuman, 'Human Rights and Constitutional Rights' (n 79) 1868.
[140] See, among others, B Weston and D Bollier, 'Toward a Recalibrated Human Right to a Clean and Healthy Environment: Making the Conceptual Transition' (2013) 4 *Journal of Human Rights and the Environment* 116.
[141] M Saward, 'Constituting Sustainability' (2008) 17(2) *The Good Society* 12, 16.
[142] Kotzé, 'Human Rights and the Environment' (n 55) 145–69.

Rights in 1948.[143] Environmental rights only really began to feature in domestic constitutional orders following the United Nations Conference on the Human Environment in 1972, which provided the impetus for couching environmental concerns in rights terms through its Principle 1.[144] It took only a relatively short period of time for the current worldwide adoption of human rights to a healthy environment, environmentally-related procedural rights, other substantive political and socio-economic human rights bearing on environmental interests, and more recently rights of nature,[145] which is testimony to their increasing popularity.[146] Boyd recently estimated that three-quarters of the world's constitutions (150 out of 193) include explicit references to environmental rights and/or environmental responsibilities.[147] This is a surprisingly large number if one considers that the right to a clean or healthy environment is one of the few rights widely recognised in constitutions today that have no 'ancestral claim' in the International Bill of Rights.[148]

The latter proliferation predominantly occurs at a domestic constitutional level, suggesting that constitutions are almost always the legal avenue of choice to entrench environmental human rights. The significance of this trend lies in the consideration that 'domestic bills of rights are also typically granted constitutional status—and often placed at the beginning of a constitutional text—for expressive reasons, to reflect a collective commitment to fundamental rights as the most important legal norms within that system'.[149] The South African Constitution cited throughout this chapter exemplifies this. As a juridically elevated expression of constitutionalism through rights, environmental protection (including those human-related interests encapsulated by environmental justice) therefore has the constitutional possibility, as it were, of assuming greater status within the protective realm of legal systems worldwide.

While there are many others, a specific issue that is reflective of historical developments in constitutional environmental protection discussed above, and that remains contentious today, is the ecocentric/anthropocentric orientation of rights.

---

[143] Kotzé, 'Anthropocene's Global Environmental Constitutional Moment' (n 55).

[144] Principle 1 states, among others: 'Man has the fundamental right to freedom, equality and adequate conditions of life, in an environment of a quality that permits a life of dignity and well-being'.

[145] See arts 10 and 71–74 of the Constitution of Ecuador 2008. Bolivia is similarly exploring the possibility to enact a 'Mother Earth Law' which draws on the indigenous concept of *Pachamama* (Mother Earth) and which aims to provide nature rights including the right to life, regeneration, biodiversity, water, clean air, balance and restoration. See N Buxton, 'The Law of Mother Earth: Behind Bolivia's Historic Bill' (date unknown) therightsofnature.org/bolivia-law-of-mother-earth/.

[146] Environmental human rights are generally understood to include: rights to the environment; incidental substantive rights such as the rights to life and dignity that bear on the environment; and concomitant procedural rights such as rights of access to information and access to courts that are used to enforce substantive environment-related entitlements.

[147] Boyd, 'Constitutions, Human Rights, and the Environment' (n 49) 171–75.

[148] May and Daly (n 61) 691/11268.

[149] S Gardbaum, 'Human Rights and International Constitutionalism' in J Dunoff and J Trachtman (eds), *Ruling the World: Constitutionalism, International Law, and Global Governance* (Cambridge, Cambridge University Press, 2009).

To this end, constraints placed upon environmental constitutionalism are reflected by regulatory realties circling around juridical resistance to a shift in the legal system's deep ideological commitments. For example, Kysar attributes United States law-makers' reticence to adopt constitutional environmental protection provisions to a concern that is also expressed globally, namely that 'expanding the reach of constitutional protection to encompass future generations or non-human life-forms—not to mention the environment as such—would require significant adjustment to the anthropocentric, individualistic, and instrumentalist outlook upon which liberal ordering strongly depends'.[150] Such a profound shift would require a fundamental sea change of law, politics and social ordering as we know it; a change that governments do not seem to be willing to embrace just yet. To date, with the notable exception of Ecuador's Constitution and Bolivia's Mother Earth Law, rights are most usually cast in anthropocentric terms. Article 71 of the Ecuadorian Constitution provides: 'Nature or Pachamama, where life is reproduced and exists, has the right to exist, persist, maintain and regenerate its vital cycles, structure, functions and its processes in evolution'.

The regulatory reluctance to open up towards more ecocentric orientations only serves to deepen the tensions between ecocentrism and anthropocentrism that continue to pervade the human rights-environment arena.[151] If it is not reoriented towards a more ecocentric orientation, environmental constitutionalism thus could reinforce, preserve and even legitimise those existing approaches to human rights fulfilment that tend to be utilitarian in focus—thus grounding attempts to improve access to, and expand, human claims to resources with a view to ensuring unbridled economic development in its widest sense (a possibility that Bosselmann has warned about in his treatment of the ecological *Rechtsstaat* above).[152] If we accept Kysar's point that 'many of environmental law's subjects are not politically represented in the usual liberal fashion',[153] one could reasonably expect the environmental constitutionalism movement to turn inwards and question its own long-held tradition, which predominantly focuses on the state and humans as its only legitimate legal subjects. Because environmental human rights are part of the broader environmental constitutionalism paradigm, such introspectivity could manifestly influence how environmental rights would approach the issue of legal subjectivity in future, acting as a point of departure from which to contemplate a fundamental reordering of traditional environmental, constitutional and human rights law's construction of legal subjectivity. Such introspection could also carry more fully the debate about environmental constitutionalism's own ecological orientation.

---

[150] DA Kysar, 'Global Environmental Constitutionalism: Getting There from Here' (2012) 1 *Transnational Environmental Law* 83, 84.

[151] L Feris, 'Constitutional Environmental Rights: An Underutilised Resource' (2008) 24 *South African Journal on Human Rights* 29.

[152] K Bosselmann, 'Human Rights and the Environment: Redefining Fundamental Principles?' (2005) http://www.ais.up.ac.za/health/blocks/HET870/Fundamentalprinciples.pdf.

[153] Kysar, 'Global Environmental Constitutionalism' (n 150) 89.

VI. Conclusion

Based on the foregoing analysis it is impossible to agree with Tarlock's view that 'much of environmental law remains a very contested, radical idea which sits outside of the western constitutional and common law tradition'.[154] There is hardly a domestic law system that does not contain a set of environmental laws. More importantly, environmental care as an explicit or implicit regulatory function and objective is now part and parcel of most domestic constitutional systems. Various authorities cited throughout this chapter have convincingly argued this. Environmental constitutionalism clearly has become a crucial addition to the state's traditional panoply of constitutionally embedded regulatory objectives such as protection of personal freedom, the rule of law, democracy and provision of social welfare guarantees. While it is still in its conceptual formative years, discursive developments to date indicate that environmental constitutionalism is gaining increased traction as an independent term of art that encapsulates all the elements of constitutionalism and which connects them to ecological concerns.

The chapter has also shown that environmental constitutionalism is not only about rights. It can also be understood in a (often-overlapping) formal and substantive sense as relating to the various other elements that traditionally resort under the conceptual umbrella of the constitutional state including, the rule of law, constitutional supremacy, judicial independence and the review functions of courts, and democracy. While this chapter has sought to historically describe and contextualise and conceptually map and trace environmental constitutionalism along the lines of these constitutional features, Chapter 6 provides a more detailed justification of why environmental constitutionalism, as a specific regulatory response, is appropriate to help address the global socio-ecological crisis of the Anthropocene. Chapter 7 then transposes the insights gained in all previous chapters, and specifically those distilled in Chapters 6 and 7, to the global regulatory domain in an effort to determine the existence and to appraise the potential of global environmental constitutionalism in the Anthropocene.

---

[154] D Tarlock, 'The Future of Environmental "Rule of Law" Litigation' (2002) 19 *Pace Environmental Law Review* 575, 587.

6

The Prospects of Environmental Constitutionalism in the Anthropocene

I. Introduction

If ever there has been a clarion call for far-reaching regulatory interventions to halt, minimise and remediate ecological damage as a result of human actions and to adapt to Earth system changes, it is now. To do so we will, among other interventions such as technology, have to change human behaviour by means of our social regulatory institutions. Usually crafted alongside a particular ethical framework, such regulatory institutions are at once a way of expressing responsibility towards human and non-human constituents and towards the Earth system itself, while simultaneously addressing vulnerability and socio-ecological insecurity. While its emergence has an obvious relationship with and implications for the natural sciences, the elaboration of the Anthropocene mindset and its imagery (reinforced by the empirical evidence of its emergence offered in Chapter 2), are destabilising society's perceptions and expectations of the classic regulatory institutions that are situated in the humanities and that we usually employ to mediate the human-environment interface:

> The framing of world order by reference to a global crisis associated with a troublesome and highly dangerous transition from state-centric borders to globally allocated limits is a fundamental challenge that human society has never before faced on a global scale ... the present crisis is mainly a product of anthropocene [sic] activities: carbon emissions, population growth, nuclear weapons and nuclear energy, resource depletion.[1]

Acting as a framework, the Anthropocene's imagery is evidence of both the scale and severity of human-driven ecological destruction, as well as an urgent reminder of Earth system limits, vulnerability and human fragility that are vividly expressed

---

[1] R Falk, 'Can We Overcome the Global Crisis: Obstacles, Options, and Opportunities' (Keynote Address Delivered at the Tanner Conference on Global Crisis, University of Utah, 2012) www.global.ucsb.edu/climateproject/publications/pdf/Richard,%20Falk.%20Can%20We%20Overcome%20the%20Global%20Crisis.pdf.

through fast-approaching planetary boundaries.[2] At the same time its imagery 'challenges us to think differently about many things';[3] it calls for restorative and less fatalistic approaches to the future; it challenges the idea of human development; and it highlights the urgency to start thinking about human responsibilities in relation to the global socio-ecological crisis.

Questions that arise consequent upon this realisation include: what role must regulatory institutions play in mediating the human-environment interface in a possible new geological epoch; are our existing regulatory interventions sufficiently geared towards confronting Anthropocene exigencies; how should regulatory institutions for the Anthropocene be designed; should they continue down their traditional path, or become more radical and interventionist? Questions such as these provide a unique opportunity to revisit our expectations of law as a social institutional means to address the events and redirect human behaviour that are causing the Anthropocene. The central hypothesis of this book is that 'ordinary' non-constitutional law, while crucial to mediating the human-environment interface, will not be sufficient to do so on its own in the Anthropocene. A form of constitutional law, most clearly explicated by environmental constitutionalism, is required to confront Anthropocene exigencies because of the social, political, juridical and regulatory advantages that constitutionalism holds out over 'ordinary' non-constitutional law.

II. About this Chapter

While there is ample evidence of constitutional approaches to environmental protection at the domestic level, as was explained in Chapter 5, the remaining question is whether our domestic-based understanding of environmental constitutionalism can be expanded to spaces beyond the state, and if so, how could this happen alongside the roadmap that the notion of global constitutionalism offers us (see Chapter 4). Before addressing this question directly in Chapter 7 and following on from the introduction to the Anthropocene in Chapter 2, the present chapter ties the ideas of the Anthropocene and constitutionalism by critically appraising the prospects of environmental constitutionalism as an apex juridical approach to mediating the human-environment interface in the Anthropocene.

In doing so, Part 3 below first offers a discussion of the regulatory implications of viewing law through the Anthropocene lens and what this means for constitutional modes of law and governance in a generic sense. Through this discussion it will be illustrated that the expectations of law, when law is situated in the Anthropocene's cognitive framework, are arguably so far-reaching that

---

[2] See Ch 2.
[3] L Head, 'Contingencies of the Anthropocene: Lessons from the "Neolithic"' (2014) 1 *The Anthropocene Review* 113, 113.

environmental constitutionalism is, and should be, an inevitably crucial part of the global juridical response to Anthropocene exigencies. Part 4 concludes the discussion by weighing the perceived advantages of environmental constitutionalism against its perceived disadvantages with a view to critically appraising the potential of a constitutional approach to global environmental law and governance in the Anthropocene.

III. Revisiting Law in the Anthropocene: The Urgency of Constitutional Transformations

Zalasiewicz and Vidas believe that '[a]s human institutions try to come to terms with a rapidly evolving Earth system, the Anthropocene will be a defining factor in 21st century policy'.[4] Accepting this possibility and the potential of Anthropocene imagery to open up for a range of possible options for addressing the global socio-ecological crisis, we could tackle this crisis either by means of technological ingenuity that should facilitate Cornucopian-like mitigation of Anthropocene events and adaptation to Anthropocene eventualities;[5] and/or through myriad socially constructed institutions that order a society, that determine its values and common goals and that create futures for societies, including through economics, philosophy, religion and, importantly for present purposes, through law. How could the Anthropocene as a cognitive framework alter our vision of law's potential role in mediating the human-environment interface in this new epoch, and what are the resultant constitutional implications, if any?

A. Law and Order: The Anthropocene's Constitutional Moment

In stark contrast to the harmonious Holocene, in the Anthropocene the Earth system is described as being erratic, unpredictable, unstable and as operating in a 'no-analogue state'.[6] The present disorder in the Earth system and its resultant socio-ecological impacts are replicated in our social systems and are increasingly

---

[4] J Zalasiewicz and D Vidas, 'The Anthropocene—Why does it Matter for Policy-makers?' (*Government Gazette*, 24 April 2015) http://governmentgazette.eu/?p=6273.

[5] See, among others, PJ Crutzen, 'Albedo Enhancement by Stratospheric Sulfur Injections: A Contribution to Resolve a Policy Dilemma?' (2006) 77 *Climate Change* 211. Scientific and technological interventions to survive the Anthropocene are ironically concrete manifestations of human mastery over nature themselves, because it is through science and technology that humans have caused the Anthropocene, and it is through innovations such as geoengineering which is a 'seemingly perfect embodiment of the human-mastery-of-nature ethos' that humans seek to guarantee a future: B Minteer, 'Geoengineering and Ecological Ethics in the Anthropocene' (2012) 62 *BioScience* 857, 857.

[6] PJ Crutzen and W Steffen, 'Editorial Commentary: How Long have We been in the Anthropocene Era?' (2003) 61 *Climate Change* 251, 253.

being observed and confirmed by humans, working at once to impact society's notions of order and stability. Climate change is an example of an Anthropocene event that is opening up epistemic closures in our understanding of societal, political and world order, stability and security. Some already argue that climate change has the potential to threaten peace and security in the way that other major catastrophes such wars have, and that it could lead to far-reaching socio-ecological insecurity in the Anthropocene.[7] Admittedly the threats of the Anthropocene, as expressed through the example of climate change, are less immediate or sudden than a terrorist attack or a nuclear war when observed from a human lifetime perspective. In terms of geological time, however, Anthropocene events occur far more rapidly. Richardson correctly notes that 'most environmental problems and threats, such as climate change, are catastrophes in relative slow motion; although in geological time their emergence and impact can be exceptionally rapid, they remain perceptibly rather long-term for humankind'.[8] As such, the Anthropocene allows us to experience and contemplate the speed, scale and depth of global socio-ecological change much more rapidly than would have been the case if we only were to view such change as an issue of long term climate change, for example. Both in terms of human experience and perceptions of time as well as in terms of the geological timescale, the Anthropocene's sense of global socio-ecological disorder is increasingly agitating for more urgent, responsive and effective regulatory interventions to counter such disorder.[9]

Law is a social institution that has the potential not to change the Earth system, but to influence the human impact on the Earth system, while enabling humans to adapt to an increasingly erratic Earth system. To this end, law as a regulatory social institution is a crucial ingredient in any response strategy to the Anthropocene, notably to the extent that it could work to increase resilience, enable society to sustain and absorb socio-ecological stress and impacts, external interference, complex and unpredictable changes, and to confront the many complex uncertainties of the Earth system.[10] Young famously defined regulatory social institutions, such as law, as:

> sets of rules of the game or codes of conduct that serve to define social practices, assign roles to the participants in these practices, and guide the interactions among occupants of these roles ... all institutions are social artefacts created by human beings-consciously

---

[7] It has been pointed out that '[t]hough the link between climate change and breaches of international security has often been muddied by the apparent disparity between climate change and, for instance, terrorism and nuclear attacks, the parallels may in fact be much stronger. The cascading effects of climate change—its ability to inflame social, economic and political dilemmas—make it a core threat to international peace and security': T Ng, 'Safeguarding Peace and Security in our Warming World: A Role for the Security Council' (2010) 15 *Journal of Conflict and Security Law* 275, 283.

[8] B Richardson, 'A Damp Squib: Environmental Law from a Human Evolutionary Perspective' (2001) Osgoode CLPE Research Paper Series Vol 07(3) ssrn.com/abstract=1760043.

[9] J Ebbesson, 'The Rule of Law in Governance of Complex Socio-ecological Changes' (2010) 20 *Global Environmental Change* 414.

[10] ibid 414.

or unconsciously-to cope with problems of coordination and cooperation that arise as a result of interdependencies among the activities of distinct individuals or social groups.[11]

A principal aim of institutions is to provide order, societal structure and stability. In this sense law is an ancient institution that is a crucial part of society and which provides order, structure and stability to society: *ubi societas ibi jus* (where people form associations, there law is to be found).[12] There are many views on what law is and what its purpose in society is or should be.[13] For present purposes it is useful to realise that law has a human dimension in the sense that it is made and changed by humans, enforced by humans and that it applies to humans.[14] Taking a broader view, however, the core of law and of law's activity reaches beyond the human dimension to the entire cosmos where it is best understood as a means to create order: 'Juridical law deals primarily with humanity. Law is at the disposal of people to establish order within the confines of their abilities and of the capacity and suitability of the law as a means to achieve order under particular circumstances'.[15] Where humanity is therefore confronted by situations where disorder prevails or by circumstances which could disrupt prevailing order such as the Anthropocene's socio-ecological crisis, law, and in this case the constitutional aspects of law, become relevant as a means to (re-)establish order.

Of all of law's manifestations, perhaps no other juridical impulse exudes the idea of hope, order and a new, better social and political reality in a time of crisis, disorder, instability and insecurity, than that of constitutionalism. As was stated in Chapters 1 and 3, constitutionalism is a juridical construct that has historically been a central foundation of the law, and it continues to be so, today even experiencing a new-found energy that only intensifies its relevance, application and popularity around the world. One could therefore expect that, along with the recent and broader Anthropocene-induced re-interrogations into law, that the constitutional aspects of law that apply to the human-environment interface should justifiably nurture overdue conversations about the extent to which a constitutional approach could be part of the global environmental law and governance response to Anthropocene exigencies. In short: if we accept that constitutionalism is a counter-reaction to disorder, insecurity and instability, then a global constitutional

---

[11] O Young, *International Governance: Protecting the Environment in a Stateless Society* (Ithaca, Cornell University Press, 1994) 3.

[12] A maxim ascribed to Hugo Grotius, Venter explains it further as follows: 'The law operates in and for a specific community of people, because it is relevant only where the relationships between and among various persons must be regulated for the purpose of establishing and maintaining order': F Venter, *Constitutional Comparison: Japan, Germany, Canada and South Africa as Constitutional States* (Cape Town, Juta, 2000) 4.

[13] Writers such as Hart, Kelsen and Fuller, among others, have devoted extensive scholarship to these issues. See, eg, HLA Hart, *The Concept of Law*, 2nd edn (Oxford, Clarendon Press, 1994); LL Fuller, *Anatomy of the Law* (New York, FA Praeger, 1968); H Kelsen, *General Theory of Law and State* (Cambridge, Harvard University Press, 1945).

[14] Venter, *Constitutional Comparison* (n 12) 2–3.

[15] ibid 3.

form of law that applies to the human-environment interface would arguably be well-placed to more fully address the socio-ecological crisis of the Anthropocene.

Such a realisation ultimately opens up the possibility and the discursive space to consider that the Anthropocene could herald the latest, and possibly the most defining, constitutional moment in the history of world politics. To be sure, some believe that 'the emergence of the Anthropocene concept can be read as a constitutional moment in the constellation of powers' where 'rights, powers and responsibilities are openly or (more often) tacitly re-negotiated'.[16] With reference to the creation of the Charter of the United Nations in 1945, an event that fundamentally changed the world order, the Anthropocene's constitutional moment is also equated to a 'charter moment' to express the type of far-reaching and urgent institutional changes that the arrival of the Anthropocene is likely to demand.[17]

Suggesting that the Anthropocene might herald a constitutional moment should not be done frivolously though. A term that owes its existence to the American constitutional lawyer Ackerman,[18] a constitutional moment after all is typically an event that announces sweeping regime change; realignment of power structures; a wholesale reform of the legal system including the shared values and aspirations of a society that are embedded in law; and usually an entirely new approach to law, order and governance generally.[19] In addition to offering an opportunity when ordinary politics of interest group rivalry temporarily give way to a broader based consensus in favour of fundamental reforms,[20] constitutional moments herald 'new beginnings' where an idyllic 'after' stands in stark contrast with a terrible 'before';[21] they signify drastic departures from the past:

> Thus a 'constitutional moment' is characterized not as a mere inflection along the timeline of a State but by a more or less complete rupture: a new beginning, even the birth of a new nation. From the expulsion of the Etruscan kings and the founding of the Roman republic to the regime changes in the Arab Spring, it is natural that a new order rips up the old rules and writes new ones.[22]

---

[16] M Mahony, 'The Anthropocene: Reflections on a Concept—Part 1' (Topograph: Contested Landscapes of Knowing: Blogspot, 12 April 2013) thetopograph.blogspot.de/search?updated-min=2013-01-01T00:00:00-08:00&updated-max=2014-01-01T00:00:00-08:00&max-results=14. See also, F Biermann et al, 'Navigating the Anthropocene: Improving Earth System Governance' (2012) 335 *Science* 1306, 1307.

[17] N Kanie et al, 'A Charter Moment: Restructuring Governance for Sustainability' (2012) 32 *Public Administration and Development* 292.

[18] BA Ackerman, *We the People, Volume 1: Foundations* (Cambridge, Harvard University Press, 1993); BA Ackerman, *We the People, Volume 2: Transformations* (Cambridge, Harvard University Press, 1998).

[19] S Choudhry, 'Ackerman's Higher Lawmaking in Comparative Constitutional Perspective: Constitutional Moments as Constitutional Features?' (2008) 6 *Icon* 193, 199.

[20] G Miller, 'Constitutional Moments, Precommitment, and Fundamental Reform: The Case of Argentina' (1993) 71 *Washington University Law Quarterly* 1061, 1075.

[21] B Ackerman, 'The Rise of World Constitutionalism' (1997) 83 *Virginia Law Review* 771, 778–80.

[22] J Stevens, 'Constitutional Moments: The Key to Britain's Uncodified Constitution' (*Student Journal of Law*, 2013) https://sites.google.com/site/349924e64e68f035/issue-5/constitutional-moments-the-key-to-britain-s-uncodified-constitution.

Illustratively, in addition to the United Nations Charter of 1945 noted above, other constitutional moments are those of countries following a great war (Germany, for example), or of countries that have transitioned from oppressive regimes to constitutional democracies (for example, South Africa), where a constitution emerges 'as a symbolic marker of a great transition in the political life of a nation'.[23] In Germany's case, the Basic Law of the Federal Republic of Germany 1949 has become a symbol of an entire nation's break with and loathing of a National Socialist past.[24] In South Africa, likewise, the Constitution of the Republic of South Africa is a symbol of the country's ideological and *de jure* break from its oppressive apartheid past and of its new-found commitment to transformation within the parameters of constitutionalism.[25] As well, while these are examples of abrupt constitutional moments, the same type, degree and extent of constitutional change (and all that goes with that impulse) can occur, not following an abrupt single event, but also as part of a more gradual and incremental process that could span hundreds of years.[26] The British Constitution is an example of such a protracted and disaggregated, as it were, constitutional moment.[27]

In addition to effecting large-scale legal, governance and societal transformations, during constitutional moments people are generally thought to be more thoroughly and enthusiastically engaged in deliberation about the public interest, politics, law and regulation, whereas during periods of 'ordinary politics' people are more uninterested in whatever may constitute collective concerns, as they take greater interest in their private affairs.[28] To this end, and as evidenced by the former domestic examples, constitutional moments (perhaps because they carry with them the promise of change and hope for a better future) have the ability to rouse and to ignite public excitement in and thorough engagement with critical regulatory issues that concern order, stability and security. At the same time, a constitutional moment, 'even if a 'mythical' fiction in part, provides a measure of shared vision'.[29]

---

[23] Ackerman, 'Rise of World Constitutionalism' (n 21) 778.
[24] See, more generally, J Brady, B Crawford and SE Wiliarty (eds), *The Postwar Transformation of Germany: Democracy, Prosperity and Nationhood* (Ann Arbor, University of Michigan Press, 1999).
[25] See, for a cogent description of post-apartheid reconciliation and transformation in South Africa, K Henrard, 'Post Apartheid South Africa's Democratic Transformation Process: Redress of the Past, Reconciliation and "Unity in Diversity"' (2002) 1(3) *Global Review of Ethnopolitics* 18.
[26] Contiades and Fotiadou note that the change a constitutional moment seeks to effect 'may happen gradually, it may happen episodically, and perhaps it may occur through the combination of both tardiness and abruptness, forged slowly but coming to light and becoming apparent instantaneously': X Contiades and A Fotiadou, 'Models of Constitutional Change' in X Contiades (ed), *Engineering Constitutional Change: A Comparative Perspective on Europe, Canada and the USA* (New York, Routledge, 2012) 418.
[27] See, among others, C Jeffery, 'Devolution in the United Kingdom: Problems of a Piecemeal Approach to Constitutional Change' (2009) 39 *Publius: The Journal of Federalism* 289.
[28] M Tushnet, 'Potentially Misleading Metaphors in Comparative Constitutionalism: Moments and Enthusiasm' in J Weiler and C Eisgruber (eds), *Altneuland: The EU Constitution in a Contextual Perspective* (New York, NYU School of Law, 2004) 3.
[29] Stevens, 'Constitutional Moments' (n 22).

Measured against the foregoing generic descriptions of constitutional moments, could the arrival of the Anthropocene actually be the next big constitutional moment? While one must be wary of overstatement, the potential impact and significance of the Anthropocene on our broader regulatory institutions, and on law specifically, cannot be overstressed, the Anthropocene is opening up 'new understandings of the world and associated ways of governing and ordering'.[30] As such, it has the potential, at least as a cognitive framework, to elicit the type of thinking that we require to instil major transformative regulatory and world order shifts, including the creation of far-reaching domestic and global constitutional legal norms (both in a substantive and formal sense) and accompanying institutional arrangements that characterised the post-Second World War period, for example. Its increased conceptual and analytical popularity, along with its vivid imagery of socio-ecological upheaval, disorder and the many consequent insecurities and vulnerabilities it constructs, indicates that we might be facing a historical socio-ecological rupture within society, a tipping point as it were, where a business-as-usual understanding of our regulatory interventions is now giving way to a broader-based consensus in favour of fundamental reforms through, among others, constitutional arrangements resulting from emotionally shared responses to the Anthropocene's threatening exigencies. As Bosselmann more recently suggested:

> The question of whether the world is at a tipping point might be rhetorical, but should alert us to an entirely new dimension of the human experience. If it is true that we are about to undermine our own conditions of survival, we must ask what the role of the human species is in the grand scheme of things … If the current system of governance is insufficient, we should have the courage to explore and demand a new or much improved system.[31]

Statements like these suggest that like a typical constitutional moment, ours is a time of heightened existential awareness (evidenced by the growing epistemological exercise that focuses on the Anthropocene), where people, in the hope of survival, are more thoroughly and enthusiastically engaged in deliberation about the socio-institutional interventions that mediate the human-environment interface. The creation of the word 'Anthropocene', arguably more than anything else, signifies a rupture in our existential consciousness, marked as it is by a destructive, disorderly past dominated by people on the one hand, and on the other hand, hope for a future that is somehow better than the socio-ecological mayhem and insecurity we are witnessing today. To this end, the Anthropocene provides a measure of shared vision for a regulatory future and it presents us with an opportunity to open up the hitherto closed discursive spaces that relate to global environmental change and our (constitutional) regulatory responses to this change.

---

[30] ibid.
[31] K Bosselmann, *Earth Governance: Trusteeship of the Global Commons* (Cheltenham, Edward Elgar, 2015) 3.

This may not happen overnight or in any drastic fashion. The Anthropocene is after all not (yet) itself a normative concept; it remains only a trope, but a powerful one at that. Yet as a powerful trope, the Anthropocene, as a result of the severity of its imagery, is already altering the landscape of our thinking in a way that reaches further and deeper than any existing political leitmotif such as sustainable development has been able to do. Acting as a collective term encapsulating apocalyptic planetary-scale exigencies through its expression of urgency, the Anthropocene 'is a concept which is perhaps big enough to urge transformation on the level of values and ontology in a way that could never have happened in response to one singular societal or environmental challenge, from globalisation to climate change'.[32]

B. The 'Global' Regulatory Space of the Anthropocene

The Anthropocene invites a holistic perspective on a globally interconnected and reciprocally related Earth system, Earth system changes and the connection between the Earth system, its changes and the increasingly globalised human social system and the impact of humans on the Earth system. The expanding human social system is a result of globalisation and it has become a central feature of the Anthropocene.[33] More particularly, the 'planetary-scale social–ecological–geophysical system' inter-relationship underlying the Anthropocene and its human-inclusive view of the Earth system, suggest that human-driven socio-economic processes are becoming an integral part of natural Earth system process,[34] and are able to change Earth systems in profound ways, as the discussion of globalisation in Chapter 4 suggested.

Part of the imagery that the Anthropocene offers accordingly requires an expanded spatial cognition of what the Earth and its systems are, of global Earth system transformations, how Earth systems are connected globally, and how an increasingly integrated global human society is related to, dependent on, and how it impacts the Earth system. This global imperative of the Anthropocene demands not only localised regulatory interventions, but also global ones which transcend borders and which are sensitive to cause-and-effect relationships in the Earth system.

While the global imagery of the Anthropocene should not be generalised by implying that the same socio-ecological conditions occur and are experienced by everyone everywhere in exactly the same way (Whitehead correctly suggests that

---

[32] Mahony, 'The Anthropocene' (n 16).
[33] F Oldfield et al, 'The Anthropocene Review: Its Significance, Implications and the Rationale for a New Transdisciplinary Journal' (2014) 1 *The Anthropocene Review* 1, 4.
[34] W Steffen et al, 'The Anthropocene: From Global Change to Planetary Stewardship' (2011) 40 *Ambio* 739, 740.

the consequences, effects and severity of Anthropocene exigencies are felt with varying degrees of intensity in different places),[35] the arrival of the Anthropocene arguably requires of us to start thinking about law, politics and social ordering in planetary terms:

> Discussions of the Anthropocene necessarily require thinking at the scale of the biosphere and over the long term. This is a planetary issue, matters at the large scale require some consideration of ethical connection and, perhaps, the implicit invocation of a single polity, however inchoate.[36]

One way to think about law revolving around a single global polity in planetary terms is through the lens of Earth system science, and more specifically through the lens of Earth system governance. Recognising the connectivity, non-linearity and complexity of socio-ecological processes, Earth system science is concerned with the 'study of the Earth's environment as an integrated system in order to understand how and why it is changing, and to explore the implications of these changes for global and regional sustainability'.[37] Fundamentally rooted in Earth system science, Earth systems governance has been developed as a reactive counter-narrative to localised, state-based and narrowly focused regulatory approaches to environmental issues through the trite application of an issue-specific environmental governance regime that focuses on pollution control, nature conservation and wildlife, among others, and that predominantly employs formal, state-based law and state institutions. It is a way of thinking about global governance and recognising that climate change, for example, is not only a matter of rising temperatures in the United States. Climate change is also a matter of water governance, trade, armed conflict and nutrition; it impacts everyone everywhere and could be addressed by multiple state and non-state actors through a whole range of regulatory interventions of which law is only a small, but crucial, part.

With reference to a more open, holistic, flexible, multi-scalar and multi-actor regulatory approach that is better able to capture and address the many complex global developments that transform the bio-geophysical cycles and processes of the Earth, the complex relations between global transformations of social and natural systems and the multi-scale consequences of socio-ecological transformation, Biermann et al define Earth system governance as:

> the interrelated and increasingly integrated system of formal and informal rules, rule-making systems and actor networks at all levels of human society (from local to global)

---

[35] M Whitehead, *Environmental Transformations: A Geography of the Anthropocene*, Kindle edn (New York, Routledge, 2014) 4219/5354.

[36] S Dalby, 'Anthropocene Ethics: Rethinking "The Political" after Environment' (International Studies Annual Convention, Montreal, Canada, 2004) www.yumpu.com/en/document/view/42485216/anthropocene-ethics-rethinking-the-political-after-environment/3.

[37] A Ignaciuk et al, 'Responding to Complex Societal Challenges: A Decade of Earth System Science Partnership (ESSP) Interdisciplinary Research' (2012) 4 *Current Opinion in Environmental Sustainability* 147, 147.

that are set up to steer societies towards preventing, mitigating and adapting to global and local environmental change and, in particular, earth system transformation.[38]

Earth systems governance clearly is not only concerned with ways to influence and direct the Earth system (the governance of aspects of technological innovations that are able to change the Earth system might resort under its ambit): 'Earth System governance is [also] about the human impact on planetary systems. It is about the societal steering of human activities with regard to the longterm stability of geobiophysical systems'.[39] Because law is particularly adept at steering human behaviour, it is a crucial aspect of Earth systems governance. Any Earth system governance-based regulatory response, including its juridical elements, must respond to persistent Earth system uncertainty; nurture new responsibilities and modes of cooperation as a result of inter- and intra-generational, spatial and socio-ecological interdependence between people, countries, species and generations; respond to the functional interdependence of Earth systems and Earth system transformations; respond to the needs of an increasingly integrated globalised society; and respond to extraordinary degrees of socio-ecological harm.[40]

What does the foregoing mean for law? In line with the global imagery of the Anthropocene, the epistemological shift caused by Earth system governance that seeks to avoid the state-bound, localised and issue-specific 'territorial trap' to which (environmental) law is often falling victim, challenges this regulatory territorial trap by suggesting alternative mappings of social and political phenomena on a planetary scale that might contribute to better understanding and responding to contemporary regulatory transformations such as those in the Anthropocene.[41] In so doing, the Anthropocene challenges the 'cartographic imagination of the social sciences'[42] and more specifically of law, by inviting a global regulatory perspective that acknowledges the interconnectedness and reciprocity of Earth system processes and phenomena; a perspective that moves away from an issue-specific governance approach to a more holistic one.[43] It is also a perspective that discards the prevailing primacy of localised and territorially bound administrative categories of the (local) nation state that are used to govern global environmental problems

---

[38] F Biermann et al, 'Navigating the Anthropocene: The Earth System Governance Project Strategy Paper' (2010) 2 *Current Opinion in Environmental Sustainability* 202, 203. See also for a more detailed conceptual analysis, F Biermann, '"Earth System Governance" as a Cross-cutting Theme of Global Change Research' (2007) 17 *Global Environmental Change* 326; and more recently, F Biermann, *Earth System Governance: World Politics in the Anthropocene* (Cambridge, MIT Press, 2014).

[39] F Biermann, 'The Anthropocene: A Governance Perspective' (2014) 1 *The Anthropocene Review* 57, 59.

[40] Biermann, '"Earth System Governance" as a Cross-cutting Theme' (n 38) 329–30.

[41] S Dalby, 'Geographies of the International System: Globalization, Empire and the Anthropocene' in P Aalto, V Harle and S Moisio (eds), *International Studies: Interdisciplinary Approaches* (New York, Palgrave Macmillan, 2011) 126.

[42] ibid 143.

[43] Hill notes that 'there is an increasing focus from the global change community on the need for human society and the governance systems that moderate our actions and decisions to operate within multiple inter-connected earth systems': M Hill, *Climate Change and Water Governance: Adaptive Capacity in Chile and Switzerland* (Dordrecht, Springer, 2013) 5.

(such as climate change);[44] and a perspective that sees the regulatory space not only as one defined by sovereign territories, but increasingly as one that is also being shaped by global environmental phenomena and change.[45] An intrinsically rooted regulatory advantage of thinking about environmental issues in these interconnected global Earth system terms is that we are able to 'build a unified political project, based upon the common ecological fate we all share'.[46]

When viewing law though the Earth system lens, the foregoing paradigm-shifting impulses will arguably have to counter environmental law's issue-specific nature; its complete dependence for its legitimacy on the state and state sovereignty; its imprisonment by national borders; and its being mostly a product of formal state and inter-state political processes where the state functions as law's key referent object.[47] Such countering in the global discursive space of the Anthropocene could open up the possibilities for thinking about law in global terms if law were to meaningfully address the exigencies of the Anthropocene at the appropriate planetary scale that the latter demands within the context of the Earth system.

Through the Anthropocene's global lens and in tandem with the Earth systems governance metaphor, it becomes possible to envision an intermeshed global regulatory space for law that must address a whole range of multi-level, reciprocal and interconnected regulatory environmental problems. This space also includes various governance levels, normative arrangements and multiple state and non-state actors, which manifest in a multi-level spatial (geographic), temporal (applicable to present and future generations), and causal setting (interacting Earth system processes). Ideal characteristics of this global regulatory space could include: global hybrid law (including interacting legal and quasi-legal structures);[48] multi-scalarity where a range of actors in a variety of interactions contributes to internalise norms transnationally through a process of interpretation, internalisation and enforcement; and ultimately, greater regulatory responsiveness to better address the type of socio-ecological transformations that characterise the Anthropocene.[49]

The most obvious consequence of the Anthropocene and the related idea of Earth system governance's global imperative for environmental constitutionalism, is that they force the idea of domestically bound environmental constitutionalism into a global cognitive space where it is possible to construct notions of

---

[44] Dalby, 'Geographies of the International System: Globalization' (n 41) 144.

[45] HG Brauch, S Dalby and Ú Oswald Spring, 'Political Geoecology for the Anthropocene' in HG Brauch et al (eds), *Coping with Global Environmental Change, Disasters and Security: Threats, Challenges, Vulnerabilities and Risks* (Berlin, Springer, 2011) 1453.

[46] Whitehead, *Environmental Transformations* (n 35) 481/5354.

[47] LJ Kotzé, 'Fragmentation Revisited in the Context of Global Environmental Law and Governance' (2014) 131 *South African Law Journal* 548.

[48] Law could be hybrid to the extent that it is state-orchestrated rather than state-centered; decentralised rather than centralised; based on dispersed rather than bureaucratic expertise; and integrating a mix of hard and soft law rather than focusing solely on mandatory rules: H Osofsky, 'Scales of Law: Rethinking Climate Change Governance' (PhD dissertation, Oregon University, 2013) 39.

[49] ibid 45–49.

global environmental constitutionalism. To this end, the global regulatory space of the Anthropocene has formal and substantive constitutional implications for law. Following the description of environmental constitutionalism in Chapter 5, from a formal constitutionalism point of view, the Anthropocene could instigate a rethink of the constitutive and architectural design and functions of the global environmental law and governance order, including the rules that create and steer governing powers, rules about law-making and rules about conflict resolution and law enforcement. This might include discussions around a global environmental governance organisation and a global environmental constitution, as well as creating and/or strengthening regional environmental governance regimes, among others.

In terms of the substantive elements, the Anthropocene could refocus attention on those aspects of global environmental law and governance that make it constitutional in a substantive sense. The substantive environmental constitutionalism elements of the global environmental law and governance must provide certain higher-order, protective guarantees through the entrenchment into a supreme norm of particular substantive content such as provisions on the rule of law, the limitation and control of authority, measures to ensure accountability such as judicial redress, principally shared ethical values, and rights. At a more concrete level this could, for example, include the development of (a) global environmental right(s), global environmental judicial structures, and processes to enhance environmental democracy and the rule of law. Chapter 7 describes in considerably more detail these formal and substantive aspects of global environmental constitutionalism, how they current exist in the global sphere and how they could possibly come about in the light of the Anthropocene.

C. Ethics, Vulnerability and Responsibility of Care

Some argue that humans are ingenuous and that we have survived many Anthropocene-like events in the past.[50] Taking comfort in this hubris and the power of precedent, they believe we will also survive the Anthropocene. The Cornucopian argument, premised as it is on a neo-liberalist Boserupian ethic and ontology, seems to be that the Anthropocene will require little else than scientific innovation and the clever application of technologies to enable human survival. These could include mild technological interventions such as carbon capture and storage, and inventions to cope with rising water levels such as floating houses; and more invasive ones such as geo-engineering, genetic engineering, nanotechnology and synthetic biology.[51]

---

[50] See, among others, G Visconti, 'Anthropocene: Another Academic Invention?' (2014) 25 *Rendiconti Lincei* 381.
[51] Whitehead (n 35) 413/5354.

While they obviously have merit to the extent that we will also need technological innovations to survive the Anthropocene's socio-ecological crisis, these arguments seem to provide easy answers that avoid a stark reality of limits and consequentially deeper questions underlying the Anthropocene; notably questions of ethics, of responsibility and of care. In the cautionary words of Whitehead:

> [W]hile we may worry over the long-term environmental impacts of human development over the last 6000 years, some may take solace in the fact that humans are now in charge of the biosphere and are better placed than ever to address the ecological problems they have created. But this immodesty can lead us to forget that humans are still only one part of the planetary system they are transforming so rapidly. Failing to acknowledge the natural limits that exist to human development could have dreadful consequences for both the health of the planet and human wellbeing.[52]

The Cornucopian approach to surviving the Anthropocene thus ignores at least two considerations: limits exist in the biosphere's ability to supply resources and to absorb the impacts of resource use;[53] and dramatic scientific innovations such as the idea to add lead to petrol to increase engine efficiency, while solving one problem, have created a host of (arguably more severe) other problems such as the disappearance of the ozone layer and exponential increases in respiratory diseases since the widespread use of leaded petrol.[54] At the same time, the Cornucopian-inclined arguments seem to fall victim to the 'either-or' trap by ignoring the possibility that human ingenuity in science and technology can and must always work in tandem with the regulatory institutions that aim to change human behaviour, including alongside a new ethic of responsibility and care in the Anthropocene that could be expressed through our legal institutions. Technology is therefore necessary in a new geological epoch, but it cannot be the complete and final answer to ensure the continuation of life on Earth.

There is consequently no convincing reason to take assurance in hubris by solely relying on human ingenuity to secure our survival. To the extent that we need to change human behaviour as a matter of moral inter- and intra-generational and inter-species responsibility, we will also have to revisit our socio-juridical institutions that mediate the human-environment interface, including the ethical and moral foundations of these institutions. As the Amsterdam Declaration on Global Change suggests: 'An ethical framework for global stewardship and strategies for Earth System management are urgently needed. The accelerating human transformation of the Earth's environment is not sustainable'.[55] In fact, if we accept

---

[52] ibid 4219/5354.
[53] See, for a neo-Malthusian approach to limits on growth and resource use, the seminal publication by D Meadows et al, *The Limits to Growth: A Report for the Club of Rome's Project on the Predicament of Mankind* (New York, Universe Books, 1972).
[54] Whitehead (n 35) 1256/5354.
[55] International Geosphere-Biosphere Programme (IGBP) et al, 'The Amsterdam Declaration on Global Change' (2001) www.colorado.edu/AmStudies/lewis/ecology/gaiadeclar.pdf.

that '[t]he collapse of any credible distinction between humans and nature forces humanity to modify ethical codes or political aspirations',[56] as is currently the case in the Anthropocene, then an Anthropocene ethic of care that is instead cast in Malthusian-like terms is probably long overdue. One of the clearest ways to give expression to such an ethic is through law and, more importantly, through constitutional forms of law such as rights, as we have seen in preceding chapters.

Law is an expression of society's shared ethics. Law is crafted as a result of being based on a specific ethic; and law has a distinct ethical orientation that is broadly reflective of a certain attitude that members of society have towards each other as well as of the attitude towards other non-human, but living, and non-living constituents of the Earth system. Environmental law likewise derives in part its legitimacy from ethics, where a specific ethical orientation steers environmental law and associated institutions and processes to achieve a specific outcome; it justifies the existence of an environmental law system; it determines the relationship between environmental law and other socio-institutional regulatory institutions such as religion; and it helps to determine the rules that structure environmental law and governance. Ranging from a pure anthropocentric to a pure ecocentric orientation, environmental ethics usually fall out in three (potentially overlapping) strands: human rights and obligations towards other humans and towards the non-human environment; rights and obligations among states with respect to the global environment; and rights and obligations within a generation and between generations with respect to the environment.[57]

To date, there is neither any systemised and generally accepted ethical framework that has gained universal acceptance for the purpose of the Anthropocene (although some, like Kim and Bosselmann, have made tentative proposals in this regard);[58] nor is any Anthropocene-specific ethic currently expressed through global environmental law and governance. Questions pertaining to what is right and wrong, just and unjust, and the multiple potential duties and responsibilities vis-à-vis the Earth system and Earth constituents that are suitable for the Anthropocene, are increasingly being asked. The formulation of an ethical framework has accordingly just begun, and it will likely continue along an undulating path of which neither the direction, nor the final destination, is yet clear.

While the precise content of an Anthropocene ethic is (still) unclear, it is however possible at this stage to speculate about this ethic's general orientation.

---

[56] S Dalby, 'Ecology, Security, and Change in the Anthropocene' (2007) 8 *Brown Journal of World Affairs* 155, 161.

[57] See for an overview on ethics and environmental law, C Stone, 'Ethics and International Environmental Law' in D Bodansky, J Brunnée and E Hey (eds), *The Oxford Handbook of International Environmental Law* (Oxford, Oxford University Press, 2007) 292–312.

[58] They propose that ecological integrity should become the *Grundnorm* of the international environmental law order in the Anthropocene. See R Kim and K Bosselmann, 'International Environmental Law in the Anthropocene: Towards a Purposive System of Multilateral Environmental Agreements' (2013) 2 *Transnational Environmental Law* 285.

The central tenet of much of the work that is concerned with formulating an Anthropocene ethic revolves around key themes such as ecological resilience, ecological integrity, greater human responsibility, ecocentrism and inter- and intra-species justice.[59] These broader themes collectively suggest that an Anthropocene ethic is possibly turning its back on the orthodox preservationist ethos that is cast in traditional environmentalism, and often in neo-liberalist terms, where wealth creation is solely dependent on the transformation of the Earth and its resources from their natural forms and on the conservation of these resources for human benefit. If one accepts that the Anthropocene is the clearest expression yet of anthropocentric behaviour and its affects, and that anthropocentrism is the main cause of the current socio-ecological crisis as some believe it is,[60] an Anthropocene ethic should be discarding palliatives such as weak sustainable development and the pervasive constructions of anthropocentrism that are permeating law and other regulatory institutions, thus working to reinforce claims for a universal morality and some responsibility to care for the biosphere. This responsibility of care must be considered through the lens of the Anthropocene which shows us a new living reality of human domination of the biosphere where humans are no longer external observers and beneficiaries of a vulnerable Earth and its systems from which they are somehow removed. As Chapter 2 has shown, humans have become an integral part of a vulnerable biosphere and in the process we are becoming vulnerable ourselves as a result of our own activities and the power we exert over the vulnerable biosphere and its many and varied components.

As an ideal form of law that forebodes progressive social orderings that are characterised by righteousness, order, security and good rule, constitutionalism is aptly placed to counter domination of the Earth and its human and non-human constituents, especially insofar as it is able to act as an expression through its component parts such as rights, of a particular ethic that underlies juridical interventions through which it promotes human responsibility towards other humans and towards the non-human environment in an inter and intra-generational sense. To this end a constitutional approach to law in the Anthropocene could provide a mediated deliberative framework that is firmly based on an ecological orientation of responsibility and care where:

> competing notions of the common good can be made compatible or arbitrated in a manner acceptable to all, thereby balancing democratic concerns with the control of the political process by a few with the risk of a tyranny by the many.[61]

---

[59] See, eg, LJ Kotzé, 'Human Rights and the Environment in the Anthropocene' (2014) 1 *The Anthropocene Review* 1.

[60] Already in 1992, Bosselmann warned that '[d]er Anthropozentrismus ist die tiefste Ursache der ökologischen Krise': K Bosselmann, *Im Namen der Natur: Der Weg zum ökologischen Rechtsstaat* (Bern, Scherz, 1992) 14.

[61] M Maduro, 'The Importance of Being Called a Constitution: Constitutional Authority and the Authority of Constitutionalism' (2005) 3 *International Journal of Constitutional Law* 332, 333.

IV. The Prospects of Environmental Constitutionalism in the Anthropocene

The potential impact of the Anthropocene on our understanding of juridical regulatory interventions and their constitutional aspects has been sketched in broad terms above. If we accept that law needs to change in the Anthropocene and that part of this change will involve constitutional transformations flowing from constitutional moments, the question to be addressed in the remainder of this chapter is: why would a constitutional approach to environmental protection, on balance, be preferable to a non-constitutional approach in times of unprecedented socio-ecological upheaval?

The failures of environmental constitutionalism have not received anywhere near the depth of attention that the successes or advantages of environmental constitutionalism have. This is perhaps understandable considering that the proponents of environmental constitutionalism would prefer to portray this apex juridical mode of law and governance in the best possible light (as this book also seeks to do). Admittedly though, environmental constitutionalism will always be plagued by the same problems and deficiencies that beset constitutionalism generally, including those already listed in Chapters 1 and 3. For example, constitutionalism is accused of being politically idealist and scientifically naïve; it can and often does come down to semantical gymnastics as a result of its terms being vague or passive, which in turn impedes potential for creating responsibilities and for enforcement. Because it is mostly cast in human rights terms, the environmental constitutionalism movement also runs the risk of being labelled as being too anthropocentric; and while it is an 'intellectually and emotionally fulsome'[62] exercise, its practical successes do not always back up its claims.

Yet, as determined from a domestic perspective, there is a strong case to be made in favour of environmental constitutionalism based on its numerous advantages that, on balance, arguably outweigh the disadvantages. Building on from those generic advantages of environmental constitutionalism highlighted in Chapter 5, the following advantages render environmental constitutionalism particularly suitable for the Anthropocene's socio-ecological crisis. Because this is a generic determination, these benefits could be equally translated to the global regulatory sphere; an issue that is explored in Chapter 7.

A. Higher-order Juridical Guarantees and Care

Because it is considerably more difficult to amend, overrule or nullify constitutional law (as opposed to normal legislation), constitutional environmental

---

[62] JR May and E Daly, *Global Environmental Constitutionalism*, Kindle edn (New York, Cambridge University Press, 2015) 1000/11268–1036/11268, 1222/11268.

protection is the highest juridical level for a society (and governments more specifically as public trustees of the environment) to express the importance of and to give effect to environmental protection: constitutional protection 'is a necessary [foundational] first step to ensure that government policy reflects the need to forego some material prosperity in the interest of environmental preservation'.[63] May and Daly add that because of environmental constitutionalism's normative superiority, the regulated community is more likely to respond to environmental constitutional provisions than to any other normative command:

> Because constitutionalism bespeaks of shared national values rather than more narrowly conceived limitations on the activities of private enterprise, the likelihood of compliance with constitutional directives increases while resistance and challenges to such obligations may decrease.[64]

As we have seen in Chapter 5, a constitution also remains the only juridically superior instrument that deeply entrenches, at the highest possible level, a collective ethical recognition of the need for environmental protection in the same way that the importance of equality or life is recognised in a polity and expressed through a constitution. Just as a post-constitutional society such as South Africa would value and seek to protect through its constitution human dignity, the achievement of equality and the advancement of human rights and freedoms[65] (as opposed to a pre-constitutional South Africa where these values were absent), a constitution that is oriented towards environmental care would seek to recognise the inextricable connection between humans and the environment, and the importance of protecting the environment as an enduring matter of constitutional importance, also for the sake of maintaining a sense of socio-ecological order and stability. Environmental constitutionalism could therefore put environmental care on the same footing as 'traditional' constitutional values and goals such as elimination of inequality by recognising the environment as either the basis of the (ecological) constitutional state, or as being inextricably interlinked with these traditional constitutional values and goals which depend for their own realisation on the environment. At a practical level the constitutional superiority of environmental care could, for example, mediate conflict between constitutional and statutory law where a more protective constitutional environmental provision would prevail as a result of its superior status.

B. A Foundational Determinant of Secondary Regimes

Environmental constitutionalism creates, terminates, determines and directs the secondary environmental law regime including its statutes, principles, common

---

[63] JYP Jnr, 'Toward a Constitutionally Protected Environment' (1970) 56 *Virginia Law Review* 458, 486.
[64] May and Daly, *Global Environmental Constitutionalism* (n 62) 812/11268.
[65] Constitution of the Republic of South Africa, s 1.

and customary laws, as well as this regime's relationship with international and foreign environmental law. To this end environmental constitutionalism could provide an impetus for stronger environmental laws that are based on and legitimised through a constitution by providing and regulating the institutional machinery that creates these laws and by setting certain minimum standards to which environmental law and governance must aspire.[66] Environmental constitutionalism could bolster the implementation and enforcement of environmental laws by affording the appropriate state institutions the necessary powers to do so in a way that simultaneously respects the general tenets of constitutionalism such as rule of law and rights protection requirements. It could also offer a safety net by filling gaps in environmental laws and a general protective measure where the secondary regime fails.[67] An incidental, but no less important, function of environmental constitutionalism is to promote coordination of environmental protection in a specific legal system by providing a unifying constitutional foundation and overarching legal and normative framework for directing silo-based and institutionally fragmented environmental policy, law and governance.[68] Environmental constitutionalism could provide an imprimatur to ensure and promote complementarity of different regimes that are situated at various governance levels.[69]

C. Benchmarking Environmental Protection Through Transnationalism

As a result and as a potentially integral part of the emerging phenomenon of transnational comparative constitutionalism that sees an increasingly transnational migration, interdependence, crosspollination and sharing of constitutional features between many countries, environmental constitutionalism could foster greater global coordination and cooperation between the actors in global governance as far as environmental protection is concerned, including the development of a more unified or even universal standard of environmental protection in various countries across the world.[70] After all, there are various common aspects

---

[66] eg, the South African environmental right (s 24 of the Constitution of the Republic of South Africa), is set as the minimum aspirational standard in virtually all of South Africa's environmental laws. See, among others, the provisions of the country's environmental framework law, the National Environmental Management Act, 107 of 1998.

[67] DR Boyd, *The Environmental Rights Revolution: A Global Study of Constitutions, Human Rights, and the Environment* (Vancouver, UBC Press, 2012) 28–33.

[68] JYP Jnr, 'Toward a Constitutionally Protected Environment' (n 63) 486. Not only the international, but also numerous domestic environmental law systems, are considered to be severely fragmented which leads to myriad regulatory problems such as duplication of governance efforts, regulatory uncertainty, lengthy administrative delays, human and financial resources implications and shifting of environmental problems from one environmental medium to another without holistically solving it. See, among others, Kotzé, 'Fragmentation Revisited' (n 47) 548–83.

[69] May and Daly (n 62) 1131/11268.

[70] LJ Kotzé, 'Arguing Global Environmental Constitutionalism' (2012) 1 *Transnational Environmental Law* 199.

inherent to the protection of, for example, human dignity and equality among the world's constitutional democracies that collectively work towards a more universal and unified global recognition of the importance of protecting human dignity and equality (as expressed, for example, through the Universal Declaration of Human Rights 1948); a trend that could extend into the environmental domain as well. In addition, specific provisions in domestic constitutions, especially those related to human rights, have been influenced by globally applicable international law instruments such as those in the 'international Bill of Rights' discussed in Chapter 4. Yet, the international Bill of Rights does not contain explicit environmental provisions, which suggests that environmental rights in domestic constitutions are mainly a result of transnational legal processes between countries.

An additional advantage of environmental constitutionalism from a transnational comparative perspective is the potential it has over time to inform the creation of supra-national environmental constitutionalism provisions, such as a global environmental right.[71] The development of a strong supra-national environmental rights regime, whether in the form of a single global instrument and/or through regional human rights treaties, could provide an important benchmark to countries in terms of which they could measure and improve their respective domestic environmental law regimes. Environmental constitutionalism could thus play a compensatory role by filling interstitial gaps in other legal systems that have been created by inadequate international, regional and domestic environmental laws.[72] Conversely, as we have seen with the phenomenon of transnational comparative constitutionalism in Chapter 4, constitutional instruments are particularly receptive to external influences from international, regional and foreign legal systems especially insofar as domestic and regional courts rely on the latter legal regimes to guide their interpretation of a constitution. Such practices could significantly contribute to aligning domestic environmental constitutional regimes with prevailing supra-national good practices and provide the impetus for a globalised notion of environmental rights and justice.

D. Regulatory Longevity

Constitutional environmental protection is far more enduring and long-lasting than a non-constitutionalised approach because a constitution, as the *lex suprema*, deeply entrenches at a much higher juridical level the strategically important long-term socio-political ethos and objectives of a society, thus achieving a measure of longevity that would have been less likely to achieve under the auspices of narrow political majorities working through legislative processes, and that tend to change

---

[71] See, more generally on the potential of a global environmental right, SJ Turner, *A Global Environmental Right* (Abingdon, Routledge, 2014).
[72] May and Daly (n 62) 1000/11268.

after each election.[73] In other words, environmental constitutionalism guarantees some degree of long-lasting environmental protection that is more immune to the whimsical onslaughts of daily politics. At a more practical level, by preventing regulatory rollbacks because superior constitutions are difficult to amend, environmental constitutionalism could prevent future governments from weakening environmental laws and standards.[74]

E. Environmental Awareness and Societal Involvement

Because constitutions often embody the soul and spirit of a nation, a constitutional approach could play a cultural and educational role that is removed from, yet complementary to, its more traditional regulatory function, thus working to instil broader societal environmental care where it sets an example for people:

> [C]onstitutional provisions promote a model character for the citizenry to follow, and they influence and guide public discourse and behavior. On a practical level, the public tends to be more familiar with constitutional provisions than specific statutory laws.[75]

A related point is that constitutional environmental protection enables participative environmental governance through various procedural entitlements that seek to guarantee and promote a citizenry's inclusivity and representation in decision-making,[76] thus enhancing the critical aspects of good environmental governance and realising substantive environmental objectives.[77] This aspect has much to do with democracy and the formal aspects of the rule of law that are necessary to protect and realise substantive entitlements.

F. Inter-generational Reach

Constitutions could work prospectively to the extent that they are 'intergenerational compacts' or 'agreements that one generation makes both to bind and [to] benefit future generations'.[78] Based on their special historical contexts and their temporally forward-looking view, constitutions act now to make possible a certain

---

[73] J Bruckerhoff, 'Giving Nature Constitutional Protection: A Less Anthropocentric Interpretation of Environmental Rights' (2008) 86 *Texas Law Review* 616, 623.

[74] Boyd, *Environmental Rights Revolution* (n 67) 30.

[75] E Brandl and H Bungert, 'Constitutional Entrenchment of Environmental Protection: A Comparative Analysis of Experiences Abroad' (1992) 16 *Harvard Environmental Law Review* 1, 4.

[76] T Hayward, *Constitutional Environmental Rights*, e-book (Oxford, Oxford University Press, 2005) ch 1, p 4/15–5/15.

[77] Understood here as environmental governance that more or less strives towards the ideals of inclusiveness, democracy, deliberation, fairness, legitimacy, efficiency and effectiveness. See S Bernstein, 'Globalization and the Requirements of "Good" Environmental Governance' (2005) 4 *Perspectives on Global Development and Technologies* 645.

[78] May and Daly (n 62) 1107/11268.

kind of world and society for the present and for the future. Ekeli points out that constitutions are considered to be able to steer the direction of future politics because they are difficult to amend, and because they constrain the actions of a present government that is (also) bound by the decisions of earlier electorates, while decisions that might impact the environment are simultaneously withdrawn from the immediate control of present majorities and state authorities.[79] Ackerman refers to this temporal characteristic of constitutions more generally as a 'conversation between generations'[80] which opens up, in the words of Kysar, the possibility for any polity to 'seek to better hear the diachronic expressions of future generations'.[81] While this temporality does not necessarily equate to a situation where future generations are afforded rights per se (although such a possibility should not be discounted), it does offer a present society and its constitution a unique opportunity to establish possible futures for a society,[82] with society's theories, values and purposes that should ideally be long-termist and therefore better able to respond to the futures of yet-to-be-born generations in the Anthropocene. This temporality often finds clearest expression through environmental rights when they 'express a preference for long term values over the decisions that a majority or a minority may make for short-term gain'.[83] For example, while stopping short of providing future generation with rights, the South African environmental right reveals its future-facing normative orientation by stating that everyone has the right 'to have the environment protected, for the benefit of present and future generations'.[84] A constitutional statement such as this could also engender some longevity by expressing a preference for long-term ecological values to prevail over short-term, and often decidedly self-interested, claims.[85]

G. Legitimisation of Environmental Law and Governance

Environmental constitutionalism creates and situates a specific polity and it defines a political community by providing people with a specific legal identify and connecting them with the environmental regulatory regime in a specific geographic area.[86] The environmental interests of people living in a specific space are therefore connected with the obligations of a government and there is a legitimate

---

[79] K Ekeli, 'Green Constitutionalism: The Constitutional Protection of Future Generations' (2007) 20 *Ratio Juris* 378, 380–81.
[80] B Ackerman, 'The Living Constitution' (2007) 120 *Harvard Law Review* 1737, 1793–809.
[81] DA Kysar, 'Global Environmental Constitutionalism: Getting There from Here' (2012) 1 *Transnational Environmental Law* 83, 90.
[82] P Allot, 'The Concept of International Law' in M Byers (ed), *The Role of Law in International Politics: Essays in International Relations and International Law* (Oxford, Oxford University Press, 2001) 69–89.
[83] May and Daly (n 62) 1119/11268.
[84] S 24(b).
[85] May and Daly (n 62) 1116/11268.
[86] ibid 1063/11268.

basis to take legislative, executive and judicial action to fulfil these obligations. This in turn, works to legitimise the environmental governance actions of the polity and of a government that they have developed to protect their interests and to reinforce the trustee obligations that a government has.[87]

H. Levelling the Sustainable Development Playing Field

Finally, environmental constitutionalism could work to 'level the playing field' by affording environmental considerations the same status as socio-economic considerations in decision-making.[88] Because of its superior constitutional status, a constitutionally protected environment would carry equal weight and demand equal consideration by environmental authorities, including courts, where there is a conflict between social, economic and environmental interests. This could be achieved, among others, by constitutionally entrenching the concept of sustainability in a constitution (mostly in the form of an environmental right), as South Africa has done. As a result, the South African Constitutional Court[89] has confirmed that sustainable development is a constitutional issue:

> This case raises an important question concerning the obligation of State organs when making decisions that may have a substantial impact on the environment … The need to protect the environment cannot be gainsaid. So, too, is the need for social and economic development. How these two compelling needs interact, their impact on decisions affecting the environment and the obligations of environmental authorities in this regard, are *important constitutional questions*.[90]

Following a detailed interrogation of sustainable development in South African statutory and constitutional law (notably in the context of the environmental right), including an assessment of international law, the Court found that:

> development cannot subsist upon a deteriorating environmental base. Unlimited development is detrimental to the environment and the destruction of the environment is detrimental to development. Promotion of development requires the protection of the environment. Yet the environment cannot be protected if development does not pay attention to the costs of environmental destruction. The environment and development are thus inexorably linked.[91]

---

[87] Bosselmann, *Earth Governance* (n 31) 155–97.
[88] Boyd (n 67) 30.
[89] *Fuel Retailers Association of Southern Africa v Director General: Environmental Management, Department of Agriculture, Conservation and Environment, Mpumalanga Province* 2007 (6) SA 4 (CC). See for a detailed discussion, LJ Kotzé, 'Sustainable Development and the Rule of Law for Nature: A Constitutional Reading' in C Voigt (ed), *Rule of Law for Nature: New Dimensions and Ideas in Environmental Law* (Cambridge, Cambridge University Press, 2013) 130–42.
[90] Para I at p 20–para A at p 21.
[91] Paras E–H at p 21.

Here the Court clearly recognises that socio-economic development cannot be divorced from ecological considerations. In this sense, sustainable development is not only a constitutional objective, it is also a constitutional mediating principle and approach to resolve the conflict that inevitably arises between competing social, economic and ecological considerations. The integration principle which has been squarely located within the parameters of constitutionalism by the Court 'implies the need to reconcile and accommodate these three pillars of sustainable development' through which '[s]ustainable development provides a framework for reconciling socio-economic development and environmental protection'.[92]

V. Conclusion

Biermann argues that in the course of the twenty-first century 'the Anthropocene is likely to change the way we understand political systems both analytically and normatively, from the village level up to the United Nations'.[93] This shift in how we perceive the world, order, politics, governance and security is already occurring. To this end, the Anthropocene notably provides us with an intellectual space to better understand global socio-ecological changes, and the myriad insecurities and vulnerabilities that arise as a result, while offering ways to contemplate the (re)design of our regulatory interventions that must address this change. At an ethical level the Anthropocene imagery creates a new position of responsibility for humans who, as destroyers of ecosystems, are ironically uniquely situated to design and implement regulatory interventions that must respond to the global socio-ecological crisis of the Anthropocene that humans have created in the first place. This places a profound responsibility of care on us to address our vulnerabilities and those of the entire Earth system while offering us an opportunity to create possible futures through, among others, our institutional interventions such as law.

The significance of the Anthropocene mindset for law and constitutionalism lies in its potential to instigate a global constitutional moment, which could see a wholesale restructuring of global institutions, norms and the global legal order itself. To this end, constitutionalism is important for regulation in the Anthropocene epoch because it provides a familiar way of thinking about, designing and applying laws that must establish and maintain order; provide long-term societal and political stability and socio-ecological security; and achieve integration and unification as far as a global identity that is based on a specific ethic of care is concerned, including consensus on matters of common public concern

---

[92] Paras E–F at p 25.
[93] Biermann, 'The Anthropocene: A Governance Perspective' (n 39) 60.

that will increasingly arise as a result of the Anthropocene's global socio-ecological crisis.

On balance it seems that a law and governance order that provides for environmental constitutionalism is more preferable to respond to the Anthropocene than one that does not. This is clear from the various advantages that environmental constitutionalism holds out. If we consider that a constitutional moment might be possible in the Anthropocene, to what extent is it possible to trace elements of environmental constitutionalism in the global regulatory space and what should these global environmental constitutional aspects ideally be so that they could respond to the Anthropocene's global socio-ecological crisis in the best possible way? These questions are addressed in the following, penultimate, Chapter 7.

7

A Vision of Global Environmental Constitutionalism in the Anthropocene

I. Introduction

Global constitutionalism has not yet been meaningfully situated in the environmental law and governance domain. With rare exceptions, environmental lawyers have been surprisingly reluctant to explore comprehensively the potential of the burgeoning global constitutionalism movement for their own globally relevant regulatory concern (ie the environment).[1] Conversely, there is reluctance among global constitutionalists to invite environmental conversations into their specialist discourse.[2] While significant inroads have been made to provide for domestic constitutional environmental protection, as we have seen in Chapter 5, 'the environment' has been unable to grab the attention of global constitutionalists in the same way that global constitutionalism has managed to do with human rights, for example. Reflecting on this lack of sustained and critical mutual engagement, Bosselmann points out that:

> we can think of the environment as a universal concern. Arguably, the environment is even more fundamental than human rights as it represents the natural conditions of all life including human beings. Both the protection of human rights and the protection of the environment are constitutionally relevant precisely because of their fundamental importance ... If we accept that the twenty-first century will be defined by its success or failure of protecting human rights and the environment, then global environmental constitutionalism, like global constitutionalism in general, becomes a matter of great urgency.[3]

---

[1] Examples of environmental law publications are J May and E Daly, *Global Environmental Constitutionalism*, Kindle edn (New York, Cambridge University Press, 2015); LJ Kotzé, 'Arguing Global Environmental Constitutionalism' (2012) 1(1) *Transnational Environmental Law* 199–233; K Bosselmann, 'Global Environmental Constitutionalism: Mapping the Terrain' 2015 (21) *Widener Law Review* 171–85; L Kotzé, 'The Conceptual Contours of Global Environmental Constitutionalism' (2015) 21 *Widener Law Review* 187–200.

[2] Environmental concerns are dealt with to a limited extent in C Schwöbel, *Global Constitutionalism in International Legal Perspective* (Leiden, Brill Nijhoff, 2011).

[3] Bosselmann, 'Global Environmental Constitutionalism' (n 1) 173.

The global constitutionalism discourse and the environmental law and governance fraternity are arguably poorer for not more deliberately creating common epistemological spaces to merge the increasingly pressing and overlapping themes of global constitutionalism and environmental protection.

II. About this Chapter

As an amalgamation of the different thoughts and findings that have thus far been offered in this book, this penultimate chapter endeavours to create such a common epistemological space to think about global environmental constitutionalism; to translate environmental constitutionalism to the global regulatory domain; and to propose a more systematic and comprehensive understanding of global environmental constitutionalism, its possible manifestations, its components and approaches thereto. It does so firstly in Part 3 by constructing a motivation in support of opening closed epistemic spaces in the global constitutionalism and environmental discourses that could be more receptive to 'radical' ideas such as global constitutionalism and the Anthropocene. For this purpose the argument focuses on the three main drivers behind global constitutionalism in the context of the Anthropocene ie globalisation, fragmentation and enhanced regulation of global problems that have been identified in Chapter 4.[4]

Taking a *lex lata* and *lex ferenda* stance, Part 4 investigates the environmental aspects of the different (related and often overlapping) approaches to global constitutionalism elaborated in Chapter 4 including: the internationalist approach, the regionalist approach, the international regulatory regime approach, the global civil society constitutionalism approach and, finally, the transnational comparative constitutionalism approach.[5] This discussion paints global environmental constitutionalism in various regulatory settings and contexts where it is continuously being shaped and driven by divergent state, global civil society and regional environmental governance agendas.

Continuing this chapter's backward- and forward-looking approach, with reference to the general features of the constitutional state that were distilled in Chapter 3 and their application in the domestic environmental constitutionalism domain set out in Chapter 5, the final part discusses in detail how these features currently do, and ideally should, manifest in the global environmental constitutionalism paradigm. In doing so, a framework is constructed for envisioning global environmental constitutionalism in terms of its component parts, ie a global environmental constitution, global environmental rule of law, separation of global environmental powers, the global environmental judiciary, global environmental

---

[4] See Ch 4, pts IV.A–IV.C.
[5] See Ch 4, pt V.

democracy, global environmental constitutional supremacy and, finally, global environmental rights.

III. From Domestic to Global Environmental Constitutionalism

Domestic environmental constitutionalism is a familiar paradigm that could provide a blueprint for global environmental constitutionalism. Global environmental constitutionalism, in turn, could potentially enable the state to extend its environmental regulatory abilities to the global space beyond its borders and sphere of direct influence and control, to a space where its abilities and influence are far more tentative, but no less important. This global regulatory space is one where (a) law and governance arrangements are deemed insufficient or inappropriate to deal with the environment-related regulatory challenges of a globalised world; (b) one where there is an increasingly urgent need for enhanced regulation of global environmental problems; and (c) one where a fragmented global environmental law and governance regime is evident. All three of these motivations for global constitutionalism, that have been dealt with generically in Chapter 4, could require the extension of environmental constitutionalism globally in a nuanced way that is sensitive to, and that could accommodate, criticisms generally levelled against attempts to transplant domestic conceptions of constitutionalism to the global level.[6]

With respect to (a), the impact of globalisation on our traditional systems of order, and our axiomatic conceptions of the latter, have been and continue to be immense. Globalisation is challenging how we view age-old doctrines with respect to the state, law and governance, visions of global anarchy and order, and familiar ways to co-exist sustainably, also in the environmental context.[7] It was already pointed out in Chapter 4 that in a globalised world, as an issue that affects all states everywhere, the environment goes beyond the state as a regulatory concern in the sense that borders do not confine it or the many associated processes, impacts and externalities resulting from globalisation that affect the environment. As is the case with other areas of international law such as trade, in the global regulatory space beyond the state, the extent, depth and intensity of environmental legal regulation is not as clear or comprehensive as it might be in domestic jurisdictions. Adding to regulatory challenges, globalisation and its impacts exacerbate the type and severity of socio-ecological conditions that arise in the Anthropocene, with amplified

---

[6] Including that an exact and complete translation of domestic constitutionalism to the global sphere might be inappropriate, inconceivable and improbable. See Ch 4, pt III.

[7] LJ Kotzé, *Global Environmental Governance: Law and Regulation for the 21st Century* (Cheltenham, Edward Elgar, 2012), specifically Ch 2.

human activity globally that increasingly impact an interconnected Earth system. This is especially true for the economic growth aspects associated with globalisation that are fundamentally neo-liberal and that seek to liberate people from overbearing state interventions so that they are able to pursue their economic self-interests.[8] Climate change is a typical example of an issue that arises as a result of increased globalised economic activities and it strains the regulatory machinery of a state to the extent that climate change cannot be governed by a single state, its constitution and its legal order alone. It is an interconnected global problem that demands a collective global response by many states and a diverse range of non-state actors at multiple geographically and functionally defined governance levels.[9]

With respect to (b), the Anthropocene and its imagery, supported by evidence of its emergence (see Chapter 2), today serve as evidence that our existing global environmental law and governance arrangements have been unable to preserve Holocene conditions, and to prevent human-induced Anthropocene events from affecting Earth system integrity. The deepening socio-ecological crisis requires a radical alternative to the business-as-usual global environmental law and governance approach if we are to preserve life on Earth. For lawyers and juridical science, an alternative mindset is only possible if we open up epistemological closures that currently prevent us from thinking differently about global environmental law and governance. Such an alternative mindset must allow us to think creatively about the potential of juridical constructions such as constitutionalism that could function as an apex regulatory intervention to counter domination, create order and strive for better regulatory outcomes in the Anthropocene. To this end, one of the many reasons for pursuing the global constitutionalism agenda and to transpose domestic conceptions of constitutionalism globally to the environmental context, would be to enable regulators to benefit from the advantages of environmental constitutionalism as a response to the exigencies of the Anthropocene. These advantages have been detailed in Chapter 6. While environmental constitutionalism and its potential regulatory advantages will not suddenly solve all global socio-ecological problems, the constitutional arsenal is available to address the regulatory deficits that lead to, perpetuate and exacerbate these problems. To this end, global environmental constitutionalism could help to reform the foundational regulatory make-up of global laws, ethics, politics and of society itself, with a view to opening up possibilities for preventing and mitigating ecological damage and facilitating adaptation. The constitutional moment of the Anthropocene has the long-term potential to be as paradigm-shifting as the post-Second World War constitutional moment was.[10]

---

[8] D Gray and L Colucci-Gray, 'Globalisation and the Anthropocene: The Reconfiguration of Science Education for a Sustainable Future' (2014) 2(3) *Sisyphus Journal of Education* 14–31, 18.

[9] See most recently, R Lyster, *Climate Justice and Disaster Law* (Cambridge, Cambridge University Press, 2015).

[10] See Ch 6 for a detailed discussion.

Finally, as far as (c) is concerned, various scholars have pointed out that the global environmental law and governance order is fragmented.[11] Fragmentation manifests as conflict between specialised environment-related law regimes such as the trade regime vis-à-vis the environmental governance regime; conflicts within the global environmental law and governance regime that exist between issue-specific sub-regimes such as biodiversity and climate change; the proliferation of multilateral environmental agreements; the concomitant mushrooming of inter-state structures and treaty regimes to govern these instruments; the fragmentary growth of secondary or procedural rules as a result of the fragmentation of primary substantive rules; treaty congestion; and conflicts between various adjudication bodies.[12] Biermann indicates that:

> Since 1972, when UNEP was set up, the increase in international environmental regimes has led to ... considerable fragmentation of the entire system. Norms and standards in each area of environmental governance are created by distinct legislative bodies—the conferences of the parties to various conventions—with little respect for repercussions and links with other fields. While the decentralized negotiation of rules and standards in separate functional bodies may be defensible, this is less so regarding the organisational fragmentation of the various convention secretariats, which have evolved into quite independent bureaucracies with strong centrifugal tendencies.[13]

Fragmentation as such is, however, not necessarily problematic when one thinks about global environmental law and governance from an Earth system governance perspective.[14] It could possibly be desirable to the extent that a fragmented global environmental law and governance order is more responsive to highly complex Anthropocene exigencies. Chapters 2 and 6 indicated that the Earth and its systems are unpredictable, non-linear, unstructured and complex, with diverse externalities that could probably be better addressed by means of an equally hybrid, diverse, responsive and flexible normative regulatory approach. The regulatory complexities of the Anthropocene would require, among others, disaggregated multi-actor governance that is entrenched in a multi-scalar global context and that consists of hybrid forms of state and non-state laws and hybrid normative options. In the context of the Anthropocene, fragmentation, as meaning a regulatory context for adaptive, reflexive, flexible, responsive, and dynamic global environmental law and governance, could:

> act to support emergent and self-organizing processes instead of constraining them ... create bridging functions and frame creativity for adaptive governance [as a result of

---

[11] See for an in-depth discussion, L Kotzé, 'Fragmentation Revisited in the Context of Global Environmental Law and Governance' (2014) 131 *South African Law Journal* 548–83.

[12] See, among others, R Wolfrum and N Matz, *Conflicts in International Environmental Law* (Heidelberg, Springer Verlag, 2003).

[13] F Biermann, 'The Rationale for a World Environment Organization' in F Biermann and S Bauer (eds), *A World Environment Organization: Solution or Threat for Effective International Environmental Governance?* (Aldershot, Ashgate, 2005) 120.

[14] See Ch 6, pt III.B.

which] dynamic efficiency is enhanced by systems of governance that exist at multiple levels with some degree of autonomy complemented by modest overlaps in authority and capability ... A polycentric decision-making structure allows for testing of rules at different scales and aids resource users at multiple levels in the crafting of new institutions to cope with changing situations.[15]

Having said that, fears about fragmentation of global environmental law and governance are likely to remain and to mirror the general apprehension international lawyers have about fragmentation of the international legal order. As was indicated in Chapter 4, these include that fragmentation could be a threat to the consistency, stability, credibility, reliability and ultimately the authority and legitimacy of the international legal order.[16] Constitutionalism, while it will not necessarily integrate this order, is a normative and analytical approach to work towards greater stability, legitimacy, predictability and ultimately effectiveness of the global environmental law and governance order.

IV. Global Environmental Constitutionalism's Five Approaches

The different (often overlapping) tracks in terms of which global constitutionalism could manifest have been discussed in Chapter 4.[17] The following part situates these tracks in the environmental domain with a view to constructing a roadmap of global environmental constitutionalism's potential diverse approaches.

A. The Internationalist Approach

The mainstream internationalist approach to global environmental constitutionalism mostly focuses on the constitutionalisation of international environmental law and its institutions, including on aspects related to the existence or

---

[15] C Folke et al, 'Reconnecting to the Biosphere' (2011) 40(7) *Ambio* 719–38, 729. This optimism about fragmentation is shared by Kanie, who believes that:

> Current research on institutions has shown that the best institutional design for managing complex problems such as the global environment is a loose, decentralized and dense network of institutions and actors that are able to relay information and provide *sufficient redundancies* in the performance of functions so that *inactivity of one institution does not jeopardize the entire system. Multiple forums allow multiple opportunities for multiple actors to hold discussions and to take action*. This increases the visibility of environmental governance and results in norm diffusion.

N Kanie, 'Governance with Multilateral Environmental Agreements: A Healthy or Ill-equipped Fragmentation?' in L Swart and E Perry (eds), *Global Environmental Governance: Perspectives on the Current Debate* (Centre for UN Reform Education, 2007) 73.

[16] M Koskenniemi and P Leino, 'Fragmentation of Internal Law? Postmodern Anxieties' (2002) 15(3) *Leiden Journal of International Law* 553–79, 560.

[17] See pt V.

emergence of: an international environmental organisation, a global environmental constitution and a hierarchy of environmental norms such as environmental *jus cogens* and *erga omnes* obligations and rights. Prominent commentators pursuing this approach include, among others, Bosselmann, Bodansky and Biermann.[18] The extent to which it is possible to state the existence or emergence of a global environmental constitution, global environmental rights and associated higher-order global norms is examined in greater detail below. The remainder of this discussion reflects on the issue of a global environmental authority as part of the internationalist approach to global environmental constitutionalism.

Whether a global environmental authority exists or should exist has been and continues to be a contentious issue in the literature and in global environmental diplomacy.[19] While the most obvious candidate for such an authority is the United Nations Environment Programme, it is believed that its 'mandate, power and resources to undertake the task of integrating environment and development within the UN system of institutions, programs and activities ... was almost set up to fail as a leader in GEG [global environmental governance]'.[20] The majority view today remains that UNEP is not a powerful international environmental organisation in the true sense of the word, and that it is unlikely that global environmental diplomacy will lead to the creation of such a powerful institution in the short or medium term:

> The organizations on which we depend [for global environmental governance], especially UNEP, have narrow mandates, small budgets, and limited support. No one organization has the authority or political strength to serve as the center of gravity for international environmental efforts. Nor does any organization have the mission or resources to respond to global environmental externalities and to establish norms for behavior in international environmental relations.[21]

While there are minor initiatives afoot to contemplate the establishment of a world environmental organisation,[22] if the current lack of political will to establish such an organisation is anything to go by, the guiding and coordinating functions of UNEP are more likely to be gradually strengthened and supplemented in

---

[18] Bosselmann (n 1); D Bodansky, 'Is There an International Environmental Constitution?' (2009) (16)(2) *Indiana Journal of Global Legal Studies* 565–84, 567; F Biermann, 'Reforming Global Environmental Governance: From UNEP towards a World Environmental Organization' in Swart and Perry (eds), *Global Environmental Governance: Perspectives on the Current Debate* (n 15) 103–23.

[19] See for a definitive account, Biermann and Bauer (eds), *A World Environment Organization: Solution or Threat for Effective International Environmental Governance?* (n 13).

[20] D Craig and M Jeffery, 'Integrating Sustainable Development into Global Institutions: Reforming the United Nations' (2009) 7(4) *Chinese Journal of Population, Resources and Environment* 3–14, 4.

[21] Yale Center for Environmental Law and Policy, 'Research Program- Global Environmental Governance: Strengthening Global Environmental Governance' www.yale.edu/gegdialogue/docs/dialogue/jun98/june1998report.html.

[22] In May 2007, approximately 25 representatives of civil society and the private sector met with representatives of the French Government in New York to discuss the idea of transforming UNEP into a United Nations Environment Organisation (UNEO). See www.un-ngls.org/IMG/pdf/ReformingInternationalEnvironmentalGovernance-mtg_report.pdf

the short and medium term, possibly through the High-Level Political Forum on Sustainable Development (HLPF) that replaced the Commission on Sustainable Development (CSD) at the Rio+20 Conference of Sustainable Development in 2012. To this end, the HLPF aims to:

> provide political leadership, guidance and recommendations for sustainable development, follow up and review progress in the implementation of sustainable development commitments, enhance the integration of the three dimensions of sustainable development in a holistic and cross-sectoral manner at all levels and have a focused, dynamic and action-oriented agenda, ensuring the appropriate consideration of new and emerging sustainable development challenges.[23]

The HLPF also aims to allow a variety of modes of participation by representatives of interested and affected parties; to follow up and review progress in the implementation of the sustainable development commitments of all the major United Nations conferences and summits; and to strengthen the science-policy interface.[24] While it is too soon to appraise the impact that the Forum is having on global environmental law and governance and its supportive role to UNEP, its creation is encouraging and it could provide a platform for the longer-term development of a consolidated international environmental organisation that could be, at least in terms of its status and competencies, on a par with other United Nations organisations. These organisations include, among others, the World Trade Organization, the Food and Agriculture Organization, the World Health Organization and the International Maritime Organization which all have mandates that overlap, and often include, environmental concerns that could be shifted to an international environmental organisation.

According to Biermann, 'upgrading' UNEP to full-fledged United Nations organisation status could result in increased financial and human resources, competencies and a broadened legal mandate; provide a venue for the integration and joint administration of the myriad convention secretariats, thus addressing fragmentation concerns as well; provide innovative use of future innovative financial mechanisms, such as revenues from emissions trading regimes; and offer awareness raising, technology transfer and the provision of environmental expertise to international, regional and domestic governance bodies.[25]

---

[23] United Nations General Assembly A/Res/67/290, para 2.

[24] S Bernstein, 'The Role and Place of the High-Level Political Forum in Strengthening the Global Institutional Framework for Sustainable Development' https://sustainabledevelopment.un.org/content/documents/2331Bernstein%20study%20on%20HLPF.pdf. The HLPF will possibly be supported in this respect at a political-strategic level by the work of the recently created United Nations Environment Assembly (UNEA). UNEA establishes 'a groundbreaking platform for leadership on global environmental policy ... [aiming to provide] the environment the same level of global prominence as issues such as peace, poverty, health, security, finance and trade'. The Assembly enjoys the universal membership of 193 UN Member States and it convened for the first time in Nairobi in 2014. See www.unep.org/docs/UNEA_2_Brochure.pdf

[25] Biermann, 'Reforming Global Environmental Governance (n 18) 104.

Even though a case could be made that it was short-sighted, in all fairness, one probably cannot fault states for not having created an international environmental organisation in the aftermath of the Second World War when, in a period where environmental concerns were decidedly not on the global political agenda, states instead focused on addressing critical humanitarian and socio-economic development issues that were mostly meant to respond to the ravages of two world wars. Today, however, considering that the Anthropocene's global socio-ecological crisis may be the most profound challenge facing humanity, it only makes sense for states to actively and more determinedly explore the creation of an international environmental organisation with international legal personality that could act more decisively in global environmental norm creation and implementation.[26] As with early post-Second World War institutional reforms in the other focus areas of global governance such as trade, health and agriculture, it might even be relatively easy for states to embark on the eventual creation of an international environmental organisation simply because they could more or less start from a clean slate.

Collectively, the foregoing suggests that the constitutional moment of the Anthropocene may not be as far-fetched as one might have imagined, and that it possibly is as urgent as the global constitutional moment that followed the Second World War. As part of the Anthropocene's constitutional moment, and in addition to its possible regulatory advantages, the creation of an international environmental organisation could open future analytical discursive tracks in the global environmental constitutionalism debate by instigating discussions about the formal and substantive constitution of this institution, and its relationship and normative status vis-à-vis the legal systems of other international organisations and states. Several questions that might arise include: to what extent does the environmental decision-making competencies of this institution rank higher than that of other organisations, if they do at all? Should it only have a formal constitution, or a more substantive one as well that sets out higher-order environmental norms such as a global environmental right, and if so, how should these substantive norms be formulated? Should this organisation also include the establishment of a specialised global environment court, and if so, what could the jurisdiction and competencies of this court be and its relation with other global courts? Within the evolving paradigm of state sovereignty and an increasing need to reorient global environmental law and governance towards a greater ecological ethic of care, how would it be able to ensure better state and non-state actor compliance with global environmental norms? Finally, what would such an organisation's powers be to overhaul and eventually to enforce the global environmental law system, including the elaborate set of treaties, to ultimately render their provisions more responsive to the socio-ecological crisis of the Anthropocene?

---

[26] M Drumbl, 'Actors and Law-making in International Environmental Law' in M Fitzmaurice, D Ong and P Merkouris (eds), *Research Handbook on International Environmental Law* (Cheltenham, Edward Elgar, 2010) 6–8.

B. The Regionalist Approach

Regional environmental governance is now a fully recognised manifestation or aspect of global environmental governance. It has emerged as a response from regionally grouped states to shared environmental problems and as a means to exert greater influence as a regional collective in global environmental diplomacy, law-making and governance. To this end, regional environmental governance is especially desirable under circumstances:

> when the global seems to fail (or, at least, is not an appropriate level to deal with collective action problems) and states simply cannot solve their own environmental problems through unilateral action or where scaling up has the potential to deliver more effective outcomes, then the 'goldilocks principle' kicks in; regionalism becomes attractive as it is neither 'too hot' nor 'too cold' but 'just right'.[27]

Other benefits include that regional environmental governance has the potential to provide for enhanced commonalities to address a particular environmental challenge; greater familiarity with key actors; the ability to tailor mitigating and adaptation actions to a smaller global constituency; and the ability to focus on ecologically defined regions such as river basins, rather than political-administrative entities.[28]

In a narrow sense, regional environmental governance could be made up of a regional environment treaty regime that governs a specific environmental aspect or shared resource in a specific region. An example is the body of norms and institutions that have been set up to govern Lake Konstanz that is shared between Germany, Switzerland and Austria.[29] Expansively considered, the regionalist approach to global environmental constitutionalism seeks constitutionalism in broader regional environmental governance orders, especially with respect to their normative and institutional environmental aspects, such as in the European Union, the African Union and the Association of Southeast Asian Nations. Chapter 4 indicated that the European Union, currently more than any other regional governance organisation, exudes some global constitutional characteristics.[30] As a benchmark for regional governance and consequently for the expansive regionalist approach to global constitutionalism:

> the EU remains highly significant. This is partly because as the most institutionalized regional organization it provides a solid example of actual regional governance. It is also

---

[27] L Elliot and S Breslin, 'Researching Comparative Regional Environmental Governance Causes, Cases and Consequences' in L Elliot and S Breslin (eds) *Comparative Environmental Regionalism* (New York, Routledge, 2011) 4.

[28] J Balsiger and S VanDeveer, 'Navigating Regional Environmental Governance' (2012) 12(3) *Global Environmental Politics* 1–17, 3.

[29] See for detail, www.worldlakes.org/uploads/10_Lake_Constance_27February2006.pdf.

[30] In addition to the sources cited in Ch 4, see M Maduro, 'How Constitutional can the European Union be? The Tension Between Intergovernamentalism and Constitutionalism in the European Union' in J Weiler and C Eisgruber (eds), *Altneuland: The EU Constitution in a Contextual Perspective*, Jean Monnet Working Paper 5/04, www.jeanmonnetprogram.org/archive/papers/04/040501-18.pdf.

because the experience of the EU informs policy debates elsewhere over how to emulate the successes and/or avoid some of the problems of Europe in the construction of regional forms. And it is also because, through contingent aid and 'interregional' partnership arrangements, there is a deliberate and active attempt to promote the EU 'model' of regional governance in other parts of the world.[31]

With some questioning whether an 'ever closer ecological union' could be observed in Europe,[32] the European Union's global constitutionalism debate is relevant for the environmental domain. The focus of this debate is on the environmental aspects of the European Union's institutional and normative architecture, and it seeks to find environmental constitutionalism elements in a regional organisation that does not have a constitution setting out elaborate environmental provisions.

Despite the absence of such explicit constitutional provisions, it is sufficiently clear by now that the European Union is a very influential environmental governance actor internally with respect to its Member States and externally vis-à-vis the rest of the world, and there are several considerations acting in support of the notion of regional European environmental constitutionalism. These considerations collectively play at the idea of the Union becoming, or being, a regional constitutional federation (*Verfassungsverbund*) that also focuses on environmental regulation. First, the 28 Member States of the Union could increasingly be seen acting as a unified, if still imperfect, collective, reminiscent of the idea of an 'international community' that acts collectively on behalf of its members and in their environment-related interests.[33] As evidence of its post-state unified regional approach to environmental law and governance, the European Union maintains permanent diplomatic missions in various countries across the world and it is represented as a collective at the United Nations, the World Trade Organization and in important global networks of influential states such as the G8. In the environmental context, the European Union is a party to the United Nations Framework Convention on Climate Change (UNFCCC), the Kyoto Protocol and the recent Paris Agreement of 2015, as are all European Union Member States in their own right.[34] Its representative collectivity is, however, not always absolute or even sufficient during global climate negotiations and the European Union has been

---

[31] Elliot and Breslin, 'Researching Comparative Regional Environmental Governance Causes, Cases and Consequences' (n 27) 1.

[32] A Weale et al, *Environmental Governance in Europe: an Ever Closer Ecological Union?* (Oxford, Oxford University Press, 2000).

[33] Used here in the sense to 'denote the repository of interests that transcend those of individual states ... In this conception, the element which distinguishes a "community" from its components is a "higher unity", as it were, the representation and prioritization of common interests as against the egoistic interests of individuals'. To this end, an international community 'needs to have certain interests common to all its members and a certain set of common values, principles and procedures'. For present purposes, such common values, principles and procedures could revolve around the environment. See B Simma and A Paulus, 'The 'International Community' Facing the Challenge of Globalization' (1998) 9 *European Journal of International Law* 266–77, 268.

[34] European Commission 'Climate Action' http://ec.europa.eu/clima/.

criticised for lacking a unified voice, and that it is often difficult to determine 'who is talking in the name of the EU, and who is doing it to defend national interests while proclaiming to represent the EU as a whole'.[35]

Secondly, formally the Union derives its environmental governance mandate from what could be considered its constituting instruments. Article 4(2) of the Treaty on the Functioning of the European Union provides that the Union shall share competence with Member States, inter alia, in the areas of the environment and energy. Article 3 of the Treaty on European Union declares that the Union 'shall work for the sustainable development of Europe based on … a high level of protection and improvement of the quality of the environment'. This suggests that environmental protection and achieving sustainable development have been laid down 'constitutionally' in a formal sense as two of the main goals of the European Union. There is also a significant degree of distribution of powers evident between the Member States and the Union as a result of the principles of proportionality and subsidiarity.[36] Based on the foregoing, a unified and more or less uniform environmental normative framework is continuously created through environmental regulations and directives according to which Member States are required to align their domestic legal systems.[37] While the foregoing is an example of formal constitutional provisions that enable regional governance, from a rule of law perspective, this also results in the emergence of a more predictable, consistent, legitimate and binding environmental law and governance framework that is becoming increasingly unified, influential and coherent across Europe.

Thirdly, in terms of substantive higher-order environmental norms, none of the European Union's constituting treaties provide for an explicit environmental right or any other explicit form of higher-order environmental norm. Based on the imperative that human rights protection is a primary aim of the Union,[38] environmental rights protection is rather to be found in several rights-related instruments. The European Convention for the Protection of Human Rights and Fundamental Freedoms of 1950 does not provide for an explicit environmental right,[39] but environmental entitlements are nevertheless raised and protected through the assertion of other incidental rights.[40] The European Court of Human Rights is very active in protecting environmental interests such as through the Convention's right to privacy (article 8), as can be seen from its rich jurisprudence

---

[35] R Martin, 'The European Union and International Negotiations on Climate Change: A Limited Role to Play' (2012) 8(2) *Journal of Contemporary European Research* 192–209, 193.

[36] See TEU, art 5.

[37] TFEU, art 288.

[38] TEU, art 6.

[39] Available at www.coe.int/t/dghl/standardsetting/hrpolicy/Publications/Manual_Env_2012_nocover_Eng.pdf.

[40] O Pedersen, 'European Environmental Human Rights and Environmental Rights: A Long Time Coming?' (2008) (21) *The Georgetown International Environmental Law Review* 73–111.

on human rights in the environmental context.[41] The extent to which the European Court of Human Rights has been able to contribute to the development of substantive regional environmental constitutionalism in Europe is evident from Haas' view that: 'in some instances environmental decisions have been elevated above the political level of contending domestic interests'.[42] The more recently adopted Charter of Fundamental Rights of the European Union of 2000, includes under its section on solidarity rights an environmental provision which states: 'A high level of environmental protection and the improvement of the quality of the environment must be integrated into the policies of the Union and ensured in accordance with the principle of sustainable development'.[43] This provision, which has become binding on all Union Member States since 2009 along with all the other provisions of the Charter,[44] although relatively weak and devoid of the classic rights-jargon, 'may become a benchmark for judicial review by the EU Court of Justice of legislative and executive EU acts as well as national measures implementing EU environmental obligations'.[45] Also, the United Nations Economic Commission for Europe (UNECE) Convention on Access to Information, Public Participation in Decision-making and Access to Justice in Environmental Matters (Aarhus Convention) 1998 provides an environmental right, although this right is non-justiciable.[46] In doing so, the Convention significantly strengthens the force of substantive regional environmental constitutionalism by allowing communications to be brought before its Compliance Committee by one or more members of the public concerning any party's compliance with the Convention.[47] It is accordingly entirely in a position to enforce higher-order rights-based provisions aimed at environmental protection (see also the discussion below).

The foregoing suggests that despite the absence of a European environmental constitution and an explicit substantive environmental right in the Union's more general constituting instruments, the European Union exudes various formal and substantive environmental constitutionalism characteristics that allow it collectively as a regional organisation, and its Member States individually, to steer environmental regulatory outcomes in a regional setting. But this

---

[41] See for a summary of environment related cases the summary in European Court of Human Rights http://www.echr.coe.int/Documents/FS_Environment_ENG.pdf.

[42] P Haas, 'Regional Environmental Governance' in T Börzel and T Risse (eds), *The Oxford Handbook of Comparative Regionalism* (Oxford, Oxford University Press, 2016) 437.

[43] Art 37.

[44] The Charter has been incorporated as a binding legal text in the Lisbon Treaty of 2007 and as a result it has become binding on all EU Member States since 2009.

[45] J Verschuuren, 'Contribution of the Case Law of the European Court of Human Rights to Sustainable Development in Europe' in W Scholtz and J Verschuuren (eds), *Regional Environmental Law: Transnational Comparative Lessons in Pursuit of Sustainable Development* (Cheltenham, Edward Elgar, 2015) 363–84.

[46] See, generally, S Kravchenko, 'The Aarhus Convention and Innovations in Compliance with Multilateral Environmental Agreements' (2007) 18(1) *Colorado Journal of International Environmental Law and Policy* 1–50.

[47] United Nations Economic Commission for Europe http://www.unece.org/env/pp/pubcom.html.

is not the case with all regional governance regimes. Some regional organisations such as the African Union still have a long way to go before they achieve any meaningful, coherent or influential measure of regional global environmental constitutionalism.[48] It will arguably be these comparatively poorer regions and countries with least adaptive capacity, that are most likely to be affected by global environmental change in future. While it is unrealistic and probably undesirable to suggest that the European model should be replicated elsewhere to the letter, the obvious regulatory advantages that global environmental constitutionalism hold out in the European context could serve regions such as Africa well in their efforts to augment environmental protection in the wake of the Anthropocene's socio-ecological crisis.

As global environmental constitutionalism increasingly infiltrates specific regions, various constitutional questions could arise, such as: where they are absent, should environmental provisions be included as formal and/or substantive provisions in a regional governance organisation's constituting treaties? What is the normative status of such regional environmental provisions vis-à-vis Member State legal systems on the one hand, and vis-à-vis international law on the other? What powers should a regional environmental authority have internally in relation to its Member States and externally in relation to other states and regional organisations? If an international environmental organisation is eventually established, what should the relationship be between such an organisation and regional environmental authorities? What role should a regional (environmental) court play in ensuring accountability, compliance and the rule of law and how would it function in relation to other courts at the international, regional and domestic levels?

C. The International Environmental Regulatory Regime Approach

The international regulatory regime approach to global constitutionalism traces constitutionalism in increasingly autonomous clustered regimes of international law that are organised around a broadly defined regime such as global trade or the environment. The focus of this approach could also be more specific in that it looks for constitutionalism in narrower regimes that are components or building blocks of the more encompassing general environmental or global trade regimes. Examples in the environmental context are the biodiversity and climate change

---

[48] While the African Union has developed an impressive array of regional agreements pursuant to the goal of sustainable development, national implementation of these instruments in general is a problem, since effective regional, sub-regional and domestic compliance and enforcement mechanisms are often lacking or are ignored completely: L Kotzé and W Scholtz, 'Environmental Law-Africa, Sub-Saharan' in K Bosselmann, D Fogel, and JB Ruhl (eds), *The Berkshire Encyclopaedia of Sustainability, Vol. 3: The Law and Politics of Sustainability* (Great Barrington, Berkshire Publishers, 2010) 179–87.

regimes. Usually, these regulatory regimes are either made up of a cluster of treaties and their concomitant institutions, or they could revolve around a fully-fledged and more powerful international organisation such as the World Trade Organization, its norms and institutional apparatus.

While the World Trade Organization has international legal personality, which means that it has the capacity to perform international legal acts, no international environmental institution has a similar degree of international legal personality or independence.[49] UNEP comes closest to such a construction, even though it is not nearly comparable to other United Nations organisations in terms of its capacity and authority to create and enforce international environmental law and adjudicate environmental disputes. Thus, the international regulatory regime approach to global environmental constitutionalism in a broad sense will probably only take deliberate shape when a more influential international environmental organisation with international legal personality is considered in line with previous suggestions in this chapter. It is only then that meaningful expansive regulatory regime constitutional conversations could be had. The global constitutionalism debate that revolves around the World Trade Organization nevertheless foreshadows constitutional issues that may in future arise in the environmental context including, among others: the founding treaty of such an organisation, its authority and capacity to create and enforce global environmental norms, issues of legitimacy, the oversight and enforcement role of its adjudicatory bodies, and its relationship with other international organisations and states.

Traces of global environmental constitutionalism could arguably be found more clearly in the narrower international regulatory regime approach. As an intergovernmental body, despite its lack of United Nations organisation status, UNEP plays an important role in initiating and supporting global environmental governance among states *inter se* and among states and other international organisations.[50] To its credit, various multilateral environmental agreements, and even entire environmental treaty regimes, have been developed under the coordinating leadership of UNEP. It is estimated that there are approximately 500 environment-related multilateral agreements in existence today.[51] It is within the aggregated collection of this burgeoning body of agreements that one finds narrowly clustered normative and institutional constructions such as the ocean governance, climate change and biodiversity regimes that could have global environmental constitutionalism characteristics. While the successes and failures of multilateral environmental agreements are debatable and often debated, there is sufficient evidence that '[i]ssue specific regimes have achieved a relatively high level of performance in a wide range of dimensions'.[52]

---

[49] See, on the juridical and political details in relation to international organisations generally, including aspects related to their international legal personality, J Klabbers and Å Wallendahl (eds), *Research Handbook on the Law of International Organizations* (Cheltenham, Edward Elgar, 2011).
[50] Drumbl, 'Actors and Law-making in International Environmental Law' (n 26) 7–8.
[51] Kanie, 'Governance with Multilateral Environmental Agreements' (n 15) 68.
[52] ibid 73.

With the possible exception of the ocean governance regime with its International Maritime Organization (that only partly deals with environmental matters), none of these narrowly clustered issue-specific regimes revolve around a strong centralised international organisation that in terms of their status and power are equivalent to United Nations organisations. Taking the biodiversity regime as an example, several multilateral environmental agreements perform basic formal constitutive functions by establishing institutions, specifying the rules that guide and constrain these institutions, and entrench these rules through amendment procedures. These include the Ramsar Convention on Wetlands 1971; the Bonn Convention on Migratory Species 1979; and the Convention on Biological Diversity 1992. In addition to regular Conferences of the Parties, these instruments and their protocols constitute and regulate various treaty institutions such as Standing Committees, Advisory Committees, Scientific Councils, Working Groups and Convention Secretariats, which in turn are responsible for implementing treaty provisions and for monitoring compliance and creating new and amending existing treaty provisions, among many other governance functions.[53] To this end, it is possible to observe a degree of formal global environmental constitutionalism that is embedded in these regimes, notably to the extent that their 'constitutional' treaties and protocols comprehensively constitute them, provide their governance institutions and associated governance procedures, and other formally constitutive provisions that make them work, as it were.

It is also possible to observe substantive constitutional aspects in these treaty regimes in the sense that they constrain behaviour, limit free will and counter arbitrary actions, however minimal this may be. To this end, Bodansky believes that 'international environmental agreements do not effectively limit the institutions they establish'.[54] While this is true, Bodansky's view of substantive constitutionalism is a narrow one, which ignores the fact that these treaty regimes have expressly been designed to limit the actions of those states to which they apply. Limiting the actions/authority of a treaty-related governance institution is only one aspect of constitutionalism, whereas limiting the actions of states is another, arguably far more important, objective. To this end, treaties are able to constrain behaviour, not only through formal global constitutional institutions

---

[53] See, for a detailed discussion of the role of Conferences of the Parties in global environmental governance, including their potential constitutional roles in this respect, A Wiersema, 'The New International Law-makers? Conferences of the Parties to Multilateral Environmental Agreements' (2009) 31 *Michigan Journal of International Law* 232–87.

[54] He elaborates:

> international environmental agreements ... are constitutions in the thin sense that they establish ongoing systems of governance and default rules for how those systems of governance will operate. They are not constitutions in the thicker sense, however, because they fail to establish institutions with significant independence from states, or to take issues outside the zone of politics by imposing effective constraints, either procedural or substantive, on the behavior of international environmental institutions.

Bodansky, 'Is There an International Environmental Constitution?' (n 18) 577–78.

and processes, but also through setting substantive limitations on what states can and cannot do. Of course the constraints that these treaties impose are not comparable to the normative force, authority and ethical/moral urgency of typical higher-order constitutional instruments such as rights or *jus cogens* norms (see the discussion below). States could also admittedly be more inclined to ignore or breach treaty provisions than they would be in the case of rights or *jus cogens* norms. It is therefore probably more appropriate to speak in this instance of a softer form of substantive global environmental constitutionalism, or constitutionalism with a 'little "c" rather than a big "C"';[55] but it is a minimal incarnation of substantive global environmental constitutionalism nevertheless.

As matters for future debate, several pertinent questions arise in the light of Anthropocene imagery that directly or indirectly relate to the global environmental constitutionalism aspects of the international regulatory regime approach. For example: should existing environmental treaty regimes be reformed to be more compatible with Earth systems governance, and if so how and to what extent? Relatedly, with a view to achieving a more comprehensive and holistic Earth systems governance approach, to what extent should additional treaty regimes be designed to address hitherto unregulated Earth system issues such as transboundary underground aquifers, and how could these treaty regimes be connected? In the light of concerns about fragmentation, how could the diverse treaty regimes be reformed to ensure normative consistency, stability, credibility, reliability and the authority and legitimacy of these regimes? Should treaty regimes be designed to cater specifically for technological interventions to mitigate and to adapt to Anthropocene eventualities, and if so, how? If an international environmental organisation is established, how could the architecture of the existing collection of environmental treaty regimes be brought in line with, or under the authority of, such an organisation? If such an organisation is not created in future, how could the institutions responsible for governing these treaty regimes be strengthened in pursuit of efforts to increase state accountability, and ultimately, the effectiveness of international environmental law?

D. Global Civil Society Environmental Constitutionalism

Famously abstract, amorphous and indeterminate, the civil society approach to global constitutionalism focuses on the emergence of pockets of non-state 'law' or 'civil constitutions' as a result of informal normative processes and (often self-regulatory) instruments and structures emanating from non-state entities such as non-governmental organisations. These global civil society actors usually share common characteristics in that they are organisations with an institutional presence and structure; they function separately from the state and thus exercise private instead of public authority; they usually operate on a non-profit basis; and

---

[55] ibid 578.

they are self-governing to the extent that they control their own affairs alongside (or sometimes in the absence of) more formal state regulation.[56] In terms of these generic characteristics, it is not entirely impossible to think of global civil society in global constitutional terms especially insofar as they are constituted entities with their own internal rules, have the ability to make softer forms of regulatory norms, and have the ability to exert some regulatory influence in global regulatory spaces beyond the state; however minimal this may be in practice.[57] These actors generally focus their energies on the externalities resulting from globalisation and create voluntary, non-juridical but law-like norms to influence specific global governance challenges.

Further reflecting on the evolution of global civil society institutions in a global constitutional sense, notably as a counter-reaction to the deficiencies of state-led global governance, Salamon and Anheier believe the fact that:

> these organizations have attracted so much attention in recent years is due in large part to the widespread 'crisis of the state' that has been underway for two decades or more in virtually every part of the world, a crisis that has manifested itself in a serious questioning of traditional social welfare policies in much of the developed North, in disappointments over the progress of state-led development in significant parts of the developing South, in the collapse of the experiment in state socialism in Central and Eastern Europe, and in concerns about the environmental degradation that continues to threaten human health and safety everywhere.[58]

The environment clearly has also become a proper concern of global civil society actors and it is gradually appealing to social movement energies and energetic global solidarities. Is it possible to observe the emergence of global civil society environmental constitutionalism?

Acting outside of the formal government setting, environmental non-governmental organisations 'affirm values that are universally recognized but politically manipulated in their own interest by political agencies'.[59] Aiming to 'undo evil or to do good',[60] non-governmental environmental organisations are popular and enjoy broad-based public support; their activities focus on practical

---

[56] L Salamon and H Anheier, 'Civil Society in Comparative Perspective' in L Salamon et al (eds), *Global Civil Society Dimensions of the Nonprofit Sector* (The Johns Hopkins Center for Civil Society Studies Baltimore, 1999) 3–4.

[57] While their influence is growing, global civil society actors unfortunately remain at the periphery of the processes through which states determine global environmental law and governance outcomes: 'Within multi-level negotiation systems governments retain the main authority for environmental foreign policies, whereas participation in, or control of, these political processes by societal actors ... run the risk of being undermined': H Breitmeier and V Rittberger, *Environmental NGOs in an Emerging Global Civil Society* (Tübinger Arbeitspapiere zur Internationalen Politik und Friedensforschung, 1998) https://bibliographie.uni-tuebingen.de/xmlui/bitstream/handle/10900/47202/pdf/tap32.pdf?sequence=1&isAllowed=y.

[58] Salamon and Anheier, 'Civil Society in Comparative Perspective' (n 56) 4.

[59] M Castells, 'The New Public Sphere: Global Civil Society, Communication Networks, and Global Governance' (2008) 616 *The ANNALS of the American Academy of Political and Social Science* 78–93, 84.

[60] ibid 85.

and current matters, specific cases and concrete expressions of human solidarity. While global non-state actors remain unable to participate fully in global environmental law-making and diplomacy as a result of them lacking international legal personality, these actors increasingly influence the outcomes of the more formal global juridical processes, thereby indirectly contributing to the development of global environmental constitutional norms and structures beyond the state.[61] As is the case in a domestic polity, the involvement of civil society actors also has the potential to strengthen democratic participation and representation in the global environmental governance system to the extent that not only states, but also a broader range of other interested and affected parties are represented in decisions that affect them and the environment. An added benefit would be that the legitimacy of global environmental governance is enhanced as a consequence. The United Nations Conference on Environment and Development in 1992 saw approximately 2,400 non-governmental organisations and 17,000 participants taking part in the parallel non-governmental organisation forum.[62] Through these instances of deliberate and broad-based civil society participation in global environmental governance and law-making, it is possible to indirectly influence the content and design of global environmental norms; to change the ideational context of an issue and enhance the sensitivity of society for new problem-solving approaches;[63] and to expand and enrich whatever notions of global democracy may be at play in the global regulatory domain which, in turn, could increase the legitimacy and effectiveness of global environmental law and governance (see also the discussion below). To this end, global civil society environmental constitutionalism is a deliberate approach that shifts the hitherto predominant focus on the state, as the main and most important actor in global environmental governance, to other, increasingly assertive and important, non-state actors.

In addition to their broader global policy influence at a strategic political and advocacy level, global environmental civil society actors also sometimes engage in the development of softer, law-like norms that aim to bolster environmental protection. One example is the voluntary ISO 14000 environmental standard that has been developed by the International Organization for Standardization (ISO) as a means to enhance the environmental performance of businesses. ISO is an independent, non-governmental international organisation with a membership of 162 national standards bodies.[64] Today there is little doubt that ISO 14001 'has become the international benchmark by which corporations can voluntarily

---

[61] The number of non-governmental environmental organisations at global United Nations conferences has steadily increased, notably since the Stockholm Conference on the Human Environment in 1972. See www.un-documents.net/aconf48-14r1.pdf, 43.

[62] K Morrow, 'Sustainability, Environmental Citizenship Rights and the Ongoing Challenges of Reshaping Supranational Environmental Governance' in A Grear and LJ Kotzé (eds), *Research Handbook on Human Rights and the Environment* (Cheltenham, Edward Elgar, 2015) 202.

[63] Breitmeier and Rittberger, *Environmental NGOs in an Emerging Global Civil Society* (n 57).

[64] See http://www.iso.org/iso/home/about.htm.

develop and assess their environmental practices'.[65] An example of a non-state regulatory instrument aimed at influencing the social and environmental behaviour of the banking industry is the Equator Principles. These were adopted in 2003 as a basic voluntary framework for governing social and environmental risks in project finance.[66] The Principles provide a minimum standard for due diligence to support responsible risk decision-making, and currently 82 Equator Principles Financial Institutions in 36 countries have officially adopted the Principles.[67]

Thirdly, and arguably most representative of a global civil society environmental constitution, is the Earth Charter. Global civil society actors adopted the Charter in 2000, and it provides an inclusive, integrated, ethical framework to guide the transition to a sustainable future.[68] It mainly acts as a response to the continued failure of states to respond adequately to the deepening socio-ecological crisis, including the state-driven neo-liberal consumerist growth-without-limits agenda. While the Earth Charter does not have the normative force of a multilateral environmental agreement, *jus cogens*, customary international law, or even soft law, it is: 'increasingly recognised as a global consensus statement on the meaning of sustainability, the challenge and vision of sustainable development, and the principles by which sustainable development is to be achieved'.[69] Acknowledging its potential global constitutional qualities, one of its fiercest proponents has even touted the Charter as 'a starting point for a dialogue on a future global constitution';[70] an issue to which the chapter returns to below.

Understandably, it might be difficult to imagine that these examples of voluntary non-juridical norms exude any constitutional characteristics; especially when considered in the light of the axiomatic domestic meaning of constitutionalism and when compared to the more trite internationalist, regionalist and regulatory regime approaches discussed above. But if one were to pursue a line of thinking about global constitutionalism outside the epistemological closures erected by self-serving states, it is possible to envisage an alternative complementary form of non-state environmental authority that exists within its own unique set of non-state norms, processes and structures, often underpinned by a deeply ethical-moral orientation of ecological integrity and care. For example, a widely endorsed global civil society instrument such as the Earth Charter, unlike the Rio Declaration of 1992, is fundamentally ecocentric and seeks to dissolve anthropocentric inter- and

---

[65] D Rondinelli and G Vastag, 'Panacea, Common Sense, or Just a Label? The Value of ISO 14001 Environmental Management Systems' (2002) 18(5) *European Management Journal* 499–510, 499.

[66] F Amalric, *The Equator Principles: A Step Towards Sustainability?* (2005) Centre for Corporate Responsibility and Sustainability: Working Paper No 01/05 of 2005, www.nachhaltigkeit.info/media/1317385761phpOHcawW.pdf, 1.

[67] See www.equator-principles.com/.

[68] See for a definitive account, K Bosselmann and R Engel (eds), *The Earth Charter: A Framework for Global Governance* (Amsterdam, KIT Publishers, 2010).

[69] See http://earthcharter.org/discover/history-of-the-earth-charter/.

[70] K Bosselmann, 'Outlook: The Earth Charter- A Model Constitution for the World?' in Bosselmann and Engel (eds), *The Earth Charter: A Framework for Global Governance* (n 68) 239.

intra-species hierarchies.[71] It has been stated that the Earth Charter has managed to guide soft law environmental instruments and even influence implementation processes related to several multilateral environmental agreements, such as the Convention on Biological Diversity and the United Nations Framework Convention on Climate Change.[72] While there is no tangible evidence for this, it is conceivable that instruments such as the Earth Charter could strengthen the hands of those agitating for more radical ecocentric-oriented constitutional and statutory reforms in the law. Ecuador's constitutional affirmation of the rights of nature in 2008[73] and Bolivia's Law of Mother Earth of 2009[74] are two possible examples of what could be achieved domestically on the basis of global initiatives. Bolivia's Law of Mother Earth recognises, is also aligned with, and has been designed as a response to, the notion of Earth system science and governance discussed in Chapter 6.[75]

Collectively considered, the foregoing institutional and normative aspects of the global civil society sphere are therefore constitutional in the sense that they formally constitute global civil society entities, regulate their activities, regulate activities of a target group such as banks where there are no or insufficient state laws available to do so, and create substantive (albeit non-enforceable but often morally inclined) restrictions on free will. That said, realistically one must recognise global civil society environmental constitutionalism for what it is: popular, non-enforceable, non-coercive, but persuasive, non-juridical normative impulses that could gradually change public opinion, engender a sense of moral and ethical ecological responsibility, increase the legitimacy of global environmental governance, enhance global environmental democracy and, eventually initiate bottom-up global environmental law and governance reforms.

E. Transnational Comparative Environmental Constitutionalism

It was explained in Chapter 4 that transnational comparative constitutionalism has to do with the emergence of environmental norms around the globe. 'Transnational' or 'global' describes both a space and a process, which entail finding constitutional elements in domestic, international and regional regimes from around the world and then comparing them with a view to comparative interpretation that could lead to law reform. Several provisions of the South African Constitution, for example, are based on provisions found in the German, American and Canadian

---

[71] See for other examples of ecocentric quasi-juridical global civil society instruments, Gaia Foundation at www.gaiafoundation.org/earth-law-precedents.
[72] Bosselmann, 'Outlook' (n 70) 250.
[73] See https://therightsofnature.org/wp-content/uploads/pdfs/Rights-for-Nature-Articles-in-Ecuadors-Constitution.pdf.
[74] See http://www.worldfuturefund.org/Projects/Indicators/motherearthbolivia.html.
[75] See, for a general discussion, K Zimmerer, 'Environmental Governance through "Speaking Like an Indigenous State" and Respatializing Resources: Ethical Livelihood Concepts in Bolivia as Versatility or Verisimilitude?' (2013) *Geoforum* 1–11.

Constitutions.[76] As well, whereas the South African Constitution explicitly obliges courts to 'prefer any reasonable interpretation of the legislation that is consistent with international law over any alternative interpretation that is inconsistent with international law',[77] courts also 'may consider foreign law'[78] when interpreting the Bill of Rights. Provisions such as these mean that the further development of domestic constitutionalism is inherently tied to a vision of international and foreign law, as it is continuously being developed through a process of cross-learning consensus between nations across the globe.

This approach accordingly has a strong comparative, cross-jurisdictional or transnational focus that is collectively seen as a global amalgamation of variously situated domestic norms around the globe. Arguably more than any of the previous four approaches to global environmental constitutionalism discussed above, transnational comparative environmental constitutionalism is emerging as a result of globalisation. In an integrally connected globalised world, the actors that contribute to developing environmental constitutional norms, including judiciaries, legislatures and scholars, are more connected than ever before. Social media, global academic conferences and access to scholarly publications, among others, collectively work to facilitate cross-jurisdictional learning, comparison, legal transplantation, transnational migration of norms and sharing of environmental constitutionalism ideas between countries.[79]

The transnational comparative approach therefore predominantly traces an emerging global constitutional dialogue that is mostly carried by domestic courts, legislatures and scholars who, through processes consisting of cross-jurisdictional learning, comparative interpretation and legal transplantation, are increasingly developing a more uniform (if not absolutely identical) normative approach to specific elements of global environmental constitutionalism, such as approaches to environmental rights and sustainable development. While there are many others,[80] one example is the South African Constitutional Court's significant reliance on the burgeoning body of international law pertaining to sustainable development that guided its interpretation of this environmental law principle in South Africa's domestic legal regime in a landmark decision in 2007.[81] The Court

---

[76] See, for a detailed discussion, D Davis, 'Constitutional Borrowing: The Influence of Legal Culture and Local History in the Reconstitution of Comparative Influence—The South African Experience' (2003) 1(2) *International Journal of Constitutional Law* 181–95.

[77] South African Constitution, s 233.

[78] ibid, s 39(1).

[79] See, for a political science perspective, M Howlett and S Joshi-Koop, 'Transnational Learning, Policy Analytical Capacity, and Environmental Policy Convergence: Survey Results from Canada' (2011) 21 *Global Environmental Change* 85–92.

[80] See the definitive and most current work on comparative environmental constitutionalism in a global context, May and Daly, *Global Environmental Constitutionalism* (n 1).

[81] *Fuel Retailers Association of Southern Africa v Director-General: Environmental Management, Department of Agriculture, Conservation and Environment, Mpumalanga Province and Others* (CCT67/06) [2007] ZACC 13, paras 46–56.

ultimately concluded that '[s]ustainable development is an evolving concept of international law' and that it:

> has a significant role to play in the resolution of environmentally related disputes in our law. It offers an important principle for the resolution of tensions between the need to protect the environment on the one hand, and the need for socio-economic development on the other hand.[82]

As a second example, Boyd indicates that the 1976 Portuguese formulation of a 'right to a healthy and ecologically balanced human living environment' is now found in 21 other constitutions and that the Supreme Court of India's decisions on environmental rights have significantly influenced other courts in Bangladesh, Pakistan, Sri Lanka, Uganda and Kenya.[83]

But it is not only domestic legal systems that are set to gain from transnational comparative environmental constitutionalism. Regional judiciaries are increasingly borrowing from one another, which indicates that these global judicial conversations are not the exclusive domain of domestic courts. In its famous Social and Economic Rights Action Center Communication of 2001 (SERAC),[84] the African Commission on Human and Peoples' Rights, for example, delivered the first substantive interpretation of regional environmental rights. Recognising that certain provisions of the African Charter on Human and Peoples' Rights 1981 were adopted as a reaction to the 'aftermath of colonial exploitation [that] has left Africa's precious resources and people still vulnerable to foreign misappropriation',[85] the Commission, relying on European Court of Human Rights and Inter-American Court of Human Rights jurisprudence, confirmed that governments have a duty to protect their citizens, not only through appropriate legislation and effective enforcement, but also by protecting them from damaging acts that may be perpetrated by foreign oil companies.[86] Within an increasingly interconnected globalised world, transnational comparative environmental constitutional conversations such as these will increase. The Anthropocene, acting as a common framework for global socio-ecological change, while creating a shared understanding of and justification for regulatory urgency, will be a factor that drives these conversations.

---

[82] ibid, paras 46, 57.
[83] D Boyd, *The Environmental Rights Revolution: A Global Study of Constitutions, Human Rights, and the Environment* (Vancouver, UBC Press, 2012) 108.
[84] Communication 155/96: Social and Economic Rights Action Center (SERAC) and Center for Economic and Social Rights (CESR)/Nigeria www.achpr.org/files/sessions/30th/comunications/155.96/achpr30_155_96_eng.pdf.
[85] ibid, para 56.
[86] ibid, para 57; Inter-American Court of Human Rights, *Velàsquez Rodríguez v Honduras* 19 July 1988, Ser C, no 4.14; and European Court on Human Rights *X and Y v Netherlands* (1985) Ser A no 91.

V. The Elements of Global Environmental Constitutionalism

Departing from the multiple regulatory advantages of constitutionalism and environmental constitutionalism that have been detailed in Chapters 3, 5 and 6, the remainder of this chapter identifies how the elements of environmental constitutionalism currently manifest in the global regulatory domain within the context of the various approaches to global environmental constitutionalism outlined above. The analysis is extended to indicate how these elements possibly could be re-imagined in the light of the Anthropocene's global socio-ecological crisis.

The various elements of global environmental constitutionalism discussed here cannot constitute a complete checklist to state the existence of an environmental constitutional state, or offer a final typology and topography of global environmental constitutionalism. The utility of finding and describing these elements rather lies in that they could be used as a framework to inform an evaluation that determines in broad terms the emergence of global environmental constitutionalism. Naturally, because there is no example of a perfectly constitutionalised domestic legal order, all the elements need not be present to state the existence of some 'complete' global environmental constitutional order; some could be absent or present in a less forceful way, while others may overlap or compensate for another's absence.

A. A Global Environmental Constitution

In one of the first publications that focused on global environmental constitutionalism, Bodansky asked: 'Is there an International Environmental Constitution?'[87] He concluded that there is not. The analysis thus far in this book supports such a conclusion: there is currently no single universal global environmental constitution sporting formal and substantive provisions, and some have indicated that the 'prospect of a global environmental constitution may not be realistic for many years to come'.[88] One reason for the absence of a global environmental constitution, and doubt as to its immediate emergence, is related to the absence of a strong, centralised international environmental organisation, a consideration that was canvassed above. These two issues are intimately related and it is likely that conversations and reform efforts in this respect will only gain more deliberate traction once sufficient political will is mustered to overcome the prevailing political reticence that is hampering the creation of such an

---

[87] Bodansky (n 18).
[88] Bosselmann (n 1) 182.

organisation and an accompanying constitution. To this end, the unprecedented socio-ecological decline globally, as evidenced by the Anthropocene, should in theory serve as sufficient motivation for states and global civil society actors to embark on paradigm-shifting reforms of global environmental law, governance and its institutions. While the recent Paris Climate Agreement in 2015 has been criticised for being too weak,[89] it is an indication, however slight, that global environmental governance actors (notably states) might eventually be willing to forego some unhindered economic expansion in favour of reforms that support growth within limits.

If a remote possibility does exist for the eventual creation of a global environmental constitution, how could it look? One example that might serve as a blueprint for a global environmental constitution is the ecocentric-oriented Earth Charter. Currently the Charter neither has the required level of state-backed support and universal state-endorsement to render it sufficiently influential at the high strategic political level, nor does it collectively represent shared ecological values that all states endorse in order for it to gain widespread support. But in a possible new geological epoch that signifies socio-ecological upheaval affecting all life on Earth, there is a chance that global civil society driven initiatives such as the Earth Charter might be taken up by more formal United Nations political and law-making processes. After all, one of the most influential global human rights instruments that has managed to instigate paradigm-shifting changes in the global order, the Universal Declaration of Human Rights of 1948, was developed as a response to shared global civil society and state-led human rights concerns in the aftermath of the Second World War. The Declaration revolved around, and sought to address, unprecedented human suffering by providing higher-order guarantees in the form of rights that have moved centre stage as shared concerns affecting everyone everywhere. The Declaration, and what it seeks to champion, was also seen to be serving the common good by elevating human rights protection to a higher juridical level.

Similar to the type of language used in the Declaration, the Earth Charter is fashioned around four foundational themes that are reflective of typical environmental constitutionalism language including: respect and care for the community of life; ecological integrity; social and economic justice; and democracy, non-violence and peace.[90] The Charter also contains both formal and substantive constitutional aspects alongside which a global environmental constitution could be fashioned. While there is no clear division, the substantive aspects are broadly outlined in the first three themes that entrench commitments towards the Earth, ecological processes and the community of life, including aspects of inter-species

---

[89] See, among others, Centre for Research on Globalization 'The COP21 Climate Summit: The Ambitions and Flaws of the Paris Agreement. Outcome of Deception and Bullying' www.global-research.ca/the-cop21-climate-summit-the-ambitions-and-flaws-of-the-paris-agreement-outcome-of-deception-and-bullying/5495512.

[90] See the text of the Charter at http://earthcharter.org/discover/the-earth-charter/.

justice and justice between humans. Part four, while it does not establish a responsible institution for global environmental governance, provides formal constitutional aspects including the need to strengthen democratic institutions at all levels, and to provide transparency and accountability in governance, inclusive participation in decision-making, and access to justice.

In line with what has already been proposed above, and while initiatives such as the Earth Charter gain increased traction as potential key elements of global environmental constitutionalism, it would be necessary to utilise, expand and significantly improve multilateral environmental agreements and their institutions. To date, these agreements remain the principal widely endorsed juridical instruments that set out some measure of formal and substantive global environmental constitutionalism provisions that establish and regulate global environmental governance and determine some limitations on the free will of states vis-à-vis the environment. A potential first step could be to focus on existing treaty regimes and to reform these to create greater synergies between their provisions and institutions, thereby improving their effectiveness. Such a short-term solution is not entirely unrealistic, considering that multilateral environmental agreements could form a collective 'unwritten' global environmental constitution (similar to the United Kingdom model), thus fulfilling the formal constitutive functions of a dispersed global environmental constitution, as well as the substantive functions of constitutionalism, however incoherent or incomplete at this stage.

An example of such an initiative is the Strategic Approach to International Chemicals Management (SAICM) that is partly being driven by UNEP. One of the objectives of SAICM is to respond to several regulatory challenges in the international chemicals governance regime including: the international law and policy framework for chemicals is fragmented and inadequate and needs to be further strengthened; implementation of international laws and policies is uneven; coherence and synergies between existing institutions and processes are not fully developed and should be improved; and several countries lack the capacity to adequately govern chemicals at the national, sub-regional, regional and global levels.[91] While this initiative does not aim to create one multilateral environmental agreement with a single governing body that should be responsible for global chemical governance, it does aim, in a bottom-up way, to facilitate greater synergies between the normative and institutional machinery of the Montreal Protocol on Substances that Deplete the Ozone Layer 1987; the Basel Convention on the Control of Transboundary Movement of Hazardous Wastes and their Disposal 1989; the Rotterdam Convention on the Prior Informed Consent Procedure for Certain Hazardous Chemicals and Pesticides in International Trade 1998; the Stockholm Convention on Persistent Organic Pollutants 2001; and the International Labour

---

[91] UNEP, 'Strategic Approach to International Chemicals Management: SAICM Texts and Resolutions of the International Conference on Chemicals Management' www.saicm.org/images/saicm_documents/saicm%20texts/New%20SAICM%20Text%20with%20ICCM%20resolutions_E.pdf, 12.

Organization's Convention No 170 1990, concerning safety in the use of chemicals at work.[92] The approach that SAICM foresees in order to achieve its objectives is very much a 'softer' bottom-up one that includes, among others: an enabling phase to build necessary capacity; to develop a national strategic approach implementation plan for participating countries; to develop regional strategic approach implementation plans; and a drive to encourage intergovernmental organisations, international financial institutions and private actors to support these activities and to consider the development of their own action plans as appropriate.[93]

Another option could be to create and/or strengthen regional environmental governance regimes, their founding treaties, normative environmental frameworks, and their governance institutions, including their adjudicating bodies. It would be crucial that the constituting treaties of these regional governance bodies and their subsequent environmental instruments, including those related to higher-order norms such as rights, are revised to cater more comprehensively for environmental concerns. Where they do not exist yet, they must be established. These reforms, which should also include initiatives for inter-regional alignment, should run concurrently with efforts to reform global environmental treaties and their regimes and they could contribute to creating regional pockets of constitutionally more coherent and effective environmental governance in a formal and substantive sense. As was intimated above, the European Union already provides a good practice example of a regional constitutional ecological federation that could guide reforms elsewhere in the world.

B. Global Environmental Rule of Law

Chapter 3 explained that the rule of law essentially consists of formal/procedural and substantive/material aspects. Whereas the formal/procedural aspects of the rule of law provide for and determine those elements that are necessary to establish and maintain a governance order on the basis of positive law, the material/substantive aspects of the rule of law bind those that exercise governance power to substantive standards, including states and to a lesser extent treaty secretariats. The formal aspects have several objectives: legality, functional delimitation of governance competencies and clear allocation of powers. The primary objectives of the substantive aspects are to ensure limited government, justice and morality through, among others, rights protection, judicial oversight, as well as the general principles of justice.

Measured against this core meaning of the rule of law, the existence of the global environmental rule of law could depend on, among others: the extent to which it could be said that (a) global environmental authority(ies) exist; the extent to which the entire collection of global laws regulating the human-environment

---

[92] ibid 20.
[93] ibid 21.

interface is available, clear and effective and able to ensure adequate compliance and enforcement; the extent to which state and non-state actor accountability with respect to environmentally damaging acts is ensured through checks and balances such as strengthened judicial control and citizen suits; and the extent to which the law is able to protect higher-order rights-based environmental guarantees.[94]

In a global setting, the formal aspects of the environmental rule of law could be regulated by constitution-like instruments in the global environmental governance sphere containing provisions that seek to provide for and determine the constitutive/formal elements that are necessary to establish and maintain the global environmental governance order; in other words, those provisions that enable and carry global environmental governance. These formal provisions focus on both the powers of environmental governance entities such as treaty secretariats themselves, and on the institutional arrangements that facilitate the involvement of states in each treaty's governance effort. Although it would have been far easier to determine these in terms of a hitherto non-existent single international environmental organisation and its constitution, such formal aspects are currently evident to some extent in the disaggregated collection of multilateral environmental agreements that create environmental governance institutions, regulate their internal functions and guide the actions of states parties, and consequently the manner in which states regulate those residing in their jurisdictions, including individuals and corporations (see the discussion above). The formal global environmental rule of law aspects should be strengthened in future in line with earlier proposals in this chapter to reform the body of multilateral environmental agreements, with the ultimate view to establishing an international environmental organisation.

Substantive global environmental rule of law aspects would aim to achieve some measure of limitation on all entities that exercise power in the global environmental governance domain including states, treaty bodies and international organisations; separation of these powers; checks, balances and judicial oversight; processes and institutions to advance democratic participation and legitimacy; and the provision and protection of rights-based guarantees. To date, as with the formal aspects of the global environmental rule of law, the global environmental law and governance order lacks a single all-encompassing instrument through which these goals could collectively be achieved. While treaties do set out some limitations on the free will of states and sanctions for non-compliance, these provisions are not absolute or sufficiently comprehensive, and on their own, treaties would not be solely up to the task of determining and enforcing higher-order normative obligations. The substantive aspects of the global environmental rule of law, such as rights and *jus cogens* norms exist to some extent, but they are scattered across the global regulatory landscape, as we will see below.

---

[94] Garver proposes an alternative view of 'ecological rule of law', which combines the notion of ecological law with the notion of the rule of law. Ecological law emphasises ecological integrity and the need for the law to ensure such integrity by making clear that global ecological limits constrain the economic and social spheres: G Garver, 'The Rule of Ecological Law: The Legal Complement to Degrowth Economics' (2013) 5 *Sustainability* 316–37.

C. Separation of Global Environmental Governance Powers

The separation of powers doctrine entails that the authority to govern should be divided among different government powers ie the executive, the legislature and the judiciary. For reasons outlined in Chapter 3, the degree of separation that this element of constitutionalism foresees is not an absolute one; the *trias politica* only needs to be 'sufficiently' separated. Related to the formal aspects of the rule of law, this doctrine essentially seeks to counter centralisation and abuse of authority, to promote accountability and to enhance governance efficiency. Separation of powers is hardly ever determined through a single explicit provision in a constitution. It usually emerges from the collective formal constitutional provisions that establish these powers and that determine and delimit their authority.[95]

Globally, it is far more difficult to determine a measure of separation of powers than it is in the domestic sphere: there is no unitary global government based on a unified constituted power with a clearly defined judiciary, executive and legislature that derive their powers from a single constituent power or instrument. Such a separation of global powers can only be vaguely detected in the United Nations and European Union's constitutional architecture. Considering, however, that domestic understandings of constitutionalism should be applied globally in a nuanced way, a close connection between three distinct separate global powers arguably need not exist, as long as the separation of powers doctrine more or less fulfils its objectives. Globally this could entail: preventing the concentration of power in any single state, group of states, an international governance organisation or a treaty body; creating accountability by requiring (a) limited global government(s) to justify decisions and actions and to act responsibly towards the international community; and increasing global governance efficiency where some global governance institutions are better placed to perform certain governance functions than others.[96]

Measured against these broad characteristics of the separation of powers doctrine outlined in Chapters 3, 4 and 5, how could the separation of powers doctrine be understood in the global environmental governance domain? There are at least two possible scenarios. The first is the most evident, but for reasons outlined above still the most unlikely scenario, where a global environmental government, or a global government with a distinct environmental arm, is created. Such a construction would create an opportunity to establish three distinct nodes revolving around executive, legislative and judicial functions that need not be entirely separated, but that allows for some form of convergence, within the confines of constitutionalism more generally, where this is necessary and permissible to ensure optimal global environmental governance of a complex and integrated Earth system in a balanced manner.

---

[95] See Ch 3.
[96] See Ch 4.

The second, and more likely option, is fashioned around O'Donoghue's proposition outlined in Chapter 4, namely to think about the separation of existing global environmental powers in geographical terms.[97] In terms of this description, vertical separation of global environmental powers would result in a clear distinction being drawn between local, federal (provincial or state), national, regional (such as the European Union) and international (the United Nations) centres of power. Because it includes the national sphere of powers and that sphere's unique horizontal division of powers as well, by necessary implication, geographical division of powers would include the traditional horizontal division of powers within a state, while including the national horizontal division of powers within the regional and international 'territorial centres'.[98] At the same time, the geographical separation of powers would include whatever minimal form of separation of powers is evident in the United Nations and European Union context as well. Such a construction might provide the means to limit the concentration of environmental governance powers at any single geographical level by divesting each sphere of some power through the multi-levelled geographical arrangement. The objectives of separation of powers in this construction could ultimately be improved by: constituting where they are absent, and improving existing legislative, executive and judicial functions in each geographical sphere; clearly delineating the relationships and measures for cooperation between the local, domestic, regional and international spheres themselves; and clearly delineating within each sphere the executive, legislative and judicial functions of the responsible environmental governance authority and providing measures for cooperation.

D. The Global Environmental Judiciary

Many domestic courts around the world have been active in adjudicating environmental disputes, interpreting environmental laws and, more generally, upholding the dictates of environmental constitutionalism by, for example, restricting state activities that could harm the environment.[99] While these are usually courts with general jurisdiction, there are examples of specialised domestic environmental courts such as the Australian New South Wales Land and Environment Court.[100] Apart from developing domestic environmental jurisprudence, these courts also contribute, through processes of trans-jurisdictional comparison, to the steady growth of transnational comparative environmental constitutionalism, as was shown above. In doing so, some latent degree of uniformity is developing globally

---

[97] A O'Donoghue, *Constitutionalism in Global Constitutionalisation* (Cambridge, Cambridge University Press, 2014) 34–35.
[98] ibid 35.
[99] See for a comprehensive discussion, May and Daly (n 1).
[100] See B Preston, 'Benefits of Judicial Specialization in Environmental Law: The Land and Environment Court of New South Wales as a Case Study' (2012) 29 *Pace Environmental Law Review* 396–440.

with respect to the interpretation, application and development of environmental law, including constitutional aspects such as environmental rights.[101] Processes associated with transnational comparative environmental constitutionalism are set to increase as globalisation and its effects deepen around the world; a possibility that bodes well for the expansion of global environmental constitutionalism in a transnational sense.

While not nearly comparable to the efforts of domestic courts, regional courts and adjudicating bodies have also in recent years increasingly engaged with environmental concerns, including the enforcement and development of substantive higher-order rights-based norms. Even though the European Convention on Human Rights of 1950 does not entrench an explicit environmental right, the European Court of Human Rights has been remarkably active in protecting environmental and related concerns through a range of other rights enshrined in the Convention.[102] In doing so, the Court is intensifying the development of higher-order rights-based norms and it provides checks and balances on power within the emerging European constitutional ecological federation, while it contributes to strengthening global environmental constitutionalism at the regional level. The Court of Justice of the European Union is the judicial institution of the Union. As a more general judicial forum, it focuses on disputes related to the legality of EU measures and ensures the uniform interpretation and application of EU law. In the environmental domain, the Court busies itself with the interpretation and application of EU environmental law, notably actions for failure to fulfil binding legal obligations.[103] As was mentioned above, the Court is likely to become an active role player in interpreting, protecting and enforcing the environment-related rights-based provision in the Charter of Fundamental Rights of the European Union of 2000.

Regional judicial bodies in the Americas are also asserting themselves as guardians of higher-order environmental constitutional norms encapsulated in rights. For example, in 1985 the Inter-American Commission on Human Rights' (IACommHR) recognised the link between environmental quality and the right to life by determining that a proposed highway and authorisations for the exploitation of natural resources in Brazil violated the rights of the Yanomani Indians to

---

[101] This is not to suggest, however, that some unqualified uniformity is emerging as it would be unrealistic to expect courts all over the world to become entirely uniform in their approaches to interpretation and the subsequent development of law. In fact, as Stephens suggests, 'some level of diversity is not only tolerable but desirable ... major points of jurisprudential difference can readily be overcome through a "transjudicial" dialogue': T Stephens, 'Multiple International Courts and the "Fragmentation" of International Environmental Law' (2006) 25 *Australian Year Book of International Law* 227–71, 231.

[102] These cases are too numerous to list here. See for a comprehensive overview, European Court of Human Rights, www.echr.coe.int/Documents/FS_Environment_ENG.pdf; and for a comprehensive discussion, J Jans and H Vedder, *European Environmental Law after Lisbon*, 4th edn (Groningen, Europa Publishing, 2012).

[103] See, for a detailed exposition of the Court's decisions on nature and biodiversity, European Commission, http://ec.europa.eu/environment/nature/info/pubs/docs/others/ecj_rulings_en.pdf.

health, life, liberty, personal security and free movement.[104] The Inter-American Court of Human Rights' (IACHR) decisions mostly revolve around indigenous peoples' rights; because of its limited justiciability, the Court's decisions have not directly focused on the environmental right articulated in article 11 of the 1999 San Salvador Protocol to the American Convention on Human Rights of 1969.[105] An example is the case of *Saramaka People v Suriname*.[106] The case involved the Government of Suriname's decision to grant mining and logging concessions in the territory of the Saramaka people.[107] The IACHR found that the concessions granted by the state failed to comply with certain necessary safeguards and that they violated the right to property of the Saramaka people.[108]

Despite the hesitance of the African Union to develop into a more clearly defined and influential regional constitutional ecological federation, its African Commission on Human and Peoples' Rights (ACHR) was the first regional judicial institution in the world to adjudicate matters that revolved around the environmental right ('the most explicit normative statement of an environmental right in any binding human rights instrument')[109] and related rights in the African Charter on Human and Peoples' Rights of 1981.[110] In the SERAC communication,[111] the Nigerian Government, during its involvement in oil production through the state-owned Nigerian National Petroleum Company (NNPC), caused environmental degradation and health problems among the Ogoni people.[112] The ACHR held that the environmental right 'imposes clear [positive] obligations upon a government. It requires the state to take reasonable and other measures to prevent pollution and ecological degradation, to promote conservation, and to secure an ecologically sustainable development and use of natural resources'.[113] In a 'negative' way, the environmental right obliges governments to desist from directly threatening the health and environment of their citizens, and it asks of governments to respect

---

[104] *Yanomami Case*, Case 7615, Inter-Am CHR Res No 12/85, OEA/Ser.L/V/II.66, doc 10, rev 1, 24 (1985).

[105] S Thériault, 'Environmental Justice and the Inter-American Court of Human Rights' in A Grear and LJ Kotzé (eds), *Research Handbook on Human Rights and the Environment* (Cheltenham, Edward Elgar, 2015) 309–29.

[106] *Case of the Saramaka People v Suriname*, 2007 Inter-Am CHR (ser C) no 172 (28 November 2007).

[107] D Shelton, 'Environmental Rights and Brazil's Obligations in the Inter American Human Rights System' (2009) 40 *The George Washington International Law Review* 733–77, 764–68.

[108] *Case of the Saramaka People v Suriname* (n 106) para 158.

[109] W Scholtz, 'Human Rights and the Environment in the African Union Context' in A Grear and LJ Kotzé, *Research Handbook on Human Rights and the Environment* (Cheltenham, Edward Elgar, 2015) 405; L Kotzé, 'Human Rights, the Environment, and the Global South' in S Alam et al (eds), *International Environmental Law and the Global South* (Cambridge, Cambridge University Press, 2015) 171–91.

[110] Esp arts 16, 21 and 24 of the Charter. See, for a comprehensive discussion of regional African judicial bodies, their decisions and key issues, F Viljoen, *International Human Rights Law in Africa*, 2nd edn (Oxford, Oxford University Press, 2012).

[111] Communication 155/96 (n 84).

[112] ibid, para 10.

[113] ibid, para 52.

the environmental right through non-interventionist conduct. The Commission subsequently found the Nigerian Government liable for violation of all the alleged human rights provisions and instructed it to make reparations. Unfortunately, the ACHR's findings are neither binding nor enforceable;[114] a reality which questions the practical influence of such a regional quasi-judicial body.[115] The African Court on Human and Peoples' Rights was subsequently established as a complimentary body to the Commission in 1998, with the view to providing an additional enforcement mechanism through its final and binding judgments.[116] The Court remains in operation, but while it has a broad jurisdiction *ratione materiae*, it has not delivered any significant environmental judgments to date, and considerable scope remains for it to do so.[117]

While the International Court of Justice (ICJ) serves as the pre-eminent international judicial forum, it is not an international environmental court. An opportunity for it to fulfil this role presented itself with the creation of the Court's Special Chamber for Environmental Matters in 1993.[118] While it was periodically reconstituted since its creation, it was unfortunately dismantled in 2006 and by that time had not adjudicated any environmental dispute. At least the fact that a judicial institution such as the ICJ contemplated the establishment of a specialised chamber was then, and today remains significant, especially to the extent that it indicates some state recognition of the political importance of the environment in international politics, law and governance.[119] And, as Sands further intimates, '[t]he very fear of its creation may serve as an inducement for various courts to demonstrate their ability to address environmental issues'.[120] The failure of the Chamber is not to suggest, however, that the ICJ has not dealt with environmental disputes between states, or that it does not remain crucially important as an institution in this respect. The complex body of ICJ environmental jurisprudence is too burgeoning to discuss here and others have extensively done such an analysis.[121] What is clear is that the ICJ has significantly contributed to

---

[114] F Viljoen and L Louw, 'State Compliance with the Recommendations of the African Commission on Human and Peoples' Rights 1994–2004' (2007) 101(1) *American Journal of International Law* 1–34.

[115] D Boyd, *The Environmental Rights Revolution* (n 83) 104.

[116] This was done in terms of the 1998 Protocol to the African Charter on Human and People's Rights on the Establishment of an African Court on Human and People's Rights.

[117] Importantly, the Constitutive Act of the African Union 2000, provided for an African Court of Justice and Human Rights to be established as one of the Union's principal organs, but the Court never became operational. It was decided in 2008 to merge the African Court of Justice and Human Rights with the African Court on Human and Peoples' Rights into an African Court of Justice and Human Rights but the protocol in terms of which this decision was made is still not in force. See http://www.au.int/en/organs/cj.

[118] See the discussion in Ch 6.

[119] P Sands, 'International Environmental Litigation and its Future' (1999) 32 *University of Richmond Law Review* 1619–41, 1626.

[120] ibid 1640.

[121] See among the many publications, T Stephens, *International Courts and Environmental Protection* (Cambridge, Cambridge University Press, 2009), esp Ch 2; J Viñuales, 'The Contribution of the International Court of Justice to the Development of International Environmental Law: A Contemporary Assessment' (2008) 32 *Fordham International Law Journal* 232–58.

developing international environmental law through its judgments,[122] advisory opinions[123] and, more creatively, through separate and dissenting opinions by some of its judges (notably those of Judge Weeramantry).[124] Its initial decisions broadly focused on transboundary environmental injuries to states and later, more encouragingly, on the environment as an international common good to be preserved by all states for the benefit of all.[125] With respect to the ICJ's contribution to the development of higher-order customary international environmental law, its affirmation of the no-harm principle is especially noteworthy.[126] This issue is discussed further below.

Acting complementary to domestic criminal systems, the International Criminal Court is not part of the United Nations system, but a treaty-based regime that aims to 'help end impunity for the perpetrators of the most serious crimes of concern to the international community'.[127] It focuses specifically on adjudicating 'the most serious crimes of concern to the international community as a whole', including genocide, crimes against humanity, war crimes and acts of aggression.[128] It is unclear from this wording whether, and none of its past judgments suggest, that environmental crimes could be included within its jurisdictional reach.[129] If they could be included, an important avenue will be created to ensure greater accountability where states, for example, commit acts of aggression that have an environmental impact or dimension.

Stephens indicates that internationally, 'environmental dispute settlement is increasingly dominated by issue-specific, judicial bodies called upon to determine essentially environmental disputes, often essentially by default'.[130] There

---

[122] Including, eg, *Corfu Channel (United Kingdom of Great Britain and Northern Ireland v Albania)* 1949; *Nuclear Tests Case (New Zealand v France)* 1974; *Gabčíkovo-Nagymaros Project (Hungary v Slovakia)* 1997; Certain Phosphate Lands in Nauru *(Nauru v Australia)* 1992; *Pulp Mills on the River Uruguay (Argentina v Uruguay)* 2006.

[123] eg, *Advisory Opinion on the Legality of the Threat or Use of Nuclear Weapons* 1996.

[124] See, for a detailed discussion, D French, 'The Heroic Undertaking? The Separate and Dissenting Opinions of Judge Weeramantry during his Time on the Bench of the International Court of Justice' (2006) 11 *Asian Yearbook of International Law* 35–68.

[125] Viñuales, 'The Contribution of the International Court of Justice to the Development of International Environmental Law' (n 121).

[126] The ICJ has endorsed the principle in its *Nuclear Weapons* Advisory Opinion, and specifically emphasised the *erga omnes* obligations that flow from it: 'The existence of the general obligation of States to ensure that activities within their jurisdiction and control respect the environment of other States or of areas beyond national control is now part of the corpus of international law relating to the environment': *Legality of the Threat or Use of Nuclear Weapons (Advisory Opinion)* ICJ Reports (1996) 268, para 29.

[127] International Criminal Court /www.icc-cpi.int/en_menus/icc/about%20the%20court/Pages/about%20the%20court.aspx. The Court was established by the adoption of the Rome Statute of the International Criminal Court 1998.

[128] Rome Statute of the International Criminal Court 1998, art 5.

[129] See further, T Smith, 'Creating a Framework for the Prosecution of Environmental Crimes in International Criminal Law' in W Schabas, Y McDermott and N Hayes (eds), *The Ashgate Research Companion to International Criminal Law* (Aldershot, Ashgate, 2013) 45 *et seq*.

[130] Stephens, 'Multiple International Courts and the "Fragmentation" of International Environmental Law' (n 101) 227–71, 233.

are various bodies of this nature such as the World Trade Organization and its General Agreement on Tariffs and Trade Panels, the International Tribunal on the Law of the Sea, the Permanent Court of Arbitration and the International Centre for the Settlement of Investment Disputes that are contributing to the normative development of international environmental law. While the jurisprudence of these institutions is too vast to deal with here, it has since become clear that despite their divergent focus areas, they have 'established an embryonic framework within which issues of international environmental law could be raised in the context of international litigation'.[131] The judgments of these judicial bodies do not necessarily contribute to develop higher-order environmental constitutional norms; they are far more effective in integrating environmental considerations with various globalised processes such as trade, and to some extent, they restrict the free will of states to engage in activities that may cause environmental harm.

An example of a civil society institution that endeavours to 'enforce' a more ecocentric ethic of environmental care is the International Rights of Nature Tribunal. In its own words, this people's tribunal:

> gives a vehicle for re-framing and adjudicating prominent environmental and social justice cases within the context of a Rights of Nature based earth jurisprudence. It gives people from all around the world the opportunity to testify publicly as to the destruction of the Earth—destruction that governments and corporations not only allow, but in some cases encourage.[132]

Civil society actors created the Tribunal in 2014, and it functions entirely within the global civil society environmental constitutionalism paradigm. To date, it has been convened thrice: in Ecuador, Peru and more recently in Paris for the 2015 global climate negotiations. It is based on a methodology that allows concerned citizens to 'testify', even in the physical absence of an 'accused' party, such as a state, that has allegedly infringed the rights of nature. While it is by no means a traditional court, it serves an important educational and awareness-raising function. A second example is the Permanent Peoples' Tribunal, which is the successor to the 1967 Bertrand Russell-Jean Paul Sartre Vietnam War Crimes Tribunal that exposed war crimes during the Vietnam War. Similar to the foregoing body, it functions as a public opinion tribunal and its judgments have no binding force. Yet, it could significantly raise global awareness of environmental issues. In March 2017, the Tribunal will hold a session on hydraulic fracturing; an initiative that was initiated by the Global Network for the Study of Human Rights and the Environment, the Environment and Human Rights Advisory and the Human Rights Consortium.[133] Initiatives such as these, while they cannot significantly strengthen

---

[131] Sands, 'International Environmental Litigation and its Future' (n 119) 1625.
[132] Global Alliance for the Rights of Nature 'International Rights of Nature Tribunal' http://therightsofnature.org/rights-of-nature-tribunal/.
[133] See https://www.tribunalonfracking.org/news/media-release/.

or expand the more traditional global judicial functions, do provide a forum for global civil society actors to voice their concerns in non-state spaces. As well, such initiatives could contribute to enhance global environmental democracy by providing a platform for global civil society to influence, however marginally, the actions of states and international organisations (see also the discussion below).

What emerges from the foregoing discussion is that 'there is no established international environmental jurisdiction, much as there is no global environmental organisation',[134] and global environmental dispute settlement remains a fragmented affair. This insight is particularly important for global environmental constitutionalism: clearly there are multiple judicial fora at various geographical levels available to enforce environmental law, to assert higher-order rights-based claims and to integrate environmental considerations into the multifarious rubric of concerns that domestic, regional and international law seeks to address. These judicial institutions simultaneously act to enforce the rule of law and in particular, accountability by keeping the actions of (mostly) states in check. Considering the many diverse dimensions and interrelated complexity of global environmental concerns, it is unlikely and probably even undesirable that one global court that has jurisdiction over all environmental disputes beyond the borders of states will or should ever exist. While there are concerns about the fragmented global environmental judiciary[135] (understood as including the panoply of the institutions discussed above), the current set-up provides the means for global judicial bodies to extend their influence into numerous global governance spaces at various geographical levels where environmental concerns might arise. In time it will be necessary, however, to create judicial bodies where they do not exist or strengthen existing ones; expand the jurisdictions of these bodies; and create specialised environmental units within each to deal with highly technical and specialised environmental issues. The Anthropocene after all requires a greater measure of scientific and technical specialisation to deal with the comprehensive range of Earth system changes that it evinces.[136]

If an international environmental organisation were established, it would be prudent to create an independent judicial body for that organisation which, while it will have a more limited jurisdiction than an all-encompassing global environmental court, must be sufficiently independent and separated from the organisation's executive and legislative functions. While global civil society actors should expand initiatives to build creative 'judiciaries' that are used to serve their agenda, processes of transnational comparative environmental constitutionalism should also be strengthened by promoting the means for domestic courts around the globe to interact more intensively.

---

[134] Stephens (n 101) 227–71, 234.
[135] ibid.
[136] See Ch 2.

E. Global Environmental Democracy

Chapter 3 indicated that democracy serves as an enabler of constitutionalism, as an expression of the majority will of people and as a necessary condition for the establishment and legitimacy of a constitutional state to the extent that democratic processes are required to constitute a structured polity. Democracy in the global context is more difficult to discern than at the domestic level because of the absence of a single global government and a constituent power, and it takes on a more nuanced meaning in the global governance sphere. Departing from an enlarged notion of an 'international community' consisting of states and non-state actors, an aggregated global constituent power should ideally be enabled to drive participative, representative, inclusive and transparent modes of global environmental governance in the spaces where states and their citizens, international organisations as global representatives of states, and global civil society actors operate.[137] The potentially potent link between democracy and what we seek to achieve through constitutionalism in the environmental law and governance domain is evident:

> Most scholarship envisions environmental politics as the pursuit of already fixed interests. That approach ignores the power of political communities to change both their values and their interests through the self-interpreting activity of democratic politics. In that politics, new forms of normative identity—who we take ourselves to be and what matters most to us—arise from reciprocal efforts at persuasion, arguments about the meaning of shared ideas and commitments. *Nature*, like *liberty* and *equality*, is a centerpiece of public language.[138]

How can the actors in global environmental governance contribute, through a more sustained and influential 'public language' that is carried by processes of democratic deliberation, to change prevailing and deep-seated values and interests? Moreover, how can global environmental democracy play out and be enhanced? First, in the state-dominant domain measures should be put in place to more equally represent all countries and regional groupings in environmental law and governance. Global environmental governance remains a matter of unequal partners and the global climate change negotiation arena is an example of an instance where states and regional organisations are disproportionally represented as a result of capacity concerns and hegemonic struggles. For example, with respect to the African grouping of states, it has been said that:

> Despite some notable contributions, Africa's impact on the UNFCCC process, as a whole, has been characterized by severe limitations. The most important appear to be weak capacity and limited resources. Furthermore, technical negotiators' organizational

---

[137] See Ch 5 and F Biermann and A Gupta, 'Accountability and Legitimacy in Earth System Governance: A Research Framework' (2011) 70 *Ecological Economics* 1856–64, 1856.

[138] J Purdy, 'The Politics of Nature: Climate Change, Environmental Law, and Democracy' (2010) 119 *Yale Law Journal* 1125–209, 1125.

structure is somewhat fragmentary and transient; the link between the different levels of negotiation is not always very clear and their approach to some issues is less strategic and more ad-hoc. There is also scope for more systematic engagement with climate change and the UNFCCC process by African political leaders.[139]

Anthropocene events are particularly evident in under-developed and developing countries such as those in Africa, and the Anthropocene's socio-ecological crisis is set to affect these countries the most. There is accordingly now, more than ever before, sufficient justification and motivation to level the global environmental political playing field by affording all states, including their global representatives, equal recognition and power in the processes and structures that determine global human-environment relations.

Secondly, in a transnational sense, and as Chapter 4 indicated, it is likely that the many actors in global governance will themselves be more democratic and inclined to observe the minimum dictates of democracy and constitutionalism in the global regulatory realm when these actors hail from domestic constitutional democracies. Acting as an ideological orientation for states in the global domain, the extent to which the citizens of a state are thus able to constitute, interact with and legitimise a constituted domestic power, including the aspects of that power responsible for domestic environmental governance, may have a meaningful persuasive bottom-up impact on how states act in and through global environmental governance. Efforts to transform non-democratic states and to strengthen domestic democratic regimes where they fall short, could thus contribute indirectly to the expansion of global environmental democracy in post-state spaces.

Thirdly, while it is not the only one,[140] a binding instrument that comes closest to comprehensively regulating and improving the participation, transparency and accountability aspects of global environmental democracy is the Convention on Access to Information, Public Participation in Decision-Making and Access to Justice in Environmental Matters 1998 (Aarhus Convention). The significant potential of the Aarhus Convention to enhance global environmental democracy lies, among others, in the effectiveness of its Compliance Committee and the fact that it is open for ratification to all members of the United Nations.[141] The Convention provides extensive measures and remedies to promote access to

---

[139] ClimDev-Africa 'Africa's Journey in the Global Climate Negotiations' www.climdev-africa. org/sites/default/files/DocumentAttachments/Africa%E2%80%99s%20Journey%20in%20the% 20Global%20Climate%20Negotiations,%20SPM%20-%20EN_0.pdf.

[140] The procedural aspects of global environmental governance currently exist in a much more comprehensive and complex global regulatory regime consisting of soft law instruments and regional and global treaties. See, for a detailed discussion, J Razzaque, 'Human Right to a Clean Environment: Procedural Rights' in Fitzmaurice, Ong and Merkouris (eds), *Research Handbook on International Environmental Law* (n 26) 284–300; and, more succinctly, U Beyerlin and T Marauhn, *International Environmental Law* (Oxford, Hart Publishing, 2011) 234–39.

[141] See, generally, E Hey, 'The Interaction between Human Rights and the Environment in the European Aarhus "Space"' in A Grear and LJ Kotzé (eds), *Research Handbook on Human Rights and the Environment* (Cheltenham, Edward Elgar, 2015) 353–76.

environmental information, public participation and access to justice in environmental matters. Importantly, these provisions are predicated on an explicit substantive, albeit non-justiciable, environmental right. Parties to the Convention are encouraged to protect the 'right of every person of present and future generations to live in an environment adequate to his or health and well-being'[142] by means of those measures that relate to the procedural aspects of environmental governance. Through the expansion of binding multilateral agreements such as the Aarhus Convention, and the encouragement of non-Member States to sign up to these agreements, a greater measure of accountable and democratic global environmental governance could possibly take root in future.

Fourthly, outside of the more formal state-driven global law and governance arena, global civil society is able to assert itself as an observer during global conferences and to cooperate more closely with states to achieve global governance objectives; an aspect that has been dealt with above where the benefits of global civil society environmental constitutionalism have also been highlighted. Multi-actor transnational networks are also increasingly created that contribute to realising some of the goals of global environmental governance in a bottom-up way. In relation to multinational corporations, the United Nations Global Compact provides a platform that engages corporations, governments and other stakeholders to collectively work towards sustainability goals.[143] Gradually expanding non-governmental organisations and global epistemic communities, such as the Global Network for the Study of Human Rights and the Environment, encouragingly evince more deliberate and possibly influential collective civil society energies that could influence and legitimise the predominantly state-driven global environmental governance agenda.

F. Global Environmental Constitutional Supremacy

The idea of constitutional supremacy assumes that there is no higher juridical norm in a state than the constitution and its provisions. Such a construction creates a normative and institutional hierarchy in terms of which all laws, decisions and acts of government are subject to the constitution and in terms of which these laws, decisions and acts could be declared unconstitutional and invalid. In domestic constitutions, such norms are usually encapsulated within rights and it is mainly the judiciary that will play a key role in upholding and protecting constitutional supremacy.[144] Constitutional supremacy is best understood in the global sphere by determining whether a normative hierarchy exists in terms of which

---

[142] Art 1.
[143] B Richardson, *Socially Responsible Investment Law: Regulating the Unseen Polluters* (Oxford, Oxford University Press, 2008).
[144] See Ch 3.

higher-order non-derogable norms supersede other norms and which bind states to the extent that their free sovereign will is limited.[145] In the absence of a global constitution that would have made this determination fairly straightforward, such norms are most likely to be found as human rights that are contained in regional and international human rights instruments, in *jus cogens* norms, customary international law and *erga omnes* obligations.[146]

Focusing for present purposes on *jus cogens* norms, Chapter 4 indicated that the rules of international law generally accepted as having *jus cogens* status include, among others: the prohibition of the threat or use of force against the territorial integrity or political independence of any state; the prohibition of genocide; the prohibition of torture; crimes against humanity; the prohibition of slavery and slave trade; the prohibition of piracy; the prohibition of racial discrimination and apartheid; and the prohibition of hostilities or force directed at a civilian population. It remains unclear if explicit environment-related *jus cogens* norms exist and/or if future peremptory norms could emerge in international environmental law.[147] There is, for example, no norm that prohibits severe and widespread pollution; or a norm that prohibits states from transgressing a minimum threshold of sustainability; or a norm that prohibits states from changing the climate through greenhouse gas emissions. Various scholars have confirmed this view. According to Birnie, Boyle and Redgwell:

> What cannot be supposed is that environmental rules have any inherent priority over others save in the exceptional case of *ius cogens* norms ... No such norms of international environmental law have yet been convincingly identified, nor is there an obvious case for treating them in this way.[148]

Beyerlin and Marauhn have also expressed their doubts about the recognition of environmental *jus cogens* norms. With reference to article 19 of the 1980 Draft Articles on State Responsibility,[149] which introduced the notion of an international crime that is seen as a violation of *jus cogens*, they argue that environmental pollution cannot at this stage be considered an international crime: 'only very few rules can actually be considered as peremptory norms and that hardly any of them is part of international environmental law'.[150] To date, no international court or tribunal has explicitly identified any norm that has, or that could in future gain, peremptory status in the environmental domain; nor has any international court or tribunal invoked articles 53 and 64 of the VCLT in practice to settle an

---

[145] Ch 4; and E de Wet and J Vidmar (eds), *Hierarchy in International Law: the Place of Human Rights* (Oxford, Oxford University Press, 2012).

[146] See for a definitive account on these issues, E de Wet, 'The International Constitutional Order' (2006) 55(1) *International and Comparative Law Quarterly* 51–76.

[147] See for a detailed discussion, LJ Kotzé, 'Constitutional Conversations in the Anthropocene: In Search of Environmental *Jus Cogens* Norms' *Netherlands Yearbook of International Law* (forthcoming).

[148] P Birnie, A Boyle and C Redgwell, *International Law and the Environment* 3rd edn (Oxford, Oxford University Press, 2009) 109–10.

[149] International Law Commission, 'Report of the International Law Commission on the Work of its 32nd Session' (5 May–25 July 1980) UN Doc A/35/10, 32.

[150] Beyerlin and Marauhn, *International Environmental Law* (n 140) 362.

environment-related treaty dispute. The closest that the ICJ came in doing so was in its *Gabčikovo-Nagymaros* judgment where it accepted by implication Slovakia's contention that none of the norms on which Hungary relied was of a peremptory nature.[151]

If we accept that a global hierarchy of constitutional-like environmental norms could be useful in restricting the free will of states in their actions that impact the environment, we need to ask if it is possible for environmental *jus cogens* norms to develop over time? The gradual Anthropocene-induced epistemological shift is redirecting our attention away from territorially limited and individual state-bound environmental concerns to a more globally collective conception of Earth system changes, their impacts on the international community of states and the collective responsibility of states in this respect. The ICJ in the *Nuclear Weapons* Advisory Opinion, has made tentative steps to connect more directly *jus cogens*, *erga omnes* obligations and the common heritage of mankind in the context of a globalised community of states that should be seeking collective responses to shared environmental problems. The Court noted that we are witnessing:

> the gradual substitution of an international law of co-operation for the traditional law of co-existence, the emergence of the concept of 'international community' and its sometimes successful attempts at subjectivization. A token of all these developments is the place which international law now accords to concepts such as obligations *erga omnes*, rules of *jus cogens*, or the common heritage of mankind. The resolutely positivist, voluntarist approach of international law still current at the beginning of the [twentieth] century has been replaced by an objective conception of international law, a law more readily seeking to reflect a collective juridical conscience and respond to the social necessities of states organised as a community.[152]

At a practical level and in light of the epistemological freedom that such pronouncements provide, article 53 of the 1969 Vienna Convention on the Law of Treaties (VCLT) offers states an opportunity to determine themselves what are peremptory norms and what are not.[153] In practice, this would occur through a process that first identifies a norm as customary international law and then an agreement on whether derogation is permitted from that customary norm or not.

Considering the deep controversy that surrounds the burgeoning debate on which international environmental law norms have or have not attained customary law status,[154] this discussion focuses for present purposes on the one rule that has unequivocally been recognised as customary environmental law, namely the no-harm rule (or *sic utere tuo ut alienum non laedas*) that imposes a negative obligation on states (as *jus cogens* norms typically do) not to cause environmental harm to another state. The rule was first recognised by an international court in

---

[151] *Gabčikovo-Nagymaros*, ICJ Reports (1997), para 97.
[152] *Legality of the Threat or Use of Nuclear Weapons (Advisory Opinion)* (n 126) 270–71 (per President Bedjaoui).
[153] E de Wet, '*Jus Cogens* and Obligations *Erga Omnes*' in D Shelton (ed), *The Oxford Handbook on International Human Rights Law* (Oxford, Oxford University Press, 2015) 542.
[154] See for a general discussion, Beyerlin and Marauhn (n 140) 47–84.

the *Trail Smelter* arbitration, which settled an environmental utilisation conflict between Canada and the United States.[155] The ICJ has subsequently endorsed the rule in its *Nuclear Weapons* Advisory Opinion, and specifically emphasised the *erga omnes* obligations that flow from it:

> The existence of the general obligation of States to ensure that activities within their jurisdiction and control respect the environment of other States or of areas beyond national control is now part of the corpus of international law relating to the environment.[156]

Today the no-harm rule:

> has been so widely accepted in international treaty practice, numerous declarations of international organisations, the codification work of the ILC [International Law Commission], and in the jurisprudence of the ICJ that it can be considered to be a customary substantive rule at the universal level.[157]

It should thus satisfy the VCLT peremptory requirement of being 'a norm accepted and recognised by the international community of States as a whole' (the first stage of acceptance).[158] Whether it has attained the status of a norm 'from which no derogation is permitted'[159] (the second stage of acceptance) is, however, debatable. It is still unlikely that states have universally accepted any 'strong ethical [ecological] underpinning'[160] that should be associated with the no-harm rule. Yet, because of its customary status, the fact that it applies at an inter-state level to environmental resources within state territories as well as to the global environmental commons, and that it imposes negative obligations, suggest that at least theoretically, it has the potential to become a peremptory norm in future. In the light of the Anthropocene and various implicit ethical obligations to desist from causing irreversible ecological harm, there is increasing motivation auguring support for universal recognition of the no-harm rule's potential strong ethical underpinning that is necessary for enhanced global ecological care. At the same time, there is sufficient justification for broadening the scope of existing *jus cogens* norms, *erga omnes* obligations and customary international law, to explicitly include environmental norms as well.

G. Global Environmental Rights

Rights are also part of the international normative hierarchy's set of apex norms. The discussion thus far has shown that an increasingly burgeoning body of

---

[155] *Trail Smelter Arbitration* (1949) 3 RIAA 1903.
[156] *Legality of the Threat or Use of Nuclear Weapons (Advisory Opinion)* (n 126) para 29.
[157] Beyerlin and Marauhn (n 140) 44.
[158] VCLT, art 53.
[159] ibid.
[160] J Vidmar, 'Norm Conflicts and Hierarchy in International Law: Towards a Vertical International Legal System?' in de Wet and Vidmar (eds), *Hierarchy in International Law: the Place of Human Rights* (n 145) 26.

environmental and related rights exists and that this body of norms is gradually expanding through trans-jurisdictional cross-pollination and the explicit entrenchment of environmental rights in regional instruments. Domestically, the transnationalisation of global environmental rights presents rich opportunities for the cross-fertilisation of legal ideas and best practices and it has the potential to influence the creation of common global legal rules on environmental rights that are at least based on the same ideas and influences, if not exactly on the same content. Regionally, in addition to environmental rights provisions in the European Union instruments, the African Charter on Human and People's Rights and the American Convention on Human Rights' San Salvador Protocol, article 3(2) of the Asian Human Rights Charter of 1998 provides for the right to a 'clean and healthy environment'.[161] The Arab Charter on Human Rights 2004 also includes a right to a healthy environment as part of the right to an adequate standard of living that ensures well-being and a decent life.[162] It was further shown that the Aarhus Convention declares a non-justiciable environmental right and it provides a whole set of procedural guarantees to facilitate inclusive and participative environmental governance.

These domestic and regional initiatives, and their relatively active judicial oversight bodies, are set to be bolstered by the increasingly vocal and influential global civil society movements that champion environment-related rights protection. Often working from their domestic jurisdictions and increasingly beyond these, such as in the case of the International Rights of Nature Tribunal discussed above, it is global civil society actors in particular that contribute to cementing, strengthening and further expanding environment-related rights at the global level through their core functions.[163]

To date, however, there is neither a universally applicable global treaty that explicitly provides for an environmental right,[164] nor has such a right been accepted into the corpus of customary international law.[165] As an ultimate expression of constitutionalism, and specifically with the view to providing greater global ecological care that is premised on strong sustainability, it will be crucial to commence with discussions about eventually creating such a right, either in a future global environmental constitution or as an element of an existing or new treaty.

---

[161] Available at http://www.refworld.org/pdfid/452678304.pdf.

[162] Art 38. Notably, neither the Asian Human Rights Charter, nor the Arab Charter on Human Rights has enforcement mechanisms.

[163] B Gemmill and A Bamidele-Izu, 'The Role of NGOs and Civil Society in Global Environmental Governance' in D Esty and M Ivanova (eds), *Global Environmental Governance: Options and Opportunities* (Yale, Yale Centre for Environmental Law and Policy, 2002) 77–100.

[164] See, generally, S Turner, *A Global Environmental Right* (Abingdon, Routledge, 2014).

[165] At most, environmental entitlements are inferred indirectly from the provisions of other human-focused but environment-related rights treaties, such as the International Covenant on Economic, Social and Cultural Rights 1966 (arts 7(b), 10(3) and 12); the Convention on the Rights of the Child 1989 (art 24); and the International Labour Organization Convention Concerning Indigenous and Tribal Peoples in Independent Countries 1989 (arts 2, 6, 7, 15). See D Shelton, 'Human Rights and the Environment: Substantive Rights' in Fitzmaurice, Ong and Merkouris (n 26) 266–67.

Considering the Anthropocene's demands for current regulatory institutions and higher-order norms to become more ecocentric, part of this discussion must also reflect on the orientation of this right. The Bolivian and Ecuadorean legal systems provide examples of ecocentric domestic environmental rights, while the Earth Charter also provides a generic framework for such a discussion. Another possibility is to contemplate a 'human right to commons- and rights-based ecological governance' that has been taken up in the recently proposed Universal Covenant Affirming a Human Right to Commons- and Rights-Based Governance of Earth's Natural Wealth and Resources. This right provides a system:

> for using and protecting all the creations of nature and related societal institutions that we inherit jointly and freely, hold in trust for future generations, and manage democratically in keeping with human rights principles grounded in respect for nature as well as human beings, including the right of all people to participate in the governance of wealth and resources important to their basic needs and culture.[166]

The Bolivian Government has recently proposed to the United Nations an even more extreme ecocentric rights reformulation in terms of the Universal Declaration of Rights of Mother Earth of 2010.[167] The Declaration recognises that the Earth is a living entity and as a result 'Mother Earth' could lay claim to the full range of fundamental rights normally attributed to humans including, among others: the right to life and to exist; the right to be respected; the right to regenerate bio-capacity and to continue her vital cycles and processes free from human disruptions; the right to maintain her identity and integrity as a distinct, self-regulating and interrelated being; the right to water as a source of life; the right to clean air; the right to integral health; the right to be free from contamination, pollution and toxic or radioactive waste; the right to not have her genetic structure modified or disrupted in a manner that threatens her integrity or vital and healthy functioning; and the right to full and prompt restoration.[168] Considering the legal fraternity's continued apprehension about such an ecological formulation and its possible legal and governance implications, as well as the prevailing strong political resistance to such a drastic proposal, it is understandably unlikely that it will gain any credence soon. Yet, the fact that the debate has been initiated in the global political arena, suggests that it could make it less difficult in future to negotiate for a global environmental right that is at once also more ecocentric in its orientation.

In sum, an ecological reorientation of rights evinces the potential that rights have to refocus exclusive attention away from serving human needs, to an approach that instead seeks to ensure care for human well-being, while simultaneously

---

[166] See art 1(1) of the Commons Law Project, *Universal Covenant Affirming a Human Right to Commons- and Rights-based Governance of Earth's Natural Wealth and Resources* (2013) www.elgaronline.com/view/journals/jhre/4-2/jhre.2013.02.05.xml.

[167] http://therightsofnature.org/bolivia-experience/.

[168] Art 2 of the Declaration. See World People's Conference on Climate Change and the Rights of Mother Earth, *Proposed Universal Declaration of the Rights of Mother Earth*, http://pwccc.wordpress.com/programa/.

respecting the limits of Earth's life supporting systems and the well-being of other species. At the very least it is one, among other attempts, to give 'ethico-juridical significance to the material situations of countless human beings, non-human animals and living eco-systems placed in unprecedented danger by the irresponsible pursuit of profit and by its associated ecological legacies'.[169]

VI. Conclusion

The analysis in this penultimate chapter was based on the various insights that were distilled throughout the book. In drawing these thoughts together, the chapter sought to provide a systemised account of global environmental constitutionalism and it outlined several motivations to search for traces of constitutionalism in the global environmental law and governance sphere. The chapter also discussed the different approaches to global environmental constitutionalism and the various elements that it could consist of. The conclusions and proposals included views on what the regulatory and normative status quo is and what type of short-, medium- and long-term future-oriented reforms would be needed in light of the Anthropocene's imagery of global socio-ecological decay. Admittedly, some of these options are more drastic than others, and it is likely that the less drastic options will be more popular policy choices for states and other global environmental governance actors in the short term. The more drastic, long-term reforms, notably the creation of an international environmental organisation with a comprehensive formal and substantive constitution that addresses the elements of global environmental constitutionalism outlined in Part 5 of this chapter, would be as close as it comes to creating an ideal form of global environmental constitutionalism. In the final analysis, it is sufficiently clear that not only is there a need for the global environmental law and governance order to be constitutionalised, but also that this process is already underway and that it should be augmented in future.

---

[169] A Grear, 'Human Bodies in Material Space: Lived Realities, Eco-crisis and the Search for Transformation' (2013) 4(2) *Journal of Human Rights and the Environment* 111–15, 111.

8

Conclusion

Global environmental constitutionalism is a comparatively radical juridical intervention to address a critical global regulatory problem: the socio-ecological crisis of the Anthropocene. Understandably, while it is much easier to situate constitutionalism in the domestic environmental law and governance sphere, it is far more difficult to do so with respect to global environmental law and governance. We need to accept that:

> The barriers to facilitating such global rethinking remain immense and must be challenged both individually and collectively by those who wish to reform the existing order ... the barriers we need to identify and dismantle are ones created by ideologies and modes of reasoning that funnel thinking and keep us from acting on these common sensibilities.[1]

The ideas that were canvassed in this book, including its numerous proposals, sought to prise open some of the epistemological closures that continue to shut out more radical thinking in the constitutional and global environmental law and governance domains respectively. While the analysis emphasised the positive contribution that environmental constitutionalism could make to improve global environmental law and governance, it also fully accepts that the mere incorporation of environmental concerns into a global constitutional framework, or conversely, the constitutionalisation of the global environmental law and governance framework, is only part of many strategies that would be necessary to counter Anthropocene exigencies. While environmental constitutionalism cannot therefore be the *panacea* for all the Anthropocene's regulatory challenges, as a value-laden manifestation of law carrying with it substantial normative force, the promise of 'new beginnings' and the potential to change polities to the core, there is an argument to be made out in support of thinking about global environmental law and governance reforms in constitutional terms, and to identify and further develop environmental constitutionalism elements in the global regulatory space beyond the state. Clearly there are sufficient fertile spaces for future critical thinking to take this debate forward. The Anthropocene's socio-ecological crisis will demand nothing less.

---

[1] S Jasanoff, 'A World of Experts: Science and Global Environmental Constitutionalism' (2013) 40(4) *Boston College Environmental Affairs Law Review* 439–52 at 443–44.

Those who wish to engage in future thinking about law, constitutionalism and the Anthropocene might want to consider, in addition to the various rhetorical questions that have been posed in Chapter 7, some of the following themes: considering that the analysis in this book was oriented towards a liberal Western-oriented understanding of constitutionalism, how could other cultures and approaches to constitutionalism infuse global environmental constitutionalism's analytical and normative project? Accepting that the Anthropocene demands a more ecocentric oriented form of global environmental governance, to what extent is it necessary to change the anthropocentric orientation of international environmental law as the main formal and substantively constitutional body of law that undergirds global environmental governance, and how could this be done? What could be an appropriate universal ethic for the Anthropocene that must orientate global environmental law and governance, and how could such an ethic be entrenched constitutionally in global environmental law and governance? As a response to the need for greater multi-disciplinary analyses, in what ways could law, ethics, ecology and political science, among others, converge to provide more holistic solutions to the regulatory challenges of the Anthropocene? Accepting that an international environmental organisation and a global environmental constitution are difficult to establish and with reference to the more flexible Paris Climate Agreement of 2015, to what extent could a bottom-up approach be adopted in which countries do what they feel is necessary and achievable while enabling greater opportunities for a non-hierarchical, diffuse movement of all kinds of actions by a variety of state and non-actors? And finally, considering the centrality of the Earth systems governance scientific agenda to the Anthropocene debate, how could global environmental constitutionalism contribute to and/or be re-imagined through the Earth systems governance paradigm?

BIBLIOGRAPHY

A

Ackerman, B, 'The Storrs Lectures: Discovering the Constitution' (1984) 93 *Yale Law Journal* 1013
——, *We the People, Volume 1: Foundations* (Cambridge, Harvard University Press, 1993)
——, 'The Rise of World Constitutionalism' (1997) 83 *Virginia Law Review* 771
——, *We the People, Volume 2: Transformations* (Cambridge, Harvard University Press, 1998)
——, 'The Living Constitution' (2007) 120 *Harvard Law Review* 1737
Albert, R, 'The Cult of Constitutionalism' (2012) 39 *Florida State University Law Review* 373
Alexy, R, *A Theory of Constitutional Rights* (Oxford, Oxford University Press, 2002)
Allen, M, 'Globalization and Peremptory Norms in International Law: From Westphalian to Global Constitutionalism' (2004) 41 *International Politics* 341
Allot, P, 'The Concept of International Law' in M Byers (ed), *The Role of Law in International Politics: Essays in International Relations and International Law* (Oxford, Oxford University Press, 2001) 69–89
Almeida, F, 'The Emergence of Constitutionalism as an Evolutionary Adaptation' (ExpressO, 2014) works.bepress.com/fabio_almeida/3/
Alston, PG, 'Against a World Court for Human Rights' (2014) papers.ssrn.com/sol3/papers.cfm?abstract_id=2344333
Amalric, A, 'The Equator Principles: A Step Towards Sustainability?' (2005) Centre for Corporate Responsibility and Sustainability Working Paper No 01/05 of 2005
Anastaplo, G, 'Constitutionalism and the Good: Explorations' (2003) 70 *Tennessee Law Review* 738
Anderson, GW, *Constitutional Rights after Globalization* (Oxford, Hart Publishing, 2005)
Arato, A, 'Forms of Constitution Making and Theories of Democracy' (1995) 17 *Cardozo Law Review* 191
Armesto, JJ et al, 'From the Holocene to the Anthropocene: A Historical Framework for Land Cover Change in Southwestern South America in the Past 15,000 Years' (2010) 27 *Land Use Policy* 148
Arts, K and Handmaker, J, 'Cultures of Constitutionalism: An Introduction' in M Frishman and S Muller (eds), *The Dynamics of Constitutionalism in the Age of Globalisation* (The Hague, Hague Academic Press, 2010) 49–56
Autin, W and Holbrook, L, 'Is the Anthropocene an Issue of Stratigraphy or Pop Culture?' (2012) July *GSA Today* 60
Ayestaran, I, 'The Second Copernican Revolution in the Anthropocene: An Overview' (2008) 3 *Revista Internacional Sostenibilidad, Technologia y Humanismo* 146

B

Backer, LC, 'From Constitution to Constitutionalism: A Global Framework for Legitimate Public Power Systems' (2008/2009) 113 *Penn State Law Review* 671

Baghel, R, 'Knowledge, Power and the Environment: Epistemologies of the Anthropocene' (2012) 3(1) *Transcience* 1

Baker, S, 'Adaptive Law in the Anthropocene' (2015) 90 *Chicago-Kent Law Review* 563

Balsiger, J and VanDeveer, S, 'Navigating Regional Environmental Governance' (2012) 12(3) *Global Environmental Politics* 1

Barnosky, AD et al, 'Approaching a State Shift in Earth's Biosphere' (2012) 486 *Nature* 52

—— et al, 'Introducing the Scientific Consensus on Maintaining Humanity's Life Support Systems in the 21st Century: Information for Policy Makers' (2014) 1 *The Anthropocene Review* 78

Barry, J, 'Towards a Green Republicanism: Constitutionalism, Political Economy, and the Green State' (2008) 17(2) *The Good Society* 3

Baskin, J, 'Paradigm Dressed as Epoch: The Ideology of the Anthropocene' (2015) 24 *Environmental Values* 9

Baykal, S, 'The Rule of Law in the European Union Context and Turkey's Accession Process' in P Müller-Graff and H Kabaalioglu (eds), *Turkey and the European Union: Different Dimensions* (Baden-Baden, Nomos Verlag, 2011) 37–51

Becker, E, 'Socio-ecological Systems as Epistemic Objects' (Institut für sozial-ökologische Forschung, 2010) www.isoe.de/ftp/publikationen/eb_socecsystem2010.pdf.

Benhör, H, '1. Arbeitsbereich: Umweltrecht in Deutschland im 19. Jahrhundert' in M Kloepfer (ed), *Umweltstaat als Zukunft: juristische, ökonomische und philosophische Aspekte* (Bonn, Economica Verlag, 1994) 108–10

Bernstein, S, 'Globalization and the Requirements of "Good" Environmental Governance' (2005) 4 *Perspectives on Global Development and Technologies* 645

——, 'The Role and Place of the High-Level Political Forum in Strengthening the Global Institutional Framework for Sustainable Development' (2013) https://sustainabledevelopment.un.org/content/documents/2331Bernstein%20study%20on%20HLPF.pdf

Bettini, G, Brandstedt, E and Thorén, H, 'Sustainability Science and the Anthropocene: Re-negotiating the Role for Science in Society' (2010) edocs.fu-berlin.de/docs/servlets/MCRFileNodeServlet/FUDOCS_derivate_000000001299/Bettini-Sustainability_Science_and_the_Anthropocene-305.pdf?hosts=

Bexell, M, Tallberg, J and Uhlin, A, 'Democracy in Global Governance: The Promises and Pitfalls of Transnational Actors' (2010) 16 *Global Governance* 81

Beyerlin, U and Marauhn, T, *Law Making and Law-Enforcement in International Environmental Law after the 1992 Rio Conference* (Berlin, Erich Schmidt Verlag, 1997)

—— and Marauhn, T, *International Environmental Law* (Oxford, Hart Publishing, 2011)

Biermann, F, 'The Rationale for a World Environment Organization' in F Biermann and S Bauer (eds), *A World Environment Organization: Solution or Threat for Effective International Environmental Governance?* (Aldershot, Ashgate, 2005)

——, '"Earth System Governance" as a Cross-cutting Theme of Global Change Research' (2007) 17 *Global Environmental Change* 326

——, 'Reforming Global Environmental Governance: From UNEP towards a World Environmental Organization' in L Swart and E Perry (eds), *Global Environmental*

Governance: Perspectives on the Current Debate (Centre for UN Reform Education, 2007) 103–23
——, *Earth System Governance: World Politics in the Anthropocene* (Cambridge, MIT Press, 2014)
——, 'The Anthropocene: A Governance Perspective' (2014) 1 *The Anthropocene Review* 57
—— and Gupta, A, 'Accountability and Legitimacy in Earth System Governance: A Research Framework' (2011) 70 *Ecological Economics* 1856
—— et al, 'Navigating the Anthropocene: The Earth System Governance Project Strategy Paper' (2010) 2 *Current Opinion in Environmental Sustainability* 202
—— et al, 'Navigating the Anthropocene: Improving Earth System Governance' (2012) 335 *Science* 1306
Birnie, P, Boyle, A and Redgwell, C, *International Law and the Environment* 3rd edn (Oxford, Oxford University Press, 2009)
Bodansky, D, 'Is There an International Environmental Constitution?' (2009) 16 *Indiana Journal of Global Legal Studies* 565
Bondy, W, *The Separation of Governmental Powers in History, in Theory, and in the Constitutions* (New York, Columbia College, 1896)
Bosselmann, K, *Im Namen der Natur: Der Weg zum ökologischen Rechtsstaat* (Bern, Scherz, 1992)
——, 'Der Ökologische Rechtsstaat: Versuch einder Standortbestimmung' in H Baumeister (ed), *Wege zum ökologischen Rechtsstaat: Umweltschutz ohne Öko-Diktatur* (Taunusstein, Eberhard Blottner Verlag, 1994) 53–69
——, *Ökologische Grundrechte: Zum Verhältnis zwischen individueller Freiheit und Natur* (Baden-Baden, Nomos Verlagsgesellschaft, 1998)
——, 'In Search of Global Law: The Significance of the Earth Charter' (2004) 8 *Worldviews* 62
——, 'Human Rights and the Environment: Redefining Fundamental Principles?' (2005) http://www.ais.up.ac.za/health/blocks/HET870/Fundamentalprinciples.pdf
——, 'Outlook: The Earth Charter—A Model Constitution for the World?' in K Bosselmann and R Engel (eds), *The Earth Charter: A Framework for Global Governance* (Amsterdam, KIT Publishers, 2010) 239
——, *Earth Governance: Trusteeship of the Global Commons* (Cheltenham, Edward Elgar, 2015)
——, 'Global Environmental Constitutionalism: Mapping the Terrain' (2015) 21 *Widener Law Review* 171
—— and Schröter, M, *Umwelt und Gerechtigkeit: Leitlinien einer ökologischen Gesetzgebung* (Baden-Baden, Nomos Verlagsgesellschaft, 2001)
—— and Engel, R (eds), *The Earth Charter: A Framework for Global Governance* (Amsterdam, KIT Publishers, 2010)
Boyd, DR, *The Environmental Rights Revolution: A Global Study of Constitutions, Human Rights, and the Environment* (Vancouver, UBC Press, 2012)
——, 'Constitutions, Human Rights, and the Environment: National Approaches' in A Grear and LJ Kotzé (eds), *Research Handbook on Human Rights and the Environment* (Cheltenham, Edward Elgar, 2015) 170–99
Boyd, W, 'Climate Change, Fragmentation, and the Challenges of Global Environmental Law: Elements of a Post-Copenhagen Assemblage' (2010) 32 *University of Pennsylvania Journal of International Law* 457

Boyle, K, 'Linking Human Rights and Other Goals' in J Morison, K McEvoy and G Anthony (eds), *Judges, Transition, and Human Rights* (Oxford, Oxford University Press, 2007) 401–22

Brady, J, Crawford, B and Wiliarty, SE (eds), *The Postwar Transformation of Germany: Democracy, Prosperity and Nationhood* (Ann Arbor, University of Michigan Press, 1999)

Brandl, E and Bungert, H, 'Constitutional Entrenchment of Environmental Protection: A Comparative Analysis of Experiences Abroad' (1992) 16 *Harvard Environmental Law Review* 1

Brandon, M, 'Constitutionalism and Constitutional Failure' (1999) 9(2) *The Good Society* 61

Brauch, HG, Dalby, S and Oswald Spring, Ú, 'Political Geoecology for the Anthropocene' in HG Brauch et al (eds), *Coping with Global Environmental Change, Disasters and Security Threats, Challenges, Vulnerabilities and Risks* (Berlin, Springer, 2011) 1453–86

Breitmeier, H and Rittberger, V, *Environmental NGOs in an Emerging Global Civil Society* (Tübinger Arbeitspapiere zur Internationalen Politik und Friedensforschung, 1998)

Brook, B et al, 'Does the Terrestrial Biosphere have Planetary Tipping Points?' (2013) 28(7) *Trends in Ecology and Evolution* 396–401

Brown Weiss, E, *In Fairness to Future Generations: International Law, Common Patrimony; and Intergenerational Equity* (Dobbs Ferry, Transnational Publishers, 1989)

Bruckerhoff, J, 'Giving Nature Constitutional Protection: A Less Anthropocentric Interpretation of Environmental Rights' (2008) 86 *Texas Law Review* 616

Brundtland GO, 'Report of the World Commission on Environment and Development: Our Common Future' (1987) www.un-documents.net/our-common-future.pdf

Bryde, B, 'International Democratic Constitutionalism' in R St John Macdonald and D Johnston (eds), *Towards World Constitutionalism: Issues in the Legal Ordering of the World Community* (Leiden, Martinus Nijhoff, 2005) 103–26

Buchanan, J, *The Collected Works of James Buchanan: Volume 7—The Limits of Liberty: Between Anarchy and Leviathan* (Indianapolis, Liberty Fund, 1999–2002)

Burge-Hendrix, B, 'Plato and the Rule of Law' in I Flores and K Himma (eds), *Law, Liberty and the Rule of Law* (Dordrecht, Springer, 2013) 27–47

C

Caldwell, E and Nardin, T, 'Methodological Approaches to Asian Constitutionalism: Introduction' (2012) 88 *Chicago-Kent Law Review* 3

Castells, M, 'The New Public Sphere: Global Civil Society, Communication Networks, and Global Governance' (2008) 616 *The ANNALS of the American Academy of Political and Social Science* 78

Castiglione, D, 'The Political Theory of the Constitution' (1996) XLIV *Political Studies* 417

Choudhry, S, 'Ackerman's Higher Lawmaking in Comparative Constitutional Perspective: Constitutional Moments as Constitutional Features?' (2008) 6 *Icon* 193

Claus, L, 'Separation of Powers and Parliamentary Government' in V Amar and M Tushnet (eds), *Global Perspectives on Constitutional Law* (New York, Oxford University Press, 2009) 48–58

Code, L, *Ecological Thinking: The Politics of Epistemic Location* (Oxford, Oxford University Press, 2006)

Cohen, J and Sabel, C, 'Global Democracy?' (2005) 35 *International Law and Politics* 763

Contiades, X and Fotiadou, A, 'Models of Constitutional Change' in X Contiades (ed), *Engineering Constitutional Change: A Comparative Perspective on Europe, Canada and the USA* (New York, Routledge, 2012) 417–68

Conway, G, 'Recovering a Separation of Powers in the European Union' (2011) 17 *European Law Journal* 304

Cottier, T and Hertig, M, 'The Prospects of 21st Century Constitutionalism' (2003) 7 *Max Planck Yearbook of United Nations Law* 261

Craig, D and Jeffery, M, 'Integrating Sustainable Development into Global Institutions: Reforming the United Nations' (2009) 7(4) *Chinese Journal of Population, Resources and Environment* 3

Craig, P, 'Constitutional Foundations, the Rule of Law and Supremacy' (2003) Spring *Public Law* 92

Criddle, EJ and Fox-Decent, E, 'A Fiduciary Theory of *Jus Cogens*' (2009) 34 *Yale Journal of International Law* 331

Crist, E, 'On the Poverty of our Nomenclature' (2013) 3 *Environmental Humanities* 129

Crutzen, PJ, 'Albedo Enhancement by Stratospheric Sulfur Injections: A Contribution to Resolve a Policy Dilemma?' (2006) 77 *Climate Change* 211

——, 'The Anthropocene: Geology by Mankind' in HG Brauch et al (eds), *Coping with Global Environmental Change, Disasters and Security: Threats, Challenges, Vulnerabilities and Risks* (Heidelberg, Springer Verlag, 2011) 3–4

—— and Stoermer, EF, 'The "Anthropocene"' (2000) 41 *IGBP Global Change Newsletter* 17

——, PJ and Steffen, W, 'Editorial Commentary: How Long have We been in the Anthropocene Era?' (2003) 61 *Climate Change* 251

Currie, I and De Waal, J, *The Bill of Rights Handbook*, 6th edn (Cape Town, Juta, 2013)

D

Dalby, S, 'Anthropocene Ethics: Rethinking "The Political" after Environment' (Paper presented at the 45th International Studies Annual Convention, Montreal, Canada, 17–20 March 2004) www.yumpu.com/en/document/view/42485216/anthropocene-ethics-rethinking-the-political-after-environment/3

——, 'Ecology, Security, and Change in the Anthropocene' (2007) 8 *Brown Journal of World Affairs* 155

——, 'Geographies of the International System: Globalization, Empire and the Anthropocene' in P Aalto, V Harle and S Moisio (eds), *International Studies: Interdisciplinary Approaches* (New York, Palgrave Macmillan, 2011) 125–48

Daly, E, 'Constitutional Protection for Environmental Rights: The Benefits of Environmental Process' (2012) 17(2) *International Journal of Peace Studies* 71

Davis, D, 'Constitutional Borrowing: The Influence of Legal Culture and Local History in the Reconstitution of Comparative Influence—The South African Experience' (2003) 1(2) *International Journal of Constitutional Law* 181

De Búrca, G and Scott, J (eds), *The EU and the WTO: Legal and Constitutional Issues* (Oxford, Hart Publishing, 2001)

De Vattel, E, *Le droit des gens ou principes de la loi naturelle appliqué's à la conduite et aux affaires de Nations et des Souverains* (Washington, Carnegie Institution of Washington, 1758, 1916 reprint)

De Wet, E, 'The International Constitutional Order' (2006) 55(1) *International and Comparative Law Quarterly* 51

——, 'Jus Cogens and Obligations Erga Omnes' in D Shelton (ed), *The Oxford Handbook on International Human Rights Law* (Oxford, Oxford University Press, 2015) 541–61

——, 'The Implications of President Al-Bashir's Visit to South Africa for International and Domestic Law' (2015) 13 *Journal of International Criminal Justice* 1

——, 'Sources and the Hierarchy of International Law' in S Besson and J D'Aspremont (eds), *Oxford Handbook on the Sources of International Law* (Oxford, Oxford University Press, forthcoming)

—— and Vidmar, J (eds), *Hierarchy in International Law: The Place of Human Rights* (Oxford, Oxford University Press, 2012)

—— and Vidmar, J, 'Introduction' in E de Wet and J Vidmar (eds), *Hierarchy in International Law: The Place of Human Rights* (Oxford, Oxford University Press, 2012) 1–14

Di Fabio, U, 'Verfassungsstaat und Weltrecht' (2008) 39 *Rechtstheorie* 399

Dicey, AV, *Introduction to the Study of the Law of the Constitution*, 8th edn (London, Macmillan, 1915; reprinted Indianapolis, Liberty Fund, 1982)

Domingo, R, 'The New Global Human Community' (2012) 12 *Chicago Journal of International Law* 563

Drahozal, C, *The Supremacy Clause: A Reference Guide to the United States Constitution* (Westport, Praeger, 2004)

Drumbl, M 'Actors and Law-making in International Environmental Law' in M Fitzmaurice, D Ong and P Merkouris (eds), *Research Handbook on International Environmental Law* (Cheltenham, Edward Elgar, 2010) 6–8

Du Toit, P, *State-building and Democracy in Southern Africa: A Comparative Study of Botswana, Zimbabwe and South Africa* (Pretoria, HSRC Publishers, 1995)

Dunhoff, J, 'Why Constitutionalism Now? Text, Context and the Historical Contingency of Ideas' (2004/05) 1 *Journal of International Law and International Relations* 191

——, 'Constitutional Conceits: The WTO's "Constitution" and the Discipline of International Law' (2006) 17 *European Journal of International Law* 647

——, 'The Politics of International Constitutions: The Curious Case of the World Trade Organization' in J Dunhoff and J Trachtman (eds), *Ruling the World: Constitutionalism, International Law, and Global Governance* (Cambridge, Cambridge University Press, 2009) 178–205

—— and Trachtman, J, 'A Functional Approach to International Constitutionalization' in J Dunhoff and J Trachtman (eds), *Ruling the World: Constitutionalism, International Law, and Global Governance* (Cambridge, Cambridge University Press, 2009) 3–25

Dupper, O, 'In Defence of Affirmative Action in South Africa' (2004) 121 *South African Law Journal* 187

Dyzenhaus, D, 'The Pasts and Future of the Rule of Law in South Africa' (2008) 124 *South African Law Journal* 734

E

Ebbesson, J, 'The Rule of Law in Governance of Complex Socio-ecological Changes' (2010) 20 *Global Environmental Change* 414

Ekeli, KS, 'Green Constitutionalism: The Constitutional Protection of Future Generations' (2007) 20 *Ratio Juris* 378

Eleftheriadis, P, 'Parliamentary Sovereignty and the Constitution' (2009) 22 *Canadian Journal of Law and Jurisprudence* 1

Elkins, Z, Ginsburg, T and Melton, J, 'Comparative Constitutions Project: Characteristics of National Constitutions' (2014, version 2.0) comparativeconstitutionsproject.org/ccp2015/download-data/

Elliot, L and Breslin, S, 'Researching Comparative Regional Environmental Governance Causes, Cases and Consequences' in L Elliot and S Breslin (eds), *Comparative Environmental Regionalism* (New York, Routledge, 2011) 4

Enzmann, B, *Der Demokratische Verfassungsstaat: Entstehung, Elemente, Herausforderungen* (Wiesbaden, Springer, 2012)

European Environment Agency (EEA), *The European Environment: State and Outlook—Synthesis* (Luxembourg, Office for Official Publication of the European Union, 2010)

F

Farred, G, 'Disorderly Democracy: An Axiomatic Politics' (2008) 8(2) *New Centennial Review* 43

Fassbender, B, 'The United Nations Charter as the Constitution of the International Community' (1998) 36 *Columbia Journal of International Law* 529

Fenske, H, *Der Moderne Verfassungsstaat: Eine vergleichende Geschichte von der Entstehung bis zum 20. Jahrhundert* (Paderborn, Ferdinand Schöning, 2001)

Ferejohn, J, 'Independent Judges, Dependent Judiciary: Explaining Judicial Independence' (1999) 72 *Southern California Law Review* 353

Feris, L, 'Constitutional Environmental Rights: An Underutilised Resource' (2008) 24 *South African Journal on Human Rights* 29

Fisher, E, 'Towards Environmental Constitutionalism: A Different Vision of the Resource Management Act 1991?' (Resource Management Law Association of New Zealand Inc, 2014) www.rmla.org.nz/upload/files/annual_conference/2014_papers/lfisher.pdf

Fiss, O, 'The Limits of Judicial Independence' (1993) 25 *Inter-American Law Review* 57

Fitch, F, Forster, S and Miller, J, 'Geological Time Scale' (1974) 37 *Reports on Progress in Physics* 1433

Flores, I, 'Law, Liberty and the Rule of Law (in a Constitutional Democracy)' in I Flores and K Himma (eds), *Law, Liberty and the Rule of Law* (Dordrecht, Springer, 2013) 77–101

—— and Himma, K, 'Introduction' in I Flores and K Himma (eds), *Law, Liberty and the Rule of Law* (Dordrecht, Springer, 2013) 1–9

Folke, C et al 'Reconnecting to the Biosphere' (2011) 40(7) *Ambio* 719

Fombad, C, 'The Separation of Powers and Constitutionalism in Africa: The Case of Botswana' (2005) 25 *Boston College Third World Law Journal* 301

——, 'Challenges to Constitutionalism and Constitutional Rights in Africa and the Enabling Role of Political Parties: Lessons and Perspectives from Southern Africa' (2007) 55 *American Journal of Comparative Law* 1

——, 'Internationalization of Constitutional Law and Constitutionalism in Africa' (2012) 6 *American Journal of Comparative Law* 439

Food and Agricultural Organization (FAO), *The State of the World's Land and Water Resources for Food and Agriculture: Managing Systems at Risk* (Abingdon, Earthscan, 2011)

Fredriksson, P and Wollscheid, J, 'Democratic Institutions versus Autocratic Regimes: The Case of Environmental Policy' (2007) 130 *Public Choice* 381

French, D, 'The Heroic Undertaking? The Separate and Dissenting Opinions of Judge Weeramantry during his Time on the Bench of the International Court of Justice' (2006) 11 *Asian Yearbook of International Law* 35

Friedman, N, 'The South African Common Law and the Constitution: Revisiting Horizontality' (2014) 30 *South African Journal of Human Rights* 69

Friedrich, C, *Der Verfassungsstaat der Neuzeit* (Berlin, Springer, 1953)

——, *The Philosophy of Law in Historical Perspective* (Chicago, University of Chicago Press, 1953)

Frishman, M and Muller, S (eds), *The Dynamics of Constitutionalism in the Age of Globalisation* (The Hague, Hague Academic Press, 2010)

Fuller, LL, *The Morality of Law* (New Haven, Yale University Press, 1964)

——, *Anatomy of the Law* (New York, FA Praeger, 1968)

G

Galindo, G, 'Constitutionalism Forever' (2010) 21 *Finnish Yearbook of International Law* 137

Gardbaum, S, 'Human Rights and International Constitutionalism' in J Dunoff and J Trachtman (eds), *Ruling the World: Constitutionalism, International Law, and Global Governance* (Cambridge, Cambridge University Press, 2009) 233–57

Gareau, BJ, 'Global Environmental Constitutionalism' (2013) 40 *Boston College Environmental Affairs Law Review* 403

Garver, G, 'The Rule of Ecological Law: The Legal Complement to Degrowth Economics' (2013) 5 *Sustainability* 316

Gearty, C, 'Do Human Rights Help or Hinder Environmental Protection?' (2010) 1 *Journal of Human Rights and the Environment* 7

Gellers, J, 'Explaining the Emergence of Constitutional Environmental Rights: A Global Quantitative Analysis' (2015) 6 *Journal of Human Rights and the Environment* 75

Gemmill B and Bamidele-Izu, A, 'The Role of NGOs and Civil Society in Global Environmental Governance' in D Esty and M Ivanova (eds), *Global Environmental Governance: Options and Opportunities* (Yale, Yale Centre for Environmental Law and Policy, 2002) 77–100

Gethmann, CF, '3. Arbeitsgruppe: Freiheit und Rechtsstaatlichkeit im Umweltstaat' in M Kloepfer (ed), *Umweltstaat als Zukunft: juristische, ökonomische und philosophische Aspekte* (Bonn, Economica Verlag, 1994) 114–17

Giddens, A, *The Politics of Climate Change*, 2nd edn (Cambridge, Polity, 2011)

Glikson, AY, *Evolution of the Atmosphere, Fire and the Anthropocene Climate Event Horizon* (Heidelberg, Springer Verlag, 2014)

Globaïa, 'A Cartography of the Anthropocene: Mens Agitat Molem' (2013) globaia.org/portfolio/cartography-of-the-anthropocene/

Goldsworthy, J, 'Legislative Sovereignty and the Rule of Law' in T Campbell, KD Ewing and A Tomkins (eds), *Sceptical Essays on Human Rights* (Oxford, Oxford University Press, 2001)

Gosseries, A, 'Constitutions and Future Generations' (2008) 17(2) *The Good Society* 32

Gradstein, G and Ogg, J, 'Geological Time Scale 2004—Why, How and Where Next!' (2004) 37 *Lethaia* 175

Grant, E, Kotzé LJ and Morrow, M, 'Human Rights and the Environment: In Search of a New Relationship. Synergies and Common Themes' (2013) 3 *Oñati Socio-legal Series* 953

Gray, D and Colucci-Gray L 'Globalisation and the Anthropocene: The Reconfiguration of Science Education for a Sustainable Future' (2014) 2(3) *Sisyphus Journal of Education* 14

Grear, A, *Redirecting Human Rights: Facing the Challenge of Corporate Legal Humanity* (New York, Palgrave Macmillan, 2010)
——, 'The Vulnerable Living Order: Human Rights and the Environment in a Critical and Philosophical Perspective' (2011) 2 *Journal of Human Rights and the Environment* 23
——(ed), *Should Trees have Standing? 40 Years on* (Cheltenham, Edward Elgar, 2012)
——, 'Human Bodies in Material Space: Lived Realities, Eco-crisis and the Search for Transformation' (2013) 4(2) *Journal of Human Rights and the Environment* 111
——, 'Deconstructing Anthropos: A Critical Legal Reflection on "Anthropocentric" Law and Anthropocene "Humanity"' (2015) *Law and Critique* 1
Greer, SC, *The European Convention on Human Rights: Achievements, Problems and Prospects* (Cambridge, Cambridge University Press, 2006)
Greiber, T (ed), *Judges and the Rule of Law: Creating the Links—Environment, Human Rights and Poverty* (Gland, IUCN, 2006)
Grimm, D, 'The Achievement of Constitutionalism and its Prospects in a Changed World' in P Dobner and M Loughlin (eds), *The Twilight of Constitutionalism?* (Oxford, Oxford University Press, 2010) 3–22
Grinlinton, D and Taylor, P (eds), *Property Rights and Sustainability: The Evolution of Property Rights to meet Ecological Challenges* (Boston, Martinus Nijhoff, 2011)
Guillaume, B, 'Vernadsky's Philosophical Legacy: A Perspective from the Anthropocene' (2014) *The Anthropocene Review* 1
Gwyn, W, *The Meaning of the Separation of Powers: An Analysis of the Doctrine from its Origin to the Adoption of the United States Constitution* (The Hague, Martinus Nijhoff, 1965)

H

Haas, P, 'Regional Environmental Governance' in T Börzel and T Risse (eds), *The Oxford Handbook of Comparative Regionalism* (Oxford, Oxford University Press, 2016) 437
Häberle, P, 'The Constitutional State and its Reform Requirements' (2000) 13 *Ratio Juris* 77
Habermas, J, *The Divided West* (Cambridge, Polity, 2006)
——, 'The Crisis of the European Union in the Light of a Constitutionalization of International Law' (2012) 23 *European Journal of International Law* 335
—— and Rehg, W, 'Constitutional Democracy: A Paradox Union of Contradictory Principles?' (2001) 29 *Political Theory* 766
Halmai, G, *Perspectives on Global Constitutionalism: The Use of Foreign and International Law* (The Hague, Eleven International Publishing, 2014)
Hamara, C, 'The Concept of the Rule of Law' in I Flores and K Himma (eds), *Law, Liberty and the Rule of Law* (Dordrecht, Springer, 2013) 11–26
Hart, HLA, *The Concept of Law*, 2nd edn (Oxford, Clarendon Press, 1994)
Haus der Kulturen der Welt, 'The Anthropocene Project: An Opening' (10–13 January 2013) www.hkw.de/media/en/texte/pdf/2013_2/programm_6/anthropozaen/booklet_anthropozaen_eine_eroeffnung.pdf
Hayward, T, *Constitutional Environmental Rights*, e-book(Oxford, Oxford University Press, 2005)
Head, L, 'Contingencies of the Anthropocene: Lessons from the "Neolithic"' (2014) 1 *The Anthropocene Review* 113
Henkin, L, *The Age of Rights* (New York, Columbia University Press, 1990)

Henrard, K, 'Post Apartheid South Africa's Democratic Transformation Process: Redress of the Past, Reconciliation and "Unity in Diversity"' (2002) 1(3) *Global Review of Ethnopolitics* 18

Hey, E, 'The Interaction between Human Rights and the Environment in the European "Aarhus Space"' in A Grear and LJ Kotzé (eds), *Research Handbook on Human Rights and the Environment* (Cheltenham, Edward Elgar, 2015) 353–75

Hill, M, *Climate Change and Water Governance: Adaptive Capacity in Chile and Switzerland* (Dordrecht, Springer, 2013)

Hodson, M and Marvin, S, 'Urbanism in the Anthropocene: Ecological Urbanism or Premium Ecological Enclaves?' (2010) 14 *City* 299

Howlett, M and Joshi-Koop, S, 'Transnational Learning, Policy Analytical Capacity, and Environmental Policy Convergence: Survey Results from Canada' (2011) 21 *Global Environmental Change* 85

Howse, R and Teitel, R, 'Global Judicial Activism, Fragmentation, and the Limits of Constitutionalism in International Law' in U Fastenrath et al (eds), *From Bilateralism to Community Interest: Essays in Honour of Judge Bruno Simma* (Oxford, Oxford University Press, 2011) 961–74

Hudson, B, 'Structural Environmental Constitutionalism' (2015) 21 *Widener Law Review* 201

Hunt, M, 'Reshaping Constitutionalism' in J Morison, K McEvoy and G Anthony (eds), *Judges, Transition, and Human Rights* (Oxford, Oxford University Press, 2007) 467–78

I

Ignaciuk, A et al, 'Responding to Complex Societal Challenges: A Decade of Earth System Science Partnership (ESSP) Interdisciplinary Research' (2012) 4 *Current Opinion in Environmental Sustainability* 147

Ignatieff, M, 'Reimagining a Global Ethic' (2012) 26 *Ethics and International Affairs* 7

International Geosphere-Biosphere Programme (IGBP) et al, 'The Amsterdam Declaration on Global Change' (2001) www.colorado.edu/AmStudies/lewis/ecology/gaiadeclar.pdf

Isensee, J, 'Staat und Verfassung' in J Isensee and P Kirchhof (eds), *Handbuch des Staatsrechts: Verfassungsstaat* (Heidelberg, Müller, 2014)

J

Jacobs, J, 'Community Participation, the Environment, and Democracy: Brazil in Comparative Perspective' (2002) 44(4) *Latin American Politics and Society* 59

Jans, J and Vedder, H, *European Environmental Law after Lisbon*, 4th edn (Groningen, Europa Publishing, 2012)

Jasanoff, S, 'A World of Experts: Science and Global Environmental Constitutionalism' (2013) 40 *Boston College Environmental Affairs Law Review* 439

Jeffery, C, 'Devolution in the United Kingdom: Problems of a Piecemeal Approach to Constitutional Change' (2009) 39 *Publius: The Journal of Federalism* 289

Jerome, S, 'The Philosophical Foundations of Human Rights' (1998) 20 *Human Rights Quarterly* 201

Jonas, H, *Das Prinzip Verantwortung: Versuch einer Ethik für die technologische Zivilisation* (Frankfurt am Mein, Suhrkamp, 1988)

JYP Jnr, 'Toward a Constitutionally Protected Environment' (1970) 56 *Virginia Law Review* 458

K

Kanie, N, 'Governance with Multilateral Environmental Agreements: A Healthy or Ill-equipped Fragmentation?' in L Swart and E Perry (eds), *Global Environmental Governance: Perspectives on the Current Debate* (Centre for UN Reform Education, 2007) 73

—— et al, 'A Charter Moment: Restructuring Governance for Sustainability' (2012) 32 *Public Administration and Development* 292

Kay, R, 'Constitutional Chrononomy' (2000) 13 *Ratio Juris* 31

Kelsen, H, *General Theory of Law and State* (Cambridge, Harvard University Press, 1945)

Kende, MS, *Constitutional Rights in Two Worlds: South Africa and the United States* (Cambridge, Cambridge University Press, 2009)

Kersch, K, 'The New Legal Transnationalism, the Globalized Judiciary, and the Rule of Law' (2005) 4 *Washington University Global Studies Law Review* 345

Kim, R and Bosselmann, K, 'International Environmental Law in the Anthropocene: Towards a Purposive System of Multilateral Environmental Agreements' (2013) 2 *Transnational Environmental Law* 285

Kjaer, P, *Constitutionalism in the Global Realm: A Sociological Approach* (New York, Routledge, 2014)

Klabbers, J, 'Constitutionalism Lite' (2004) 1 *International Organizations Law Review* 31

——, 'Setting the Scene' in J Klabbers, A Peters and G Ulfstein (eds), *The Constitutionalization of International Law* (Oxford, Oxford University Press, 2009) 1–44

——, Peters, A and Ulfstein, G (eds), *The Constitutionalization of International Law* (Oxford, Oxford University Press, 2009)

—— and Wallendahl Å (eds), *Research Handbook on the Law of International Organizations* (Cheltenham, Edward Elgar, 2011)

Klarman, M, 'What's so Great about Constitutionalism?' (1998) 93 *Northwestern University Law Review* 145

Kleinlein, T, 'Alfred Verdross as a Founding Father of International Constitutionalism?' (2012) 4 *Goettingen Journal of International Law* 385

Kloepfer, M, 'Auf dem Weg zum Umweltstaat' in M Kloepfer (ed), *Umweltstaat: Ladenburger Diskurs* (Berlin, Springer Verlag, 1989) 39–78

——, 'Droht der autoritäre ökologische Staat?' in H Baumeister (ed), *Wege zum ökologischen Rechtsstaat: Umweltschutz ohne Öko-Diktatur* (Taunusstein, Eberhard Blottner Verlag, 1994) 42–50

——, 'Eröffnungsvortrag: Das Ladenburger Kolleg Umweltstaat: Resultate und Perspektiven' in M Kloepfer (ed), *Umweltstaat als Zukunft: juristische, ökonomische und philosophische Aspekte* (Bonn, Economica Verlag, 1994) 3–41

—— (ed), *Umweltstaat als Zukunft: juristische, ökonomische und philosophische Aspekte* (Bonn, Economica Verlag, 1994)

Kobayashi, N, 'Constitutional Studies and World Problems: A Study of Japan's Constitutional History as a Starting Point' in T Fleiner (ed), *Five Decades of Constitutionalism: Reality and Perspectives (1945–1995)* (Bale, Helbing and Lichtenhahn, 1999) 3–17

Kolb, R, 'Does Article 103 of the Charter of the United Nations Apply only to Decisions or also to Authorizations Adopted by the Security Council?' (2004) 64 *Zeitschrift für ausländisches öffentliches Recht und Völkerrecht* 21

Koskenniemi, M and Leino, P, 'Fragmentation of Internal Law? Postmodern Anxieties' (2002) 15 *Leiden Journal of International Law* 553

Kotzé, LJ, 'The Application of Just Administrative Action in the South African Environmental Governance Sphere: An Analysis of Some Contemporary Thoughts and Recent Jurisprudence' (2004) 7(2) *Potchefstroom Electronic Law Journal* 58

——, 'Arguing Global Environmental Constitutionalism' (2012) 1 *Transnational Environmental Law* 199

——, *Global Environmental Governance: Law and Regulation for the 21st Century* (Cheltenham, Edward Elgar, 2012)

——, 'Sustainable Development and the Rule of Law for Nature: A Constitutional Reading' in C Voigt (ed), *Rule of Law for Nature: New Dimensions and Ideas in Environmental Law* (Cambridge, Cambridge University Press, 2013) 130–42

——, 'Crossing Boundaries: Water and the Rights Paradigm' (2014) 5 *Journal of Human Rights and the Environment* 1

——, 'Fragmentation Revisited in the Context of Global Environmental Law and Governance' (2014) 131 *South African Law Journal* 548

——, 'Human Rights and the Environment in the Anthropocene' (2014) 1 *The Anthropocene Review* 1

——, 'Rethinking Global Environmental Law and Governance in the Anthropocene' (2014) 32 *Journal of Energy and Natural Resources Law* 121

——, 'Transboundary Environmental Governance of Biodiversity in the Anthropocene' in LJ Kotzé and T Marauhn (eds), *Transboundary Governance of Biodiversity* (Boston, Brill, 2014) ch 2

——, 'The Conceptual Contours of Global Environmental Constitutionalism' (2015) 21 *Widener Law Review* 187

——, 'Human Rights and the Environment through an Environmental Constitutionalism Lens' in A Grear and LJ Kotzé (eds), *Research Handbook on Human Rights and the Environment* (Cheltenham, Edward Elgar, 2015) 145–69

——, 'Human Rights, the Environment and the Global South' in S Alam et al (eds), *International Environmental Law and the Global South* (New York, Cambridge University Press, 2015) 171–90

—— and Paterson, AR (eds), *The Role of the Judiciary in Environmental Governance: Comparative Perspectives* (Alphen aan den Rijn, Kluwer, 2009)

—— and Scholtz, W, 'Environmental Law-Africa, Sub-Saharan' in K Bosselmann, F Fogel and JB Ruhl (eds), *The Berkshire Encyclopaedia of Sustainability, Vol. 3: The Law and Politics of Sustainability* (Great Barrington, Berkshire Publishers, 2010) 179–87

Kravchenko, S, 'The Aarhus Convention and Innovations in Compliance with Multilateral Environmental Agreements' (2007) 18(1) *Colorado Journal of International Environmental Law and Policy* 1

Kumm, M, 'The Legitimacy of International Law: A Constitutionalist Framework of Analysis' (2004) 15 *European Journal of International Law* 907

——, 'The Jurisprudence of Constitutional Conflict: Constitutional Supremacy in Europe before and after the Constitutional Treaty' (2005) 11 *European Law Journal* 262

Kysar, DA, *Regulating from Nowhere: Environmental Law and the Search for Objectivity* (New Haven, Yale University Press, 2010)

——, 'Global Environmental Constitutionalism: Getting There from Here' (2012) 1 *Transnational Environmental Law* 83

L

Larkins, C, 'Judicial Independence and Democratization: A Theoretical and Conceptual Analysis' (1996) 44 *American Journal of Comparative Law* 605

Latour, B, 'Agency at the Time of the Anthropocene' (2014) 45 *New Literary History* 1

Law, D and Versteeg, M, 'The Ideology and Evolution of Global Constitutionalism' (2011) 99 *California Law Review* 1163

Limbach, J, 'The Concept of the Supremacy of the Constitution' (2001) 64 *Modern Law Review* 1

Lord Bingham, 'The Rule of Law' (2007) 66 *Cambridge Law Journal* 67

Loughlin, M, 'Rights, Democracy, and Law' in T Campbell, KD Ewing and A Tomkins (eds), *Sceptical Essays on Human Rights* (Oxford, Oxford University Press, 2001)

——, 'What is Constitutionalisation?' in P Dobner and M Loughlin (eds), *The Twilight of Constitutionalism* (Oxford, Oxford University Press, 2010) 47–72

Lövbrand, E, Stripple, J and Wiman, B, 'Earth System Governmentality: Reflections on Science in the Anthropocene' (2009) 19 *Global Environmental Change* 7

Lovelock, JE, 'Geophysiology, the Science of Gaia' (1989) 27 *Reviews of Geophysics* 215

——, 'Hands up for the Gaia Hypothesis' (1990) 344 *Nature* 100

Lutz, D, 'Thinking About Constitutionalism at the Start of the Twenty-First Century' (2000) 30(4) *Publius* 115

Lyster, R, *Climate Justice and Disaster Law* (Cambridge, Cambridge University Press, 2015)

M

Maathai, W, 'An Unbreakable Link: Peace, Environment, and Democracy' (2008) Winter *Harvard International Review* 24

Macdonald, R, 'Fundamental Norms in Contemporary International Law' (1987) 25 *Canadian Yearbook of International Law* 115

—— and Johnston, D (eds), *Towards World Constitutionalism: Issues in the Legal Ordering of the World Community* (Leiden, Martinus Nijhoff, 2005)

Mackenzie, R and Sands, P, 'International Courts and Tribunals and the Independence of the International Judge' (2003) 44 *Harvard International Law Journal* 271

Maduro, M, 'How Constitutional can the European Union be? The Tension Between Intergovernmentalism and Constitutionalism in the European Union' in J Weiler and C Eisgruber (eds), *Altneuland: The EU Constitution in a Contextual Perspective* (Jean Monnet Working Paper 5/04)

——, 'The Importance of Being Called a Constitution: Constitutional Authority and the Authority of Constitutionalism' (2005) 3 *International Journal of Constitutional Law* 332

Magraw, D, 'Rule of Law and the Environment' (2014) 44 *Environmental Policy and Law* 201

Mahony, M, 'The Anthropocene: Reflections on a Concept—Part 1' (Topograph: Contested Landscapes of Knowing: Blogspot, 12 April 2013) thetopograph.blogspot.de/search?updated-min=2013-01-01T00:00:00-08:00&updated-max=2014-01-01T00:00:00-08:00&max-results=14

Malm, A and Hornborg, A, 'The Geology of Mankind: A Critique of the Anthropocene Narrative' (2014) 1 *The Anthropocene Review* 62

Mandel, M, 'A Brief History of the New Constitutionalism, or "How we Changed Everything so that Everything Would Remain the Same"' (1998) 32 *Israel Law Review* 250

Mansfield, H, 'Separation of Powers in the American Constitution' in B Wilson and P Schramm (eds), *Separation of Powers and Good Government* (Lanham, Rowman and Littlefiel, 1994) 3–6

Martin, R, 'The European Union and International Negotiations on Climate Change: A Limited Role to Play' (2012) 8(2) *Journal of Contemporary European Research* 192

Martineau, A, 'The Rhetoric of Fragmentation: Fear and Faith in International Law' (2009) 22 *Leiden Journal of International Law* 1

Masterman, R, *The Separation of Powers in the Contemporary Constitution: Judicial Competence and Independence in the United Kingdom* (Cambridge, Cambridge University Press, 2011)

May, JR and Daly, E, *Global Environmental Constitutionalism*, Kindle edn (New York, Cambridge University Press, 2015)

McConnell, M, 'The Forgotten Constitutional Moment' (1994) 11 *Constitutional Commentary* 115

——, 'A Moral Realist Defense of Constitutional Democracy' (1998) 64 *Chicago-Kent Law Review* 89

McHarg, A, 'Climate Change Constitutionalism? Lessons from the United Kingdom' (2011) 2 *Climate Law* 469

McIlwain, C, *Constitutionalism: Ancient and Modern* (Amagi, Liberty Fund, 2007)

Meadows, D et al, *The Limits to Growth: A Report for the Club of Rome's Project on the Predicament of Mankind* (New York, Universe Books, 1972)

Merkel, W, 'Measuring the Quality of the Rule of Law: Virtues, Perils, Results' in M Zürn, A Nollkaemper and R Peerenboom (eds), *Rule of Law Dynamics in an Era of International and Transnational Governance* (Cambridge, Cambridge University Press, 2012) 21–47

Midlarsky, M, 'Democracy and the Environment: An Empirical Assessment' (1998) 35 *Journal of Peace Research* 341

Milewicz, K, 'Emerging Patters of Global Constitutionalization: Toward a Conceptual Framework' (2009) 16 *Indiana Journal of Global Legal Studies* 413

Miller, G, 'Constitutional Moments, Precommitment, and Fundamental Reform: The Case of Argentina' (1993) 71 *Washington University Law Quarterly* 1061

Minteer, B, 'Geoengineering and Ecological Ethics in the Anthropocene' (2012) 62 *BioScience* 857

Moore, K, 'Anthropocene is the Wrong Word' (Earth Island Journal, Spring 2013) www.earthisland.org/journal/index.php/eij/article/anthropocene_is_the_wrong_word/

Morrow, K, 'Sustainability, Environmental Citizenship Rights and the Ongoing Challenges of Reshaping Supranational Environmental Governance' in A Grear and LJ Kotzé (eds), *Research Handbook on Human Rights and the Environment* (Cheltenham, Edward Elgar, 2015) 202

Mowbray, A, 'The Creativity of the European Court of Human Rights' (2005) 5 *Human Rights Law Review* 57

Murkens, J, 'The Quest for Constitutionalism in UK Public Law Discourse' (2009) 29 *Oxford Journal of Legal Studies* 427

Murswiek, D, '2. Arbeitsgruppe: Staatliche Umweltverantwortung' in M Kloepfer (ed), *Umweltstaat als Zukunft: juristische, ökonomische und philosophische Aspekte* (Bonn, Economica Verlag, 1994) 111

N

Nedelsky, J, *Private Property and the Limits of American Constitutionalism: The Madisonian Framework and its Legacy* (Chicago, University of Chicago Press, 1990)

Nemesio, I, 'Strengthening Environmental Rule of Law: Enforcement, Combatting Corruption, and Encouraging Citizen Suits' (2015) 27 *Georgetown International Environmental Law Review* 321

Nergelius, J, *The Accession of the EU to the European Convention on Human Rights: A Critical Analysis of the Opinion of the European Court of Justice* (Stockholm, Swedish Institute for European Policy Studies, 2015)

Neuman, GL, 'Human Rights and Constitutional Rights: Harmony and Dissonance' (2003) 55 *Stanford Law Review* 1863

Ng, T, 'Safeguarding Peace and Security in our Warming World: A Role for the Security Council' (2010) 15 *Journal of Conflict and Security Law* 275

Nollkaemper, A, 'The Independence of the Domestic Judiciary in International Law' (2006) XVII *Finnish Yearbook of International Law* 261

Nyman Metcalf, K and Papageorgiou, I, *Regional Integration and Courts of Justice* (Antwerp, Intersentia, 2005)

O

O'Donoghue, A, *Constitutionalism in Global Constitutionalisation* (Cambridge, Cambridge University Press, 2014)

Oldfield, F et al, 'The Anthropocene Review: Its Significance, Implications and the Rationale for a New Transdisciplinary Journal' (2014) 1 *The Anthropocene Review* 1

Ophuls, W, *Ecology and the Politics of Scarcity* (San Francisco, WH Freeman Press, 1977)

Osofsky, H, 'Scales of Law: Rethinking Climate Change Governance' (PhD dissertation, Oregon University, 2013)

P

Paczolay, P and Bitskey, B (eds), *Separation of Powers Regarding the Jurisdiction of the Constitutional Court: The 10th Conference of the European Constitutional Courts, Budapest, 6–9 May, 1996* (Budapest, Hungarian Constitutional Court, 1997)

Pattberg, P, 'Conquest, Domination and Control: Europe's Mastery of Nature in Historic Perspective' (2007) 14 *Journal of Political Ecology* 1

Paulus, A, 'Commentary to Andreas Fischer-Lescano and Gunther Teubner: The Legitimacy of International Law and the Role of the State' (2004) 25 *Michigan Journal of International Law* 1047

Peabody, B and Nugent, J, 'Toward a Unifying Theory of the Separation of Powers' (2003) 53 *American University Law Review* 1

Pease, PS, *International Organizations: Perspectives on Governance in the Twenty-First Century*, 3rd edn (Upper Saddle River, Pearson Prentice Hall, 2008)

Pedersen, O, 'European Environmental Human Rights and Environmental Rights: A Long Time Coming?' (2008) 21 *The Georgetown International Environmental Law Review* 73

Pernice, I, 'Multilevel Constitutionalism in the European Union' (2002) 27 *European Law Review* 511

Peters, A, 'Global Constitutionalism in a Nutshell' in K Dicke et al (eds), *Weltinnenrecht: Liber Amicorum Jost Delbrück* (Kiel, Walther Schücking Institut für Internationales Recht, 2005) 535–50
——, 'Compensatory Constitutionalism: The Function and Potential of Fundamental International Norms and Structures' (2006) 19 *Leiden Journal of International Law* 579
——, 'The Constitutionalist Reconstruction of International Law: Pros and Cons' (2006) NCCR International Trade Working Paper No 11(07-2006)
——, 'The Merits of Global Constitutionalism' (2009) 16 *Indiana Journal of Global Legal Studies* 397
Preston, B, 'Benefits of Judicial Specialization in Environmental Law: The Land and Environment Court of New South Wales as a Case Study' (2012) 29 *Pace Environmental Law Review* 396
Preuss, U, 'Disconnecting Constitutions from Statehood: Is Global Constitutionalism a Viable Concept?' in P Dobner and M Loughlin (eds), *The Twilight of Constitutionalism* (Oxford, Oxford University Press, 2010) 23–46
Pring, G and Pring, C, *Greening Justice: Creating and Improving Environmental Courts and Tribunals* (The Access Initiative, 2009) www.eufje.org/images/DocDivers/Rapport%20Pring.pdf
Purdy, J, 'The Politics of Nature: Climate Change, Environmental Law, and Democracy' (2010) 119 *Yale Law Journal* 1125

Q

Quinn, G, 'Dangerous Constitutional Moments: The "Tactic of Legality" in Nazi Germany and the Irish Free State Compared' in J Morison, K McEvoy and G Anthony (eds), *Judges, Transition, and Human Rights* (Oxford, Oxford University Press, 2007) 223–49

R

Ramcharan, B, 'Constitutionalism in an Age of Globalisation and Global Threats' in M Frishman and S Muller (eds), *The Dynamics of Constitutionalism in the Age of Globalisation* (The Hague, Hague Academic Press, 2010) 15–47
Razzaque, J, 'Human Right to a Clean Environment: Procedural Rights' in M Fitzmaurice, D Ong and P Merkouris (eds), *Research Handbook on International Environmental Law* (Edward Elgar, Cheltenham 2010) 284–300
Reith, G, 'Uncertain Times: The Notion of "Risk" and the Development of Modernity' (2004) 13 *Time Society* 383
Revkin, A, *Global Warming: Understanding the Forecast* (New York, Abbeville Press, 1992)
Richardson, B, 'A Damp Squib: Environmental Law from a Human Evolutionary Perspective' (2001) Osgoode CLPE Research Paper Series Vol 07(3) ssrn.com/abstract=1760043
——, *Socially Responsible Investment Law: Regulating the Unseen Polluters* (New York, Oxford University Press, 2008)
Richardson, HJ, 'Self-determination, International Law and the South African Bantustan Policy' (1978) 17 *Columbia Journal of Transnational Law* 185
Ristroph, E, 'The Role of Philippine Courts in Establishing the Environmental Rule of Law' (2012) 42 *Environmental Law Reporter* 10866

Rivers, J, 'A Theory of Constitutional Rights and the British Constitution: Translator's Introduction' in R Alexy, *A Theory of Constitutional Rights* (Oxford, Oxford University Press, 2002) i–xvii

Robin, L and Steffen, W, 'History for the Anthropocene' (2007) 5 *History Compass* 1694

Robinson, N, 'Beyond Sustainability: Environmental Management for the Anthropocene Epoch' (2012) 12 *Journal of Public Affairs* 181

——, 'Fundamental Principles of Law for the Anthropocene?' (2014) 44 *Environmental Policy and Law* 13

Rockström, J et al, 'A Safe Operating Space for Humanity' (2009) 461 *Nature* 472

—— et al, 'Planetary Boundaries: Exploring the Safe Operating Space for Humanity' (2009) 14(2) *Ecology and Society* 1

Rogers, AD (ed), 'The Global State of the Ocean; Interactions between Stresses, Impacts and Some Potential Solutions. Synthesis Papers from the International Programme on the State of the Ocean 2011 and 2012 Workshops' (2013) 74 *Marine Pollution Bulletin* 491

Rondinelli, D and Vastag, G, 'Panacea, Common Sense, or Just a Label? The Value of ISO 14001 Environmental Management Systems' (2002) 18(5) *European Management Journal* 499

Rosas, A, 'Separation of Powers in the European Union' (2007) 41 *The International Lawyer* 1033

Rosenfeld, M, 'The Rule of Law and the Legitimacy of Constitutional Democracy' (2001) 74 *Southern California Law Review* 1307

——, 'Is Global Constitutionalism Meaningful or Desirable?' (2014) 25 *European Journal of International Law* 177

Rosenn, K, 'The Protection of Judicial Independence in Latin America' (1987) 19 *University of Miami Inter-American Law Review* 1

Rosenne, S, 'Establishing the International Tribunal for the Law of the Sea' (1995) 89 *American Journal of International Law* 806

Ruddiman, W, 'Orbital Insolation, Ice Volume, and Greenhouse Gases' (2003) 22 *Quaternary Science Reviews* 1597

——, 'The Anthropocene' (2013) *Annual Review of Earth and Planetary Sciences* 45

S

Sahu, G, 'Implications of Indian Supreme Court's Innovations for Environmental Jurisprudence' (2008) 4 *Law, Environment and Development Journal* 1

Sajó, A, 'Constitution without the Constitutional Moment: A View from the New Member States' (2005) 3 *International Journal of Constitutional Law* 243

Salamon, L, and Anheier, H, 'Civil Society in Comparative Perspective' in L Salamon et al (eds), *Global Civil Society Dimensions of the Nonprofit Sector* (The Johns Hopkins Center for Civil Society Studies Baltimore, 1999) 4

Sand, PH, 'The Concept of Public Trusteeship in the Transboundary Governance of Biodiversity' in LJ Kotzé and T Marauhn, *Transboundary Governance of Biodiversity* (Boston, Brill, 2014) 34–64

Sands, P, 'International Environmental Litigation and its Future' (1999) 32 *University of Richmond Law Review* 1619

——, 'On Being 40: A Celebration of "Should Trees have Standing?"' (2012) 3 *Journal of Human Rights and the Environment* 2

Sartori, G, 'Constitutionalism: A Preliminary Discussion' (1962) 56 *American Political Science Review* 853

Saward, M, 'Constituting Sustainability' (2008) 17(2) *The Good Society* 12

Scholtz, W, 'Human Rights and the Environment in the African Union Context' in A Grear and LJ Kotzé (eds), *Research Handbook on Human Rights and the Environment* (Cheltenham, Edward Elgar, 2015) 405

Scott, K, 'International Law in the Anthropocene: Responding to the Geoengineering Challenge' (2013) 34 *Michigan Journal of International Law* 309

Schwöbel, C, 'Situating the Debate on Global Constitutionalism' (2010) 8 *International Journal of Constitutional Law* 611

——, *Global Constitutionalism in International Legal Perspective* (Leiden, Martinus Nijhoff, 2011)

——, 'The Appeal of the Project of Global Constitutionalism to Public International Lawyers' (2012) 13 *German Law Journal* 1

Secretariat of the Convention on Biodiversity, *Global Biodiversity Outlook 3* (Montreal, Secretariat of the Convention on Biodiversity, 2010)

Sen, A, 'Elements of a Theory of Human Rights' (2004) 32 *Philosophy and Public Affairs* 315

Shauer, F, 'Judicial Supremacy and the Modest Constitution' (2004) 92 *California Law Review* 1045

Shelton, D, 'Normative Hierarchy in International Law' (2006) 100 *American Journal of International Law* 291

——, 'Environmental Rights and Brazil's Obligations in the Inter American Human Rights System' (2009) 40 *The George Washington International Law Review* 733

——, 'Human Rights and the Environment: Substantive Rights' in M Fitzmaurice, D Ong and P Merkouris (eds), *Research Handbook on International Environmental Law* (Cheltenham, Edward Elgar, 2010) 265–83

Showstack, R, 'Scientists Debate Whether the Anthropocene Should be a New Geological Epoch' (2013) 94(4) *Eos* 41

Simma, B, 'From Bilateralism to Community Interest in International Law' (1994) 250 *Recueil des Cours de l'Académie de Droit International* 6

—— and Paulus, A 'The "International Community" Facing the Challenge of Globalization' (1998) 9 *European Journal of International Law* 266

Slaughter, A, and Burke-White, W, 'An International Constitutional Moment' (2002) 43 *Harvard International Law Journal* 1

Slaughter, RA, 'Welcome to the Anthropocene' (2012) 44 *Futures* 119

Smith, N, *Uneven Development: Nature, Capital and the Production of Space* (New York, Blackwell, 1984)

Smith, T, 'Creating a Framework for the Prosecution of Environmental Crimes in International Criminal Law' in W Schabas, Y McDermott and N Hayes (eds), *The Ashgate Research Companion to International Criminal Law* (Aldershot, Ashgate, 2013) 45

Spike, P, 'Whose Rights? A Critique of the "Givens" in Human Rights Discourse' (1990) 15 *Alternatives* 303

Standing, A, *Corruption and the Extractive Industries in Africa: Can Combatting Corruption Cure the Resource Curse?—ISS Paper 153* (Pretoria, Institute for Security Studies, 2007)

Steffen, W et al, 'The Anthropocene: Conceptual and Historical Perspectives' (2011) 369 *Philosophical Transactions of the Royal Society* 842

—— et al, 'The Anthropocene: From Global Change to Planetary Stewardship' (2011) 40 *Ambio* 739

——, Crutzen, P and McNeill, J, 'The Anthropocene: Are Humans Now Overwhelming the Great Forces of Nature?' (2007) 36 *Ambio* 614

Steinberg, R, *Der ökologische Verfassungsstaat* (Frankfurt am Main, Suhrkamp, 1998)

Stephens, T 'Multiple International Courts and the "Fragmentation" of International Environmental Law' (2006) 25 *Australian Year Book of International Law* 227

——, *International Courts and Environmental Protection* (Cambridge, Cambridge University Press, 2009)

Stevens, J, 'Constitutional Moments: The Key to Britain's Uncodified Constitution' (*Student Journal of Law*, 2013) https://sites.google.com/site/349924e64e68f035/issue-5/constitutional-moments-the-key-to-britain-s-uncodified-constitution

Stone, C, 'Should Trees have Standing? Towards Legal Rights for Natural Objects' (1972) 45 *California Law Review* 450

——, 'Ethics and International Environmental Law' in D Bodansky, J Brunnée and E Hey (eds), *The Oxford Handbook of International Environmental Law* (Oxford, Oxford University Press, 2007) 292–312

Stone Sweet, A, 'Constitutionalism, Legal Pluralism, and International Regimes' (2009) 16 *Indiana Journal of Global Legal Studies* 621

Swyngedouw, E, 'Whose Environment? The End of Nature, Climate Change and the Process of Post-Politicization' (2011) XIV *Ambiente & Sociedade Campinas* 69

Syvitski, J, 'Anthropocene: An Epoch of our Making' (2012) 78 *Global Change* 11

T

Tarlock, D, 'The Future of Environmental "Rule of Law" Litigation' (2002) 19 *Pace Environmental Law Review* 575

Taylor, P, '"The Imperative of Responsibility" in a Legal Context: Reconciling Responsibilities and Rights' in R Engel, L Westra and K Bosselmann (eds), *Democracy, Ecological Integrity and International Law* (Newcastle upon Tyne, Cambridge Scholars Publishing, 2010) 198–225

Teubner, G, 'Societal Constitutionalism: Alternatives to State-Centred Constitutional Theory?' in C Joerges, I Sand and G Teubner (eds), *Transnational Governance and Constitutionalism* (Oxford, Hart Publishing, 2004) 3–28

—— and Fischer-Lescano, A, 'Regime-Collisions: The Vain Search for Legal Unity in the Fragmentation of Global Law' (2004) 25 *Michigan Journal of International Law* 999

Thériault, S, 'Environmental Justice and the Inter-American Court of Human Rights' in A Grear and LJ Kotzé (eds), *Research Handbook on Human Rights and the Environment* (Cheltenham, Edward Elgar, 2015) 309–29

Tomuschat, C, 'International Law: Ensuring the Survival of Mankind on the Eve of a New Century' (1999) 281 *Recueil des Cours de l'Académie de Droit International* 63

Tsagourias, N, 'Introduction—Constitutionalism: A Theoretical Roadmap' in N Tsagourias (ed), *Transnational Constitutionalism: International and European Models* (Cambridge, Cambridge University Press, 2007)

Tully, J, 'The Unfreedom of the Moderns in Comparison to their Ideals of Constitutional Democracy' (2002) 65 *Modern Law Review* 204

Turner, SJ, *A Global Environmental Right* (Abingdon, Routledge, 2014)

Tushnet, M, 'Potentially Misleading Metaphors in Comparative Constitutionalism: Moments and Enthusiasm' in J Weiler and C Eisgruber (eds), *Altneuland: The EU Constitution in a Contextual Perspective* (New York, NYU School of Law, 2004)

U

Uhrqvist, O and Lövbrand, E, 'Seeing and Knowing the Earth as a System: Tracing the History of the Earth System Science Partnership' (*Earth System Governance*, 3 December 2009) www.earthsystemgovernance.org/ac2009/papers/AC2009-0107.pdf

United Nations, 'Documents of the Second Part of the Seventeenth Session and of the Eighteenth Session Including the Reports of the Commission to the General Assembly (UN Doc A/CN.4/SER.A/1966/Add.1)' (1966) 2 *Yearbook of the International Law Commission* 1

United Nations Environment Assembly (UNEA), 'Delivering on the 2030 Agenda' www.unep.org/docs/UNEA_2_Brochure.pdf

United Nations Environment Programme (UNEP), 'Global Environment Outlook: Environment for the Future We Want' (*GEO 5*, 2012) www.unep.org/geo/geo5.asp 23

——, *Vital Water Graphics: An Overview of the State of the World's Fresh and Marine Waters*, 2nd edn (Nairobi, UNEP, 2008)

V

Venter, F, *Constitutional Comparison: Japan, Germany, Canada and South Africa as Constitutional States* (Cape Town, Juta, 2000)

——, 'Die Staat, Staatsreg en Globalisering' (2008) 3 *Tydskrif vir die Suid-Afrikaanse Reg* 412

——, *Global Features of Constitutional Law* (Nijmegen, Wolf Legal Publishers, 2010)

——, 'South Africa: A Diceyan Rechtsstaat?' (2012) 57 *McGill Law Journal* 722

——, 'Konstitusionalisme in Suid-Afrika' (2014) 11 *LitNet Akademies* 91

——, 'Re-imagining the Role of the Sovereign State and Individual Rights in Mitigating the Effects of the Deterioration of the Environment' in A Grear and LJ Kotzé (eds), *Research Handbook on Human Rights and the Environment* (Cheltenham, Edward Elgar, 2015) 121–40

Verdross, A, 'Zur Konstruktion des Völkerrechts' (1914) 8 *Zeitschrift für Völkerrecht* 329

——, *Die Verfassung der Völkerrechtsgemeinschaft* (Vienna, Springer, 1926)

Vernadsky, V, 'The Transition from the Biosphere to the Noösphere: Excerpts from Scientific Thought as a Planetary Phenomenon 1938' (2012) Summer-Spring *21st Century* 10 (trans W Jones)

Verschuuren, J, 'The Constitutional Right to Environmental Protection' (1994) 12(2) *Current Legal Theory* 23

—— (ed), *Research Handbook on Climate Change Adaptation Law* (Cheltenham, Edward Elgar, 2013)

——, 'Contribution of the Case Law of the European Court of Human Rights to Sustainable Development in Europe' in W Scholtz and J Verschuuren (eds), *Regional Environmental Law: Transnational Comparative Lessons in Pursuit of Sustainable Development* (Cheltenham, Edward Elgar, 2015) 363–84

Vidas, D et al, 'International Law for the Anthropocene: Shifting Perspectives in Regulation of the Oceans, Environment and Genetic Resources' (2015) 9 *Anthropocene* 1

Vidmar, J, 'Norm Conflicts and Hierarchy in International Law: Towards a Vertical International Legal System?' in E de Wet and J Vidmar (eds), *Hierarchy in International Law: The Place of Human Rights* (Oxford, Oxford University Press, 2012) 14–41

Viljoen, F, *International Human Rights Law in Africa*, 2nd edn (Oxford, Oxford University Press, 2012)

—— and Louw, L 'State Compliance with the Recommendations of the African Commission on Human and Peoples' Rights 1994–2004' (2007) 101(1) *American Journal of International Law* 1

Viñuales, J, 'The Contribution of the International Court of Justice to the Development of International Environmental Law: A Contemporary Assessment' (2008) 32 *Fordham International Law Journal* 232

Visconti, G, 'Anthropocene: Another Academic Invention?' (2014) 25 *Rendiconti Lincei* 381

Voigt, C (ed), *Rule of Law for Nature: New Dimensions and Ideas in Environmental Law* (Cambridge, Cambridge University Press, 2013)

Volk, C, 'Why Global Constitutionalism does not Live up to its Promises' (2012) 4 *Goettingen Journal of International Law* 551

Von Bogdandy, A, 'Constitutionalism in International Law: Comment on a Proposal from Germany' (2006) 47 *Harvard International Law Journal* 223

W

Wagler, R, 'The Anthropocene Mass Extinction: An Emerging Curriculum Theme for Science Educators' (2011) 73 *The American Biology Teacher* 78

Walker, J, 'A Critique of the Elitist Theory of Democracy' (1966) 60 *American Political Science Review* 285

Walker, N, 'Taking Constitutionalism Beyond the State' (2008) 56 *Political Studies* 519

——, 'Reframing EU Constitutionalism' in J Dunhoff and J Trachtman (eds), *Ruling the World: Constitutionalism, International Law, and Global Governance* (Cambridge, Cambridge University Press, 2009) 149–76

Walter, C, 'International Law in a Process of Constitutionalization' in J Nijman and A Nollkaemper (eds), *New Perspectives on the Divide between National and International Law* (Oxford, Oxford University Press, 2007) 191–215

Waters, CN et al, 'A Stratigraphical Basis for the Anthropocene' (2014) 395 *Geological Society of London Special Publications* 1

Waters, M, 'Mediating Norms and Identity: The Role of Transnational Judicial Dialogue in Creating and Enforcing International Law' (2005) 93 *Georgetown Law Journal* 487

Weale, A et al, *Environmental Governance in Europe: an Ever Closer Ecological Union?* (Oxford, Oxford University Press, 2000)

Weber-Fas, R, *Der Verfassungsstaat des Grundgesetzes: Entstehung, Prinzipien, Gestalt* (Tübingen, Mohr Siebeck, 2002)

Weinrib, L, 'Constitutionalism in the Age of Rights: A Prolegomenon' (2004) 121 *South African Law Journal* 278

Weston, B and Bollier, D, 'Toward a Recalibrated Human Right to a Clean and Healthy Environment: Making the Conceptual Transition' (2013) 4 *Journal of Human Rights and the Environment* 116

Whitehead, M, *Environmental Transformations: A Geography of the Anthropocene* (New York, Routledge, 2014)

——, *Environmental Transformations: A Geography of the Anthropocene*, Kindle edn (New York, Routledge, 2014)
Wiener, A, 'Editorial: Evolving Norms of Constitutionalism' (2003) 9 *European Law Journal* 1
—— et al, 'Global Constitutionalism: Human Rights, Democracy and the Rule of Law' (2012) 1 *Global Constitutionalism* 1
Wiersema, A, 'The New International Law-makers? Conferences of the Parties to Multilateral Environmental Agreements' (2009) 31 *Michigan Journal of International Law* 232
Winslow, M, 'Is Democracy Good for the Environment?' (2005) 4 *Journal of Environmental Planning and Management* 771
Witteveen, W, 'Doctrinal Stories' (1993) 6 *International Journal for the Semiotics of Law* 179
Wolfrum, R and Matz, N, *Conflicts in International Environmental Law* (Heidelberg, Springer Verlag, 2003)
World Meteorological Organization, 'The State of Greenhouse Gasses in the Atmosphere Based on Global Observations through 2013' (2014) 10 *WMO* 1
Wotipka, CM and Tsutsui, K, 'Global Human Rights and State Sovereignty: State Ratification of International Human Rights Treaties, 1965–2001' (2008) 23 *Sociological Forum* 724

Y

Young, O, *International Governance: Protecting the Environment in a Stateless Society* (Ithaca, Cornell University Press, 1994)

Z

Zalasiewicz, J et al, 'Are we Now Living in the Anthropocene?' (2008) 18(2) *Geological Society of America Today* 4
—— and Vidas, D, 'The Anthropocene—Why does it Matter for Policy-makers?' (Government Gazette, 24 April 2015) http://governmentgazette.eu/?p=6273
Zimmerer, K, 'Environmental Governance through "Speaking Like an Indigenous State" and Respatializing Resources: Ethical Livelihood Concepts in Bolivia as Versatility or Verisimilitude?' (2015) 64 *Geoforum* 314–24
Zoethout, CM, *Constitutionalisme: Een Vergelijkend Onderzoek naar het Beperken van Overheidsmacht door het Recht* (Arnhem, Gouda Quint, 1995)
—— and Boon, P, 'Defining Constitutionalism and Democracy: An Introduction' in CM Zoethout, ME Pietermaat-Kros and PWC Akkermans (eds), *Constitutionalism in Africa: A Quest for Autochthonous Principles* (Deventer, Gouda Quint, 1996) 1–15

INDEX

Aarhus Convention to Access to Information, Public Participation in Decision-making and Access to Justice in Environmental Matters (1998) (Aarhus Convention), 108
  global environmental democracy and, 238–9
  non-justiciable environmental right, 213
accountability and separation of government powers, 72–3
African Charter on Human and Peoples' Rights 1981, 130, 223, 243
African Commission on Human and Peoples' Rights (ACHR), 115, 223, 232
African Union and global environmental constitutionalism, 214
allocation of powers and rule of law, 71
Amsterdam Declaration on Global Change (2001), 3–4, 189
Anthropocene:
  definition and alternative terms, 4, 32–4
  derivation of term, 36–7
  history and ideology of, 26–9, 38
  implication of, 39
  onset date, 28
  significance of, 183
  stages of, 28
  uncertainty and, 40–1
  see also specific subjects

Basic Law of the Federal Republic of Germany (1949), 60, 157
Bill of Rights (South Africa), 82, 163
  courts and, 120, 168, 222
  democratic rights and values and, 169
  environmental protection, 157–8
  limitation of, 85
biodiversity, 205, 215
  global law and governance, 98
  loss of, 22–3, 37
biodiversity regime, 216
biogeochemical cycles modified, 22, 34
biophysical thresholds, 22
biosphere:
  humans and, 29, 30
  limits of resources, 189

Bolivia:
  domestic environmental rights, 244
  Universal Declaration of Rights of Mother Earth (2010), 244–5
central government, global governance order lacks, 92
Charter of Fundamental Rights of the EU (2000) and environmental protection, 213
Charter of the United Nations (1945), 8, 181
  global constitution, as, 112
  global government, as, 112
  supreme norm, as, 122
civil society:
  global environmental governance and law-making, 219
  see also global civil society
civil society actors:
  democratic participation and representation, 219
  environmental protection and, 219–20
climate change, 1, 3, 179, 185, 204–5
  Tunisian Constitution and, 12
constituent powers, domestic and global levels, 79, 92
constituted powers, domestic and global levels, 79, 92
Constitution of the Republic of South Africa (1996), 8, 49, 60, 156, 157–9
  environmental protection, 193
  human rights and, 158–9
  judicial independence, on, 165
Constitution of the Tunisian Republic (2014) and climate change, 12
constitutional democracy, UK is, 78
constitutional environmental protection, 146
  longevity of, 195–6
  United States, in, 174
'constitutional moments', 63–4
  Anthropocene's, 181
  definition, 63–4
  Germany, in, 182
  political and legal order and, 64
  public interests and, 182
  reforms and, 64
  South Africa, in, 182
constitutional state, 54–6

contemporary, 56, 61–87
  democratic justification and, 80
  objectives of, 139–40
  stages of, 143–4
constitutional supremacy, 77–9, 239–40
  definition, 77
  environmental rule of law and, 168–9
  parliamentary sovereignty and, 78
  separation of powers and, 77–8
  South Africa, 79, 169
constitutionalisation, 52–4
  definition, 47, 52–3
  fragmentation and, 99
  institutional socio-cultural framework and, 53–4
  process of, 53
  socio-legal process, as, 53
constitutionalism, 43–87
  advantages of, 57
  American, 59–60
  Anthropocene and, 7–11
  component parts, 46
  constitution, supporting, 51
  counter-constitutionalist trend, 100–1
  criticism of, 9–10, 61
  definition, 8, 9, 47, 50–1
  democracy and, 81, 169
  domestic perspective, 45
  environmental *see* environmental constitutionalism
  environmental protection and, 11, 147
  environmentalism and, 133–4
  European Union and 104–6
  expectations of, 95
  foreign jurisdictions and, 46–7
  global *see* global constitutionalism
  good governance and, 58
  government and, 58, 164
  human-environment interface and, 18
  individual autonomy and, 59–60
  individualism and, 60
  law and *see* constitutionalism and law
  legal and political order and, 58
  legal certainty and, 58–9
  limitations, 102
  local to global, 91–5
  morality and, 57–8
  perception, insular, 91
  'political technology', as, 57
  politics and, 59
  process, as, 94
  rights and, 83
  state and, 45, 94
  World Trade Organisation and, 107, 108
constitutionalism and law, 44, 180–1
  global socio-ecological crisis and, 44–5
  governance and, 10–11

constitutions, 48–9
  authority of, 48–9
  bill of rights in, 65
  'constitutional moments', 63–4
  constitutionalism supports, 51
  definition of, 42–3, 47, 48, 62, 154–5
  domestic, 156
  environmental protection and, 193
  formalistic, 52
  functions of, 149
  governance, enabling, 48
  government and people and, 43–4
  human rights and, 84, 110, 146, 173
  legitimacy of, 50
  living (New Zealand), 63
  nation state and, 62–3
  no formal (United Kingdom), 63
  organisation of states, documents for, 65
  preamble, 64–5
  separation of powers and, 72
  supremacy of upheld by judiciary, 78–9
  written and unwritten, 63
  written documents as, 48
Convention on Access to Information, Public Participation in Decision-making and Access to Justice in Environmental Matters (1998) *see* Aarhus Convention (1998)
countermajoritarian dilemma projects, 9–10, 61, 76, 78
  courts and, 165
  judges and, 78
courts:
  access, unimpeded, 67
  Bill of Rights (South Africa) and, 120, 168, 222
  countermajoritarian dilemmas and, 165
  domestic, 120
  environmental, 166
  environmental constitutionalism and, 165–6
  environmental governance disputes and, 164
  environmental obligations and, 166
  environmental protection and, 167
  functions reviewed and judicial independence, 76–7
  global, 121
  impartiality of, 165
  regional, 231
  rule of law and, 68
  sustainable development and, 167–8

decision-making, 40, 198
  Earth Charter and, 226
  ecological concerns, 139, 141
  environmental, 145, 148, 163–4, 167, 209, 213
  Equator Principles and, 220
  political, 59, 113
  polycentric model, 206

Index

democracy, 79–82, 169–72
  Bill of Rights (South Africa) and democratic rights, 169
  constitutional, development of, 80
  constitutional state and, 81–2
  constitutionalism and, 81, 169
  definition, 79–80
  environmental authorities' decisions and, 171
  environmental protection and, 171
  environmental quality and, 150, 170, 231
  environmentalism and, 170–1
  expansion of, 126
  global, 125–8
  majority rule (South Africa) and, 81, 82
  majority will and, 80
  political concept, 80
  public goods and, 169–70
  separation of powers and, 71–2
  South Africa, in, 81
  sovereign self-determination, 81
dispute resolution:
  environmental *see* environmental dispute resolution
  universal global mechanism, 92
domestic bill of rights, 173
domestic constitutional orders, 153–74
domestic constitutionalism in global sphere, 95
  appropriateness, 93–5
  inappropriateness, 91–3
  translation to, 92–3
domestic constitutions, 156
  human rights and, 84, 110, 195
domestic courts:
  transnational comparative constitutionalism and, 120
  transnational comparative environmental constitutionalism and, 230–1
domestic environmental constitutionalism and global environmental constitutionalism, 203–6
domestic jurisdiction and environmental constitutionalism, 18–19
domestic legal systems and transnational comparative environmental constitutionalism and, 222–3

Earth:
  history of and Anthropocene, 24–6
  human domination of, 1–2
Earth Charter, 220, 225–6
  decision-making and, 226
  environmental instruments influenced by, 221
  themes of, 225–6
Earth system, 178–9
  Anthropocene and, 184
  driver and humanity, 5–6
  global, 184
  governance and, 164, 185–6
  human impact on, 3–4
  law and, 179–80
  science, 185
  'stewardship' *see* environmentalism
  transformation, 164
ecological constitutional state (Steinberg), 143–4
ecological disasters:
  Anthropocene and, 40
  human domination and, 1–4
ecological Rechtsstaat (Bosselmann), 140–2
economic growth and globalisation, 204
Ecuador:
  Constitution, 174
  domestic environment rights, 244
element cycles, 22–3
energy production and consumption, 2
environment:
  authorities' decisions and democracy, 171
  awareness of and societal involvement, 196
  damage to, 140–1
  freedom of state and, 134–5
  quality of, 150, 170, 231
  reports on, 21
  state, relationship between, 153
environmental care:
  constitutional support, 152
  constitutionalism and, 141
  governmental and societal responsibility for, 153
  judicial support, 153
  state governance and, 153
environmental constitution, 156
  environmental governance and, 155–6
  formal and substantive, 154–9
environmental constitutional democracy (Verschuuren), 142–3
environmental constitutionalism, 11–14, 133–75
  Anthropocene, in, 176–200
  constraints, 174
  courts and, 165–6
  definition, 13, 149
  domestic and constitutional orders and, 153–74
  domestic jurisdiction and, 18–19
  E Fisher's views of, 147–8
  environmental rights and, 172–3
  environmental statutes and, 147–8
  failure of, 192
  global cognitive space and, 187–8
  global comparative, 148–9
  global constitutionalism and, 15
  global regulation and, 19
  law and, 147–8
  1970s onwards, 151–3
  regulatory measure, as, 147
  secondary environmental law regime and, 193–4
  state's obligation, 152

structural and fundamental (Hudson), 150–1
  thick and thin, 146–7
  transnationalism and, 195
environmental dispute resolution, 233–6
  global environmental constitutionalism and, 236
  judicial bodies for, 234–5
environmental governance, 150–1
  constitutions and, 152–3
  democratic advantages of, 171–2
  disputes and courts, 164
  formal environmental constitution and, 155–6
  legitimisation of, 197–8
  mandate and EU, 212
  responsibility for, 135
  separation of powers and, 163–4
  South Africa in, 159
environmental human rights, 86, 149, 174
  constitutions and, 146, 148, 149, 173
environmental law:
  Anthropocene and, 7, 186–7
  environmental rule of law and, 162
  ethics and, 190
  legitimisation of, 197–8
environmental non-governmental organisations, 170, 218–19
environmental normative framework and EU, 212
environmental protection, 136–7
  Bill of Rights (South Africa), 157–8
  Charter of Fundamental Rights of the EU (2000), 213
  civil society actors and, 219–20
  constitutional *see* constitutional environmental protection
  constitutionalism and, 11, 147
  constitutions and, 193
  courts and, 167
  democracy and, 171
  environmental state and, 140
  human rights and, 158–9
  transnationalism and, 194–5
environmental quality, 150, 231
  democracy and, 170
environmental rights and interests, 172–4
  Aarhus Convention (1998) and, 238–9
  criticism, 172
  definition, 172
  domestic in Bolivia, 244
  environmental constitutionalism and, 172–3
  European Court of Human Rights and, 212–13
  European Union, in, 212–13
  human rights and, 173
  non-justiciable (Aarhus Convention, 1998), 213
  Yugoslavia, in (1974), 136

Environmental Rights Revolution, The (Boyd, 2012), 145–6
environmental rule of law, 159–62
  constitutional supremacy and, 168–9
  definition, 160, 161
  environmental laws and, 162
environmental state, 141
  concept and ideas of, 139
  environment protection and, 140
  future state and, 140
  Kloepfer on, 138–40
environmental statutes and environmental constitutionalism, 147–8
environmentalism, 28
  constitutionalism and, 133–4, 136–51
  democracy and, 170–1
equality:
  right to and rule of law, 68–9
  South Africa, in, 68–9
Equator Principles and decision-making, 220
ethics:
  Anthropocene, 190–1
  environmental law and, 190
European Convention on Human Rights (1950), 105
European Court of Human Rights, 105, 108, 223, 231
  environment rights and interests, 212–13
European Court of Justice, 116, 118, 231
European environmental constitutionalism, 211–12
European Union:
  constitutionalism and, 104–6
  diplomatic missions, party to, 211
  environmental governance mandate and, 212
  environmental normative framework and, 212
  environmental rights and, 212–13
  European environmental constitutionalism and, 211–12
  global constitutional debate, 211
  global separation of powers, 116
  Kyoto Protocol and, 211
  Paris Agreement (2015) and, 211
  regional governance and, 210–11
  United Nations Framework Convention on Climate Change (UNFCCC), 211
executive authorities and separation of power, 73–4
extinction of species, mass, 27

farming and Anthropocene, 27, 28
fragmentation:
  advantages of, 205–6
  constitutionalisation and, 99
  habitat transformation, 2
  international law, of, 98–9
freedom of international law, 93
freedom of state and environment, 134–5

Index

Future We Want, The (Rio+20 outcome document, 2012), 160–1

Gaia hypothesis, 34
geochronology, 24–5
German National Socialist Constitution, 52
Germany:
  Basic Law of the Federal Republic of Germany (1949), 60, 157
  'constitutional moment' and, 182
  constitutional state and, 54–6
  constitutional supremacy and, 79
'global bill of rights', contenders, 129
global change, human ingenuity and behaviour and, 189–90
global civil society:
  constitutionalism, 107–9
  environmental constitutionalism and, 217–21
  global constitutionalism and, 217–18
  global environmental democracy and, 239
  global environmental rights and, 243
  institutions and state-led global governance, 248
  networks of, 130
global cognitive space and environmental constitutionalism, 187–8
global constitution, 112–14
  Charter of the United Nations as, 112
  World Trade Organization as, 112–13
global constitutional conglomerate, 112–14
global constitutional court, International Court of Justice as, 118
global constitutional supremacy, 121–4
global constitutionalism, 14–15, 89–132
  approaches to, 103–11, 131
  civil society approach, 217–18
  classifying, 103
  critiquing, 100–2
  domestic constitutionalism, translation from, 92–3
  environmental constitutionalism and, 15
  Euro-centrism of, 101
  European Union's, 211
  global power and trade, 15, 106–7
  international regulatory regime, 106–7
  internationalist approach and International Court of Justice, 119
  law and, 110–11
  legitimacy of, 98
  political power and, 100
  regional approach and regional courts, 119–20
  regulatory regime approach, 120
  trade law and, 10–11
global constitutionalism and domestic constitutionalism, 95
global democracy, 125–8

global Earth system, 184
  change and Anthropocene, 39
global environment authority, 207–9
  United Nations Environment Programme and, 207–8
global environmental:
  constitutionalism, 204
  government and separation of global environmental government powers, 229
  indicators, 22
  judiciary, 230–6
  justice and green constitutionalism, 145
  powers and geographical division of powers, 230
global environmental constitution, 224–7
  absence of, reasons for, 224–5
  African Union and, 214
  regional environmental governance regimes and, 227
global environmental constitutional supremacy, 239–42
  overview, 240–1
global environmental constitutionalism, 201–45
  Anthropocene and, 16–17, 217
  domestic environmental constitutionalism and, 203–6
  elements of, 224–45
  environment and, 201–2
  environmental dispute resolution, 236
  global environmental problems and, 204
  International Environmental Organisation and, 209
  internationalist approach, 206–9
  regionalist approach, 210–14
  Regulatory Regime approach, 214–17
Global Environmental Constitutionalism (May and Daly, 2015), 148–9
global environmental democracy, 237–9
  Aarhus Convention (1998) and, 238–9
  development of, 237–9
global environmental governance (GEG), 207, 247
  civil society and, 219
  United Nations Environment Programme and, 215
global environmental law:
  fragmentation of, 205–6
  making and civil society, 219
global environmental rights, 242–5
  domestic applications, 243
  global civil society movements and, 243
  global treaty idea, 243
  regional applications, 243
global environmental rule of law, 227–8
  pre-conditions for, 227–8
  regulation of, 228

global governance:
  objectives, achievement of, 127–8
  procedural aspects of, 127
global government:
  absence of, 112
  Charter of the United Nations as, 112
global judiciary, 115, 118–21
  amalgamation of courts as, 119
  transnational comparative constitutionalism and, 120
global law:
  biodiversity and, 98
  constitutionalism and, 110–11
  regulatory space for, 187
  socio-ecological crisis and, 6–7, 21–42
global non-state actors influence global juridical processes, 219
global problems, enhanced regulation for, 99–100
global regulation and environmental regulation, 19
global regulatory space, 203
  Anthropocene, of, 184–8
  law and, 187
  rights prevalence in, 129
  trade and, 203–4
global rights, 128–31
global rule of law, 114–16
  formalistic elements, 114
  resistance to, 115–16
  substantive elements, 115
global separation of powers, 116–18
  European Union and, 116
  geographical, 117
  states and, 118
  vertical, 117
global social reality, 99–100
global socio-ecological crisis:
  Anthropocene's, 4–6
  constitutionalism and law and, 44–5
  law and, 6–7, 21–42
global trade and global constitutionalism and, 106–7
globalisation, 96–8
  challenges of, 97
  definition, 96
  economic growth and, 204
  order, effect on, 203
  regulatory problems, 96
  territorial borders and, 97
  transnational comparative environmental constitutionalism, 222
governance:
  creation of through constitutions, 48
  Earth system and, 164, 185–6
  efficiency, 73
  good and constitutionalism, 58
  international law and, 98

  law and, 205–6
  water, 185
government:
  accountability, 72–3
  constitutionalism and, 58
  efficiency, 73
  institutions and separation of powers, 72
  people and constitutions, 43–4
  relationship with people and separation of powers, 72
government powers:
  accountability and, 72–3
  constitutionalism and, 164
  separation of power and, 72–3
'great acceleration' of human impact, 34–5
Green Constitutionalism (Ekeli), 144–5
  advantages of, 145
  definition, 145
  global environmental justice, 145
greenhouse gas (GHG), 2, 22, 240

habitat transformation and fragmentation, 2
High-Level Political Forum on Sustainable Development (HLPF), 208
Holocene Epoch, 6–7, 24–5
  Anthropocene and, 29, 37
  law, 7
human domination:
  Anthropocene and, 37–8
  Earth, of, 1–2
  ecological disasters and, 1–4
human-environment interface, 176
  Anthropocene and, 18, 19
  constitutionalism and, 18
  non-constitutional law and, 177
human ingenuity and behaviour and global change, 189–90
human-nature relations, 30–1
'human right to commons- and rights-based ecological governance', 244
human rights, 82–7
  characteristics of, 84
  classification of, 85–6
  constitutional orders and, 86
  constitutionalism and, 83
  constitutions, 84, 110, 146, 173
  criticism of, 86–7
  definition, 84–5
  derivation of, 83
  domestic constitutions and, 84, 110, 195
  ecocentric orientation, 174
  environmental, 86, 149
  environmental protection and, 158–9
  environmental rights and, 173
  entitlements based on, 86
  fundamental rights in constitutions, 86–7
  increased consumption activities and, 86
  limitations of, 85

Index

masculine emphasis in, 86
normative, 85–6
religious roots of, 86
rule of law and, 68, 69–70
South African Constitution and, 158–9
types of, 82–3
United Nations and, 83–4
Universal Declaration of Human Rights (1948) and, 83–4
humanity:
Anthropocene and, 4, 188–9
Earth system driver and, 5–6

impartiality, 74, 121
courts, of, 165
global judges, of, 121
judicial independence and, 75
'imperative of responsibility' (*Das Prinzip Verantwortung*) (Jonas), 138
'In the Name of Nature' (*Im Namen der Natur*), 140–2
individual autonomy, constitutionalism and, 59–60
individualism:
constitutionalism and, 60
of rights, 137–8
Industrial Revolution and Anthropocene, 28, 29, 35
institutional socio-cultural framework and constitutionalisation, 53–4
inter- and intra-species, hierarchies, 12, 31, 60, 220–1
Inter-American Commission on Human Rights (IACommHR), 231–2
Inter-American Court of Human Rights (IACHR), 232
inter-generational agreements, 196–7
Intergovernmental Panel on Climate Change (IPCC), 3
'international community', 126–7
International Court of Justice, 233–4, 241
global constitutional court, as, 118
internationalist approach to global constitutionalism, 119
international crime and *jus cogens* norm, 240–1
International Criminal Court, 119, 234
international environmental agreements, 216
international environmental institutions, constitutionalisation of, 206–7
international environmental law, constitutionalisation of, 206–7
international environmental organisation, 209
global environmental constitutionalism and, 209
international environmental regimes and fragmentation, 205

international environmental regulatory regime approach, 214–17
examples of regimes, 214–15
international law:
framework of, 93
governance and fragmentation, 98–9
legitimacy of, 126
state sovereignty and, 104
transnational comparative constitutionalism and, 109–10
International Maritime Organization, 208, 216
international regulatory regime and global constitutionalism, 106–7
International Rights of Nature Tribunal (2014), 235
International Tribunal for the Law of the Sea, 120
ISO 14000 environmental standard, 219–20

judges:
countermajoritarian dilemma and, 78
global, impartiality of, 121
impartiality of, 74
independence of, 75, 121
rule of law and independence, 76
sustainability and, 166, 167
judicial authorities and separation of powers, 73–4
judicial independence (courts'), 165–8
courts' functions, review of, 76–7
definition, 74
external, 75–6
impartiality and, 75
internal, 75–6
origin of, 74
powers of review and, 74–7
principles of, 74–5
judicial review, substantive environmental constitutionalism and, 157
judiciaries, regional and transnational comparative environmental constitutionalism, 223
judiciary:
global *see* global judiciary
supremacy of constitution, upholds, 78–9
jus cogens:
rules, 118
status, rules of law have, 123
jus cogens norm, 240–1
constitutional, 123
environment-related, 240, 241
international crime and, 240–1
normative hierarchy and, 122–3
sustainability and, 240

Kyoto Protocol and European Union, 211

Land and Environment Court, New South
    Wales, 166, 230
law:
    accessibility of, 67
    constitutional approach and Anthropocene,
      191
    constitutionalism and, 10–11, 44, 180–1
    Earth system and, 179–80
    framework of international 93
    global *see* global law
    governance and, 10–11, 205–6
    obedience to, 67
    order and Anthropocene, 178–84
    promulgation of, 67
    purpose of, 180
    substantive and rule of, 68
law-making and non-state entities, 107–8
Law of Mother Earth (Bolivia, 2009), 221
legal certainty and constitutionalism, 58–9
legal order and constitutionalism, 58–9
legal right and liability, 67
legality and rule of law, 70
legislative authorities and separation of powers,
    73–4
legitimacy:
    global constitutionalisation, of, 98
    international law, of, 126
lex lata stance, 19
lex ferenda stance, 19

majority rule and democracy (South Africa),
    81, 82
morality and constitutionalism, 57–8
multilateral environment agreements, 215, 216,
    221, 226–7, 228
multi-level constitutionalism *see* transnational
    comparative constitutionalism
multi-scalarity, 187

nation state:
    constitution and, 62–3
    local, 186–7
National Socialist German constitution, 52, 64
natural resources, 144, 158, 171, 231–2
natural sciences and Anthropocene, 5
nature:
    definition, 31
    human-nature relations, 30–1
    state (Naturstaat), 141
New Zealand:
    living constitution, 63
    Resource Management Act 1991, 147
Nigerian oil production, 232–3
no-harm rule 242
non-constitutional law, human-environment
    interface and, 177
non-governmental organisation, 125, 239
    environmental, 170, 218–19

non-human living entities' rights, 137–8
non-state entities, law-making, 107–8
norms:
    creation, 125–6
    environmental, 209
    evolution of, 124
    international environmental law, 241–2
    international law, 123
    peremptory, 124, 241
    superior as rights, 128
    supreme, Charter of the United Nations as,
      122
Nuclear Weapons Advisory Opinion, 241–2

ocean governance regime, 216
Öko-Diktatur, 139, 164, 171
order:
    law and *see* law
    system of and globalisation, 203
Ordnungsform, 56

Paris Agreement (2015) and European Union,
    211
parliamentary sovereignty and constitutional
    supremacy, 78
people and government and constitution, 43
Permanent Peoples' Tribunal, 235–6
planetary boundaries, 22–3
political and legal order, 'constitutional
    moments', 64
political power:
    global constitutionalism and, 100
    order and constitutionalism and, 58
politics:
    constitutionalism and, 59
    global, 125
popular sovereignty, 79
population growth, 2, 134, 176
posterity provision, 144–5
powers of review (courts'), 165–8
    judicial independence and, 74–7
primary substantive rules, 205
Principles on the Role of Law and Sustainable
    Development (Johannesburg Principles)
    (2002), 167
private legal regimes, 108
public goods and democracy, 169–70
public interest and constitutional moments, 182

Rechtsstaat, 54–6
    ecological (Bosselmann), 140–2
regional courts:
    environment concerns and, 231
    regionalist approach to global
      constitutionalism, 119–20
regional environmental governance, 210–14
    benefits of, 210
    development of, 210

orders, 210
  regimes and global environmental constitution, 227
regional environmental treaty regime, 210
regional governance and European Union, 210–11
regional judicial bodies, environmental concerns of, 231–2
regional law and transnational comparative constitutionalism, 109–10
regionalist approach to global constitutionalism, 104–6
regulatory institutions and Anthropocene, 38–41
regulatory regime approach and global constitutionalism, 120, 215–16
regulatory social institutions, 179–80
  definition, 179–80
reports on the environment, 21
'right to a healthy and ecologically balanced human living environment' (1976), 223
rights:
  anthropocentric orientation, 173–4
  domestic constitutions, in, 130–1
  ecocentric orientation, 173–4
  fundamental, 84–5
  global, 128–31
  human *see* human rights
  prevalence in global regulatory sphere, 129
  superior norms, 128
rule of law, 65–71
  allocation of powers and, 71
  courts and, 68
  definitions, 67, 160
  elements of, 67, 70
  generalisations of, 65–6
  governance efficiency and, 73
  history of, 66–7
  human rights and, 68, 69–70
  judges' independence, 76
  judicial oversight, 71
  legality and, 70
  objectives of, 227
  procedural, 67–8, 70
  right to equality and, 68–9
  separation of powers and, 71–2
  substantive, 70
  substantive law and, 68
  sustainable development and, 160–1
  United Nations and, 160
'rule of law for nature', 160

'safe space' and uncertainty, 22
secondary environmental law regime and environmental constitutionalism, 193–4
secondary rules (procedural), fragmentary growth of, 205
self-determination, sovereign and democracy, 81

separation of global environmental governance powers, 229–30
  scenarios of, 229
separation of powers, 71–4, 117
  absolute, 73–4
  aims of, 117
  constitutions and, 72
  constitutional supremacy and, 77–8
  definition, 71
  democracy and, 71–2
  environmental governance and, 163–4
  executive authorities and, 73–4
  geographical, 117
  global *see* global separation of powers
  government institutions, 72
  government accountability, 72–3
  government's relation with people, 72
  legislative authorities, 73–4
  origin of, 71
  rule of law and, 71–2
  sufficient, 117
  vertical, 117
Should Trees have Standing? (1972), 137
Social and Economic Rights Action Center Communication (SERAC, 2001), 223
social sciences and Anthropocene, 5
South Africa:
  Bill of Rights *see* Bill of Rights (South Africa)
  constitution *see* Constitution of the Republic of South Africa (1996)
  'constitutional moment', 182
  constitutional supremacy and, 79, 169
  democracy and majority rule, 82
  democracy in, 81
  environmental governance and, 159
  equality in, 68–9
  human rights and rule of law in, 69–70
  inter-generational agreements, 197
  sustainable development as constitutional issue, 198–9
South African Constitutional Court and transnational comparative environmental constitutionalism, 222–3
South African environmental right, 150
Special Chamber for Environmental Matters (1993), 233–4
state:
  citizens and global environmental democracy, 238
  constitutional, 81–2
  constitutionalism and, 45, 94
  deconstitutionalisation of, 97
  dominant measures, 237–8
  environment, relationship between, 153
  global separation of powers and, 118
  governance and environmental care, 153
state-environment-constitutionalism relationship, 143–4

Index

state-led civil society institutions and global civil society institutions, 218
state sovereignty, 209
　global actions of, 95
　international law and, 104
　treaty regimes limit actions, 216–17
Stockholm Conference (1972) *see* United Nations Conference on the Human Environment
Stockholm Declaration (1972), 136–7
Strategic Approach to International Chemicals Management (SAICM), 226–7
　conventions and agreements, under, 226–7
sub-'constitutions', treaties as, 113
substantive environmental constitutionalism:
　features of, 156–7
　judicial review, 157
superior environmental protection and constitutional environment protection and, 146
Supreme Court of India, 166, 223
sustainability, 12
　achievement of, 146
　conflicts of, 162, 166
　ecological, 157
　global corporate, 128
　judges and, 166, 167
　jus cogens norm, 240
　sustainable society, 142
sustainable development:
　concept, 36
　constitutional issue, as, 198–9
　courts and, 167–8
　rule of law and, 160
Sustainable Development and Rights of Future Generations Commission, 12
systems of order and globalisation, 203

technology, use of, 136–7, 189
territorial borders and globalisation, 97
trade:
　global regulatory space, 203–4
　law and global constitutionalism, 10–11
transnational comparative constitutionalism, 109–10
　domestic courts and, 120
　global judiciary and, 120
　international law, 109–10
　regional law and, 109–10
transnational comparative environmental constitutionalism, 221–3
　domestic courts and, 230–1
　domestic legal systems and, 222–3
　globalisation and, 222
　overview, 221–2

regional judiciaries and, 223
transnationalism:
　environmental constitutionalism and, 195
　environmental protection, 194–5
treaties:
　regimes limiting states' actions, 216–17
　sub-'constitutions', as, 113
tribunals:
　access, unimpeded, 67
　environmental, 166
　global, 121
　treaty, 116

uncertainty:
　Anthropocene and, 40–1
　Earth system, of, 135, 186
　regulatory, 147
　'safe space' and, 22
United Kingdom:
　constitutional democracy, is, 78
　no formal constitution, 63
United Nations:
　organisation status, UNEP upgrade to, 208
　regional human rights instruments and, 129–30
　rights and, 83–4
　rule of law and, 160
United Nations Conference on Environment and Development (1992), 219
United Nations Conference on the Human Environment (1972), 11, 136, 173
United Nations Environment Programme (UNEP, 1972), 1, 160, 205
　global environmental authority and, 207–8
　global environmental governance, supporting, 215
　status of, 209
　strengthening of, 207–8
　United Nations organisation status, upgrade to, 208
United Nations Framework Convention on Climate Change (UNFCCC), 221, 237–8
　EU and, 211
United States:
　Constitution (1788), 48
　constitutional environmental protection, 174
　constitutionalism, 59–60
Universal Covenant Affirming a Human Right to Commons- and Rights-Based Governance of Earth's Natural Wealth and Resources, 244
Universal Declaration of Human Rights (UDHR, 1948), 8, 115, 172–3, 225
　rights and, 83–4

Index

Universal Declaration of Rights of Mother Earth (2010), 244–5

Verfassungsstaat, 54–5
Vienna Convention on the Law of Treaties (VCLT) 1969, 240–1, 242

'We the People', 79, 80
World Trade Organization, 245
  constitutionalism and, 107, 108
  global constitution, as, 112–13